D0153331

SUMMA PUBLICATIONS, INC.

Thomas M. Hines
Publisher

William C. Carter
Editor-in-chief

Editorial Board

William Berg
University of Wisconsin

Germaine Brée
Wake Forest University

Michael Cartwright
McGill University

Hugh M. Davidson
University of Virginia

Elyane Dezon-Jones
Washington University

John D. Erickson
Louisiana State University

Wallace Fowlie (emeritus)
Duke University

James Hamilton
University of Cincinnati

Freeman G. Henry
University of South Carolina

Norris J. Lacy
Washington University

Jerry C. Nash
University of New Orleans

Allan Pasco
University of Kansas

Albert Sonnenfeld
University of Southern California

Orders:
P.O. Box 660725
Birmingham, AL 35266-0725

Editorial Address:
3601 Westbury Road
Birmingham, AL 35223

Romantic Vision

The Novels of George Sand

Romantic Vision

The Novels of George Sand

Robert Godwin-Jones

SUMMA PUBLICATIONS, INC.
Birmingham, Alabama
1995

Copyright 1995
Summa Publications, Inc.
ISBN 1-883479-06-1

Library of Congress Catalog Number 95-69365

Printed in the United States of America

All rights reserved.

216079

To my family—
Beth, Jacob, Molly, Luke, and Emma

Contents

Contents (cont'd)

Introduction: Speaking to the Heart

George Sand as Novelist

*Les romans parlent au cœur et à l'imagination, et quand on
vit dans une époque d'égoïsme et d'endurcissement on peut,
sous cette forme, frapper fort pour réveiller les consciences
et les cœurs.*

—*Correspondance* (8: 685)

Much has been written, and continues to be written, on
George Sand's life. She was a pivotal figure of French Romanticism
and was involved professionally or personally with a wide array of
French and foreign writers, artists, and musicians. Her unorthodox
lifestyle, passionate relationships with Chopin, Musset, and others,
her ardent political involvement—she served as unofficial Minister
of Propaganda in the short-lived Second Republic—all make
George Sand an irresistible subject for scholarly and popular biography. It was not, however, the love affairs or the cigar smoking but
her novels which made her a world-wide phenomenon during her
lifetime. Her critical views on society and championship of individual freedom attracted a passionate following, not only in France,
but also in England, Germany, and Russia. It was George Sand the
radical thinker, out to destroy marriage, abolish private property,
expose the evil core of the Catholic Church, create a new social
order, who became a household word to her contemporaries.

In his study of George Sand, Pierre Salomon has little good to say about the infamous woman's character, describing her as cowardly, opportunistic, fawning, vacillating, vain. Others would add such epithets as promiscuous, hypercritical, cruel, unfaithful, and shallow—just to stop there. But Salomon respects Sand as a novelist, particularly for her commitment to use her fiction to serve a variety of serious purposes: "Le plus beau côté de sa nature, c'est précisément cette passion des idées, cette aspiration ardente vers le bien et le vrai" (158). Salomon, clearly not sentimental in his approach to George Sand, believes we should take the novelist at her word when she says that she lived more with ideas than with men. Madame Karénine's assessment was similar: "Ce qui distingue par-dessus tout George Sand pendant les quarante-cinq années de sa carrière littéraire . . . c'est son attachement passionné à toutes les grandes idées, sa prédication convaincue pour atteindre à cet idéal" (1: 8). It is this aspect of Sand's works, her novels as vehicles for the discussion of social, political, and religious issues, which this study proposes to examine. The goal is to illuminate the nature of Sand's "romantic vision," her version of the generation's desire to reshape, even recreate, the world. The guiding principle in the process was the individual creative imagination; reality is reconstructed in the poet's image. But the vision is not just turned inward, the ultimate desire is to improve the lot of mankind, to make the world whole again. As Isabelle Naginski points out, Sand endorsed an activist romantic agenda which entailed a denunciation of materialism along with a call for a new social order and moral renewal (14). This was the mission she set out to fulfill through her fiction.

It was a noble—and naive—undertaking and one which George Sand shared with writers like Balzac, Dickens, Goethe and Tolstoy. Having placed Sand in such company, I should hasten to add that only occasionally does her "vision" reach the heights attained in the works of the greatest novelists of the age. The uneven quality of her fiction stems in part from the astounding variety of novels she wrote. Her iron discipline—as well as an often empty purse—led her to produce novels and other works at a steady pace throughout her career, whether she was inspired by the work in progress or not. Few would claim for Sand the status of having been a profound and original thinker. Yet she was far from being the slavish follower of Lamennais, Leroux, or others that even today she is still portrayed as.[1] The revelation that many of the ideas supposedly borrowed from others appear in Sand's earliest fiction—before her relationships with Leroux or even Michel de Bourges—counteracts this image of servile imitation. Kristina Wingard, in her perceptive study of Sand's early novels, rightly points out that it was largely because Sand was a woman that she has been denied credit for original and independent thought (*Socialité* 4). In his study of Sand's reception Jörg Kujaw maintains that the paucity of reviews which discuss her political views reflects the attitude that Sand's political ideas could not be considered seriously because she was a woman (98).

Sand herself contributed to this negative appraisal by remarks indicating her dependence on the ideas of others.[2] This is particularly the case in reference to Pierre Leroux. If, however, other novelists' comments on their works are received critically, why is the same not true for George Sand? Here again, a different standard is applied to this woman novelist. Isabelle Naginski, it seems to me, justly sums up Sand's relation to the ideas of others when she describes her as "not a vessel, a receptacle for the logos surrounding her, but an authentic autonomous voice, insofar as anyone can be, engaged in a constant dialogue with the voice of her age" (13-14). Sand was caught up in the enthusiastic search of her age for new approaches and new solutions. The works which resulted are sterling examples of the characteristically romantic phenomenon of interdependence. Of course, Sand, like everyone, speaks in many voices, changing her discourse to fit her audience.[3] Her statements in letters and prefaces have too often been taken at face value without regard to the recipients and Sand's relationship to them. The author's prefaces which began appearing in the 1850s were written for a collected edition of her works and must be read in that context when Sand discusses her intentions in those works or even how they originated. The prefaces were often responses to reviews. As Kujaw shows, contemporary reviews can be helpful in understanding the critical discourse which contributed to shaping

Sand's fictional voices. They are also important in revealing expectations and norms. The variety of approaches Sand took in integrating her ideas and concerns into her fiction is in part a continuing response to the reception her novels enjoyed as they appeared.

Whatever one's view on the origins of the ideas manifested in her fiction, it still remains that Sand's way of viewing social problems tends often to be simplistic, her solutions sometimes self-contradictory. But how many good novelists can also be classified as great thinkers? In Sand's case we can with certainty say that here was a novelist with passionate and sincere beliefs who saw her fiction as a means of conveying those beliefs to her contemporaries. Of course there have always been readers and critics to maintain that this is precisely the problem with Sand's novels: they're too pointed, too preachy. But this view assumes that the "message" could somehow be filtered out. In fact, nothing would remain, so central is Sand's social commitment to her narrative vision. This is true even of such "innocuous" works as her rustic novels.[4] Without the central beliefs and ideas which are at the core of the most representative novels, many of the characters would lose their significance, their passion, their *raison d'être*. Given this fact, it is not surprising that Sand's most intense creative period (roughly 1838-1848) coincided with her deep involvement in social and political causes. This does not mean that Sand's most successful novels are those, like *Le Compagnon du tour de France* (1841), which offer the most direct evidence of her social or political mission. In fact, one of the most striking aspects of Sand's novels during this period is the variety of narrative approaches and voices. From *Spiridion* (1838) to *Le Meunier d'Angibault* (1845), from *Lélia* (1839 version) to *Horace* (1841), from *Consuelo* (1842) to *La Mare au diable* (1846), the variation in subject and approach is astonishing.

The present study examines all of the novels listed above; in fact twelve novels published for the first time or having undergone major revision in this ten-year period provide the fundamental focus for the study. In addition nine other novels are interpreted. This number represents less than a third of Sand's output. But the inclusive dates, 1832-72, cover the entire period of her creativity, and the examples selected provide a representative cross section of Sand's entire *œuvre*. Virtually all her best-known novels are included, but the selection was not based on popularity; those novels are examined which had a major impact on contemporary readers or offer important insights into Sand's integration of her views into her fiction. Therefore the study includes works like *Mademoiselle La Quintinie* (1863) as well as *Indiana* (1832), *Nanon* (1872) along with *Mauprat* (1837).

The novels are discussed in chronological order in an attempt to trace the development of Sand's approach to writing fiction. There is no absolute linear development in her use of the novels as vehicles for changing aspects of French society or of incorporating her religious or philosophical views. Her concern with women's place in society, particularly as manifested in marriage, is evident, for instance, in her earliest novels but also in much later works like *Constance Verrier* (1859). Likewise her critical assessment of the Catholic Church surfaces in *Lélia* (1833) and *Spiridion* but also in *Mademoiselle La Quintinie*. It is possible, nonetheless, to establish a basic pattern in her commitment to using novels to suggest and effect social change. There is a general movement from instinctive protests in the early 1830s to an awakening of social consciousness in the late 1830s to a fierce commitment to social engagement in the 1840s. Likewise there is a gradual dampening off in the direct incorporation of social and political ideas beginning after the 1848 revolution. As she grew older she generally became more restrained in the expression of her concerns. The interests of "la bonne dame de Nohant" came more and more to center around friends and family, and this is reflected to a great extent in her fiction. This was also a reflection of both the more restrictive intellectual and publishing climate under the Second Empire and of the general movement from romanticism to realism.

George Sand's earliest works (roughly 1832-35) deal, as do many throughout her career, with the nature of male-female relationships in contemporary society. *Indiana* and *Valentine* (1832) feature women trapped in unhappy, stifling marriages. One novel offers an exotic escape while the other ends in despair and death. *Lélia* and *Jacques* (1834) offer another possible solution: a complete and utter removal from the normal roles and attitudes of men and women in society. None of the novels purports to offer a definitive, realistic answer to society's unjust treatment of women. Sand repeatedly stated that she did not write these works as treatises against marriage—although that is largely how they were received—rather as individual case studies. This, of course, leaves it up to the reader to make deductions based on the characters' experiences. The reader's emotional involvement in the lives of the characters is invited by the passionate, exclamatory style of these works. They owe in this respect a considerable debt to Chateaubriand and the sentimental novel of the late eighteenth and early nineteenth centuries.

The novels of the second half of the decade (1836-39) are also characteristically romantic creations. The influence of the gothic novel, clearly present in *Lélia*, becomes even more evident in *Mauprat* and *Spiridion*. Intertwined with the gothic devices are religious elements which in these novels, as in *Les Sept cordes de la lyre* (1839), tend toward mysticism. Swedenborg's influence is evident. Sand also exhibited growing interest in the socialist thought of writers such as Michel de Bourges and Félicité de Lamennais. Critics were already beginning to view her works as demonstrations of the Saint-Simonian school's views on women. A concern with social inequality begins to manifest itself in novels of this period such as *Simon* (1836). The socialist and mystical influences combine to create the character of the *paysan illuminé* who first emerges in the figure of Patience in *Mauprat*. The changes Sand was undergoing in her approach to fiction during this period clearly emerge in the alterations made in the new edition of *Lélia*. From a nihilist work projecting a radically individualistic vision of man and woman's role in society; the novel in its new version comes to project the ideals of brotherhood and commitment to social justice.

The novels of the next phase (1840-45) incorporate even more explicitly the social and political ideas George Sand was beginning to embrace with more vigor. If critics of Sand's earliest novels complained that they offered no solutions to the problems raised, they now voiced their opposition to the extent to which Sand elaborated in her fiction a new social model which would resolve the fundamental problems of French society. By this period she had found her spiritual mentor, Pierre Leroux. Her stated ambition is to be "le vulgarisateur à la plume diligente" (*Correspondance* 6:431) of the Leroux system. In works like *Le Compagnon du tour de France* and *Le Meunier d'Angibault* the desire to convert is plainly, sometimes painfully, evident. While she expresses open concern for the welfare of the working class, she does not advocate that class conflict be resolved through violent means. The solution is instead symbolized in the projected union of a working-class man with an aristocratic woman. In place of revolution, social harmony can be achieved through mutual understanding and cooperation between the social classes. The mystical side of Leroux's system, including the belief in palingenesis and metempsychosis surfaces in *Consuelo* and *Jeanne*. These inspired women represent not only individuals but the future of the human race. In these novels, the message emerges more clearly from the action and characters. In fact, contrary to a commonly held view, there is considerable variety in the narrative strategies in the works of this period, including the technical *tour de force* of *Horace* with its unreliable narrator.

The rustic novels (1846-53) are often seen as a radical departure from the "socialist" novels. Indeed *La Mare au diable* is a very different work from that immediately preceding it, *Le Péché de M. Antoine* (1845). The former is a short, simple tale of peasant love told simply, the latter has a convoluted plot structure, many *invraisemblances*, a variety of characters from different social backgrounds and an intrusive narrator. Despite the different approaches, we must not lose sight of the fact that *La Mare au diable* and the other rustic novels continue to be vehicles for Sand's social propaganda. It is simply that the narrative strategy has evolved again. The emphasis on simplicity of incident and virtuousness of character in the rustic novels is a response to the popularity of the *roman-feuilleton* such as Eugène Sue's *Mystères de Paris*. Sand was offering an alternative to such works in her new version of the pastoral. The message is no longer explicitly evoked by the narrator; in fact, after *La Mare au diable* a peasant narrator is used. The reader now enters unimpeded into the peasant world, even sampling its idiom, with the hope of creating sympathy and social solidarity. Sand also used extensive introductions to direct reader reaction, and to establish the proper context in which to read the story.

After 1848 it is difficult to discern a pattern in Sand's literary production. The word which best summarizes her later fiction is variety, variety in subject matter, in appearance, and in quality. There are novels about artists (*Adriani*, 1854), novels about science (*Laura*, 1864), historical-mythical novels (*Les beaux messieurs de Bois-Doré*, 1857), regional novels (*Tamaris*, 1862). Some novels continue to explore the question of nature versus civilization (*Jean de la Roche*, 1859), others which seem to indicate a surprising return to the eighteenth-century novel of manners (*Le Marquis de Villemer*, 1860). A continuing source of attention are male-female relationships and the question of marriage (*Constance Verrier*, 1859). While several of her novels explore the question of romanticism and idealism (*La Daniella*, 1857), Sand wrote others which contributed to her image as a scandalous woman like the virulently anti-Catholic *Mademoiselle La Quintinie*, the personal justification of the Musset relationship in *Elle et lui* (1859) or the satiric portrait of the empress in *Malgrétout* (1870). Although few of these works are outstanding examples of nineteenth-century fiction, many of them testify to Sand's continuing concern with improving the lot of her fellow man and the conditions of life in nineteenth-century French society.

In general, however, Sand's later works place less emphasis on providing a forum for discussing social and political issues. Because of her disappointment over the outcome of the 1848 revolution, Sand lost interest in writing novels and she turned her attention increasingly to the theater. Her return to writing fiction was accompanied by a shift in her social and political views. According to Jacques Langlade, one of the few critics to have studied Sand's later novels, becoming a grandmother liberated Sand's "âme bourgeoise," always lurking in the background and evident in her attachment to home and family (15). Sand of course was not alone in this development; as Langlade points out (33) it was a time when politics in general seemed to be adjourned in fiction.

Most of the twelve chapters of the study offer a comparative/contrastive analysis of two novels from the same period. In many cases the works discussed have different plot structures or narrative approaches but reveal a similar strategy for activating reader response. In examining Sand's novels my goal is not to extract and summarize the ideas or to locate their sources—that has been done by others—but to analyze how these beliefs are shaped and presented in the novels and the effect they produce on the reader.[5] The goal is to track the change in Sand's approach to fiction which developed as her perception of how best to effect change in her readers evolved. Therefore, I will be dealing to a great extent with questions of genre, narration, and reader response. In the analysis of the reader's role, I will be examining above all the ways in which the implied or inscribed reader is signaled to receive the text, that is to say, how the narrator shapes the tale toward a given set of responses.[6] This is, of course, not to say that the real reader—then or now—will respond in the fashion dictated by the textual signals. Too many external factors condition the actual reader's reception of a text and stand between the author's vision and the real reading experience. The implied reader is also not to be confused with the characterized or fictional reader, the *cher lecteur* directly addressed in the text. The characterized reader is often evoked for satirical or humorous purposes and more often than not reveals more about the narrator than about the role that the author encoded for the reader.[7]

Studying the reader responses the author has built into the text can reveal much about the narrative strategy in the novel, that is to say, how the author hopes to convey her vision to her (real) reader. But other factors are involved as well, and in the analysis of some novels here play a larger part than the study of the reader's role. One of the most striking aspects of Sand's fiction is the way in which she uses and transforms traditional narrative forms. Sand was herself an avid reader and often complained that the demands of literary production left her so little time to read. She was a perceptive and receptive reader, acutely attuned to the literary developments of her day. Indeed, her life in the center of the literary capital, in close contact with contemporary literary giants as well as lesser lights made it inevitable that Sand become immediately exposed to literary trends and developments. Like most romantic writers, and perhaps more so than many, Sand borrowed heavily from her contemporaries. But in her case this resulted more in inspiration than imitation, giving Sand the raw material, incidents and individuals to use as starting points. More often than not the destination was quite different from that of the models. Not infrequently, her use of a narrative model results in an inversion of that genre, as is true of the *roman de mœurs* in *Indiana*, the gothic novel in *Spiridion*, the historical novel in *Mauprat* or the pastoral in *La Mare au diable*. In examining the narrative strategies, I believe it will become evident that, as Kathryn Crecelius has recently asserted, Sand was a much more careful and savvy novelist than is generally recognized (15).

Recent critics, particularly Naomi Schor and Isabelle Naginski, have discussed the nature and impact of Sand's commitment to the idealist novel.[8] As Schor points out, this was a respected literary genre in the nineteenth century, well into the period of realism and naturalism. If there is one constant in Sand's extensive literary output, it is her consistent adherence to a representational mode that prefers the general to the specific, that extracts the essential in human behavior, that imposes a moral vision on individual lives, that, in short, subsumes reality to the realm of ideas. The absence of social reality—compared, for example, to Balzac's fiction—is in itself a social protest, a refusal to acknowledge the primacy of social institutions. Schor calls for a much needed reevaluation of the idealist novel, whose importance has been devalorized by being seen as an exclusively feminine enterprise (68). The English view of the idealist novel, particularly as represented by the Brontë sisters, has long ago become accepted critically; a new look at the French idealist novel is long overdue.

The question of realism is one contemporary critics frequently raised. In reading their reviews of Sand's novels, it immediately becomes evident, however, that their notions of realism diverge sharply from the use of the term today. We have become so conditioned to view realism in the Auerbachian terms of objective representation of a (changing) contemporary reality that it is sometimes difficult to comprehend reviewers' enthusiasm for the realism of *Indiana* or *Valentine*. What the critics were referring to was above all the psychological consistency in the characterization. While modern critics and readers might well wonder at such an assessment, Sand's critics were not reading her novels of the 1830s in the light of *Madame Bovary* or *A la recherche du temps perdu*, but rather as a welcome change from the *roman noir* and the often insipid *roman intime*. Contemporary reviewers can be helpful in reminding us not to apply anachronistic standards. In Sand's case they are also important in revealing expectations and norms. The variety of approaches Sand took in integrating her ideas and concerns into her fiction is in part a continuing response to the reception her novels enjoyed as they appeared.

Modern criticism offers new insights into the nature of realism, with critics like Michael Riffaterre and Christopher Prendergast demonstrating that "mimesis" is not the simple process of imitating reality it has often been taken to be. Mimesis entails not reference to a pre-established reality but to a series of signs and conventions encoded in the text. It is the reader who interprets the signals and creates in his own imagination the sense of reality.[9] We surely have come far enough now to realize there is no inherent virtue or advantage in a "realistic" approach; rather it simply denotes a particular set of conventions, a particular kind of "contract" with the reader. Sand's fiction is so rich because her novels invoke the reader's involvement in a great variety of ways. She was not incapable of Balzacian "realism"; she was simply not interested in being strait-jacked to one approach: "Her form of 'making real' was not so much being 'realistic' as it was 'making visible' " (Naginski 51). There is no question that in this attempt she was successful. It is the nature of this "vision" that this study proposes to examine.

1

Chaste Volupty

Passion and Religion in *Indiana* and *Valentine*

*Livrée à des pensées douces et pures comme son cœur, elle
savourait le bien-être de cette soirée de mai si pleine de
chastes voluptés pour une âme poétique et jeune.*
—*Valentine* (41)

George Sand's first two novels were greeted with high praise
in the French press. Critics sensed the arrival of an important new
voice in French fiction, bringing a fresh approach to the *roman de
mœurs*.[1] They praised the "haute moralité" which the lives of the
heroines projected[2]; Sainte-Beuve and others lauded the realistic
treatment of character. They tended to group the novels together:
"L'idée génératrice de *Valentine*, c'est comme dans *Indiana* . . . le
duel implacable de la passion contre la société" (qtd. in Kujaw 83).
The reviews of *Indiana* generally saw the implied social criticism in
the novel in a positive light; in fact, the reviews are remarkably free
of ideological discussion (*Indiana* xlix).[3] It was only after the appearance of a series of works dealing with matrimonial misery—
and especially after the publication of *Jacques*—that many critics
began to view and attack Sand's fiction as a premeditated campaign against the institution of marriage. The fact that these early
novels do indeed deal with the plight of women in society—inside

and outside marriage—has led in recent years to a great deal of critical interest and commentary.[4]

Sand wrote three different prefaces to *Indiana*, spaced ten years apart, in 1832, 1842, and 1852. Each reveals quite well Sand's views on the role of fiction at the time it was written. The 1832 preface emphatically denies any intent to "instruct": "[L'écrivain] n'a point la prétention de cacher un enseignement grave sous la forme d'un conte. . . . Il ne renonce point à remplir quelque jour cette tâche honnête et généreuse; mais jeune qu'il est aujourd'hui, il vous raconte ce qu'il a vu, sans oser prendre ses conclusions" (5). The 1852 preface, written in the politically cautious period after 1848, is similar in tone, although less rhetorically charged: "On voulut y voir un plaidoyer bien prémédité contre le mariage. Je n'en cherchais pas si long, et je fus étonné au dernier point de toutes les belles choses que la critique trouva à dire sur mes intentions subversives" (1). Sand wrote the 1842 preface in a period of intense missionary zeal, and it offers a very different perspective on the work's purpose: "J'ai écrit *Indiana* avec le sentiment non raisonné, il est vrai, mais profond et légitime, de l'injustice et de la barbarie des lois qui régissent encore l'existence de la femme dans le mariage, dans la famille et la société" (19-20). This is the emphatic and radical language of the socialist novels of the 1840s; it is certainly not the tone of *Indiana*.

It is of course only the 1832 preface which offers insight into Sand's vision of what her novel was to express at the time it was written. It introduces a male authorial persona whose ostensible role is to serve as a neutral observer and provide an even-handed treatment of the characters. Characters who transgress against social laws are not cast in a more favorable light than those who represent authority: "Vous verrez enfin que, s'il n'a pas effeuillé des roses sur le sol où la loi parque nos volontés comme des appétits de mouton, il a jeté des orties sur les chemins qui nous en éloignent" (6). This approach corresponds to the narrative stance of the novel's opening. In the first chapter the narrator creates an aura of objective reporting through an insistence on the visual aspect of the scene. The situation is static; the three characters are seated, staring into the fire. The immobility—as well as the sparse narrative introduction—imitate the initial scene of a play, an impression reinforced by the later description of Lelièrre's entry into the room, which resembles a stage direction (31). The reader occupies the position of spectator or observer. The narrator's first direct appeal to the reader emphasizes this role: "Si vous l'eussiez vue enfoncée sous le manteau . . . si vous l'eussiez vue, toute fluette . . ." (25). The narrator shapes the reader's response through the extended comparison of the scene to a Rembrandt painting (27-28). The characters themselves seem almost aware of being subjects in a painting or a *tableau vivant*: "On eût dit, à voir l'immobilité des deux personnages [Ralph and Indiana] en relief devant le foyer, qu'ils craignaient de déranger l'immobilité de la scène" (28). The narrator's obsession with the visual aspect of the opening scene suggests a reliance on sensory perception as a means of interpreting reality. Early reviewers singled out the "realism" of *Indiana* as one of its most appealing qualities.[5] This is an impression created early on by the narrator's insistence on exteriors and by the resulting implication that the reader rely on this perspective as his source of "truth," of information about the characters.

The narrator of *Indiana* not only presents the characters and tells the story in line with the principles enunciated in the first preface, he also represents the continuation of the male persona of the preface.[6] He exhibits a much higher degree of narrative visibility than the narrator of *Valentine*. On several occasions he engages in extended digressions, discussing politics or small town mentality. He frequently makes general statements and reflections, inspired by the action or the characters. The narrator of *Indiana* must clearly be differentiated from the author—not always the case in Sand's fiction—and not just because of the difference in sex, but above all because of considerable divergences in fundamental views and attitudes. The narrator has a condescending view of women and often goes out of his way to find justification for the behavior of the male characters.[7]

In the early part of the novel the narrator emphasizes objectivity and even-handedness. The balancing even extends to stylistic traits, as in the use of parallel syntactic structures.[8] The narrator often couches his comments on the characters in terms which suggest rather than dictate, making rich use of subjunctive forms and qualifying statements or adverbs (particularly "peut-être"). This creates the impression that it is the reader who is interpreting the events. In fact the narrator explicitly states this: "Nous ne vous invitons point à vous prendre d'affection ou de haine pour ce personnage [Raymon], pas plus que pour tel ou tel autre de cette chronique. C'est à nous de les faire passer devant vous, c'est à vous de vous prononcer sur eux" (370-71). This was a passage in the first edition deleted in subsequent editions, as were a number of other passages in which the narrator directly addressed the reader. But many passages remain which characterize the relationship between narrator and implied reader. Some of these are at the rhetorical and conventional level, as when the narrator professes ignorance over the thoughts or emotions of a character. Of course, the narrator proceeds to provide the information all the same. The narrator's disclaimers serve to emphasize his claim of objectivity and of reliance on observable facts. In revealing—seemingly in spite of himself—the thoughts and emotions of the characters, the narrator breaks through the veneer of surface reality.

Even if they are qualified—made in a veiled or indirect manner—the statements the narrator makes about the characters' inner worlds tend to subvert the objective realist code so carefully established. Of Indiana and Ralph immobile before the fire he writes: "Fixes et pétrifiés comme les héros d'un conte de fées, on eût dit que la moindre parole, le plus léger mouvement allait faire écrouler sur eux les murs d'une cité fantastique; et le maître au front rembruni, qui d'un pas égal coupait seul l'ombre et le silence, ressemblait assez à un sorcier qui les eût tenus sous le charme" (28). The fantastic is here only a vision, a momentary impression, but the point is made that Indiana and Ralph are both under the control of Delmare. In the process a kind of subtext is established which defines, albeit in hypothetical terms, a different relationship among the characters than that given in the principal narrative. The accompanying implication is that the outward immobility of the characters masks the dynamic tension of their relationship. Soon thereafter the narrator makes clear that the character of Indiana conceals more than she reveals: "Si quelqu'un alors eût observé de près madame Delmare, il eût pu deviner, dans cette circonstance minime et vulgaire de sa vie privée, le secret douloureux de sa vie entière. Un frisson imperceptible parcourut son corps" (29). Here again the truth about Indiana can only be apprehended through something more than a cursory external view. A slight shiver—in response to Delmare's treatment of her dog—is seen as revelatory of "le secret douloureux de sa vie."

The suggestion that behind the passive exterior there is an active inner life is eventually brought to the surface at the end of the chapter when Indiana reacts "avec feu" to Delmare's assertion that he has the right to kill an intruder like a dog: "C'est une affreuse loi" (32). What began in the realm of the visionary and hypothetical—the indication of an inner life in Indiana opposed in some way to Delmare—erupts into a passionate condemnation of authority. In the process the reader is confronted with a perspective on the characters which challenges the impartial view from above established by the narrator. By gradually entering into the emotional turmoil and fermenting rebellion of Indiana's world, the reader draws closer to her, a movement reinforced by the description of Delmare; he is almost a caricature of the husband as absolute master for whom a wife's obedience is as much a matter of course as that of his dog and other animals.

The realist code is violated outright in the second chapter when Indiana demonstrates her "seconde vue," sensing and anticipating accurately the violent confrontation between Delmare and Raymon. Despite the evidence regarding the reliability of Indiana's presentiments, the narrator, true to his adherence to objective realism, couches his description of Indiana's "gift" in cautious, even skeptical language: "Je ne sais quelle attente vague pesait sur cette âme impressionnable et sur ses fibres délicates. Les êtres faibles ne vivent que de terreurs et de pressentiments. Madame Delmare avait toutes les superstitions d'une créole nerveuse et maladive" (35). The effect of this disparity is to alert the reader to the possibility of a quite different interpretation of observable reality and invites him to distance himself from the narrator's insistence on empirical observation as the basis for truth. In other words George Sand is subverting the belief in her narrator and establishing a kind of subtextual dialogue with the reader, bypassing the narrator. This leads to what Nancy Rogers has described as the erosion of the patriarchal value system in the novel.[9]

This shift in the reader's role allows Sand to continue to maintain the pretense of neutrality in the treatment of characters and events while continuing to evoke sympathy for Indiana. The narrator, for instance, ostensibly defends Raymon's behavior toward Noun: "Aux jours où il était le plus épris de sa maîtresse, il avait bien songé à l'élever jusqu'à lui, à légitimer leur union . . . Oui, sur mon honneur! il y avait songé; mais l'amour, qui légitime tout, s'affaiblissait maintenant; il s'en allait avec les dangers de l'aventure et le piquant du mystère. Plus d'hymen possible; et faites attention: Raymon raisonnait fort bien et tout à fait dans l'intérêt de sa maîtresse. . . . Non, vous conviendrez avec lui que ce n'était pas possible, que ce n'eût été généreux, qu'on ne lutte point ainsi contre la société, et que cet héroïsme de vertu ressemble à don Quichotte" (52-53). The passage is based on an assumed identity of views between a "reasonable" narrator, with conventional, male-oriented views on morality and social behavior, and a "reasonable" reader with similar views. As the narrator continues his dialogue with the characterized reader—the reader directly addressed in the text—the distance increases between his views and those of the implied or inscribed reader, whose perspective is being shaped by the subtextual undermining of the narrator. When the narrator later again tries to justify Raymon's behavior the response is in a sense preprogrammed: "Ne croyez pourtant pas qu'il ait été insensible à la perte de Noun. Dans le premier moment, il se fit horreur à lui-même, et chargea des pistolets dans l'intention bien réelle de se brûler la cervelle; mais un sentiment louable l'arrêta. Que deviendrait sa mère . . . sa mère âgée, débile! . . . cette pauvre femme dont la vie avait été si agitée et si douloureuse, qui ne vivait plus que pour lui, son unique bien, son seul espoir? Fallait-il briser son cœur, abréger le peu de jours qui lui restaient? Non, sans doute" (112). What could have constituted praise of Raymon's filial devotion in another context, now takes on an ironic hue. It is indicative of the narrative strategy of the novel that the playful bantering of the narrator so evident in passages concerning Raymon is absent from those which deal with Indiana. The latter are on a different level of discourse, one in which both the narrator and characterized reader are virtually effaced.

This contrast between the narrator's evocation of Raymon's positive side and the built-in skepticism of the reader's response serves to emphasize the callousness and inhumanity of Raymon as representative of the male-dominated world which subsumes female desire—and even women's lives—to the "important" social duties of the male. The narrator feels that Raymon's value to society is of paramount importance and counterbalances his ungenerous behavior towards the opposite sex: "Raymon ne fut donc pas plus tôt rentré dans ce monde, son élément et sa patrie, qu'il en ressentit les influences vitales et excitantes. Les petits intérêts d'amour qui l'avaient préoccupé s'effacèrent un instant devant des intérêts plus larges et plus brillants" (106). For a man of the world like Raymon, someone with important social duties and capabilities, his blame-worthy conduct in "les petits intérêts d'amour" seems of minor concern. It is left to the reader to recall the tragic consequences of Raymon's love affairs, namely the suicide of Noun.

The narrator provides considerable insight into the thoughts of Raymon. Indeed it is the repeated account of Raymon's resolutions made and then broken which, despite the narrator's justifying remarks, paints a negative portrait. By contrast, the narrator does not enter into as much detail in rendering Indiana's state of mind until near the end of the novel.[10] In receiving a more thorough account of Raymon's thoughts and activities, the reader is able to see how much more his life offers in possibilities of action and fulfillment than is the case for Indiana. Indeed, her social position and her sex do not even allow her to express her true feelings. There is, of course, no possibility that Indiana play an important part in society the way that Raymon does. The prominence of Raymon in the novel and the account of his role in politics demonstrate the very unequal roles men and women have in French society.

The way in which the reader is led to view with skepticism the praise of Raymon's qualities also appears in the narrator's defense of Delmare. The narrator goes so far in his attempt to be even-handed and just to Delmare that he even suggests blaming

Indiana for the failure of their relationship: "Avec une femme moins polie et moins douce, il eût été craintif comme un loup apprivoisé; mais cette femme était rebutée de son sort" (122). Not only is Delmare defended, but Indiana's positive qualities—her gentleness and patience—are seen as explanations for Delmare's behavior. In fact, Indiana is criticized for not "descending" to his level of brutishness: "Indiana était la victime de ses ennuis, et il y avait, nous l'avouerons, beaucoup de sa propre faute. Si elle eût élevé la voix, si elle se fût plainte avec affection, mais avec énergie, Delmare, qui n'était que brutal, eût rougi de passer pour méchant. Rien n'était plus facile que d'attendrir son cœur et de dominer son caractère, quand on voulait descendre à son niveau et entrer dans le cercle d'idées qui était à la portée de son esprit" (198). Indiana is accused of taking a masochistic pleasure in her suffering, of taking pride in her role as slave. Through scenes such as those defending Delmare and Raymon, the reader's increasing distancing from the viewpoint of the narrator invites the condemnation of the views and conventions on which his position is based. If society censors women for being gentle and forgiving, then clearly something is amiss with society. The ultimate goal is to alert the reader to the deception behind bourgeois marriage and make him ready to accept the alternate social model which Sand provides in the novel.

This notion of breaking away from normal society is presented several times in the context of breaking a kind of spell. The first is that passage cited earlier in which Delmare is compared to a sorcerer holding Indiana and Ralph in his power (28). Later Indiana is viewed as a figure from a Hoffmannesque tale: "Les contes fantastiques étaient à cette époque dans toute la fraîcheur de leurs succès; aussi les érudits du genre comparèrent cette jeune femme à une ravissante apparition évoquée par la magie, qui, lorsque le jour blanchirait l'horizon, devait pâlir et s'effacer comme un rêve" (59). Once again an alternative to the "official" view presented by the narrator is first offered in oblique, indirect fashion; here the possibility of escape for Indiana is seen through the eyes of admirers of the fantastic tale. Such passages could not come unfiltered from the narrator since he is committed to a presentation of events opposed to such fantasy. In fact, in a passage from the first edition, concerning Noun's suicide, the narrator explains at length his refusal to take the story in this direction: "Je pourrais, pour peu que je fusse à la hauteur de mon siècle, exploiter avec fruit la catastrophe qui se trouve si agréablement sous ma main, vous faire assister aux funérailles, vous exposer le cadavre d'une femme noyée, avec ses taches livides, ses lèvres bleues, et tous ces menus détails de l'horrible et du dégoûtant qui sont en possession de vous recréer par le temps qui court. Mais chacun sa manière, et moi je conçois la terreur autrement" (377). The narrator evokes the gothic only to withdraw it and to emphasize his insistence on portraying real life.[11]

The fantastic/visionary passages, qualified or refuted by the narrator, are important in preparing the reader for Indiana's eventual escape from the "real" world.[12] In fact, her situation recalls that of the abducted damsel of gothic fiction. Indiana, a "captive" (70) and a "femme esclave" (71), dying of a "mal inconnu" (69), is looking for a "libérateur" and "messie" (69). In marrying Delmare, "elle ne fit que changer de maître" (68), passing from one form of tyranny to another. With Raymon she sees the chance of escape and of entering a different, enchanted world: "Vous qui devez être pour moi en dehors de la vie commune et me créer un monde d'enchantements, à vous seul" (143). But the savior becomes the seducer and, like the heroines of gothic romances, she comes under his hypnotic spell, at first fighting "contre cette puissance magique qu'il exerçait autour de lui, sorte d'influence magnétique que le ciel ou l'enfer accorde à certains hommes" (137). She is drawn to him despite her consciousness of moral danger: "Elle vit avec une ineffable joie échouer son plan de résistance. Elle sentit qu'elle aimait avec passion cet homme qui ne s'inquiétait point des obstacles, et qui venait lui donner du bonheur malgré elle. Elle bénit le ciel qui rejetait son sacrifice, et au lieu de gronder Raymon, elle faillit le remercier" (74). Raymon is attracted to this side of Indiana, drawn by "son esclavage et ses souffrances" (85). He sees her as becoming his slave/victim: "Il jura qu'il serait son maître, ne fût-ce qu'un jour, et qu'ensuite il l'abandonnerait pour avoir le plaisir de la voir à ses pieds" (191). Later he considers making her his sexual slave while he is married to someone else. In the pattern of violence and

passion familiar in the gothic novel, Raymon in his attempt to seduce Indiana evokes several times the circumstances under which
he and Indiana met, with repeated references to his having been
"tout sanglant" (74,77). In the end, however, Raymon refuses to
sacrifice society for the passionate, exclusive relationship Indiana
envisions. By marrying Laure de Nangy, he remains safely in the
world of respectable—and unhappy—matrimony.

While the greater part of the novel chronicles Indiana's relationship with Raymon, the conclusion of the novel shows her having successfully escaped the yoke of society and finding both
happiness and passion in an unlikely source, her cousin Ralph. This
ending has often been seen as problematic and unprepared.[13] But if
viewed from the perspective of the narrative strategy in the novel it
can be argued that the ending is neither totally unexpected nor
arbitrary.

From the beginning the narrator evinces little sympathy for
Ralph. The initial portrait is anything but flattering: "Le moins
artiste des hommes eût encore préféré l'expression rude et austère
de M. Delmare aux traits régulièrement fades du jeune homme. La
figure bouffie, gravée en relief sur la plaque de tôle qui occupait le
fond de la cheminée, était peut-être moins monotone, avec son
regard incessamment fixé sur les tisons ardents, que ne l'était dans
la même contemplation le personnage vermeil et blond de cette histoire" (19). After reproducing several statements of Ralph's, the
narrator comments: "Je vous fais grâce d'une foule d'autres lieux
communs que débita le bon sir Ralph d'un ton monotone et lourd
comme ses pensées" (27). The reader is even less likely to think
positively of Ralph in that the narrator initially suggests that
Indiana does not like him. Ralph is an outsider, an Englishman in
France, a permanent member of a family to which he does not
belong. As Kristina Wingard points out, Ralph's eccentric behavior
early on breaks the realist code; Ralph in fact plays the role of the
gothic novel's "bon génie" (*Socialité* 60-61). There are indications
from the beginning of Ralph and Indiana's spiritual affinity, such as
the passage in which they are both seen as being under the spell of
Delmare. In fact throughout the novel he is clearly acting under the
influence of thoughts and feelings not explicitly stated, shown in

startling fashion in the scene in which he is about to cut his throat believing that Indiana has died in a hunting accident.

The perceived problem with Ralph's eventual union with Indiana lies in the sudden transformation he undergoes at Bernica. Rather than being the cold egotist we have experienced, we learn that Ralph is a sensitive soul secretly in love with Indiana. The narrator finds himself in the position of having to convince the reader of the believability of this transformation, especially of the sudden emotional outpouring, so out of character to the Ralph the reader has come to know: "La première fois que cette conscience rigide se trouva délivrée de ses craintes et de ses liens, la parole vint d'elle-même au secours de la pensée, et l'homme médiocre, qui n'avait dit dans toute sa vie que des choses communes, devint, à sa dernière heure, éloquent et persuasif comme jamais ne l'avait été Raymon" (301). But the narrator realizes that the account of the new Ralph may not be convincing: "Si le récit de la vie intérieure de Ralph n'a produit aucun effet sur vous, si vous n'en êtes pas venu à aimer cet homme vertueux, c'est que j'ai été l'inhabile interprète de ses souvenirs" (319). The change in Ralph and in Indiana's relationship with him cannot be understood from the perspective of psychological realism. The novel has abandoned this conventional interpretation of behavior as it shifts away from being a *roman de mœurs*. To appreciate the nature of his transformation it must be seen in conjunction with Indiana's visionary aspirations and the novel's dependence on aspects of the gothic tradition, especially its substitution of a personalized religious belief for official dogma.

In listening to Ralph's confession, Indiana "sentit son âme pure s'élever du même vol. Une ardente sympathie religieuse l'initiait aux mêmes émotions, des larmes d'enthousiasme coulèrent de ses yeux sur les cheveux de Ralph" (320). Ralph's transformation represents a spiritual experience for her. Ralph's speech is compared to "les mystérieuses visions de l'anachorète . . . des instants d'exaltation et d'extase" (319). It is in this mystical perspective that Ralph's transformation is seen. The reader is prepared for this aspect of the conclusion through the increasingly visible role religion plays in the novel. The novel presents a basic opposition between Indiana's visionary religious beliefs and the more down-to-earth

views of Raymon, representing the male-dominated society as a whole. Raymon's God watches over him, particularly by insuring that adversity strikes others, not Raymon: "Raymon était fort content de sa providence; car il en avait une à lui, à laquelle il croyait en bon fils, et sur laquelle il comptait pour arranger toutes choses au détriment des autres plutôt qu'au sien propre. Elle l'avait si bien traité jusque-là, qu'il ne voulait pas douter d'elle. Prévoir le résultat de ses fautes et s'en inquiéter, c'eût été à ses yeux commettre le crime d'ingratitude envers le Dieu bon qui veillait sur lui" (227). Later when his mother dies and he falls out of political favor, Raymon "demanda compte à Dieu du bonheur qu'il lui devait" (265). He is reconciled with his deity only when the rich and eligible Laure de Nangy is placed in his path (292). For Raymon God is a provider of material happiness for the chosen few; God is held accountable for assuring a steady rise in his social prominence and political power.

Indiana's God stands in direct opposition to that of Raymon:

> Je ne sers pas le même Dieu, mais je le sers mieux et plus purement. Le vôtre, c'est le dieu des hommes, c'est le roi, le fondateur et l'appui de votre race; le mien, c'est le Dieu de l'univers, le créateur, le soutien et l'espoir de toutes les créatures. Le vôtre a tout fait pour vous seuls; le mien a fait toutes les espèces les unes pour les autres. Vous vous croyez les maîtres du monde; je crois que vous n'en êtes que les tyrans. Vous pensez que Dieu vous protège et vous autorise à usurper l'empire de la terre; moi, je pense qu'il le souffre pour un peu de temps, et qu'un jour viendra où, comme des grains de sable, son souffle vous dispersera . . . La religion que vous avez inventée, je la repousse: toute votre morale, tous vos principes, ce sont les intérêts de votre société que vous avez érigés en lois et que vous prétendez faire émaner de Dieu même, comme vos prêtres ont institué les rites du culte pour établir leur puissance et leur richesse sur les nations. Mais tout cela est mensonge et impiété. (242-43)

Indiana's God is universal, democratic and anti-capitalist. Against Raymon's "dieu des hommes," Indiana champions the "Dieu de

l'univers." The religion of the capitalist and aristocratic society is seen in opposition to the religious views embracing all creatures without discrimination. The opposition is not only male domination against social equality, the powerful against the oppressed, but also civilization against nature. The "Dieu des opprimés et des faibles" to whom Indiana prays (276) and whom Ralph sees as "le Dieu que nous adorons, toi et moi" (310), is, according to Ralph revealed in nature: "Pour nous, l'univers est le temple où nous adorons Dieu. C'est au sein d'une nature grande et vierge qu'on retrouve le sentiment de sa puissance, pure de toute profanation humaine. Retournons donc au désert, afin de pouvoir prier. Ici, dans cette contrée pullulante d'hommes et de vices, au sein de cette civilisation qui renie Dieu ou le mutile, je sens que je serais gêné, distrait et attristé" (312-13). When Indiana and Ralph make the decision to return to the Ile Bourbon to commit suicide, they see it as a spiritual quest: "Je sens que nous avons assez souffert l'un et l'autre ici-bas pour être lavés de nos fautes. Le baptême du malheur a bien assez purifié nos âmes: rendons-les à celui qui nous les a données" (312). In fact providence—acting through nature—seems to bless their undertaking; on the way "il semblait qu'un vent favorable fût chargé de conduire au port ces deux infortunés" (314) and on the evening of the projected suicide "le hasard voulut que ce fût une des plus belles soirées que la lune eût éclairées sous les tropiques" (316).

It is in the context of this personal and powerful "natural" religious faith that the transformation of Ralph should be viewed. The spectacular natural setting is a major contributing factor to Ralph's spiritual transformation. The experience cannot be explained in rational terms. In telling the narrator in the conclusion what he and Indiana experienced that night at Bernica, Ralph evokes divine intervention:

> J'aime mieux croire que l'ange d'Abraham et de Tobie, ce bel ange blanc, aux yeux bleus et à la ceinture d'or, que vous avez vu souvent dans les rêves de votre enfance, descendit dans la tremblante vapeur de la cataracte, il étendit ses ailes argentées sur ma douce compagne. La seule chose qu'il soit en mon

pouvoir de vous affirmer, c'est que la lune se coucha derrière les grands pitons de la montagne sans qu'aucun bruit sinistre eût troublé le paisible murmure de la cascade; c'est que les oiseaux du rocher ne prirent leur vol qu'à l'heure où une ligne blanche s'étendit sur l'horizon maritime; c'est que le premier rayon de pourpre qui tomba sur le bosquet d'orangers m'y trouva à genoux et bénissant Dieu. (349-50)

The natural setting forms an integral part of the religious vision which ends with Ralph thanking God for his deliverance and for the night spent with Indiana.[14] The evocation of passion and religion, reaching its apex in nature, will become a major aspect of *Valentine*. The recourse to nature in Sand's early novels not only signals the inadequacy of the social world but also serves to liberate sexual feelings. In *Indiana* it also marks the definitive break with the *étude de mœurs*.

The conclusion of the novel offers a different narrative vantage point; it is told in the first-person by a narrator who becomes intimately involved with Indiana and Ralph.[15] The narrator describes the walk he takes through the île Bourbon and particularly his impression of a group of large rocks he encounters on a mountain: "Au front de ce monument étrange, une large inscription semblait avoir été tracée par une main immortelle. Ces pierres volcanisées offrent souvent le même phénomène. Jadis leur substance, amollie par l'action du feu, recut, tiède et malléable encore, l'empreinte des coquillages et des lianes que s'y collèrent. De ces rencontres fortuites sont résultés des jeux bizarres, des impressions hiéroglyphiques, des caractères mystérieux, qui semblent jetés là comme le seing d'un être surnaturel, écrit en lettres cabalistiques" (341). He stops and unsuccessfully tries to decipher the message. The narrator is convinced that there is more to what he sees, something hidden beneath the surface. This stands in sharp contrast to the opening of the novel in which observable reality is presented as truth. This is one of the central movements of the narrative, toward an appreciation of the hidden world behind observable reality, of the world of pain and passion behind the calm exteriors of Indiana and Ralph. The *roman de mœurs* must step aside for the mystical novel of passion. This makes the question of interpretation central to the novel. How is one to perceive the motivation behind actions?

Raymon mistakenly believes that Indiana's romantic actions and ideas derive from novels she had read (194, 196, 210). The question of literature influencing characters' actions is raised in the novel through the large number of references to popular literature, from the vogue of gothic fiction to Samuel Richardson and Bernardin de Saint-Pierre. These references are part of the handshake between narrator and characterized reader, a demonstration that both belong to the same cultural and cultured world. The implication is made as well that this reader's views are at least in part derived from such readings. This is brought out explicitly in the narrator's discussion of Raymon's writings: "Il est temps de vous apprendre que ce Raymon, dont vous venez de suivre les faiblesses et de blâmer peut-être la légèreté, est un des hommes qui ont eu sur vos pensées le plus d'empire ou d'influence, quelle que soit aujourd'hui votre opinion. Vous avez dévoré ses brochures politiques, et souvent vous avez été entraîné, en lisant les journaux du temps, par le charme irrésistible de son style, et les grâces de sa logique courtoise et mondaine" (102f). The reader characterized here is, like the narrator, a man of the world, someone who reads political brochures and admires ambition. This is an incredible assertion, that a fictional reader was influenced—before reading the book—by the writings of an imaginary writer.[16] Literary artifice could hardly be taken further. The passage helps identify further the reader whom the narrator insists on addressing; clearly this reader is worlds away from Indiana.

While it would appear that the novel invites the implied reader to free himself from the influence of literature, nothing is so simple and straightforward in this novel claiming realism and embracing artifice, using the gothic while debunking it. While Indiana's motives are all interior, Ralph admits to the narrator that his relationship to Indiana —and many of his actions—have been determined by the influence exerted upon him of a literary work, *Paul et Virginie*. It is no accident that it is the man who is influenced from outside. Indiana is representative of Sand's women in that her feelings and thoughts are authentic, natural, and free. This is, of course, a reflection of the reality of women's lives in the period which offered scant opportunity for exposure to the world of ideas. The picturesque novel is important as an intertext in *Indiana,* although once again the narrator in the original edition declares his intention to ignore the convention of that genre: "Si vous n'avez vu jusqu'ici, dans cette véridique histoire, qu'une œuvre de caprice et d'imagination, vous allez me reprocher de n'avoir pas jeté dans cet aride récit un peu de poésie et de grâce; car l'occasion se présente, et pourtant je la néglige. Je m'abstiens des richesses de mon sujet. J'ai refusé de vous faire l'autopsie d'une femme noyée, je me refuse maintenant à vous peindre la mer des Indes et les montagnes bleues de l'Ile-Bourbon, la plus belle mer, la plus belle contrée du monde sous le ciel le plus pur et le plus beau" (394). Later he goes even further in this vein, telling the reader to put down the book and go take a walk (401). The narrator questions the value of his enterprise while inviting the reader to partake of the freedom of choice. As the reader follows Indiana's path to liberated happiness, establishing a sympathetic rapport with her, he is invited to find his own way to freedom, by not relying only on observable actions. Indiana in pursuing her own vision leaves behind the reality of social conventions and laws.

While her solution is an individual one, by involving the reader in her struggle, George Sand generalizes the experience. That observable social and political reality does not provide a solid foundation upon which to build one's existence is demonstrated in the sudden eruption of the apparently placid French society in the 1830 revolution.[17] The political aspect of the novel is important, not only in the sense that Indiana's fate is intertwined with that of the revolution and particularly with Raymon's changed position that results from it, but also in the sense that it mirrors what is demonstrated by Indiana's situation that appearances deceive, that individual freedom is paramount.

❖ ❖ ❖

Indiana and Ralph succeed in escaping the political and social realities of nineteenth-century France. Their lives in Ile

Bourbon are shaped by nature, not civilization. In her second novel
George Sand in a sense picks up where she had left off at the end of
Indiana. The action of *Valentine* takes place in the isolation of the
province of Berry, described as "ayant moins souffert que toute
autre province des envahissements de la civilisation" (7). The narrator emphasizes the untouched, unspoiled character of life there. The
extensive description of the setting offers a sharp contrast to the
abrupt opening scene of *Indiana* which introduces the characters
through a kind of *tableau vivant*. In *Valentine* the reader initially assumes a more active role by adopting the perspective of a traveler.
This perspective is evoked in the first lines of the novel: "La partie
sud-est du Berri renferme quelques lieues d'un pays singulièrement
pittoresque. La grande route qui le traverse dans la direction de
Paris à Clermont étant bordée des terres les plus habitées, il est
difficile au voyageur de soupçonner la beauté des sites qui l'avoi-
sinent. Mais à celui qui, cherchant l'ombre et le silence, s'enfon-
cerait dans un de ces chemins tortueux et encaissés qui débouchent
sur la route à chaque instant, bientôt se révéleraient de frais et
calmes paysages, des prairies d'un vert tendre, des ruisseaux
mélancoliques, des massifs d'aunes et de frênes, toute une nature
suave et pastorale" (3). The spectacular beauty of Berry lies hidden
and unsuspected beyond the view from the highway, requiring the
traveler (reader) to go beyond the immediately visible to appreciate
this hidden world. In Sand's second novel the reader is exhorted
not to take surface reality for truth. The reader's guide in this process is the narrator, whose privileged insights the reader is invited
to adopt. The narrator of *Valentine* thus establishes early on a very
different kind of relationship to the inscribed reader than is the case
in *Indiana*. This relationship is maintained throughout the novel; the
"vous" of the opening description as well as the "voyageur" of the
last sentence could refer to either narrator or reader. Co-opted from
the beginning into the special perspective of the narrator, the reader
will be invited in this novel not only to see the true side of Berri but
as well the real significance of social roles and institutions.

The hidden truth is unexpected: the traveler in Berri who
strays from the beaten path will encounter a different, surprising
world. The emphasis is on the picturesque qualities of land and

labourer; the narrator depicts the strangeness of peasant behavior as seen from a Parisian viewpoint. After the exoticism of the île Bourbon George Sand exoticizes the French hinterlands. This was, in fact, one element of the novel which almost all contemporary critics praised.[18] The perspective on the countryside is that of the urban tourist passing through, not that of the working peasant. This is maintained throughout the novel. No mention is made of any work being done on the Lhéry farm. The narrator insists instead on its visual attraction—its beautiful setting or overgrown garden. Louise, having come back to Berri from Paris, perceives the farm in this way. Like the reader, Louise is entering the farm world from the outside; the common perspective invites the reader to share in Louise's appreciation of the lack of accustomed amenities at the farm as an expression of quaint charm. Later, Bénédict dreams of being a poet-farmer with Valentine by his side. Just before the tragic conclusion of the novel, Bénédict expounds to Valentine his view of their future life as "peasants": "Te souviens-tu qu'un jour tu regrettais ici de n'être pas fermière, de ne pouvoir te soustraire à l'esclavage d'une vie opulente pour vivre en simple villageoise sous un toit de chaume? Eh bien, voilà ton vœu exaucé. Tu seras suzeraine dans la chaumière du ravin; tu courras parmi les taillis avec ta chèvre blanche. Tu cultiveras tes fleurs toi-même, tu dormiras sans crainte et sans souci sur le sein d'un paysan. Chère Valentine. Que tu seras belle sous le chapeau de paille des faneuses!" (325). This vision—as so many others in this novel—remains unfulfilled. But the perspective it offers on how the characters envision leading their lives reveals a fundamental aspect of the novel, a movement away from a concern with practical questions of work, money and social responsibility toward an embrace of an alternative vision of life, one rooted in a sentimental view of rural life and featuring characters living in natural self-isolation.

In contrast to the situation in *Indiana*, the narrator of *Valentine* early on divulges the inner worlds of the principal characters. As was the case with the landscape of Berri, the reader is shown the truth behind appearances. Through the evocation of the mysterious circumstances surrounding Louise's visit at the Lhéry farm the narrator suggests that actions have hidden motivations. By repeatedly referring to the unusual precautions Louise must take during her stay at the farm, the narrator invites the reader to solve this mystery. This differs noticeably from *Indiana*'s in which the hints about Indiana's inner life are given obliquely. In *Valentine* the difference between the private worlds and public roles of Bénédict and Valentine is clearly drawn. The novel chronicles the conflict and tragedy which arise from this dichotomy. Whereas the principal characters are scarcely affected by political events, they are not able to escape from the social hierarchy imposed by French society.[19] When Bénédict and Valentine first meet at the village dance their relationship is determined by each's respective social status. They violate social conventions when they dance together, and Valentine's mother is scandalized when Bénédict gives Valentine the customary kiss in the *bourrée*. Both characters are defined initially in terms of their socio-economic origins. The narrator's insistence on this point is an important aspect of the narrative strategy of the novel, since the subsequent action demonstrates the fundamental irrelevance of these social roles and proposes a different means of establishing personal identity, suggesting that the essence of human relations escapes social rules and convention. Later Valentine gives Bénédict another kiss, for the help he gave in setting up a clandestine meeting with Louise. In both cases the impetus for the kiss comes from a third person—Lansac or Louise— but this first contact between Valentine and Bénédict marks the beginning of a relationship which will replace the roles of peasant and aristocrat the two had been playing. The fact that the first kisses do not originate with the eventual lovers is an early indication that the responsibility for this relationship is not to be laid solely at the door of the lovers themselves.[20]

Bénédict's need to redefine himself through his love for Valentine stems in part from his failed education, a topic raised here for the first time in Sand's fiction. Bénédict's adoptive parents, the Lhérys, have arranged for him to receive a more extensive education than most peasants have. But his passionate and restless nature did not benefit from the experiences; in fact it is suggested that farming would have better served his development. This is a view radically different from that expounded in later novels concerning the ability of peasants to profit from formal education. Athénaïs, as well, has been corrupted by the education she has received; her peasant virtues have disappeared behind the vanity and petty ambition acquired in a boarding school. The best that could happen to Athénaïs and Bénédict would be to shed the "benefits" of their respective educations.

The upbringing given the characters and their prescribed social roles do not correspond to their tastes and talents. Whereas Athénaïs has learned to despise any useful domestic activities, Louise, born into the aristocracy, enjoys spinning and doing jobs around the farm. Outward appearances and apparent identities, as so often in the novel, prove to be deceptive. Valentine goes even further than her sister in the direction of domesticity. In contrast to Athénaïs, Valentine seems ideally suited to be a peasant's wife. She favors simple, domestic activities; at the Lhéry farm she shocks Athénaïs by knitting a stocking. Louise and Valentine have had a greater opportunity to find their own way because of the unique circumstances in which their lives developed. As a social outcast, Louise has had to find her identity herself. Valentine's upbringing has been neglected to such an extent that she too has had to follow this path. The necessity of self-definition through discarding of the "civilizing" effects of education is a continuation of the central message of *Indiana*, the movement away from civilization, toward nature. This is a fundamental aspect of George Sand's romantic vision.

If *Valentine* offers a condemnation of traditional education because it destroys innate virtues, the novel, quite logically, celebrates the inalienable freedom of individual thought and feeling. The *vie intérieure* emerges as a means of escape from the egotism and personal constraints of society. This is what Valentine's trips to the Lhéry farm represent to her: "Loin des regards de sa mère, loin de la roideur glaciale qui pesait sur tous ses pas, il lui semblait respirer un air plus libre. . . . Nulle n'était moins faite pour la vie d'apparat, pour les triomphes de la vanité. Ses plaisirs étaient, au contraire, tout modestes, tout intérieurs; et plus on lui faisait un crime de s'y livrer, plus elle aspirait à cette simple existence qui lui semblait être la terre promise" (105-06). The thirst for freedom forms a fundamental link between Indiana and Valentine. If greed and ambition are the motive powers of the exterior life, love is the reigning religion of the interior life. The absence of love explains the Countess's commitment to the exterior life: "Jamais elle n'avait pu concevoir les charmes de la vie intérieure; jamais son cœur vide et altier n'avait goûté les douceurs de la famille" (98). After Valentine has given Bénédict her kiss of thanks the narrator carefully notes that on that evening Valentine is sent to bed "sans avoir obtenu le baiser maternel" (68). Valentine's care in establishing the pavilion of the château as a retreat is an attempt to create in concrete terms an environment free from the corrupting presence of the social world outside. The pavilion allows Valentine considerable freedom of movement, permitting her to associate freely with her chosen circle of friends. This sanctuary of the interior life becomes a *locus amoenus*, the fertile ground for the growth of the passionate love which rules that sphere of existence. It is in this environment that authentic human relations can be established. The narrator emphasizes throughout the novel the primacy of the *vie intérieure* over the *vie extérieure*.

In *Indiana* the passion of Ralph and Indiana appears with little forewarning. The situation is quite different in *Valentine*. Intent on demonstrating the inevitability of their union and hence its naturalness and morality, the narrator gives a detailed account of the development of the lovers' feelings for each other. He meticulously documents the fact that Valentine and Bénédict initially do all they can *not* to fall in love. Bénédict does not like Valentine at first sight (30) and despite her beauty has no thoughts of love for her (49). As their friendship grows he again declares he will never love her (82) and steadfastly refuses to acknowledge the possibility of love between them (114). Valentine, on her side, is confident that her public role as Lansac's fiancée will prevent any passion developing for Bénédict. After Valentine realizes she is falling in love she takes God as her witness that she did not voluntarily enter into any action or feelings "contraire à mes devoirs" (233). Such passages have the effect of signposting the reader to the reality the lovers are trying to ignore. The lovers' futile struggle to resist their passion—carefully documented—while demonstrating the irrepressible force of passion also represents a nod in the direction of "public morality" which dictated that lovers should not plunge head-first into adultery.[21] But in the context of this novel Bénédict and Valentine's love is a natural and acceptable phenomenon of the interior life, a world free from exterior concerns such as those of social class, marital status or religious dictates. The narrator gives occasional lip service to the traditional social and moral order— such as characterizing characters' views as exaggerated—but the entire thrust of the novel from the beginning leads the reader into an active collusion with this view. The narrator's negative view of characters devoted to the exterior life (the Count de Lansac, the Countess, the Marquise) and the positive treatment of the pavilion conspirators reaffirm the position the narrator established at the outset.

The narrator goes even further in demonstrating to the reader the virtue and necessity of the *vie intérieure*; he enlists the support of forces outside society: nature, music, religion. As in *Indiana* divinely inspired love is closely tied to nature, both are seen as manifestations of God's presence on earth. Bénédict and Valentine fall in love while on an outing by the river with Louise and Athénaïs. While they are lying next to the lush river bed Valentine gives Bénédict her white handkerchief to mop his brow, a symbolic offering up of her virginity. The beauty of the natural setting acts as a fermenting agent on Valentine and Bénédict's feelings. The intertwining of religion and passion begins with the first kiss Valentine gives Bénédict, which recalls to his mind his first communion. Bénédict comes to think of his love as "un secret entre Dieu et moi" (142). Later Bénédict imagines communing with Valentine through nature after he is dead: "Si l'âme n'est pas un vain souffle que le vent disperse, la mienne habitera toujours près de vous. Le soir, quand vous irez au bout de la prairie, pensez à moi si la brise soulève vos cheveux, et si, dans ses froides caresses, vous sentez courir tout à coup une haleine embrasée; la nuit, dans vos songes, si un baiser mystérieux vous effleure, souvenez-vous de Bénédict" (200). Bénédict's religion of love is evoked through images from nature. Relations between the sexes seen in a social setting—as represented by Lansac, the Countess and the Marquise—are insincere and egotistical. In the world of Sand's early fiction it is in the freedom and isolation of nature that the faith of love can be professed and practiced. The pavilion, too, is in an emphatically natural setting.

Bénédict's love initially is disinterested; he is certain it can not be returned. But as the religious fervor of Bénédict's passion grows, his sexual desire awakens. The crucial event in this transformation is Valentine's marriage to Lansac. Resolved to prevent Lansac from consummating the marriage, Bénédict secretly slips into Valentine's bedroom on her wedding night. Bénédict feels at this moment "un culte presque divin" (192) for Valentine and kneels down next to the altar of his faith, Valentine's bed. But his "profession de foi" turns into a physical craving. The sight of Valentine's hair—a frequent sexual symbol in Sand's fiction—sends Bénédict into such a sexual rage that he bites her shoulder, then is on the point of raping her: "Il se jeta sur elle avec désespoir, et, près de céder à ses fougueuses tortures, il laissa échapper des cris nerveux et déchirants" (196). The inability to reconcile his need to keep Valentine "pure et sacrée" (198) and yet satisfy his sexual desire leads Bénédict to attempt suicide. Sexuality becomes a more overt and uncontrollable force in *Valentine* than it was in *Indiana*. This, too, is an aspect of the *vie intérieure*.

While Valentine's love for Bénédict results in a similar impasse, it develops in a different way. In her case a deeply held traditional Christian faith gradually yields to the religion of passion. Valentine is pure and innocent, spends countless hours praying and is considered a saint by Louise (149). Any passion she feels relates to the beauty of nature and it is appropriately in a natural setting that her love for Bénédict develops. In fact, Bénédict is perceived by Valentine initially as a phenomenon of nature. After meeting him at the country dance, Valentine next encounters Bénédict when she is lost in the country. While trying to find her way Valentine hears a series of sounds—the loud respiration of her horse (43), the chirping of crickets, the far-off barking of dogs, the wailful bleating of sheep and finally the murmur of the river (44-45). Then another sound greets her ears; it is Bénédict, whose voice is intertwined with the sounds of nature. His "voix des éléments" deeply effects Valentine who comes "sous le charme de ce chant mystérieux" (46).

Music is a natural but mystical force drawing Bénédict and Valentine together. Bénédict's singing affects Valentine in the same way but more deeply than her love for nature. When Bénédict sings to her after having tuned the piano, Valentine is unable to control her emotions. Music, "le langage de toute passion forte" (228), takes Valentine out of the controlled, civilized environment and places her under the sway of more immediate, primitive emotions. It is a gateway to the interior life.

Nature itself seems to conspire in creating a passion for Bénédict in Valentine, as evinced in the scene in which Valentine watches Bénédict fish: "Elle s'effrayait de le voir se hasarder sur des saules vermoulus qui se penchaient sur l'eau et craquaient sous le pied; et, lorsqu'elle le voyait échapper, par un bond nerveux, à une chute certaine, atteindre avec adresse et sang-froid à de petites places unies que l'herbe et les joncs semblaient devoir lui cacher, elle sentait son cœur battre d'une émotion indéfinissable" (108). Bénédict becomes aware of the fears Valentine is feeling and plays on them by placing himself in dangerous positions. The danger represented by water adds to the potency of its value as a symbol for sexual passion. Bénédict repeatedly uses violence as a means of control over Valentine's feelings: "Il était fier pour la première fois de sa force et de son courage. Il traversa une écluse que le courant franchissait avec furie; en trois sauts, il fut à l'autre bord. Il se retourna; Valentine était pâle: Bénédict se gonfla d'orgueil" (114). His suicide attempt points in the same direction. Afterwards he makes Valentine constantly aware of his scar, "le sceau et le symbole de mon amour" (239). The use of violence to gain sexual ascendancy is not unusual in fiction of the age; it was especially characteristic of the *roman noir*. It plays a more prominent role in Sand's later *Mauprat*.

The scene by the river demonstrates that in nature all social distinctions are meaningless. Bénédict is no longer a peasant for Valentine, but simply a man: "Bénédict, vêtu d'habits grossiers et couvert de vase, le cou nu et hâlé; Bénédict, assis négligemment au milieu de celle belle verdure, au-dessus de ces belles eaux; Bénédict, qui regardait Valentine à l'insu de Valentine, et qui souriait de bonheur et d'admiration, Bénédict alors était un homme; un homme des champs et de la nature, un homme dont la mâle poitrine pouvait palpiter d'un amour violent" (111). The two see each other through the medium of water, Valentine watching Bénédict balanced over it and Bénédict looking at Valentine's reflection in the river; this perspective provides a new appreciation of each other and marks the beginning of their passion. In this budding relationship social roles lose their significance.

If their love tends to put distance between them and society it takes them closer to God; this is what Valentine comes to believe: "Elle en vint à se dire que, loin d'être un sentiment dangereux, c'était là une vertu héroïque et précieuse, que Dieu et l'honneur sanctionnaient leurs liens, que son âme s'épurait et se fortifiait à ce feu sacré. Toutes les sublimes utopies de la passion robuste et patiente vinrent l'éblouir. Elle osa bien remercier le ciel de lui avoir donné pour sauveur et pour appui, dans les périls de la vie, ce puissant et magnanime complice qui la protégeait et la gardait contre elle-même" (254-55). The life of "chastes voluptés" (41) Valentine had lived in nature has changed its focus. Her faith as "une source de rêves ascétiques et brûlants" offers her the possibility of fervent but innocent worship. But in thinking of Bénédict as a support in her spiritual life his image becomes inseparably bound up with her devotion to God: "Ses prières devinrent plus longues; le nom et l'image de Bénédict s'y mêlaient sans cesse, et elle ne les repoussait plus; elle s'en entourait pour s'exciter à mieux prier" (254). As was the case with Bénédict's singing Valentine's association of Bénédict with her religious faith serves to break down barriers between them, but once again this is an almost unconscious process. If Bénédict as a manifestation of nature removed any social stigma from their relationship, his spiritual elevation endows the bond with divine approbation.

As Valentine becomes aware that she is losing the struggle against her passion, she tries to enlist the support of her family and even of her husband. When all her efforts fail, she seeks refuge in her faith. But on her personal altar she has placed the blood-stained handkerchief which had been on Bénédict when he attempted suicide: "La vue du sang répandu pour elle fut comme une victorieuse protestation d'amour et de dévouement, en réponse aux affronts qu'elle recevait de toutes parts. Elle saisit le mouchoir, le pressa contre ses lèvres" (299). Just as Bénédict was on his knees before Valentine's bed, Valentine now falls to her knees in front of the altar, her hair once again flowing freely as a symbol of her sexuality: "[Bénédict] vit distinctement Valentine à genoux, avec ses cheveux blonds à demi détachés, qui tombait négligemment sur son épaule, et que le soleil dorait de ses derniers feux. Ses joues étaient animées, son attitude avait un abandon plein de grâce et de candeur. Elle pressait sur sa poitrine et baisait avec amour ce mouchoir sanglant" (300-01). The loss of virginity the bloodied handkerchief represents is not long in coming. In a pattern by now familiar Bénédict risks his life swinging from a tree into Valentine's room, appearing to be near death from the effort. When Valentine brings tea to revive him, she spills it, burning her leg: "Elle s'éloigna en boîtant. Il se jeta à genoux et baisa son petit pied, légèrement rougi, au travers de son bas transparent, et puis il faillit mourir encore; et Valentine, vaincue par la pitié, par l'amour, par la peur surtout, ne s'arracha plus de ses bras quand il revint à la vie . . ." (304). The ellipsis suggest that the combination of fear and fervor have finally led to the transformation of a spiritual bond into physical union.

When Lansac dies later in a duel, the way appears open for Valentine and Bénédict to join in the kind of life which Ralph and Indiana enjoy. But Valentine's social conditioning is too deeply ingrained; she feels that she has placed herself in a situation of great guilt. In fact, the lovers pay for their transgression with their lives; Bénédict is shot by Pierre Blutty who thinks he is his wife's lover, and Valentine dies shortly thereafter. The course of the novel thus demonstrates in a variety of ways how inevitable and "natural" the union of Bénédict and Valentine is, but the ending shows the brutal revenge of society upon the lovers for following the call of nature. Society emerges as the villain because it stands in the way of a natural, divinely inspired and blessed love. Moreover, the characters who represent society have done nothing to help Valentine in her predicament, as she points out: "Ils traitaient tous ma vertu avec une incroyable légèreté. Moi seule, qu'ils accusaient, je concevais la grandeur de mes devoirs, et je voulais faire du mariage une obligation réciproque et sacrée. Mais ils riaient de ma

simplicité; l'un me parlait d'argent, l'autre de dignité, un troisième de convenances" (326). This is an indictment of conventional morality and of a social order which demands standards of conduct which are empty, hypocritical and contrary to human nature. For polite society the maintenance of conventional decorum and the social status quo are more important motivating factors in relationships than feelings. George Sand, disciple of Jean-Jacques Rousseau, is pointing to the need for a recognition of basic human instincts and passions, for a more "natural" intercourse and a rejection of the artifice and injustice of polite society. This was an aspect of the novel favorably mentioned in a number of contemporary reviews.[22]

This message is brought out as well through the figure of Louise and her treatment at the hands of her stepmother, the Countess of Raimbault. The latter is virtually a fairy-tale evil stepmother. The Countess's hatred increases since Louise's lover, by whom she has a child, was her stepmother's as well. But despite the Countess's cruelty and depravity, society does not condemn her behavior since she respects conventions. Both Valentine and Louise are guilty in the eyes of society not because they transgressed the moral code, but because they violated social convention. Valentine's marriage also shows that society permits any kind of base conduct as long as it is done within the bounds of established social institutions and conventions. Even though M. de Lansac and Valentine feel nothing for one another and, as it turns out, he is interested only in her money, society sanctions their union, since they are from the same social class.

Such marriages are unnatural, indeed, immoral in Sand's eyes. This is demonstrated dramatically through Bénédict's resolution to save the virtue of his virgin lover—Valentine's virginity is stressed in the novel—by killing Lansac before he can consummate their marriage. For Bénédict such an event would be rape: "Il y avait un moyen de sauver Valentine d'une odieuse et flétrissante tyrannie; il y avait moyen de punir cette mère sans entrailles, qui condamnait froidement sa fille à un opprobre légal, au dernier des opprobres qu'on puisse infliger à la femme, au viol.—Oui, le viol! répétait Bénédict avec fureur (et il ne faut pas oublier que Bénédict

était un naturel d'excès et d'exception)" (183). The narrator is careful to distance himself from the ideas expressed by Bénédict, which constitute a radical rejection of conventional marriage. While not following the narrator of *Indiana*'s insistence on the "balancing" representation of characters in the service of a professed realism, the narrator of *Valentine* is nevertheless careful not to identify himself with characters or positions too far out of the mainstream of accepted moral or social views.[23] But, as we have seen, the stated positions of the narrator are less important than the views he leads the reader to embrace, which are clearly those celebrating the *vie intérieure*. The message inherent in the novel's resolution is hardly strong enough to overshadow the effect of the narrator's insistence throughout the novel on the inevitability of Valentine and Bénédict's love. While the narrator is considerably less visible than in *Indiana*, rarely addressing the reader directly or indirectly, a closer relationship results through the narrator's letting the reader see "behind the scenes" into the "interior life" of Valentine and Bénédict. This makes the characters seem to be less the types that they are in *Indiana*. George Sand also portrays the characters in a more dynamic fashion through dialogue and action. As a result, the reader willingly accepts the characters's experiences as being at least psychologically plausible and thereby revelatory of a real aspect of human relationships.[24] The twentieth-century reader may find the strong emotions and radical mood swings of Bénédict and Valentine exaggerated and vitiated by rhetorical excesses. The reader's role built into the narrative is predicated on a reader comfortable with the language of passion of the romantic novel and the moral and social statement George Sand wanted the novel to make can be received only from that orientation.

2

Escape from a World Vile and Odious:

Lélia and *Jacques*

*Quand un homme comme toi naît dans un siècle où il n'y a
rien à faire pour lui; quand, avec son âme d'apôtre et sa force
de martyr, il faut qu'il marche mutilé et souffrant parmi ces
hommes sans cœur et sans but . . . il faut qu'il cède et qu'il
retourne à Dieu, fatigué d'avoir travaillé en vain, triste de
n'avoir rien accompli. Le monde reste vil et odieux; c'est ce
qu'on appelle le triomphe de la raison humaine.*

—*Jacques* (346-47)

      Contemporary critics did not know what to make of *Lélia*
and *Jacques*. They had expected Sand to continue in the vein of
Indiana and *Valentine*, novels generally viewed as compelling ver-
sions of the *roman de mœurs*. Critics praised what they perceived as
a successful combination of realism and insightful social commentary. However, when *Lélia* and *Jacques* appeared the enthusiasm
turned to expressions of dismay, even disgust. Gone were the realistic decor and the believable characters, replaced by figures far removed from the normal concerns of nineteenth-century society.
While critics praised the moral indignation of *Indiana* and *Valentine*
they were aghast at what many saw in *Lélia* and *Jacques* as a celebration of revolt and perversity. Both novels required spatial or

temporal displacement to be appreciated; *Jacques* became a sensation in Russia, *Lélia* in our time has been recognized as one of the pivotal documents of French romanticism.[1]

Both works are now viewed as offering valuable insights into Sand's evolution as a writer and her views on marriage and sexuality. While Sand was writing these works, she was undergoing a period of profound existential doubt and of personal crisis.[2] She had become disinterested in politics following the massacre at Cloître Saint-Merri and, having left the Catholic Church some time earlier, was groping for a new spiritual faith. In addition her marriage was breaking up and her new relationships proved to be stormy and brief. The result was a pessimism that permeates both novels. They demonstrate as well Sand's narrative versatility. *Lélia* is almost a prose poem, unique in French romanticism, while *Jacques* is an epistolary novel.

Contemporary reviewers of *Lélia* did not appreciate the innovations it represented and they gave their judgments in no uncertain terms: "*Lélia*, c'est la plus effroyable débauche de talent qui ne soit jamais vue dans aucune littérature" (*La Revue de l'Armorique*, qtd. in Kujaw 123). Many were as adamant in their rejection of the novel as critics had been in singing the praises of *Indiana* and *Valentine*. *L'Europe littéraire* commented: "Souillée, noircie, sentant la boue et la prostitution . . . La prostitution de l'âme et du corps! C'est LELIA" (qtd. in Kujaw 167). This reviewer is able to find only one other French author whose work is comparable to Sand's novel: the Marquis de Sade. There were positive reviews as well, but they constituted the distinct minority. One complaint that was almost universally echoed concerned the lack of realism in the novel. This had been the one aspect of the first two novels which critics had praised consistently. They appreciated the historical frame of *Indiana* and the detailed descriptions of the Berri countryside in *Valentine*. What they found in George Sand's third novel was something quite different, a work which the author herself described as a "poème confus et diffus" (*Correspondance* 2: 388). The characters no longer function in an identifiable setting. The fictional place names do not even allow for clear identification of the country in which the action takes place. There is no symbiotic relationship between characters and place of origin as was the case with Indiana and Ile Bourbon or Bénédict and Berri. The story in which the characters of *Lélia* are involved has no vital connection to a specific place. Nature, which played an important role in *Indiana* and *Valentine*, disappears from sight in *Lélia*.

The action is also not determined temporally. In a sense this aspect of the novel is a further development of what was evident in the chronology of *Valentine*, namely a turning away from temporal reality. The treatment of time points to the author's desire to escape conventional reference points. The characters view time not as a measure of hours, minutes and seconds but as a concept to indicate stages in personal development. Trenmor writes to Lélia: "Vous aimez Sténio! Cela n'est pas et ne peut pas être. Songez-vous aux siècles qui vous séparent de lui" (52). Sténio later tells Trenmor in reference to Lélia: "Cent ans se sont écoulés depuis que je l'ai quittée" (255). These are obviously not measures of elapsed time, but ways of demarcating changes in individual lives. Lélia sees herself as being a thousand years old and Sténio is old at twenty.

Lélia at one point protests against the tyranny of conventional notions of time: "Aux lieux habités s'attache, selon moi, une grande misère. C'est l'indomptable nécessité de savoir toujours à quelle heure on est de sa vie. Vainement on chercherait à s'y soustraire. On en est averti le jour par l'emploi que fait du temps tout ce qui vous entoure. Et la nuit, dans le silence, quand tout dort et que l'oubli semble planer sur toutes les existences, le timbre mélancolique des horloges vous compte impitoyablement le pas que vous faites vers l'éternité et le nombre des instants que le passé vous dévore sans retour" (130-31). This is clearly an indictment of how conventional lives are lived, determined by the regular re-occurrence of set routines. The characters in *Lélia* are far removed from such concerns. They inhabit a world in which no outside pressures are exerted to accomplish tasks at certain times, or, for that matter, to do anything at all. The activities or professions associated with the characters—poet, gambler, priest, prostitute—remove them from the normal working world. Part of the sense of *Lélia* is that these outsiders—since they are free from the pressures besetting the average man—possess a different, deeper insight into the nature of life. Lélia is the freest of all, leading her life as she chooses and making her choices based solely on her will. She has achieved the freedom which is so highly praised and passionately sought in Sand's other early novels.

The concepts of the transmigration of souls (metempsychosis) and memories of a past life ("reminiscences") to which the novel refers also undermine a conventional sense of time. If existence has no end, then time takes on quite a different meaning. Given this treatment of time it is not surprising that Lélia has no faith in progress. Wingard has shown that Lélia represents the "new" *mal du siècle* characterized by a feeling of abandonment by God, whereas Sténio believes, like the older romantics, in an evolution of history directed by a beneficial providence (153-58). Both oppose liberalism, the prevailing position in the July Monarchy. The Lélia of 1833 sees herself living in an "âge de fer" (117) in which inertia is "le grand fléau" (103). Those few who try to remedy the situation, such as the saint-simonians, are doomed to failure. This was one of the major aspects of the novel which Sand changed in the 1839 edition of *Lélia*.

Given the temporal and spatial focus, it is not surprising that the characters in the novel could hardly be mistaken for flesh-and-blood creatures. Individual identity becomes problematic. The novel opens with the question "Qui es-tu?" (7) which Lélia addresses to Sténio. Their exchange of letters—presented with no introduction or information to the reader—does not suggest a realistic depiction of human communication. The novel is nothing if not artificial. While Sténio's question remains unanswered, he himself puts forward a number of possible answers, none of which allows any definite appreciation of Lélia's nature. His principal response is resumed in the following statement: "Tu es un ange ou un démon, mais tu n'es pas une créature humaine" (7). In the first few pages of the novel Lélia is variously portrayed as an angel, a devil, Jesus, a misanthrope, a sphinx, an agnostic and a being superior to God. No one is able to give any information on her origins. Sténio has a similar variety of identities to assign initially to Trenmor. The characters clearly depart from the conventions of the *roman de mœurs*; they are not meant to represent real people, but ideas and symbolic values. The multiplicity of identities of individual characters, and the abandonment of any pretense at psychological realism recall the gothic novel. In fact, the pessimism and condemnation of bourgeois society are characteristics which *Lélia* shares with *frénétisme*. There are a host of individual incidents ranging from murders to orgies which could have come from a variety of *romans noirs* of the period.[3]

Contemporary critics used to Sand's "caractères vrais, candides, passionnés, remplis de sentiments et de bonhomie" (*Le petit courrier des dames* on *Indiana*, qtd. in Kujaw 177) did not know what to make of the characters in *Lélia*. The *Journal de Paris* commented: "On réunit des sentiments, des idées, qui jamais ne se sont rencontrés dans un même esprit. Qu'est-ce que *Lélia*? Qui jamais a vu une pareille femme? . . . Quant à Trenmor, purifié par le bagne, peut-on se figurer un caractère plus faussement grotesque?" (qtd. in Kujaw 164). Conditioned by Sand's first two novels, critics were expecting a work incorporating elements of the *roman de mœurs* and *roman intime*. Instead, what they got was a work "en dehors de tout ce qui a été publié jusqu'ici" (Gustave Planche, qtd. in *Lélia* 586). Some critics recognized that different criteria would have to be applied to understand a work whose premises were so radically different. At least one critic saw an internal logic in *Lélia*: "Le mérite le plus réel, le plus souverainement incontestable, c'est sans contredit le rapport rigoureux et harmonieux des idées entre elles, la logique de leurs déductions et de leur conclusion" (Chaudes-Aigues in *L'artiste*, qtd. in Iknayan 165). Few critics were so flexible. Most summarily rejected the kind of fiction *Lélia* represented.

Critics unable to decipher the nature of the characters got little help from the narrator. Much is left unrevealed. Trenmor's real name, for example, is known only by Lélia. She does not reveal this information, just as she keeps other knowledge to herself. She tells Sténio at one point: "Je vous définirai la vie en deux mots, mais plus tard" (17). Lélia is a kind of oracle, a fountain of information available only to the initiated few. She instructs Sténio in a number of areas, but makes clear to him that she is not telling him all she knows. The reader is placed into a similar position to that of Sténio.

He is given no background, no introduction and is accorded con-flicting statements on the characters. This serves to create a sense of uncertainty and doubt, even insecurity in the reader, as if reason and logic no longer sufficed to apprehend reality.[4]

The novel follows no conventional or logically consistent structure. No reason is offered for the initial exchange between Lélia and Sténio to be in written form. This serves on the one hand to impart a more rhetorical and artificial character to the opening of the novel. The characters use the letters as soapboxes, opportuni-ties to accuse or justify their positions at length. On the other hand, the epistolary form distances the reader from the characters; the reader cannot experience the story as directly as in *Indiana* and *Valentine*. Indeed, much of the story in *Lélia* is "filtered" to the reader, given second-hand. As Naginski points out, the letters do not play the standard role of informing the reader, rather they "subvert any attempt at elucidation" (120). The account of Lélia's past life is not presented directly by the narrator, but brought out through the conversation between Lélia and Pulchérie. Numerous flashbacks prevent the reader from participating directly in the story. The effect adds to the aura of unapproachability and insolv-able mystery surrounding Lélia. The primacy of the *vie intérieure*, highlighted in *Valentine*, reaches its furthest extreme in Lélia. Not only are her actions insignificant, but her contact with the outside world remains cursory and inconsequential. What matters is the development of her inner life. Possible distractions—such as mar-riage, children, work, even love, are eliminated. In this sense, *Lélia* is the climax of the movement begun in *Indiana* pointing to the need to recognize the importance of women's inner lives, as distinct from their social roles.[5]

The novel's structure serves to emphasize the inviolability of Lélia's *vie intérieure* and to remove the reader further from a re-liance on logic and realism as guides. The guiding principle which underpins the construction of the novel is contrast. In the early chapters the ostensible reason that Lélia tells Sténio the life story of Trenmor is that his life serves as an example for Sténio. But what a model it provides: should Sténio devote his life to gambling so that he too can work on a galley ship and thereby find inner peace?

Clearly Trenmor's life does not convey this meaning. It does offer, however, a panoply of dramatic contrasts, designed to shock Sténio—and the reader—out of complacency and make him aware of how trivial his pursuits are by comparison. Lélia's account of Trenmor's experiences revolves around fundamental contrasts: "Il a été forçat, cet homme qui avait été si riche, si voluptueux parfois, cet homme de mœurs élégantes et de sensations poétiques, celui qui avait été artiste et dandy!" (36-37). He has won and lost millions, but he is imprisoned for a theft of a hundred francs. Trenmor's life as a prisoner doing forced labor leads him to find peace and contentment: "Et cet égout infect, où trouvent encore moyen de se pervertir le père qui a vendu ses filles et le fils qui a violé et empoisonné sa mère, le bagne, d'où l'on sort défiguré et rampant comme les bêtes, Trenmor en est sorti debout, calme, purifié, pâle comme vous le voyez, mais beau encore comme la créature de Dieu" (37). What a lesson for the bourgeois! Years of physical suffering and humiliation represent the path to happiness. For Trenmor pain turns into pleasure: "Que de trésors m'eussent été à jamais refusés sans le bienfait de ces cinq ans de pénitence et de recueillement! L'agonie du bagne fut pour moi ce qu'à une âme plus douce et plus flexible eût été la paix du cloître" (41). As so often in the novel the point is made in an extreme way, but the message remains the same as in the characterization of Lélia, namely the primacy of the inner life over outer circumstances. What matters is not social position or economic condition, not what you have, but what you are. The goals are not wealth, prestige and power but peace, contentment and self-knowledge.

Trenmor is, of course, not the only figure in the novel characterized by contrasts. Lélia—angel and devil—offers abundant examples as well. Magnus, a priest with uncontrollable lust, and Sténio's love/hate relationship with Lélia follow this pattern as well. The characters certainly offer contrasts among themselves, the fiery Sténio and dispassionate Trenmor, the frigid Lélia and passionate Pulchérie. In fact, there is evidence that George Sand thought of the characters in this way, as abstract types representing opposing principles.[6] In the process the novel relinquishes any claim to verisimilitude.

The effect is also to create a sense of detachment in the reader, an invitation to view these characters as something other than just figures in a story. Their lives—and the violent contrasts they embody—challenge comfortable, conventional views on life, inviting the reader to call into question accepted values and judgments. Conventional views of society are contested at every turn. Lélia considers Trenmor's past existence as a gambler as a valid way of life, and she even glorifies it. The insistence that Sténio has no right to judge someone who gambles has a wider social application. Lélia has an opportunity to bring this out explicitly after Sténio—voicing the views of the average bourgeois—finds fault with her for befriending a former gambler and convict: "Oh! donner un verre d'eau à celui qui a soif, porter un peu de la croix du Christ, cacher la rougeur d'un front couvert de honte, jeter un brin d'herbe à une pauvre fourmi que le torrent ne dédaigne pas d'engloutir, ce sont là de minces bienfaits! Et pourtant l'opinion nous les interdit ou nous les conteste! Honte à nous! nous n'avons pas un bon mouvement qu'il ne faille comprimer ou cacher. On apprend aux enfants des hommes à être vains et impitoyables, et cela s'appelle *l'honneur!*" (36). The call is not only for greater sympathy with our fellow-man but also for greater freedom of action and thought in what is socially accepted.

This emerges in particular in the views of Pulchérie, the prostitute. She has a saner, more balanced view of human relations than either Lélia or Sténio.[7] She is in many ways more perceptive than Lélia and a better judge of human nature. Her views on her own profession jolt the reader out of his complacent views. She thus makes a startling comparison between prostitutes and mothers: "Comparez-vous les travaux, les douleurs, les héroïsmes d'une mère de famille à ceux d'une prostituée? Quand toutes deux sont aux prises avec la vie, pensez-vous que celle-là mérite plus de gloire, qui a eu le moins de peine" (152). Pulchérie tells Lélia that society leaves women with two options: to sell themselves through prostitution or marriage. These passages caused reviewers to brand *Lélia* as immoral and dangerous, as evident in the comment of the reviewer in *l'Europe littéraire*: "Le jour où vous ouvrirez *Lélia*, renfermez-vous dans votre cabinet pour ne contaminer personne.

Si vous avez une fille dont vous voulez que l'âme reste vierge et naïve, envoyez-la jouer aux champs" (qtd. in Kujaw 589). *La France* in looking back on Sand's literary production up to 1836 classified her novels as "fruits corrompus et corrupteurs d'une monstrueuse fécondité et entre lesquels domine *Lélia*, la plus révoltante et la plus impure de toutes ces impures et révoltantes productions" (qtd. in Kujaw 124). However, Sand's letters at the time speak strongly in favor of monogamy.[8] One is reminded of Sand's reaction to Sainte-Beuve, who told her the novel frightened him: "Ne croyez trop à mes airs sataniques; je vous jure que c'est *un genre* que je me donne" (*Correspondance* 2: 277).

Lélia (and George Sand) finds more merit in the honest acceptance of Trenmor and Pulchérie's lives as gambler and prostitute than in the hypocritical virtue of polite society. Those who profess to act out of generous motives are presented as frauds. That the one selfless friend of mankind is none other than the former gambler and convict is of course an additional slap in the face of conventional social values. In fact, none of the major characters in the novel fulfill socially productive roles.

For Lélia the state of society points to a more general decline:

> Comment pouvez-vous croire, jeune homme, que nous suivons une marche progressive, lorsque vous voyez autour de vous toutes les convictions se perdre, toutes les sociétés s'agiter dans leurs liens lâches, toutes les facultés s'épuiser par l'abus de la vie, tous les principes jadis sacrés tomber dans le domaine de la discussion et servir de jouet aux enfants . . . [le monde] chancelle maintenant comme une ruine qui va crouler pour jamais; encore quelques heures d'agonie convulsive et le vent de l'éternité passera indifférent sur un chaos de nations sans frein, réduites à se disputer les débris d'un monde usé qui ne suffira plus à leurs besoins. (115-16)

Lélia herself is trapped in this downward movement but yet has no feeling for her companions in distress. Lélia's *ennui* expresses the loss of values and inevitable decline that she perceives as the characteristics of her age. At the same time she is able to use her distaste for society as a means of overcoming *ennui*. After her chosen isolation, for instance, she goes back into society because she hopes to "renaître, par la force de son courage, au milieu de ce monde qu'elle haïssait et de ces joies qui lui faisaient horreur" (135). Again the narrative progresses through opposition. For Lélia an easy acceptance of the *vie intérieure* is impossible.

Satiated desires hold no interest for Lélia; as Pulchérie observes, as soon as Lélia gets what she wants, it no longer has any significance to her. The void that her rejection of society leaves can not be filled for Lélia through a refuge in nature. The kind of life in nature Valentine enjoys at the pavilion would be unthinkable for Lélia. When spring comes to the desert, Lélia is unable to share in the general re-awakening to life; she is not one with nature. Like Faust, Lélia is continually searching for a means of personal fulfillment, creating a constantly widening gulf between herself and the rest of mankind. At the same time, Lélia takes pride and even pleasure in her isolation and suffering. Her stay at a ruined monastery points to a masochistic tendency. It is pain and suffering which make her feel alive; at the same time, suffering is a kind of purifying experience which raises the individual to a higher spiritual level. This is brought out by Trenmor's exeriences as a convict.

Lélia also takes pleasure in the suffering she imposes on herself and her lovers through her willful domination of the relationships. The power to dominate her lovers—which she demonstrates in her relationship with Sténio—makes Lélia a very different kind of woman from Indiana or Valentine. It is she, rather than the man, who sets the terms for the relationship. She gives of herself only as much as she decides. Her conception of love is spiritual and rejects the physical. In fact, Sténio considers her unable to love men; he complains that she is as cold as marble. Lélia is aware that her overemphasis on spiritual development has left her incapable of physical love: "Nourrie d'une manne céleste, moi dont le corps était appauvri par les contemplations austères du mysticisme, le sang fatigué par l'immobilité de l'étude, je ne sentis point la jeunesse enfoncer ses aiguillons dans ma chair. J'oubliai de m'éveiller. Mes rêves avaient été trop sublimes; je ne pouvais plus redescendre aux appétits grossiers de la matière. Un divorce complet s'était opéré à mon insu entre le corps et l'esprit" (167). It is a condition which increases her isolation and often causes her to feel inadequate: "Pourquoi m'avez-vous fait naître femme, si vous vouliez un peu plus tard me changer en pierre et me laisser inutile en dehors de la vie commune?" (99). The relationship she imposes on Sténio is one of mother and son, not of lovers. This was to become a frequent pattern in Sand's fiction.

For Sténio this is not enough. His love for Lélia manifests itself through complete devotion and subjugation. He gives all of himself to her and expects the same in return. In the end he sees her refusal of his love as an indication of her failed mission on earth. Lélia's refusal to give of herself to others has led to her isolation and suffering. It has also transformed Sténio's love into hatred. Sténio realizes in the end that what he worshiped in Lélia was not reality, but an elusive ideal: "Je sais aujourd'hui Lélia tout entière, comme si je l'avais possédée; je sais ce qui la faisait si belle, si pure, si divine: c'était moi, c'était ma jeunesse" (288). But losing this illusion does not mean that Sténio is able to achieve the equilibrium which Pulchérie and Trenmor have found. Instead the loss of illusion removes Sténio's reasons for living and leads him to commit suicide.

His own vision of Lélia is not the only illusion Sténio nourished and lost. Just before he dies Sténio tells Magnus at length about his obsession with Don Juan. Sténio originally saw Don Juan as "l'emblème d'une lutte glorieuse et persévérante contre la réalité" (293). In other words, this fictional figure represented for Sténio not only a possible model for his relationship with women but also an avenue of escape from reality. In fact, this is how literature in general is viewed in the novel. Lélia also relates closely to the literary world; she has the impression that she once knew Shakespeare, Tasso and Dante (113). She is guided by her readings of Longus, Anacreon and others to stay longer at the abandoned monastery. But she tells Pulchérie that it is a mistake to allow literature to guide one's life: "Vous avez raison de dire que la poésie a perdu l'esprit de l'homme; elle a désolé le monde réel, si froid, si pauvre, si déplorable au prix des doux rêves qu'elle enfante. Enivrée de ses folles promesses, bercée de ses douces moqueries, je n'ai

jamais pu me résigner à la vie positive. La poésie m'avait créé d'autres facultés, immenses, magnifiques et que rien sur la terre ne devait assouvir" (167). Similarly, Pulchérie rejects the possibility of following the path laid out by poets. She has found her own path to authenticity.

Sténio's love for Lélia had replaced his love for God. This was, in Lélia's view, a common phenomenon: "Nous refusons à Dieu le sentiment de l'adoration, sentiment qui fut mis en nous pour retourner à Dieu seul. Nous le reportons sur un être incomplet et faible, qui devient le dieu de notre culte idolâtre" (55). In fact, Lélia had experienced the same transfer in her first love. At the same time, love can be a kind of revelation of God; Lélia describes it as "l'aspiration sainte de la partie la plus éthérée de notre âme vers l'inconnu" (55). She reconnaît que "pour les âmes poétiques, le sentiment de l'adoration entre jusque dans l'amour physique" (57). If then this adoration is rebuffed, as happens in the case of Sténio and Magnus, it means that the fundamental basis for life has disappeared. Magnus attempts to cure his passion for Lélia through religion. But prayer and fasting do not quell his sexual urges, as debauchery has those of Sténio.

The impossibility of giving birth to a "new man" through religious practices is an attack on the Catholic Church. Magnus's case also calls into question the celibacy of priests. The suffering the Church imposes does not lead to a spiritual rebirth; it leads only to frustration and hypocrisy.

For Lélia Christianity is based on egotism. Lélia respects Jesus as "le Verbe divin fait homme," but she is not able to accept a conventional belief in God. For her and for Trenmor, God can only be found by individuals in solitude, emphasizing the personal, individual relationship to God rather than any community of worshipers. Lélia's worship takes unusual form, as in her prayers to the skeleton of a monk she discovers in the abandoned monastery. It is revealing of Lélia's spiritual quest that it is a disembodied man who represents the divinity. *Lélia* questions not only traditional values of society but fundamental religious tenets as well. In particular, religious beliefs and practices which lead man to hope for a reward in the next life are not only illusory, but are also signs of

egotism and moral cowardice. This emerges in Sténio's glorification of the "homme fort" just before his suicide: "L'homme fort ne prend aucune sûreté pour son avenir et ne recule devant aucun des dangers du présent. Il sait que toutes ses espérances sont enregistrées dans un livre, dont le vent se charge de tourner les feuillets, que tous les projets de sagesse sont écrits sur le sable et qu'il n'y a au monde qu'une vertu, qu'une sagesse, qu'une force, c'est d'attendre le flot et de rester ferme tandis qu'il vous inonde, c'est de nager quand il vous entraîne, c'est de croiser ses bras et de mourir avec insouciance quand il vous submerge" (281). Stoicism emerges as a more durable force than Christianity. As Wingard has pointed out, Sténio's spiritual path from pantheism to skepticism mirrors that of many of Sand's contemporaries (169). Common to all the different religious beliefs embraced by the characters of *Lélia* is a rejection of orthodox Christianity. Not surprisingly, contemporary critics charged Sand with blasphemy.[9]

The vision of *Lélia* is profoundly pessimistic. Our lives are predetermined by fate and by the inevitable downward movement of society. All that remains for the individual is to accept his fate and grow through his suffering. It is only then that one can obtain the kind of equilibrium that Trenmor has achieved: "Aujourd'hui je suis peut-être le plus heureux des hommes, parce que je vis sans projets et sans désirs" (42). It is a sad fate, indeed, if human happiness is to be equated with absolute passivity. Even Lélia's cherished freedom is questioned at the end of the novel. After Sténio's death, Lélia doubts the value of her individual path: "C'est en vain que l'homme veut lutter contre les lois célestes; en refusant son front orgueilleux au joug qui soumet ses semblables, il entre dans une liberté dangereuse. En s'éloignant des routes tracées par la volonté de Dieu, il s'égare, il se perd" (202). She sees herself as "une exception maudite" (199). But the ending can not efface the impression created by the novel up to that point that the kind of personal freedom Lélia enjoys is worth a great deal and is superior to conventional modes of existence. Sainte-Beuve criticized Sand for taking an exceptional case and generalizing it. Indeed, the abstract character of *Lélia* points the reader clearly in this direction. The author herself rejected such a view, as evident in a letter of

November, 1834: "*Lélia* n'est point un livre, c'est un cri de douleur, ou un mauvais rêve, ou une discussion de mauvaise humeur, pleine de vérités et de paradoxes, de justice et de préventions. Il y a de tout, excepté du calme, et sans calme, il n'y a pas de conclusion acceptable. Il ne faudrait pas plus demander un code moral à *Lélia*, qu'un travail d'esprit à un malade. Si quelques femmes ont cru devoir se détacher d'elle, ou s'unir à elle, elles se sont également trompées. Vous l'avez mieux compris, Mademoiselle, puisque vous n'y avez vu qu'une femme à plaindre, et que vous avez fermé le volume en le regardant comme non-avenu." (*Correspondance* 2: 741). This statement is in accord with Sand's many other declarations of this period, claiming that the author had no serious message in her fiction. The novels tell a different tale.

The last pages of the novel represent a kind of epilogue which in a symbolic way shows Lélia having given up her fiercely fought independence. Trenmor sees two lights coming together over the lake from different shores, where the two lovers are buried. This mystical union, the reconciliation of opposites, points to the superiority of the spiritual over the material sides of human existence. The two lovers, unable to come together in the flesh, succeed in the spirit. This is the realization of Lélia's concept of love as "l'aspiration sainte de la partie la plus éthérée de notre âme vers l'inconnu" (55). George Sand clearly felt it necessary to end her novels on at least a symbolically hopeful note. The union of Valentin and Athénaïs at the end of *Valentine* is a of similar symbolic significance.

❖ ❖ ❖

The dark shadows of *Lélia* extend over *Jacques* as well. It too met with considerable hostility on the part of critics, although it was a favorite book of Flaubert's.[10] It was condemned as immoral, an invitation to adultery and suicide and one more attempt to destroy the institution of marriage. In her later preface Sand defends the novel, pointing out that it is really society which wins out in the end since it survives while Jacques perishes. In fact, from her perspective of 1854, Sand views Jacques's suicide critically, as a

capitulation to society. There is at any rate a closer connection between the action of the novel and the values of society in *Jacques*
than in *Lélia*. There is not the same divorce from reality. The action
takes place in a clearly defined time frame (five years) and in identifiable and stated locales in France and Switzerland. Like *Lélia*,
however, there is no mention of contemporary events which would
serve to situate the novel's events more concretely. The characters
in *Jacques* are no more concerned with practical matters of making a
living than those in *Lélia*. They have the leisure to devote their time
to the development of their relationships. Jacques does go off from
time to time to take care of unspecified "business," but this is not
more precisely identified and simply mentioned in passing. Recent
critics have shown how Sand's refusal in her early novels to place
her characters in a concretely depicted social setting is in itself a
protest against social institutions.[11]

Like *Lélia*, *Jacques* has a limited roster of characters, although
here minor figures such as Clémence and M. Borel are introduced
and play a strategic role in the plot.[12] The center of interest is, as in
Lélia, the interaction of a small group of people who develop a
complex and unconventional relationship. It is loosely based on
Goethe's *Wahlverwandtschaften* (*Elective Affinities*).[13] Like the characters in the previous novel they live their lives to extremes.
The thoughts and actions of these characters are also, once again,
"filtered" to the reader. Jacques is an epistolary novel with the
"editor" of the letters only addressing the reader at the end of the
novel to report on Jacques's suicide. Otherwise, the reader culls his
knowledge of the characters from their written accounts which, according to the editor's footnote, are selected from a larger body of
correspondence. Given the inherent artificiality and remoteness of
the epistolary form, Sand was quite successful in finding appropriate and plausible reasons for the characters to correspond, and particularly, for them to chronicle their inner lives and past experiences. The reader learns about Jacques in the beginning of the
novel through the understandable curiosity of Fernande. She is
about to marry a man she scarcely knows and goes about finding
information about him, thus allowing Sand to incorporate reports
of old army friends of Jacques who give essential background

information on his character. Jacques's past is also resuscitated through the request of Sylvia to know the truth about the nature of her family connection to him. Jacques chronicles his relationship for Sylvia at her request because of her intense interest in Jacques and as a lesson she might apply to her own life. The letters are arranged so as to emphasize the sharp contrasts that exist in the major characters' personalities, past lives and world views. Letters in which Fernande naively describes her very limited understanding of Jacques as a suitor are followed by Jacques's cynical analysis of social conventions. The sharp contrasts are used, as in *Lélia*, as a fundamental structuring principle. Through the varied array of characters, the novel is embedded more in social reality; this is reinforced by the letters between Fernande and Clémence which deal with down-to-earth matters of marriage and decorum. Of course, Jacques seems all the more extraordinary when contrasted with such characters and especially when described from the point of view of a seventeen-year old convent girl. Fernande's invitation to Clémence in her letters to help her judge Jacques is a signal to the reader to do the same. However, the reader's privileged insight into Jacques's characters and views—not shared by Fernande and Clémence—leads to the conclusion that the conventional means Clémence uses to understand Jacques's behavior do not suffice. In the process the narrator begins to call into question conventional codes of behavior, a message explicitly reinforced through Jacques's statements on social mores. The efficiency of the message is tempered, however, in the same way as in *Lélia*, by the fact that, as the letters clearly reveal, in Jacques we are dealing with a truly exceptional individual.

The reader's interest in Jacques is stimulated in a manner similar to that used in *Lélia*, through an aura of mystery surrounding him. The first letters all deal with Jacques and his upcoming marriage; Jacques does not speak for himself until well into the novel. By then his character has been established through the letters of Fernande to her friend Clémence and of Sylvia to Jacques. However, the information the letters contain is incomplete and sometimes contradictory. While Fernande describes Jacques as considerate, generous, and intelligent, she also admits to her friend that she is largely correct in assuming Jacques is "un homme vieux, sec et sentant la pipe" (4). She also concedes that "on lui attribue quelques singularités" (6). Fernande acknowledges that she is young and flighty, telling Clémence: "Je suis encore trop pensionnaire. Il faudra que Jacques me corrige de cela, lui qui ne rit pas tous les jours" (5). In her second letter Fernande tells her that Jacques is thirty-five, making him eighteen years older than she. She admits that this has changed her perception of Jacques and led her to become more respectful but also more fearful of Jacques. The impression created by Fernande's comments is not auspicious. Their different social and economic backgrounds could also create future problems. Part of the narrative strategy of the novel hinges on the reader's perception that Jacques and Fernande were not really meant for each other, so that their eventual break-up will be seen as inevitable. This clears the way for Fernande's subsequent union with Octave. As in *Valentine*, relationships are shown not to depend on the will of the partners but on factors beyond their control. From this fact emerges then the conclusion that hard and fast social rules are impossible.

The projected union does not appear any more hopeful if viewed from Jacques's perspective. This is the role which Sylvia's letters play. She describes Jacques as possessing a "caractère insaisissable" and "esprit indompté" (13) and anticipates from his marriage "des douleurs nouvelles" (12) since he is too inflexible and demanding. Her description of Jacques leads the reader to doubt even more the success of the marriage and also increases the interest in Jacques by imbuing him with more mystery: "Vous renoncerez donc à tout ce que vous avez été jusqu'ici et à tout ce que vous auriez été encore! Car votre vie est un grand abîme où sont tombés pêle-mêle tous les biens et tous les maux qu'il est permis à l'homme de ressentir. Vous avez vécu quinze ou vingt vies ordinaires dans une seule année; vous deviez encore user et absorber bien des existences avant de savoir seulement si vous aviez commencé la vôtre" (13). Like Lélia and Trenmor, Jacques has lived his life so intensely that his chronological age is meaningless as a measure of his life's experience. He feels he has lived two or three centuries (51).

He is so out-of-the-ordinary that he creates the impression in others than he is somehow more than human. This, in fact, is explicitly evoked in comments made to Fernande by Jacques's former army comrades. His valor in battle was legendary. His abilities seem to surpass what is humanly possible, as when he fights his first duel against an accomplished swordsman without ever having used a sword before and wins. Jacques is convinced of his superiority; he calmly naps before the duel. He nonchalantly whistles while bullets are removed from his chest. He is very knowledgeable in a great variety of fields without any formal education.

His extraordinary abilities are matched by exceptional suffering and unhappiness. He knows he is different, as he tells Sylvia: "Songerais-tu à établir une comparaison entre moi et le reste des hommes? En fait de souffrance, ne suis-je pas une exception?" (52). He is more courageous than other men but also more miserable. In fact no other human could have lived his life. Like Lélia and other romantic misfits such as Mary Shelley's Frankenstein monster or Adalbert von Chamisso's Peter Schlemihl, Jacques is tragically separated from the rest of mankind. Sylvia calls him a "colosse de vertu farouche" (46). The only companion he can contemplate having in his joy or sorrow is God. Unlike other men, Jacques is unable to forget; everything he has experienced remains a part of him. Like Shelley's monster, Jacques turns into "une espèce de brute vindicative et cruelle" (316), dueling and killing in an uncontrollable thirst for blood and vengeance. Sylvia uses several times the word "abîme" to describe Jacques's character. It is in an abyss, the crevice of a glacier, that Jacques voluntarily ends his life.14 Moreover, like the Frankenstein monster, the impenetrable mountains are at best a refuge from his tormenters. Jacques is also able to climb to areas in the mountains which no human has ever reached. It is above all the extraordinary character of Jacques that takes the novel out of the realm of realism and the *roman de mœurs*. As in *Lélia*, the coherence of the novel lies in its symbolic character. This is all the more the case in that, as we shall see, the reader's perspective on Jacques changes significantly in the course of the novel.

Jacques does not expect any long-term happiness from his marriage to Fernande; he has lost all illusions concerning the permanency of relationships. If he is marrying Fernande it is not in expectation of a life-long union but "parce que c'est l'unique moyen de la posséder" (35). Like other romantic heroes, Jacques willingly enters into a pact which he knows he cannot win. He loves Fernande because he is convinced she is pure, a virgin in body and soul. His hope is to keep her in that state as long as possible, which for Jacques means battling society for her soul. It is with great reluctance that Jacques concedes to society's insistence that their union be sanctified by marriage: "Je ne suis pas réconcilié avec la société, et le mariage est toujours, selon moi, une des plus barbares institutions qu'elle ait ébauchées. Je ne doute pas qu'il ne soit aboli, si l'espèce humaine fait quelque progrès vers la justice et la raison; un lien plus humain et non moins sacré remplacera celui-là, et saura assurer l'existence des enfants qui naîtront d'un homme et d'une femme, sans enchaîner à jamais la liberté de l'un et de l'autre" (36). This is the lesson Sand hoped to impart through her novels of the early 1830's, the need for marriage to be radically redefined. Jacques believes, however, like Lélia, that those who propose an alternative model to traditional marriage are too far ahead of their time to be effective. *Lélia* and *Jacques* belong to a period of profound pessimism in Sand's fictional expression of social change. While *Indiana* and *Valentine* hold out some hope that a recognition of the importance and validity of the *vie intérieure* and its demands can redefine male-female relationships, these novels offer little more than a cry of despair.

Jacques does hope, however, in his own marriage to change the nature of that institution. He and Fernande will say the traditional vows, but Jacques will add his own as well, namely to respect her rights as an equal human being. He promises to give Fernande her freedom any time she desires it. Jacques is more than true to his word. When at one point Fernande goes down on her knees to plead with him Jacques is horrified: "Ce n'est pas ainsi que je veux être aimé; inspirer à ma femme le sentiment qu'un esclave a pour son maître!" (130-31). Later, after Fernande has begun to fall in love with Octave, Jacques refuses to sleep with her if she is not as willing a partner as he. This is a far cry from the views on marriage held by the husbands in Sand's earlier novels or, certainly from those held by the majority of Sand's contemporaries. In this sense, Jacques stands as an exemplary model, someone far enough ahead of his time to be able to anticipate the kind of union of men and women which will develop in the future. Many of Jacques's statements are calculated to provide shock value for the bourgeois reader, as when he states that it is not adultery that is the crime but rather continuing to sleep with one's wife while having an outside liaison.

Indeed, the scandal of the novel was that Jacques goes so far in granting freedom to his wife that when she falls in love with another man, he leaves to make room for him and then commits suicide so as not to be in the way. *Jacques* takes the demand for respect and freedom in marriage made in *Indiana* and *Valentine* to its final logical conclusion. Jacques, in marrying Fernande, had anticipated the day when their love would end and was prepared to accept that fate: "J'essaierai de conjurer la destinée; si cela est impossible, j'accepterai du moins mes défaites avec le stoïcisme d'un homme qui a passé sa vie à chercher la vérité et à cultiver l'amour de la justice au fond de son cœur" (98). As in *Lélia* stoicism is seen as one of the few authentic attitudes in the face of an inimical world. After only a few months of wedded life Jacques already sees that the spiritual separation has begun. But the end does not come as Jacques had anticipated. When Fernande first fell in love with Octave Jacques resolved to have everyone live together. When he discovers that Fernande is expecting Octave's child, he sees that suicide is his only option. He accepts his fate with the assurance that it is not only best for all concerned but, under the circumstances, morally justifiable. This, of course, was hardly a conclusion contemporary critics could embrace.

Beyond the ethico-religious question there is, however, another aspect of Jacques's fate that is problematic in a different sense. The reader is meant to admire Jacques's conduct, even if he may find it goes too far. In the latter part of the novel, the events are presented from Jacques's perspective so that the reader gains considerable insight into his thoughts and concerns. But the Jacques presented after Fernande falls in love with Octave is hard to reconcile with the Jacques of the first half of the novel.[15] There Jacques is presented for the most part from Fernande's perspective, so that he appears overbearing, eccentric and even insensitive. George Sand was intent early on to demonstrate how unfruitful and temporary the marriage between Fernande and Jacques was likely to be. The reader is led to see how unhappy Fernande is in their relationship; this makes it seem likely, given her need for love, that she will seek affection elsewhere. In the second half of the novel, however, the emphasis is less on Jacques's eccentricities and more on his suffering and soul-searching. Only toward the end of the novel does Jacques reveal the war-time experience that has determined his character, his disgust with the killing and the system that produced and condoned it.

Jacques does not blame Fernande and Octave for his fate. He had made a kind of pre-nuptial agreement with Fernande which anticipated such an event: "Ni toi ni moi ne connaissons ce qu'a de force et de durée en toi la faculté de l'enthousiasme, qui seule fait différer l'amour moral de l'amitié. Je ne puis te dire que chez moi cet enthousiasme survivrait à de grandes déceptions; mais la tendresse paternelle ne mourrait pas dans mon cœur avec lui. La pitié, la sollicitude, le dévouement, je puis jurer ces choses-là, c'est le fait de l'homme; l'amour est une flamme plus subtile et plus sainte, c'est Dieu qui le donne et qui le reprend" (74). If he can not assure eternal love for Fernande, then it is logical to assume that she may well love someone else. In this course of events no one is to blame, either for falling in or out of love: "Nulle créature humaine ne peut commander à l'amour, et nul n'est coupable pour le ressentir et pour le perdre" (301). According to Jacques love is different from friendship in that it is beyond the power of reason to control. The essential irrationality and unpredictability of love, clearly shown in the novel, reinforce the fundamental message of the novel, that blame can not be assessed in matters of the heart.

Fernande's views on love are radically different from those of Jacques: the distance that separates them is emphasized so as to lead the reader to anticipate their eventual break-up. Her enthusiastic love leads her to smother Jacques with concern and demonstrative affection. In contrast to Jacques and Sylvia, Fernande's views are traditional and conventional; she is far from sharing their stoic outlook. Jacques sees this as a fault of her upbringing. Her views on woman's role in marriage are diametrically opposed to those of Jacques as well. Early in their relationship she is thrilled when he uncharacteristically commands her; she looks forward to playing a subservient role to her husband. She had dreamed of marrying "un des anges sous les traits d'un homme" (69). Her need to love is mentioned repeatedly. She suffers terribly in her relationship with Jacques but can not conceive of a life without love. Therefore, when Octave appears on the scene the probability of her falling in love is apparent to all except Fernande. The danger Octave represents greatly increases because of the romantic guise in which he appears, a poacher or bandit. Octave sees that Fernande's fears make her ripe for romantic adventure while she believes she is simply serving as a go-between for Octave and Sylvia. When she realizes she may be falling in love she is naive enough to enlist Octave's help in fighting her feelings for him: "Tu m'aideras à être vertueuse et tranquille comme toi" (227). There is a heavy dose of irony at work here, as Fernande believes she can have a platonic relationship with Octave: "Je saurai m'élever jusqu'à toi, et planer du même vol au-dessus des orages des passions terrestres, dans un ciel toujours radieux, toujours pur" (229). The fatalism that hangs over the novel causes the reader to see what Fernande cannot, that it is only a matter of time before she gives in. Yet her struggle is by no means ridiculed. She eventually becomes so intent on her struggle against her passion that it makes her seriously ill. Like Bénédict and Valentine, Fernande and Octave become physically necessary to one another and thus separating them is seen as nothing less than criminal. The mutual attraction and similarity of views and tastes of the two lovers is emphasized. They have such a sympathetic rapport that speech becomes unnecessary. This is a far cry from Fernande's relationship with Jacques, in which the two utterly fail to communicate their inner feelings.

Octave in fact in many ways is a mirror image of Jacques. He is not interested in developing an ideal relationship; in his budding love for Fernande he is enticed by the trappings of his romantic adventure: "J'aurai donc pour quelques jours encore le clair de lune, les appels du hautbois, les promenades sur la mousse, les robes blanches à travers les arbres, les billets sous la pierre du grand ormeau, en un mot ce qu'il y a de plus charmant dans une passion, les accessoires" (181). He has no profession and no desire to have one: "Je ne vois pas vers quoi ma vocation m'attire. Je n'ai aucune passion violente, je ne suis ni joueur, ni libertin, ni poëte; j'aime les arts, et je m'y entends assez pour y trouver un délassement et une distraction; mais je n'en saurais faire une occupation prédominante. Le monde m'ennuie en peu de temps; je sens le besoin d'y avoir un but, et nul autre but m'y semble désirable que d'aimer et d'être aimé" (170-71). For the characters in Sand's early novels love is a vocation, nothing else matters. In pursuing Fernande despite her marriage and his friendship with Jacques, Octave is simply following the dictates of his character, which do not allow for strong resolutions or courageous actions. He admits that his actions are egotistical but defends them nonetheless: "Je suis égoïste, je le sais; mais je le suis sans honte et sans peur. L'égoïsme qui se dissimle et rougit de lui-même est une petitesse et une lâcheté; celui qui travaille hardiment au grand jour est un soldat courageux" (322). In this sense Octave differs from the scheming and deceitful Raymon in *Indiana*. In fact, Jacques sees Octave's egotism this way as well, understanding that this form of egotism is simply an instinct for self-preservation.

If Octave and Fernande share a Goethean "elective affinity," so, too, do Sylvia and Jacques. If it were not for the fact that they may be brother and sister, they would have been perfectly matched. Sylvia has the same view of society as Jacques and a very similar temperament. She is proud and, like Jacques, inexorable in her idealism : "Orgueilleuse jusqu'à la folie, elle veut agir comme si nous étions encore au temps de l'âge d'or, et prétend que tous ceux qui osent la soupçonner sont des lâches et des pervers" (169). Fernande wonders, "avec son âme de bronze, est-ce là une femme?" (184). Octave's relationship with her has been even stormier than that of Fernande and Jacques. He believes her to be incapable of returning passion; in fact, she yearns for an extraordinary passion: "Je me sens dans l'âme une soif ardente d'adorer à genoux quelque être sublime, et je ne rencontre que des êtres ordinaires; je voudrais faire un dieu de mon amant, et je n'ai affaire qu'à des hommes"

(201). She admits to Fernande that she has loved a man whom she can never possess. Such remarks, and her later reaction to Jacques's announced suicide, show that Jacques himself is the man she loves, in the same way that Chateaubriand's Aurélie loves René. But she never tells Jacques so that the delicate and taboo subject is never raised overtly in the novel.[16]

Like Octave and Fernande, Sylvia and Jacques have a special insight into each other's souls. It is through her analysis of Jacques at the end of the novel that the question of Jacques's sacrifice in relation to society is raised. On the one hand, she sees that Jacques was just too intense to survive for long: "Ton âme est trop brûlante; elle ne veut pas vieillir, elle aime mieux se briser que de s'éteindre. Trop modeste pour entreprendre d'éclairer les hommes par la science, trop orgueilleux pour pouvoir briller par le talent aux yeux d'êtres si peu capables de te comprendre, trop juste et trop pur pour vouloir régner sur eux par l'intrigue ou par l'ambition, tu ne savais que faire de la richesse de ton organisation" (346). As was the case with Lélia, his superiority bears no fruit. It is not coincidental that the twins he fathers die. Octave insists to Fernande that his child *will* live and Jacques agrees. Lélia, too, is barren. On the other hand, the age in which he was living is responsible as well: "Quand un homme comme toi naît dans un siècle où il n'y rien à faire pour lui; quand, avec son âme d'apôtre et sa force de martyr, il faut qu'il marche mutilé et souffrant parmi ces hommes sans cœur et sans but, qui végètent pour remplir une page insignifiante de l'histoire, il étouffe, il meurt dans cet air corrompu, dans cette foule stupide qui le presse et le froisse sans le voir" (347). In his final letter Jacques himself sees his death in this light:

> Dans le grand moule où il [Dieu] forge tous les types des organisations humaines, il en a mêlé quelques-uns plus austères et plus réfléchis que les autres. Il a créé ceux-là de telle façon, qu'ils ne peuvent vivre pour eux-mêmes, et qu'ils sont incessamment tourmentés du besoin d'agir pour faire prospérer la masse commune. Ce sont des roues plus fortes qu'il engrène aux mille rouages de la grande machine. Mais il est des temps où la machine est si fatiguée et si usée, que rien ne peut plus la faire

marcher, et que Dieu, ennuyé d'elle, la frappe du pied et la fracasse pour la renouveler. Dans ces temps-là, il y a bien des hommes inutiles, et qui peuvent prendre leur parti d'aimer et de vivre s'ils peuvent, de mourir s'ils ne sont pas aimés et s'ils s'ennuient. (349-50)

As in *Lélia*, a profoundly pessimistic note is struck here. Society has reached such a low point that men of great ability are simply stifled by it and never have the chance to rise up and be leaders. The future thus offers no hope. There is not even a symbolic union at the end as in *Lélia*. Jacques's life ends in profound solitude. For George Sand a worse fate could hardly be imagined.

3

Rising up from Ignorance and Imposture:

Education and Religion in *Mauprat* and *Spiridion*

Esprit de vérité, relève les victimes de l'ignorance et de l'imposture.
—*Spiridion (192)*

Lélia and *Jacques* stand as exceptional works in Sand's *œuvre*. They differ markedly from the novels that precede and from those that follow. The subsequent novels of the 1830s lack their anguish and despair and begin to offer constructive ideas for changing the social order. During this period Sand was coming under the influence of prominent socialist theorists. The year 1835 was pivotal in this sense; in the spring of that year she met Michel de Bourges, Félicité de Lamennais and Pierre Leroux. At the same time she was attending meetings of the Saint-Simonians.[1] It was also the year in which she began to write *Mauprat*. While Leroux's influence did not emerge until several years later, the ideas of Michel and Lamennais took root immediately. However, it is not the case that Sand's social consciousness suddenly sprang to life in 1835. Many of the concerns which Sand addressed in the novels of the late thirties and forties first appeared in her novels of the early 1830s. *Indiana* deals with the position of women in society as well as addressing larger social and political issues. The question of social equality pervades almost all Sand's early works. Sand's awareness of social inequality and her determination to use her fiction to fight it did not suddenly arise when she met Lamennais or Leroux. Indeed, Sand's early novels suggest that she was familiar with Saint-Simonian thought. Sand's social beliefs were personal and deep-rooted, and Leroux and others helped her to channel these concerns in certain directions and to systematize her ideas.

Mauprat and *Spiridion* are novels of spiritual growth and renewal. The protagonists travel paths diametrically opposed to those of Lélia and Jacques. Both novels celebrate achievement of personal goals through abstinence and learning and offer models of hope rather than, like Lélia and Jacques, personifications of despondency. The male-female relationships in *Mauprat* offer a stark contrast to those in the previous novels. This is, in fact, what the author says she set out to do: "La pensée me vint de peindre un amour exclusif, éternel, avant, pendant et après le mariage" (29). After attacking the institution of marriage in her early novels, in *Mauprat* George Sand wanted to celebrate "toute la beauté morale de son principe" (29). *Mauprat* was designed to be a case study of true, eternal love. The frame narrator in introducing the story can claim that although the story is not "précisément agréable et riant. . . . Il se mêle quelque chose de si consolant, et si j'ose m'exprimer ainsi, de si sain à l'âme, que vous m'excuserez, j'espère, en faveur des conclusions" (32). The wholesomeness of the story represents a radical departure from *Lélia* and *Jacques*. Not surprisingly, *Mauprat* was greeted with nearly universal praise by reviewers.[2] Modern criticism has also assessed the novel very positively.[3]

The reader's role in *Mauprat* is also quite different from that in the previous two novels. The frame narrator introduces the aged Bernard Mauprat who then tells his life story. The reader thus sees at the beginning the transformed Bernard and knows, as the story unfolds, that despite all that will happen to Bernard, everything will turn out for the best. As an added symbolic reinforcement of this message the destruction of Roche-Mauprat, the home of the Mauprats and thus the symbol of evil and ignorance, is mentioned three times in the introduction to Bernard's tale. It becomes clear before the story starts that this will be a positive, uplifting tale. Reader interest is thus not keyed so much to *what* will happen as it is to *how* this outcome will be achieved, that is to say, how Bernard is successfully educated. This puts the emphasis on the process, not the result, and invites the reader to reflect on questions of upbringing and education. The reader is reminded of the eventual outcome throughout the novel through the interruptions in Bernard's narrative. The message presented by Bernard's account of his life does not relate directly to the situation of the contemporary reader because of the Mauprats' exceptional social position and the separation from contemporary reality created through the historical setting.

This distancing is reinforced by a kind of fairy-tale aura which pervades the entire novel. The frame narrator strikes this note early in reference to the Mauprat family: "C'est que, dans mon enfance, j'ai placé le nom de Mauprat entre ceux de Cartouche et de la Barbe-Bleue, et qu'il m'est souvent arrivé alors de confondre, dans des rêves effrayants, les légendes surannées de l'Ogre et de Croquemitaine avec les faits tout récents qui ont donné une sinistre illustration, dans notre province, à cette famille des Mauprat" (32). The Mauprats are in fact avatars of a mythic past; they are compared to "paladins du 12e siècle" (41) and Tristan, Bernard's grandfather, ressembles a medieval robber baron. The family history offers ample evidence of their cunning and cruelty and their scandalous treatment of law officials and women. They live outside the pale of legal and moral society and constitute a kind of prototypical villainous family familiar from the historical novels of Walter Scott.

Bernard gives his account of how he came to live with the Mauprats at the infamous Roche-Mauprat in a way which recalls the youth of heroes from medieval romances or fairy tales. After his mother dies—poisoned by his uncle—Bernard is whisked away on horseback at night by his grandfather:

> C'était la réalisation soudaine de toutes les terreurs que ma mère m'avait inspirées en me parlant de son exécrable beau-père et de ses brigands de fils. La lune, je m'en souviens, éclairait de temps

à autre au travers du branchage serré de la forêt. Le cheval de
mon grand-père était sec, vigoureux et méchant comme lui. Il
ruait à chaque coup de cravache, et son maître ne les lui épar-
gnait pas. . . . Enfin, vers minuit, nous nous arrêtâmes brusquement devant une petite porte aiguë, et bientôt le pont-levis se
releva derrière nous. Mon grand-père me prit, tout baigné que
j'étais d'une sueur froide, et me jeta à un grand garçon estropié,
hideux, qui me porta dans la maison. C'était mon oncle Jean, et
j'étais à la Roche-Mauprat. (37)

Bernard is rescued from his evil family by another fairy-tale figure,
whom Bernard evokes upon first seeing Edmée: "J'avais vu des
fées figurer dans mes légendes de chevalerie. Je crus presque que
Morgane ou Urgande venait chez nous pour faire justice" (71). In
fact, while Edmée is repeatedly referred to as a fairy-tale figure,
Bernard is frequently described as an animal, particularly a wolf or
lion; he is a creature in need of transformation in order to become
human. The impression created through this fairy-tale atmosphere
is that Bernard leads a charmed existence, pointing once again to
the happy outcome of Bernard being transformed by the good fairy
Edmée.[4]

    This situation contrasts sharply with the "education" he re-
ceived at Roche-Mauprat. There are no books in the family and the
knowledge passed on to him amounts to no more than anecdotes,
legends and prejudices. He has the impression that his grandfather
knew Charlemagne personally. In the perverted Mauprat family
education begets ignorance and teaching means restraining, as evident from Bernard's relationship to his uncle Jean: "Jean devint
naturellement mon gardien et mon instituteur, c'est-à-dire mon
geôlier et mon bourreau" (45). The language he is taught differs
radically from that he will later learn: "Ce qui, hors de notre
tanière, s'appelait, pour les autres hommes, assassiner, piller, et tor-
turer, on m'apprenait à l'appeler combattre, vaincre et soumettre"
(45-46). When his uncle adopts him he has considerable difficulty
expressing himself. Bernard's early neglect is emphasized in the
text since this is an essential aspect of the novel's thesis, that environment determines character. Bernard's early childhood follows

the pattern of the negative effects of education evoked in Sand's early novels. For Bénédict, too, his education, although totally different, was also something to be discarded. Bernard differs, of course, because he has the good fortune of subsequently receiving a real (positive) education. The importance of education, seen as a force for social progress, becomes a major theme for Sand in the late thirties and early forties.

What makes the Mauprat clan so detestable is that not only do they rape and pillage, but they also exploit the poor whose ignorance turns them into easy victims. The Mauprat family, however low they have sunk, are still presented as representatives of the aristocracy and hence as oppressors. Class struggle emerges in *Mauprat* for the first time as an important theme. The Mauprats resemble Jacques in the sense that they too do not recognize the validity of laws and conventions and, like Jacques, have chosen to "se retirer du monde" (38). But there the similarities end. The Mauprats do not act out of a sense of morality or justice. Beyond the demonstrated need for laws and also for the censuring force of public opinion, the Mauprats also point to a fundamental shift which differentiates *Mauprat* from the earlier *Lélia* and *Jacques*. Sand now sees the virtue of working for change within the system rather than rejecting it outright and glorifying those who refuse to abide by the rules of society. Bernard's story is one of social integration.

Bernard's uncivilized state represents the fundamental barrier between him and Edmée. Even though she has promised herself to Bernard as the price of having Bernard help her escape from Roche-Mauprat, she refuses to yield until he proves himself worthy. She encourages Bernard to earn her love by becoming civilized and educated. Only after seven years and the dramatic events surrounding Bernard's trial does Edmée finally yield. In the meantime, Bernard proves himself by becoming educated and responsible.[5] He also spends several years fighting for the Americans in the Revolutionary War. As his American friend Arthur observes, Bernard is in the position of a medieval knight who has to earn the love of his lady by successfully accomplishing assigned tasks. Indeed, an element of courtly love enters into the relationship of the two cousins. Bernard makes a keepsake he wears around his neck in which he keeps as relics her ring and letters. He refers to her as "madone" (180). But Edmée represents much more for Bernard than a woman on a pedestal. There is also a strong sexual undercurrent in their relationship. Bernard's first encounter with Edmée comes immediately after his uncles challenge him to demonstrate his virility. Edmée is to be his first hapless victim. Her vow that Bernard forces her to make: "Je jure de n'être à personne avant d'être à vous" (84) points in this direction. Later there are rumors that Edmée spent the night at Roche-Mauprat in a wild orgy. Even after Bernard has been "tamed" this aspect of their relationship remains. Edmée keeps a dagger with her at all times in case Bernard loses control. Bernard tells Edmée that he has in fact always viewed her this way: "Je n'ai eu que des désirs, et jamais je n'ai pensé à vous sans devenir fou" (127). He is surprised when Edmée mentions marriage; he had not anticipated that their physical union could develop in that direction. His incentive to be educated does not derive from a desire to marry but from the belief that it is the condition she has attached to his "possession" of her.

For her part, Edmée also shows signs of strong sexual desire for Bernard. This is not as overt as it is in the case of Bernard, but there are nevertheless unmistakable indications. Edmée tells her maid that she likes the rough-hewn look of Bernard, even though his clothes make him look like a poacher. She especially admires his hair, which she prefers unpowdered, a clear reference to Bernard's raw sexual energy. Just after Edmée's discussion of Bernard's hair a scene follows in which Bernard carries Edmée across the Indre while her fiancé looks on passively. The scene is nearly a repetition of that in *Valentine*, with the combination of water and a show of masculine strength and bravura. Afterwards Edmée must stay in bed for several days, an indication of how deeply the incident has affected her.

The change in Bernard is not, however, as complete or radical as might seem from a summary of his development. In fact, Bernard already showed positive aspects of his character when he was at Roche-Mauprat. Even though he accepts the way of life and manners of the Mauprats, he does not share their penchant for evil. He has an instinctive horror of his uncles' cruelty. When he accompanies his uncles as a bandit, he secretly helps the victims afterwards. His generosity and fair-mindedness also emerge in his first encounter with Patience; after the hermit humiliates him, Bernard does not seek revenge by reporting the affront to his uncles. At the same time, his savage ways do not entirely disappear after he is educated. On several occasions he is ready to commit murder in order to eliminate rivals for Edmée's love. It is especially in his impetuous behavior toward her that the old Bernard emerges. This reaches its climax during the hunt when Edmée and Bernard stray away from the others. He is nearly unable to control his passion: "J'étais pâle, mes poings se contractaient; je n'avais qu'à vouloir, et la plus faible de mes étreintes l'eût arrachée de son cheval, terrassée, livrée à mes désirs. Un moment d'abandon à mes instincts farouches, et je pouvais assouvir, éteindre, par la possession d'un instant, le feu qui me dévorait depuis sept années!" (252). As if it were a punishment for this relapse, he is shortly thereafter unjustly accused of having shot Edmée.

    At the trial it is not just Bernard who is being judged but also the question of whether someone in his position could really have changed for the better. This is the case the prosecutor makes: "L'avocat du roi eut beau jeu à déclamer un réquisitoire fulminant, dans lequel il me présenta comme un pervers incurable, comme un rejeton maudit d'une souche maudite, comme un exemple de la fatalité des méchants instincts" (277). Bernard's acquittal marks the triumph of Sand's thesis. That it is Edmée whose testimony assures Bernard's release highlights her role in his education. Passionate love in *Lélia* leads to despair, suicide and murder. In *Mauprat* it is a force which uplifts and sanctifies. In both novels, however, it is the woman who has in her power the fate of her lover. It is Lélia who destroys Sténio and Magnus, just as it is Edmée who saves Bernard. For Bernard, even though facing a death sentence, the question of love becomes more important than the decision of the court: "Je n'avais que cette préoccupation dans l'esprit; je ne me souvenais même plus de la cause ni du but de mon procès. Il me semblait que la question agitée dans ce froid aréopage était uniquement celle-ci: *Est-il aimé, ou n'est-il pas aimé?* Le triomphe ou la défaite, la vie ou la mort n'étaient que là pour moi" (301). Love in Sand's fiction

represents a palpable force capable of great destruction or of immense benefit. Other concerns often must yield to the power of
passion. In Bernard's case it is capable of unraveling the web of
"fatalité" which has been woven around him. The use of repeated
references to the hand of fate hovering over Bernard represents a
kind of straw man which Bernard's triumphant acquittal knocks
down definitively. His life becomes a clear demonstration of the
fact that fate does *not* control human lives, that man is free to determine his own character and destiny.

George Sand makes sure that the message the story is to
project reaches the reader. Edmée educates Bernard, Bernard educates the frame narrator. The reader's viewpoint coincides with
that of the narrator: both are hearing the story told by Bernard.
The reader's identification with the frame narrator is solidified in
the beginning of the novel through the sympathetic portrait of
Bernard and the fact that he is in the "present" like the reader. The
narrator anticipates the expected reader reaction to the *Mauprat*
family; he shudders at the mere mention of the name. He thus
serves to condition the reader's response at the outset. Crecelius
has pointed to the fact that using a male voice in the frame narration forces the actual (male) reader to take the story—and message—more seriously than if a female voice had been employed.[6]

It is difficult to escape the message the novel projects. Bernard explicitly evokes it for the narrator (and reader) at the end of
the novel. Bernard as narrator refers a number of times to the lesson
his transformation teaches: "Ne croyez pas trop à la phrénologie;
car j'ai la bosse du meurtre très-développé, et, comme disait Edmée
dans ses jours de gaieté mélancolique, on *tue de naissance* dans notre
famille. Ne croyez pas à la fatalité, ou du moins n'exhortez personne à s'y abandonner. Voilà la morale de mon histoire" (313).
This is a tone and emphasis differing markedly from *Lélia* and the
earlier novels. Now George Sand, coming increasingly under the
sway of early socialist thought, was beginning to think of her
novels as instruments for propagating ideas. *Mauprat* is fundamentally a *roman à thèse*.[7] The doctrine on which the thesis rests derives
largely from the works of Rousseau, who is repeatedly evoked in
the narrative. Indeed, in his conclusion Bernard cites Rousseau in

giving his final lesson to be gathered from his life story: "L'homme ne naît pas méchant; il ne naît pas bon non plus, comme l'entend Jean-Jacques Rousseau, le vieux maître de ma chère Edmée. L'homme naît avec plus ou moins de passions, avec plus ou moins de vigueur pour les satisfaire, avec plus ou moins d'aptitude pour en tirer un bon ou un mauvais parti dans la société. Mais l'éducation peut et doit trouver remède à tout; là est le grand problème à résoudre, c'est de trouver l'éducation qui convient à chaque être en particulier" (314). Bernard qualifies here not so much Rousseau, but a simplistic reading of the second *Discours*. In fact, Edmée bases her direction of Bernard's education on *Émile*. The novel's final lesson is an extension of the principle of the educability of man, namely a plea against the death penalty "qui n'est autre chose que la consécration du principe de la fatalité, puisqu'elle suppose le coupable incorrigible et le ciel implacable" (314). George Sand is no longer content merely to evoke social inequities, she now offers specific ideas on changing social institutions.[8]

The fact that Sand bases her vision of social justice and the inhumanity of capital punishment in *Mauprat* in part on divine mercy points to another influence in *Mauprat*, that of Lamennais. As Wingard has shown, Lamennais refocused for Sand aspects of Rousseau's religious belief (329). He added to Rousseau's religion a social dimension emphasizing equality and based on the precepts of early Christianity. The hopeful thrust of *Mauprat*—so different from *Lélia* or *Jacques*—is at least in part a reflection of Lamennais's belief in the spiritual progression of mankind. The negative portrait of conventional Christianity may reflect his influence as well. The only positive cleric—Abbé Aubert—is rejected by the Church, while the self-serving Jean Mauprat becomes almost a saint. The monks live lives of leisure and luxury; their only efforts involve extortion and vengeance.

There is a second character in the novel who travels a path roughly parallel to that of Bernard: the hermit Patience. An unschooled peasant, his natural curiosity turns into a passion for learning. In meetings with the abbé Aubert, Patience becomes enthralled with new ideas of enlightenment: "Dans ces conciliabules mystérieux, l'imagination de Patience, restée si fraîche et si ardente dans la solitude, s'enflamma de toute la magie des idées et des espérances qui fermentaient alors en France depuis la cour de Versailles jusqu'aux bruyères les plus inhabitées" (53). Part of the optimism of *Mauprat* is in its celebration of the joy of learning and of personal growth through knowledge. After becoming acquainted with Rousseau and the *philosophes*, Patience is introduced to the epic poets of antiquity. This has a dramatic effect on his outlook on life: "Avant de connaître les poëtes, disait-il dans ses dernières années, j'étais comme un homme à qui manquerait un sens. Je voyais bien que ce sens était nécessaire, puisque tant de choses en sollicitaient l'exercice. Je me promenais seul la nuit avec inquiétude, me demandant pourquoi je ne pouvais dormir, pourquoi j'avais tant de plaisir à regarder les étoiles, que je ne pouvais m'arracher à cette contemplation; pourquoi mon cœur battait tout d'un coup de joie en voyant certaines couleurs, ou s'attristait jusqu'aux larmes à l'audition de certains sons" (119). The power of imaginative literature to help the individual use his senses to perceive the world and realize his potential indicates to what extent books can help to educate and uplift man. Not surprisingly, there are a large number of allusions to literature, including specific references to Beaumarchais and Franklin.

Literature has given Patience something more, namely the faith in the possibility of educating the common man:

> Depuis que je sais qu'il est permis à l'homme sans dégrader sa raison, de peupler l'univers et de l'expliquer avec ses rêves, je vis tout entier dans la contemplation de l'univers; et, quand la vue des misères et des forfaits de la société brise mon cœur et soulève ma raison, je me rejette dans mes rêves; je me dis que, puisque tous les hommes se sont entendus pour aimer l'œuvre divine, ils s'entendront aussi, un jour, pour s'aimer les uns les autres. Je m'imagine que, de père en fils, les éducations vont en se perfectionnant. Peut-être suis-je le premier ignorant qui ait deviné ce dont il n'avait aucune idée communiquée du dehors. Peut-être aussi bien d'autres avant moi se sont inquiétés de ce qui se passait en eux-mêmes, et sont morts sans en trouver le premier mot. (119-20)

Patience himself demonstrates the thirst of the lower classes for knowledge and the waste of human potential that the lack of educational possibilities for the masses represents. Patience is himself very aware of social distinctions. His encounter with Bernard early in the novel constituted a class conflict. According to Patience, the intelligence of the lower classes has been undermined by vices which the higher classes have not discouraged. The direct corroboration between clean virtuous living and intelligence is evoked as well in Aubert's assessment of Patience: "Il connaissait toute la pureté des mœurs de Patience, et il s'expliquait l'ascendant de son esprit par le pouvoir et le charme que la vertu exerce et répand autour d'elle" (50). Patience is incensed over Bernard's cruelty to him when he was a boy largely because he mistakenly believed Bernard knew how to read and write and therefore had no excuse for behaving badly.

Patience's exemplary life has resulted not only in a rudimentary knowledge but, one may logically deduce, also in his power to perceive more than is normally possible. After Bernard kills his bird, Patience warns of the coming upheaval: "Avant cent ans, avant moins peut-être, il y aura bien des changements sur la terre. . . . Le pauvre a assez souffert; il se tournera contre le riche, et les châteaux tomberont, et les terres seront dépecées. . . . Il parlait avec énergie. Son regard brillait comme la flamme, son front était baigné de sueur; il y avait en lui quelque chose de puissant comme la parole des vieux prophètes" (134).

He predicts the coming of the revolution on other occasions as well. Patience is the first of the "paysans illuminés" whom Sand introduced into her fiction as she began to focus her energy on the liberation of the working class. They are seers who point the way of the future for the common man. This is in keeping with Sand's belief that leadership toward the new classless society she advocated would derive not from the upper but from the working classes. Beyond prophesying a coming age of equality and social justice, Patience also helps Edmée in her attempts to create such a world on her father's estate. Upon his return home from America Bernard discovers that the park of the château has been transformed into a kind of model farm. Patience has become the treasurer of Edmée's charitable works but instead of giving the poor money, the principle is "à chacun selon son besoin." Patience determines the specific needs of the peasant families and fills them. There is also another aspect to this system. The peasants are simply too ignorant to know how to use money wisely and effectively. Edmée's charitable system is another reminder of the need for universal education of the lower classes. Edmée and Patience's cooperative effort to help the poor represents as well a fusion of the two oppressed groups of society, women and working class. Their union not only foreshadows the trend in Sand's novels of the 1840s, but it also reinterprets the past, showing a different possible result of the French Revolution.[9]

Although Bernard and Patience demonstrate Sand's thesis on the desirability of educating the common man, they are not totally one-sided characters. Their constant striving encounters numerous personal and public obstacles, and their actions transform them into more human characters than the type figures of Sténio and, to a lesser extent, Jacques. However, the same observation does not apply to Edmée. She suffers from a similar more-than-human aura that surrounds Lélia. She does not need to undergo any change in the novel since her perfection is evident from the beginning: "Élevée aux champs, elle était forte, active, courageuse, enjouée: elle joignait à toutes les grâces de la beauté délicate toute l'énergie de la santé physique et morale. C'était une fière et intrépide jeune fille autant qu'une douce et affable châtelaine" (117). In contrast to Bernard she never escapes from the fairy-tale world in which he initially places her.[10] There are indications that she has the potential to evolve into a flesh-and-blood character, but these beginnings are not carried through. I am thinking particularly of the scene in which Bernard carries Edmée across the Indre. The passion that Edmée feels for Bernard during that incident seems to fade away afterwards. Other passages suggest that Edmée has no desire for a union with Bernard. She tells Aubert that she was destined to have a happy life until her encounter with Bernard has virtually destroyed everything worth living for in her life. Marrying Bernard would bring disaster: "Il n'est rien de plus possible que de se vouer au malheur et au désespoir; rien de plus possible, par conséquent, que d'épouser Bernard Mauprat" (143). There is no hint of any passion for him. Of course these statements are made to Aubert and necessarily colored by that fact. But nevertheless the force with which she states her feelings points to an inconsistency in the portrayal of her attitude toward Bernard which is something other than indecision.[11] George Sand wanted to keep the reader in the dark as to Edmée's feelings for Bernard so as to make more sensational the coup-de-théâtre at the trial in which she admits her love before a packed courtroom. However, the confession comes too late since the reader has come to experience Bernard as a human being, someone who should not be kept waiting for seven years without clear reasons; that could have been appropriate for a medieval romance. Sensing the reader's frustration, Sand has her heroine offer explanations for her refusal to acknowledge Bernard's love for so long. But her explanation does not convince: "A mesure que tu as grandi à mes yeux, j'ai senti que je pouvais attendre, parce que j'avais à t'aimer longtemps, et que je ne craignais pas de voir évanouir ma passion avant de l'avoir satisfaite, comme font les passions dans les âmes faibles. Nous étions deux caractères d'exception, il nous fallait des amours héroïques; les choses ordinaires nous eussent rendus méchants l'un et l'autre" (310). Edmée was living a heroic dream, her readings perhaps having guided her behavior. In any event, if the reader accepts Edmée's statement on the exceptional nature of her and Bernard's relationship, this calls into question the universality of Sand's thesis in the novel. Was Bernard's transformation extraordinary due to the coming together of two extraordinary individuals? If so, his case is irrelevant to the theory of the desire and ability of the common man to rise himself up intellectually. The fairy-tale aura and gothic paraphernalia work against the reader's application of the thesis to the real world. In *Mauprat* George Sand was striving to convert her fiction into a teaching tool—which demanded a certain minimum of verisimilitude—while at the same time she remained indebted for the construction of the characters and incidents to literary traditions which led in a diametrically opposite direction.

❖ ❖ ❖

Spiridion (1838) is closer in character to *Lélia* than to *Mauprat* in that it too represents a radical divorce from the real world. This is true despite the fact that time and place are clearly stated; the action takes place in a monastery in Italy during the Napoleonic era. Of course, one can hardly speak of action in discussing *Spiridion*. It is a mystical novel in the mold of Balzac's *Louis Lambert* or *Séraphita* The novel is essentially the account of a spiritual odyssey, one that stretches across time and involves several different individuals in the same quest. The story is told in the first person, first by Angel the novitiate monk and then by Alexis, the scholar-scientist who becomes Angel's mentor and finally by Angel again. The narrative form is actually even more complex in that Alexis in his account to Angel of his own spiritual journey also relates the life of Spiridion, the founder of the monastery and, to a lesser extent, of Fulgence, his own mentor. The narrative form is effective here because the frankly subjective mode of narration corresponds better to the subject matter than did the omniscient narrator of *Lélia*. The reader is immediately drawn into first the perspective of Angel and then that of Alexis. The intertwining narrations also reinforce one of the basic ideas in the novel, that of the continuation of one person's life into that of another.

Reader involvement in the opening of the novel is effected, as in *Lélia* and *Jacques*, through mystery. Angel is unaccountably being ostracized by the other monks, even by his confessor and the prior, despite the fact that he is intelligent and dedicated. His confessor even pushes Angel away, knocking him unconscious in the process. This inexplicable treatment of Angel, whose name aptly describes his character, not only raises questions as to the monks' motivations but also introduces the reader to their indiscriminate brutality. Later Alexis reinforces this initial negative impression of the monks, in his explanation to Angel of why he was mistreated: "Ils veulent te rendre pervers, stupide et infâme. . . . Ils veulent t'enseigner la haine hypocrite, la vengeance patiente, la couardise et la férocité. Ils veulent que ton âme meure pour avoir été nourrie de miel, pour avoir aimé la douceur et l'innocence. Ils veulent, en un mot, faire de toi un moine" (208-9). As in *Mauprat* there is in *Spiridion* a clear choice between characters representing good and

those dedicated to evil. After presenting the brutality and immorality of the corrupted aristocracy of the Mauprat family, Sand moves on in *Spiridion* to another group holding power under the *ancien régime*, the clergy.

Angel's relationship to the other monks is not the only obscure aspect of the novel's opening pages. Alexis's behavior appears impenetrable to Angel, through whose eyes the reader views the action. He does not lead the same life as the other monks; he does not join in prayer sessions but keeps to himself in his tower study. The novitiates are told not to have anything to do with him. Angel is at a loss as to how to interpret Alexis's actions. He sees Alexis, for instance, studying a book intently, but when he too looks at it he discovers the pages are blank. Later in the novel, the reader finds out that the book is written in invisible ink to conceal its contents from the other monks. The power and mystery of books and knowledge form a major focus in this novel. As in *Mauprat* Sand highlights learning as a major step toward mankind's elevation.

The "spirit" that Alexis continuously evokes in Angel's presence leads him to wonder whether it is the Holy Ghost or the devil that Alexis is conjuring; only later do we learn it is the spirit of Spiridion. The most striking events designed to arouse the reader's interest in pursuing the story concern Spiridion himself and Angel's encounter with his spirit. The first-person narration places such gothic occurrences—even more plentiful in this novel—in a different perspective. The reader experiences the chilling events along with the characters, rather than viewing them from outside. Moreover, the gothic elements are fully integrated into the thematic structure of the novel. The monastic setting, especially as seen through the eyes of a young boy, makes the appearance of the gothic paraphernalia natural and inevitable. The reader does not have to wait long for the fulfillment of this expectation. After being knocked unconscious, Angel is revived by a mysterious, refreshing breeze which appears from nowhere. He then hears a sigh from the prie-dieu and subsequently a voice which proclaims: "Esprit de vérité, relève les victimes de l'ignorance et de l'imposture" (192). Alexis later repeats this formula. Angel then sees a "shadow" pass out of the room. Shortly thereafter, Angel sees a stranger in the monastery whose appearance suggests an angelic quality. It is only later, however, that Angel suspects the supernatural nature of this visitor, when he sees the same figure in two paintings depicting Pierre Hébronius, alias Spiridion. What happens next is no surprise to the reader familiar with the *roman noir*: "Je regardai involontairement le portrait d'Hébronius, et je joignis les mains, emporté par un mouvement irrésistible de confiance et d'espoir. Le soleil frappait en cet instant le visage du fondateur, et il me sembla voir sa tête se détacher du fond, puis sa main et tout son corps quitter le cadre et se pencher en avant. Le mouvement fit ondoyer la chevelure, les yeux s'animèrent et attachèrent sur moi un regard vivant" (237). The figure emerging from the portrait is something more than just another gothic trick. It has been prepared by Angel's previous encounters with the voice and the figure of Spiridion. More importantly, Spiridion's ability to transform his being from inanimate to animate points both to his spiritual nature and to the idea of transformation, a central concern in the novel.

Spiridion's presence as a roving spirit is emphasized by contrast with an event which occurs immediately after Angel's experience with the portrait. When Angel is sitting with the ailing Alexis in his cell, he has what appears to be another supernatural encounter: "La porte s'ouvrit brusquement, et une figure épouvantable vint se placer en face de moi. Je demeurai terrifié au point de ne pouvoir articuler un son ni faire un mouvement. Mes cheveux se dressaient sur ma tête et mes yeux restaient attachés sur cette horrible apparition comme ceux de l'oiseau fasciné par un serpent" (238). Alexis, however, receives this purported emissary of the devil calmly; he unmasks the apparition as a fellow monk sent by the prior to try to frighten Alexis and Angel into a confession of Satanic practices. He explains to Angel that "tous ces démons, toutes ces créations infernales, dont parlent tous les jours les ignorants ou les imposteurs, sont de vains fantômes créés par l'imagination des uns pour épouvanter celle des autres" (245). The effect of this episode is not only to suggest by comparison the reality of the visions of Spiridion but also to expose the depravity of the other monks.

Other supernatural occurrences reinforce the critical vision of the Catholic Church. Alexis tries repeatedly to retrieve the manuscript that Spiridion ordered to be entombed with him when he died. When descending into the burial vaults on the second try he encounters scenes of horror that rival those of the goriest of gothic tales: "Il y avait de chaque côté une rangée d'êtres immondes, revêtus de la forme humaine, mais d'une laideur effroyable, occupés à dépecer des cadavres, à dévorer des membres humains, à tordre des viscères, à se repaître de lambeaux sanglants. De la voûte pendaient, en guise de clefs et de rosaces, des enfants mutilés qui semblaient pousser des cris lamentables, ou qui, fuyant avec terreur les mangeurs de chair humaine, s'élançaient la tête en bas" (344). Later these inanimate figures come to life and try to seize Alexis. Afterwards Spiridion appears to him and explains the significance of those visions: "Tu as vu dans cet édifice composé de figures de bronze et de marbre, tour à tour dévorantes et dévorées, un symbole des âmes que le catholicisme a endurcies et mutilées, une image des combats que les générations se sont livrés au sein de l'Église profanée, en se dévorant les unes aux autres le mal qu'elles avaient subi" (352). Here, too, the supernatural occurrences are not gratuitous, as is the case in *Lélia* or *Mauprat*, but form part of the ideological framework of the novel.

The image of the Catholic faithful devouring themselves over successive generations is in direct opposition to the mystical view of human development championed in *Spiridion*. Angel's visions of Spiridion suggest the continuation of life after death before this is presented theoretically by Spiridion to Fulgence on the former's death-bed:

> Nul n'est plus ennemi que moi, tu le sais, des grossières jongleries dont les moines se servent pour terrifier leurs adeptes . . . mais je crois aux apparitions et aux songes qui ont jeté quelquefois une salutaire terreur ou apporté une vivifiante espérance à des esprits sincères et pieusement enthousiastes. Les miracles ne me paraissent pas inadmissibles à la raison la plus froide et la plus éclairée. Parmi les choses surnaturelles qui, loin de causer de la répugnanace à mon esprit, lui sont un doux rêve et une

vague croyance, j'accepterais comme possibles les communica-
tions directes de nos sens avec ce qui reste en nous et autour de
nous des morts que nous avons chéris. (266-67)

The same contrast is made here between charlatanism and true
spiritualism. The apparent supernatural—familiar from the gothic
tradition—is relegated to the deception of dishonest monks. The
believability of the transmigration of souls is offered as an explicit
contrast. Patience had evoked metempsychosis in *Mauprat* as his
reason for being a vegetarian. Revealingly, in opposition to the
tenets of their religion, the monks cling to a superstitious and negative view of life after death, as in their fear of Spiridion: "Une superstition, qui durera tant qu'il y aura des couvents, condamnait
son spectre à errer sur la terre jusqu'à ce que les portes du purgatoire tombassent tout à fait devant son repentir ou devant les sup-
plications des hommes" (274). After the tentative suggestion put
forward by Spiridion, later statements and events evoke more
clearly the reality of this phenomenon. The possibility of continuing one's spiritual quest after death—through the incorporation of
one's spirit into that of a living person—offers the chance of reaching spiritual fulfillment, even if it takes several generations. The
evocation of metempsychosis dramatically highlights Sand's belief
in progress. Even if the mystical aspect of mankind's growth is rejected, the idea of continual development remains. It is no coincidence that the works celebrating this belief, *Mauprat* and *Spiridion*,
are both historical novels, allowing Sand to give a practical demonstration of change and growth over time. In a sense, *Spiridion* is an
amplification of the position argued in *Mauprat* that the physical
being can be controlled by the intellect. Bernard Mauprat's case
offers an extreme example of this process. The frequent use of animal images in reference to Bernard is no accident. In *Spiridion* the
idea of transformation is taken a step further, not animal to man,
but man to angel.

Alexis, as a scientist, finds nothing rationally objectionable
in the idea of metempsychosis. Just as modern science has found
explanations for phenomena previously thought supernatural, he
has faith that the transmigration of souls might too one day be

scientifically understood. Actually, science is treated in an ambiguous way in the novel. On the one hand, scientific enquiry is celebrated as a means of enlightenment. In fact, Spiridion founds his monastery "pour se livrer avec eux [les moines] à la recherche de toutes les vérités, et travailler à l'agrandissement et à la corroboration de la foi par la science" (253). Alexis becomes a scholar and scientist, excelling in the fields of astronomy, geology and physics. However, he comes to see a danger in immersing himself too deeply in science: "Dans les sciences, la difficulté vaincue est si enivrante que les résolutions consciencieuses, les instincts du cœur, la morale de l'âme, sont sacrifiés, en un clin d'œil, aux triomphes frivoles de l'intelligence" (355). The question he raises is the same one evoked in other works of the age such as *Frankenstein* or the tales of E.T.A. Hoffmann: the suppression of basic human feelings of morality and compassion which can disappear behind an over-concern with science.

Alexis begins to see the moral dangers of science after he has become seriously ill and developed a strong attachment to the monk Christophe who nursed him. When Christophe dies, his dog follows him shortly thereafter in true devotion. This leads Alexis to begin to see the value of friendship: "Je sentis alors profondément que la plus humble amitié est un plus précieux trésor que toutes les conquêtes du génie" (363). Alexis gets a chance to demonstrate his sense of fraternal love when an epidemic breaks out and he is called upon to help care for the ill. To provide more effective help, he temporarily leaves the monastery and goes to live for three months with a hermit who is devoting all his efforts to combatting the epidemic and ministering to the afflicted. His experiences during his stay lead him to change his attitude toward science. He sees that his pursuit of knowledge was essentially a form of egotism. His model becomes the hermit, whom he considers a genuine saint, but whose life and work are too obscure to be recognized by the Church.

Alexis eventually sees that fraternal love can become a kind of religion: "Ami Spiridion, tu le savais bien quand tu me disais: aime et tu comprendras! O ma science frivole! O mon érudition stérile! Vous ne m'avez pas éclairé sur le véritable sens des

Ecritures! C'est depuis que j'ai compris l'amitié, et par elle la charité, et par la charité l'enthousiasme de la fraternité humaine, que je suis devenu capable de comprendre la parole de Dieu" (436). Religious exaltation and brotherly love go hand in hand. It is significant that it is the hermit who leads Alexis to change his life. Alexis comes to realize that only in solitude can man realize his divine potential: "[Dieu] l'a [l'homme] fait perfectible dans le bien, corrigible dans le mal. Si, dans la société, l'homme peut se considérer souvent comme perdu pour la société, dans la solitude l'homme n'est jamais perdu pour Dieu; car, tant qu'il lui reste un souffle de vie, ce souffle peut faire vibrer une corde inconnue au fond de son âme" (357). The solitude evoked here is possible even when one is not alone. It is the kind of spiritual peace of mind that Trenmor (*Lélia*) achieves when he is on a slave ship and which Alexis recommends to Angel as the path he should follow at the monastery: "Cherche ta solitude au milieu d'eux" (210-11). This feeling of solitude in the midst of others is not a form of egotism, but rather a path to God.

This is the mission monasteries are supposed to accomplish, to allow the seeker of truth to concentrate all his efforts on the life of the spirit and exclude the life of the body. However, the monks have perverted this purpose by using the monastery as a place in which they can lead lives of lust and laziness. Alexis realizes that Spiridion's message to him was not to follow blindly the ways of the monks or of anyone else, but to find his own path: "La pensée de Spiridion a été celle-ci, me disais-je: Ne croyez pas sur la foi les uns des autres, et ne suivez pas comme des animaux privés de raison, le sentier battu par ceux qui marchent devant vous. Ouvrez vous-mêmes votre voie vers le ciel; tout chemin conduit à la vérité celui qu'une intention pure anime et que l'orgueil n'aveugle pas. La foi n'a d'efficacité véritable qu'autant qu'elle est librement consentie" (291). Freedom of choice is absolutely essential if man is to find himself. On his death-bed Alexis feels that his greatest accomplishment is being able to say: "Je suis libre" (422). He is able to make that statement because he returned to the monastery of his own volition after the epidemic. In the process he resists another temptation, that of worldly glory—another form of egotism—that is offered to him by the young Corsican, none other than the future emperor, whose ship stops over near the hermit's hut.

Alexis's freedom of thought and action contrasts markedly with the regimented, mindless life led by the other monks. After his return, Alexis soon discovers that a monk's life, too, is steeped in egotism. This realization crystallizes in his reaction to the approaching death of a monk who is considered a model of faith and devotion: "Tu as raison de craindre et de trembler à cette heure; tu fais bien de te tenir toujours prêt à paraître devant le juge! Puisses-tu trouver à ton heure dernière une formule qui t'ouvre la porte du ciel, ou un instant de remords qui t'absolve du pire de tous les crimes, celui de n'avoir rien aimé hors de toi" (407). His words constitute the essence of the criticism of Catholicism in the novel, that it leads its followers toward selfishness and away from a concern for their fellow-men: "Le catholique ne se rattache à rien dans l'histoire du genre humain et ne sait rien rattacher au christianisme. Il s'imagine être le commencement et la fin de la race humaine . . . aussi le catholique croit-il n'avoir ni père ni frères dans l'histoire de la race humaine" (304). The monks persecute Angel because they suspect he does not share their base instincts, and because, unlike them, he is not solely concerned with his personal welfare. Sand's perception of the Catholic Church at this time, as an institution denying the progressive development of mankind, clashed with her view of man's history and future.

Other organized religions do not fare any better in the novel. Spiridion successively rejects Judaism and Protestantism. In following Spiridion and Alexis's spiritual development, the reader receives a detailed account of their encounters with organized religion. Spiridion was born a Jew (in Austria) but rejects Judaism because of its exclusivity. He first embraces Protestantism but then, influenced above all by Bossuet, converts to Catholicism. Spiridion's need for faith makes him more inclined to accept a church which institutionalized certainty and authority. But he soon feels oppressed under the weight of the Church "et la liberté d'examen, qu'il avait autrefois dédaignée, rentra victorieusement dans son intelligence" (255). Spiridion comes to view Jesus as human which leads him to make Jesus—and God—accountable in human terms.

He finds the cruelty which results from this perspective so disturbing that it leads him to discard Christianity all together.

Alexis's spiritual path is similar and emerges in even more
detail, as he passes from the study of official church literature (292)
to the "heretic" writers (295), then to the classical authors (301) and
finally to his contemporaries, the *philosophes* (310). As he progresses in his studies, his faith evolves as well: "Dire que je passai à
Wiclef, à Jean Huss, et puis à Luther, et de là au scepticisme, c'est
faire l'histoire de l'esprit humain durant les siècles qui m'avaient
précédé, et que ma vie intellectuelle, par un enchaînement de né-
cessités logiques, résuma assez fidèlement" (300-01). This statement
points to the reason for the inclusion of this detailed account of religious theory in the novel; Sand was aspiring to provide a model
for the development which mankind in general has undergone.
The important result of this succession of religious beliefs is to
show, once again, that mankind is moving progressively toward
greater knowledge. Spiridion and Alexis provide concrete and en-
capsulated examples of western man's religious history. The argu-
mentations included also provide a means of anticipating and
possibly redirecting the reader's own religious orientation.

Despite rejecting all organized religion Alexis still inclines
toward faith: "Je gardai pour toute religion une croyance pleine de
désir et d'espoir en la divinité, le sentiment inébranlable du juste et
de l'injuste, un grand respect pour toutes les religions et pour
toutes les philosophies, l'amour du bien et le besoin du vrai" (302).
Above all, Alexis has a profound respect and love for Jesus, not as
the son of God, but as someone able to embody the noblest instincts
of mankind: "Nous pouvons adorer chez l'homme investi d'une
haute science et d'une haute vertu un reflet splendide de la Divinité. O Christ! Un temps viendra où l'on t'élèvera de nouveaux
autels, plus dignes de toi, en te restituant ta véritable grandeur,
celle d'avoir été vraiment le fils de la femme et le sauveur, c'est-à-
dire l'ami de l'humanité, le prophète de l'idéal" (420).[12] According
to Alexis, one should strive to emulate such men and even if organized religion does not hold the answer, man should still strive toward an ideal: "L'homme privé d'idéal est l'esclave de lui-même,
de ses instincts matériels, de ses passions farouches, tyrans plus

absolus, maîtres plus fantasques que tous ceux qu'il a renversés avant de tomber sous l'empire de la fatalité" (423). Alexis sees this reaching for an ideal as a manifestation of God's love, as the divine spark in man. The influence of Lamennais is evident here as it is throughout the novel. The movement from orthodox Catholicism to a kind of enlightened Christian faith coincides with Lamennais's own evolution of faith. According to Karénine (220), after the publication of the novel Lamennais was given the nickname of Spiridion.

He receives a kind of official sanction of this view at the end of the novel when Angel retrieves Spiridion's manuscript. He and Angel discover it has three parts: the Gospel according to John, the "Introduction à l'Evangile éternel" of Jean de Parme, and the manuscript of Spiridion.[13] The number three holds mystical significance, as explained in Spiridion's writing: "Le dogme de la Trinité est la religion éternelle; la véritable compréhension de ce dogme est éternellement progressive. Nous repasserons éternellement peut-être par ces trois phrases de manifestations de l'activité, de l'amour et de la science, qui sont les trois principes de notre essence même, puisque ce sont les trois principes divins que *reçoit chaque homme venant dans le monde*, à titre de *fils de Dieu*. Et plus nous arriverons à nous manifester simultanément sous ces trois faces de notre humanité, plus nous approcherons de la perfection divine" (435; George Sand's emphasis). The repeated references to the number three in the text helped prepare the reader for the mystical importance of this triad. Angel has a dream three times in which Spiridion appears to him, just as he hears Spiridion's footsteps behind him three times. Spiridion himself had three names (Samuel, Pierre, Spiridion) corresponding to the three religions through which he has passed. Alexis, too, hears Spiridion's steps three times and tries three times to retrieve his manuscript.[14] Angel is triumphant in liberating the message of Spiridion: he is the founder's third follower. What Spiridion is actually expounding here is the doctrine of Pierre Leroux; the three phases of "activité, amour, science" correspond to Leroux's "sensation, sentiment, connaissance." George Sand was thus acting as a spokesperson for the ideas of her mentor as well as celebrating the role of the mentor in Spiridion's relationship to

Alexis and that of Alexis to Angel. The revelatory nature of Spiridion's manuscript—pointing as it does to Leroux's thesis—enables her to place her own prophet's works in a larger-than-life spotlight. This is emphasized by the words in the book Spiridion holds in his portrait: "Hic est veritas" (232).

The recovery of Spiridion's manuscript corresponds to the arrival of the French revolution at the monastery in the guise of the French troops who ransack the Church and kill Alexis. The two events are not unrelated. Sand chose to set both *Mauprat* and *Spiridion* in the late eighteenth-century, so that they coincided with the coming of the revolution. To Sand the revolution represented a giant step forward for mankind in the search for the new society she and Leroux envisioned, a movement away from ignorance toward freedom and a more secular society. Alexis sees the revolution in this light: "Comme je vois les hommes du présent se faire de plus grands maux encore en vue de l'avenir que nous ne nous sommes fait en vue du passé, je me dis que tout ce mal doit amener de grands biens; car aujourd'hui je crois qu'il y a une action providentielle, et que l'humanité obéit instinctivement et sympathiquement aux grands et profonds desseins de la pensée divine" (383). The revolution is part of the plan of creation, leading ever upwards. The revolution will not only bring material well-being to the people but also represents a major shift in consciousness: "Ce travail gigantesque de la révolution française, ce n'était pas, ce ne pouvait pas être seulement une question de pain et d'abri pour les pauvres; c'était beaucoup plus haut, et malgré tout ce qui s'est accompli, malgré tout ce qui a avorté en France à cet égard, c'est toujours, dans mes prévisions, beaucoup plus haut, que visait et qu'a porté, en effet, cette révolution. Elle devait, non-seulement donner au peuple un bien-être légitime, elle devait, elle doit, quoi qu'il arrive, n'en doute pas, mon fils, achever de donner la liberté de conscience au genre humain tout entier" (399). Thus the end of the novel represents a step in the right direction, even though it means that Alexis is killed, accused of being a representative of the oppressive Catholic Church. Alexis himself sees his death as part of the universal progression toward a new society: "Ceci est l'œuvre de la Providence, et la mission de nos bourreaux est sacrée, bien qu'ils ne

la comprennent pas encore! Cependant, ils l'ont dit, tu l'as entendu: c'est au nom du *sans-culotte Jésus* qu'ils profanent le sanctuaire de l'église. Ceci est le commencement du règne de l'Evangile
éternel prophétisé par nos pères" (445f.). The positive significance
given to Alexis's death sharply contrasts with the ending of *Lélia*
and *Jacques*; there could hardly be a clearer demonstration of Sand's
newly found belief in progress.

4

The Illusive Ideal

Sacrifice and Delusion in *Le Compagnon du tour de France* and *Horace*

J'aspire à un amour sublime, je n'en éprouve qu'un misérable.
Je voudrais embrasser l'idéal, et je n'étreins que la réalité.
—Horace (242)

In 1839 George Sand published a new version of *Lélia*. The author's denials notwithstanding, the reworked *Lélia* represents a virtually complete turn-about when compared to the original: she turns from skepticism and nihilism in 1833 to faith in progress and a belief in God in 1839. The explanation for the shift is well-known: Sand's new determination to use her fiction to serve a serious social purpose, especially to spread the ideas of Pierre Leroux. In the revised *Lélia*, Lélia gives Sténio a chance to regain her love by engaging in political and social causes. Trenmor becomes the head of a secret society dedicated to social and political justice. Secret societies figure prominently in the two novels which this chapter examines. They represent the ideal of men and women working together toward a common goal of a new and more just society, something which, given the prevailing political climate, could only be undertaken clandestinely. In the 1839 edition Lélia enters a convent and becomes its abbess, a position she takes in order to fulfill the mission of instructing the rich in their social and economic duties toward the poor. But neither Lélia nor her colleague, the Cardinal, is an orthodox Catholic; they see Catholicism as "cette forme particulière de la religion universelle" (477) and as a basis from which to work toward establishing principles of equality and justice. Lélia also campaigns for women's rights. When Lélia dies, her clothes are treated like the relics of a saint, a far cry from the Lélia of 1833.

George Sand's new beliefs influenced not only the ideas presented in her novels during this period, but also her conception of her role as a novelist and of the place of literature in society. This aim is not immediately evident in the new *Lélia*. The basic form of the novel remains the same but new gothic episodes are added: Trenmor's *venta* meets in a ruined castle; Trenmor goes also by the names of Valmarina, Mario and Anselme (an echo of E.T.A. Hoffmann's *Devil's Elixir*). Sténio believes he sees Lélia's ghost, as does Trenmor as well. The echoes of Faust remain as evident as ever in Lélia's final speech: "J'ai tout cherché, tout souffert, tout cru, tout accepté. . . . J'ai évoqué tous les spectres, j'ai lutté avec tous les démons, j'ai supplié tous les saints et tous les anges, j'ai sacrifié à toutes les passions. Vérité! vérité! tu ne t'es pas révélée, depuis dix mille ans je te cherche et je ne t'ai pas trouvée! . . . Depuis dix mille ans j'ai crié dans l'infini: *Vérité, vérité!* Depuis dix mille ans, l'infini me répond: *Désir, désir!*" (541). That the German connection remained strong in the second version is evident from the fact that Sand consulted with an informed source as to various aspects of German philosophy.[1]

It is not surprising that in revising *Lélia* with the purpose of having it reflect her new views, Sand left the basic structure of the novel intact. *Le Compagnon du tour de France* and *Horace*, both published in 1841, made it clear, however, that Sand's view of the novel had undergone a radical change. The stock devices of the Sandian catalog remain—overheard conversations, exaggerated pathos. But the adoption of fictional models based on current literary fashion has yielded to a more individualized and self-conscious view of herself as novelist. Whereas in the 1830s her novels borrowed heavily from the traditions of the gothic and sentimental novels, her two novels of 1841 strike out in different directions. Her new works point to the perils of reading—and believing—conventional novels and attempt to establish a new relationship between narrator and reader. The two very different approaches taken demonstrate the surprising narrative versatility of George Sand.

In her *avant-propos* to *Le Compagnon* Sand writes: "il y aurait toute une littérature nouvelle à créer avec les véritables mœurs populaires" (6). The figure she selects to illustrate this new kind of literature can hardly be taken as representative of the working class. Pierre Huguenin is no average carpenter. He is so handsome as a youth that two painters passing by attempt to paint his portrait. His description is designed to make him appeal to the same group to which artists would have sold their portrait, the middle class, particularly women: "Ses grands yeux bleus ombragés de cils noirs et le coloris délicat de ses joues donnaient une expression douce et pensive à cette tête qui n'eût pas été indigne du ciseau de Michel-Ange" (17). While he is depicted as a worker, this characterization is nearly always qualified in some way: "Il était vêtu en ouvrier, mais avec une propreté scrupuleuse" (21). Pierre is obsessed with cleanliness. He is also very polite and respectful. His portrayal is designed neither to shock nor threaten a bourgeois readership. His disinterest in improving his social status played an important role in Sand's narrative strategy. The reader is to take a keen interest in Pierre and even to reach the point of seeing him as an equal.

Although he has received little formal education, Pierre's intelligence and curiosity induce him to learn mathematics, geometry and architecture as they apply to carpentry. He justifies his love of science to his skeptical father in terms which recall *Spiridion*: "La science exacte n'est autre chose que le résultat de l'expérience de tous les hommes raisonnée, constatée et démontrée dans des termes dont la technique vous effraie à tort; car leur précision est plus facile à retenir que toutes les vagues définitions de l'usage vulgaire" (35). Science provides evidence of mankind's progress. Important in Sand's appreciation of science is the collective view she takes of its development; rather than the individual, it is the steady accumulation of experience from generation to generation which determines scientific advances. The fact that Pierre embraces more modern and more effective methods of carpentry than his father echoes the principal theme of *Spiridion*, the onward march of mankind. Like Alexis (*Spiridion*) and Patience (*Mauprat*), Pierre has developed a genuine love of learning. This was an important function which Sand incorporated into the figure of Pierre: to serve as a symbol for the great potential of the working class.

Despite his innate gifts and considerable accomplishments, Pierre is content to remain in the same social and economic class into which he was born: "Je ne désire rien au delà de ma condition, si ce n'est quelques heures de plus par semaine pour me livrer à la rêverie et à la lecture" (83). The narrator reminds the bourgeois reader that Pierre represents no danger to the established social order. At the same time Pierre's inability to find time to improve his mind inculpates the societal structure that relegates artisans exclusively to manual labor and denies them the leisure and means to improve themselves intellectually. Although Pierre's wishes are pointedly modest and non-threatening, their fulfillment would entail a radical change in the working environment and educational opportunities of the working-class. Pierre's determination to remain in the working class derives from a sense of pride and a feeling of solidarity with his fellow artisans. He is less concerned with his new position than with the welfare of his class:

> Quant à moi, je déclare que ma pauvreté et mon obscurité ne me pèsent pas encore, et que je serais bien plus malheureux, bien plus troublé dans mon sentiment de la justice si j'étais né riche comme vous, mademoiselle. Mais se résigner au malheur d'autrui, mais supporter le joug qui pèse sur des têtes innocentes, mais regarder tranquillement le train du monde sans essayer de découvrir une autre vérité, un autre ordre, une autre morale! Oh! C'est impossible . . . impossible! Il y a là de quoi ne jamais dormir, ne jamais se distraire, ne jamais connaître un instant de bonheur; il y a de quoi perdre le courage, la raison ou la vie! (George Sand's ellipsis, 303)

As evident in this speech, Pierre has a tendency to use formal rhetorical devices to make his point. There is in fact little effort to make Pierre seem natural—or believable—as a character. His role is first and foremost to be a symbol and spokesman.

As the novel progresses, Pierre becomes increasingly aware of the injustice of the existing socio-economic structure. Pierre's espousal of socially radical views develops gradually; the narrator underscores that his personal experience with social injustice leads to his politicization, and not any desire for personal gain or ambition. This not only elevates Pierre, it also provides a possible model for the reader. Although Pierre learns from books he reads, he also has an innate wisdom and a prophetic gift reminiscent of Patience in *Mauprat*. After his speech to the *Compagnons* in Blois in which he exposes the injustice of the poor's position in society, the narrator comments: "Un esprit droit et assez cultivé, une âme ardente, une imagination poétique, faisaient de lui un être mystérieux et singulier, assez semblable aux pâtres inspirés qui naissaient dans l'ancienne tradition avec le don de prophétie, on pouvait dire, avec la Savienne, qu'il était rempli de l'esprit du Seigneur; car, dans la candeur de son enthousiasme, il touchait aux plus hautes questions humaines, sans savoir lui-même quelles étaient ces cimes voilées où son rêve l'avait porté. C'est pourquoi ses discours, dont nous ne pouvons vous donner ici que la substance sèche et grossière, avaient un caractère de prédication" (123-24). Pierre's speech moves his colleague Amaury so much that he instantly changes his views on society and on the system of *compagnons*. The narrator's role has changed from being a chronicler and neutral observer to becoming an interpreter who puts the working class characters' thoughts in terms more readily comprehensible to the middle class. This tends to change the narrator's relationship to the principal character from one of neutrality to one of partisanship.

This alteration in the narrator's status poses a problem: the reader must accept the narrator's account of the powerful effect of Pierre's speech since his actual words are not reproduced in the text. The excerpts do not match the narrator's inflated claims about the inspirational nature of Pierre's speech, and Amaury's instant conversion does not ring true. George Sand was trying to accomplish two goals here. She wanted to convey her views on the organization of society and demonstrate that the common man, when inspired like Pierre, has the ability to serve as a guiding beacon to his class and an ideal to society as a whole. In the process she created a figure who surpasses human dimensions (e.g., his frequent comparison to Jesus). The narrator exceeds the limits of verisimilitude in emphasizing Pierre's virtues. In fact, Pierre is something other than a conventional fictional character. He comes to embody all earthly wisdom, as is evident in Yseult's reaction to their discussion: "[Elle] fut frappée de la droiture de jugement avec laquelle, sans autre lumière que celle d'une conscience rigide et d'un cœur plein de charité, il réfutait l'erreur et confondait l'orgueil des savants de ce monde, n'admirant chez les poètes et les philosophes que ce qui est vraiment grand et éternellement beau, ne croyant de l'histoire que ce qui est d'accord avec la logique divine et la dignité humaine, s'élevant enfin, par sa grandeur innée, au-dessus de toutes les grandeurs décernées par le jugement des hommes" (374). Pierre's instinctive knowledge raises him not only above the other characters but above all human seers and philosophers. This is a jump which tends to leave the reader behind.

Pierre is in a sense in the wrong novel; he belongs more to the world of *Spiridion* than to the more realistic world of *Le Compagnon*. One could more easily accept his role if it were transmitted in the mystical way highlighted by the spiritual transmission in *Spiridion*. The opening of the novel leads the reader to expect a more realistic and conventional approach to characterization. Lerebours, the estate manager of the Villepreux family, has his feet, at least, firmly on the ground. It is his ironically depicted relationship with the "family" which defines him. Lerebours is part of a traditional, conventional world, seen in the exchange with Master Huguenin over the projected repairs of the chapel. Lerebours and Huguenin are socio-historically situated by their attitudes toward the aristocracy and the French revolution. Initially Pierre seems to belong to this world; he is shown for the first time working in his father's shop. But he soon breaks through the boundaries of the realistic code in a way which calls into question the coherence of the narrative. While the other major characters except Yseult are treated ironically, Pierre is always cast in a serious light.

As high as Pierre rises above the world around him, the narrator's point of view still stands above his. The narrator thus comments at one point concerning Pierre's despair over fighting between workers: "Pierre n'était pas assez avancé . . . pour faire une distinction nette entre le principe et le fait. . . . Si Pierre Huguenin avait pu se rendre bien compte du passé et de l'avenir du peuple, il ne se fût pas tant effrayé du présent où il le voyait engagé" (143-44). The narrator later makes similar comments on the lessons Pierre would learn in his life and the different systems with which he would become involved. The narrator of *Le Compagnon* differs radically from the largely self-effacing narrator of the novels of the 1830s; he is chatty and informal and seems in no particular hurry to tell the story. The leisurely opening of the novel contrasts markedly with the frantic pace in novels like *Lélia* or *Jacques*. Startlingly different from those novels as well is the great amount of humor in *Le Compagnon*. The misadventures of Lerebours's son Isidore with a horse are depicted in some detail. Humor in fact is his only *raison d'être*, as is the case as well for "le Berrichon" who works with Pierre in his father's workshop. The novel recalls Fielding's fiction in several ways including the fact that most of the minor characters play at least in part a comic role. This is true even for the secret organizer of the Carbonari, Achille Lefort, who ineptly attempts to win the hand of Yseult. The tone occasionally recalls Fielding as well, when the narrator "catches up" with the characters: "Je crois que cette digression était nécessaire à l'intelligence de mon récit. Maintenant, beaux lecteurs, et vous, bons compagnons, permettez-moi de courir après mes héros, qui ne sont pas arrêtés ainsi que moi sur la chaussée de la Loire" (101). The novel resembles also eighteenth-century models in the multiple story lines which make the structure of the novel quite different from that of most of Sand's novels up to that point. Sand's desire to write an unabashedly didactic novel may have led her to look back to models from the enlightenment.

Sand's narrator, like Fielding's, willingly interrupts the story to add commentary. There are several long explanations, for example, concerning habits and practices of the *compagnons*. There are even factual footnotes and quotations from historical treatises. At one point the narrator changes the form of the text, putting it in the form of dialogue. The continuity of the story is frequently interrupted by flashbacks, telling, for instance, of Pierre's *tour de France*, the Count's political career or Joséphine's marriage. All this makes the experience of reading *Le Compagnon* quite different from *Mauprat* or *Spiridion*, which were written accounts of oral tales. The narrative strategies were based on the reader's entering into the atmosphere and spirit of the stories as much as possible. In *Le Compagnon* this is impossible. Through the way the story is told, the reader is reminded at every turn that he is reading a novel. There is no attempt to hide the artificiality of the process. As we shall see, this accords with the fundamental message of the novel, to beware of romantic illusions.

The narrator addresses the reader directly and repeatedly, so often that a definite picture of the fictional reader emerges. *She* is someone who is accustomed to reading novels and who tends to be influenced by them: "Vous l'avez deviné, ô lectrice pénétrante! La pauvre Joséphine, ayant lu beaucoup de romans (que ceci vous soit un avertissement salutaire), éprouvait le besoin irrésistible de mettre dans sa vie un roman dont elle serait l'héroïne" (230). The narrator has a somewhat disdainful attitude toward this reader, commenting sarcastically, for example, about ideas emanating from houses "où vous ne daigneriez pas vous asseoir" (412). The novel's biting humor derives principally from figures close in character to the fictional reader. Isidore Lerebours and the Marquise de Frenays, née Joséphine Clicot, strive to rise above their classes and make themselves ludicrous in the process. Their ludicrous actions also demonstrate the dignity and wisdom of Pierre, who has no such ambitions. The narrator even pokes fun at the expectations a habitual novel reader might have; gothic conventions are mentioned only to turn them upside down. Ghosts are evoked when the count refuses to believe that they are the source of a noise he hears one night. A secret passageway does indeed exist, but instead of serving the purpose of creating mystery and terror, as in *Mauprat*, it serves the designs of love.

The narrator tries to cure the fictional reader of her prejudices and to eradicate the illusion fed by fiction:

Peut-être accuseras-tu ce pâle intermédiaire de prêter à ses héros des sentiments et des idées qu'ils ne peuvent avoir. A ce reproche, il n'a qu'un mot à répondre: informe-toi. Quitte les sommets où la muse littéraire se tient depuis si longtemps isolée de la grande masse du genre humain. Descends dans ces régions où la poésie comique puise si largement pour le théâtre et la caricature; daigne envisager la face sérieuse de ce peuple pensif et profondément inspiré que tu crois inculte et grossier: tu y verras plus d'un Pierre Huguenin à l'heure qu'il est. Regarde, regarde, je t'en conjure, et ne prononce pas sur lui l'arrêt injuste qui le condamne à végéter dans l'ignorance et la férocité. (94)

As if this appeal were not enough, the narrator even tries to frighten his female reader into paying attention: "Madame, madame! Hâtez-vous d'être belle et de faire briller vos diamants. Peut-être sont-ils trempés dans le sang d'Hiram, et peut-être faudra-t-il un jour les cacher, ou les jeter loin de vous" (96). The message to the fictional reader is clear: reform or suffer the consequences. The real readers Sand anticipated could hardly have matched the portrait of the fictional reader; if the two coincided the offended reader would likely throw the book down in disgust. The negative portrait Sand paints of the female reader is rather an invitation to the real reader to see the shallowness and prejudice of these representatives of middle class complacency. A feeling of solidarity for the lower classes is solicited instead through the figure of Pierre. Reader interest in Pierre and his fellow workers derives not only from their own intrinsic value as characters, but also from the secret organization of *compagnons* to which they belong. The narrator assumes the reader is totally ignorant of these societies and goes to some length to recreate the world of the *compagnons*. Much of Sand's information came from Agricol Perdiguier's *Livre du compagnonnage*. The *compagnons* are first seen through the suspicious eyes of Pierre's father; this places the emphasis on their mysterious practices, their violence and their possible connection with the devil. The narrator takes every opportunity to list the colorful names given the *compagnons*, Pierre for example is "l'Ami-du-trait," Amaury "le Corinthien." In general, the practices of the *compagnons* are first mentioned by the characters and then only explained subsequently by the narrator (e.g., Pierre's encounter with Jean Sauvage, a member of a rival *devoir*, or in the artisans' contest in Blois). The effect is to highlight the exoticism of the *compagnons*, how they differ from normal, middle-class society. The narrator occasionally pre-programs this response, as in qualifying a character's announcement of the upcoming battle of the *Devoirs* as "une étrange révélation" (87). The repeated use of *compagnonnage* terms in the text serves once again to interrupt the flow of the text and make the reader aware of the fact that he is reading a novel.

The point George Sand is making about losing one's illusions is not only inserted into comments by the narrator but, more importantly, is incorporated into the presentation of characters. Pierre becomes more socially and politically aware by reading, but the discovery of fiction puts romantic delusions into his head. Pierre enters into a kind of secret literary collusion with Yseult before she even appears in the novel through his nightly reading of the books in her library. What he reads changes his perspective on the world around him and on his position in it: "Un monde nouveau s'était révélé à lui depuis ses dernières lectures. Il comprenait la mélodie d'un oiseau, la grâce d'une branche, la richesse de la couleur et la beauté des lignes d'un paysage. Il pouvait se rendre compte de ce qu'il avait senti jusqu'alors confusément, et la nouvelle puissance dont il était investi lui créait des joies et des souffrances inconnues. —A quoi me sert, se disait-il souvent, de n'être plus le même dans mon esprit, si ma position ne doit pas changer? Cette belle nature, où je ne possède rien, me sourit et m'enivre aussi bien que si j'étais un des princes qui l'oppriment. . . . Travailleur infatigable, il faut que, de l'aube à la nuit, j'arrose de mes sueurs un sol qui verdira et fleurira pour d'autres yeux que les miens" (62). This perspective on nature is radically different from that in earlier novels. The link between nature and passion, so evident in *Indiana* and *Valentine*, has been replaced by a socially aware and critical view. Yseult's books also give Pierre insight into his own character by stripping away the prejudices of society: "Durant ces heures de mystérieuse étude, assis avec noblesse sur les coussins d'un sofa de velours, il contemplait un paysage admirable dont il sentait la poésie se révéler à lui à mesure que les descriptions des poètes lui traduisaient l'art divin dont la création est l'expression visible. Dans ces moments-là Pierre Huguenin se sentait le roi du monde; mais lorsqu'il retrouvait sur son front pensif, sur ses mains sèches et meurtries, les éternels stigmates de sa chaîne d'esclave, des larmes brûlantes coulaient de ses yeux" (44-45). Pierre, however, does not yield to despair; his readings help him to maintain patience and resignation.

Pierre is apparently a regular newspaper reader as well; he is aware of the latest social and political developments in France and abroad. But soon he begins to read the novels of Walter Scott, and this interest, as the narrator predicts at the end of chapter four, would prove dangerous to him. Scott leads Pierre to leave the world of hard facts and history for that of fancy and illusion, a world in which social reality ceases to exist. Later, when Pierre hears the rumor that Yseult is the illegitimate daughter of Napoleon, it stirs thoughts born of his reading of Scott: "Pierre ne pouvait se défendre de repasser dans sa tête tous les romans qu'il avait lus, et il n'en trouvait aucun aussi étrange que celui qu'il avait fait dans le secret de son cœur, lui épris et presque jaloux de la fille de César" (272). That night he realizes that he is passionately in love with Yseult. Thus the romantic associations Pierre makes between Yseult and heroines of novels lead him to forget the humiliating insult that Yseult had inflicted a short time before. Not only is Pierre's love motivated by this view of Yseult as a heroine of fiction, so is his eventual refusal of her offer of marriage: "Il avait soif de faire une grande chose; elle se présentait, il n'hésita pas. Il fut plus romanesque que tous les romans qu'il avait lus. Il crut mériter l'amour d'Yseult en y renonçant, et justifier sa préférence en prouvant qu'il était au-dessus de tous ces biens qu'elle lui offrait" (455-56). The narrator's superior vantage point enables him to see that Pierre has committed himself to a wrong course of action, but one which he claims Pierre will overcome in a promised, but never delivered, sequel.

Pierre is not the only character who harbors illusions nourished on Scott's novels. This is above all true for Joséphine: "C'est donc à sir Walter Scott qu'il faut attribuer le désordre qui s'était

organisé, si l'on peut parler ainsi, dans la cervelle de Joséphine. Elle se rêvait la dame du quinzième siècle que devait poursuivre un jeune artisan, enfant perdu de quelque grande maison, lancé prochainement dans la carrière du talent et de la gloire, en attendant qu'il recouvrât ses titres ou qu'il en acquît par son mérite et sa réputation" (243-44). Joséphine ultimately rejects Amaury as a second husband because he has no aristocratic title to offer her.[2] The passion between Joséphine and Amaury sustains itself by the romantic illusion each partner has. Amaury sees in Scott's fiction "la réalisation possible de sa propre destinée, non comme l'héritier méconnu de quelque grande fortune, mais comme le conquérant prédestiné à la gloire dans l'art" (244). The dream of future glory, which is an essential element in Amaury's relationship with Joséphine, is viewed by the narrator as leading to egotism: "Il nous est permis d'être fiers de l'objet de notre amour, et de compter sur les victoires de notre volonté intelligente. Mais ce n'est pas là toute la vie de l'homme; et si l'amour de soi n'est pas étroitement lié à l'amour des semblables, cette ambition, qui eût pu triompher de tout à l'état de dévouement, souffre, s'aigrit, et menace de succomber à chaque pas lorsqu'elle reste à l'état d'égoïsme. L'amour, qui étend cet égoïsme à deux êtres fondus en un seul, ne suffit point pour le légitimer" (350). Amaury's passion makes him a worse human being; he turns morose and unfriendly, ignoring his fellow artisans. Love in *Le Compagnon* is not, as in *Indiana* or *Valentine*, a force which needs no other justification. Love has lost its role as an exclusive, all-embracing way of life; it needs to be anchored in an ideal outside the lovers' world. This is missing in the passion of Amaury and Joséphine.

It is present, however, in the ennobling love of Pierre and Yseult. Whereas the physical predominates in the relationship of Joséphine and Amaury, the spiritual and intellectual side of Pierre and Yseult's love is paramount. Their love is intertwined with their feelings for mankind in general and their desire to reform society. After Yseult tells Pierre of her vision of a future classless society, the narrator comments: "Pierre était enivré, hors de lui; la fièvre qui brûlait dans les veines d'Yseult avait passé dans les siennes. Tous deux croyaient être transportés seulement par la foi, et n'avoir

en ce moment d'autre lien que celui de la vertu. C'était pourtant l'amour qui avait pris cette forme, et qui se chargeait d'allumer en eux la flamme de l'enthousiasme révolutionnaire" (340). Love has become here a socially beneficial force. In contrast to the relationship between Amaury and Joséphine, passion plays no role in the love of Pierre and Yseult. Pierre, the narrator tells us, "aimait trop pour désirer" (353). He idealizes Yseult, treating her as an unapproachable being. Several times Pierre is afraid of brushing up against Yseult. When Yseult asks his forgiveness for having insulted him, Pierre has what can only be called a fit: "Elle fit un cri en le voyant devenir pâle comme les lis de sa corbeille, et tomber à ses pieds, suffoqué, ivre de joie et de terreur, évanoui d'abord, et puis bientôt en proie à une crise nerveuse qui lui arracha des cris étouffés et de nouveaux torrents de larmes" (284). Pierre's state is not caused by suppressed sexual desire; his relationship to Yseult is very far removed from that of Bernard Mauprat to Edmée. For Pierre Yseult is "un être céleste" (353); he sees her in a dream as an angel. When she talks to him, "elle remuait toute son âme, et la faisait remonter à ces hautes régions de l'enthousiasme, où il n'y a plus ni trouble ni terreurs" (353). Images of flight are associated throughout the novel with Yseult's relationship to Pierre. They often meet in the park of the château where Yseult keeps a collection of birds. When a storm destroys the bird cage, Pierre rebuilds it and in the process their relationship becomes much closer.

Later Pierre and Yseult spend a great deal of time in the tower where la Savienne is housed, and again birds play a role in their relationship: "Il y avait devant la fenêtre gothique de cette tour une grande vigne, où les pigeons venaient se jouer au bord du toit. Yseult les avait apprivoisés à force de se tenir accoudée sur la fenêtre; et tandis que le capucin, le bizet ou le bouvreuil venaient becqueter sa main, elle eut souvent de grandes révélations sur la perfectibilité, et monta avec Pierre, qui pendant ce temps façonnait un ornement de boiserie, jusqu'aux plus hautes régions de l'idéal" (412-13). The stairs in the chapel function in a similar symbolic way, indicating how Pierre rises to Yseult's intellectual level. Their love is so thoroughly ensconced in the high regions of idealism that one can speculate that Pierre's refusal to marry Yseult may well stem in

part from a reluctance to exchange their ideal union for physical mating.[3] The course of their love runs opposite to that of Bernard and Edmée in *Mauprat*.

In *Mauprat* the lovers' story projects education and elevation through love, but this is largely separate from the solution to social inequity and human misery represented by Patience's eventual role in the château. In *Le Compagnon* the solution envisioned in *Mauprat* no longer seems viable: "On a rasé des châteaux, on a semé le blé dans les parcs seigneuriaux; chacun a tiré à soi un lambeau de la dépouille, et s'est cru sauvé. Mais de dessous chaque pierre est sorti un essaim de pauvres affamés, et la terre se trouve maintenant trop petite" (276). A newly proposed solution is symbolized by Pierre and Yseult's ephemeral love, a union of all men free from material considerations and based on the belief in a common ideal. This is the role Sand envisioned her novel playing, pointing to the possibility and necessity of such a *unio mystica* of mankind. By emphasizing the pernicious role that traditional fiction played in the lives of the characters, Sand invites the reader to ponder the effect novels have on readers. The inference he should draw, according to Sand's narrative strategy, is that this novel could also be leading him toward a certain behavior pattern. In attacking other forms of fiction, however, Sand implies that what she is doing in *Le Compagnon du tour de France* is quite different. The many devices which disrupt the flow of the narrative contribute to the impression she hoped to create, that *Le Compagnon du tour de France* was a totally different kind of writing from conventional fiction—represented by Scott—whose influence is seen as pernicious.

The mystical mission of *Le Compagnon* is an extension of Sand's views in *Spiridion*. Indeed, one of the sacred texts evoked at the end of that novel, *l'Evangile éternel*, is also mentioned here. *Le Compagnon*, too, is full of spiritual sentiments separated from official Church teachings. The chapel of the château is being converted into a museum and spiritual retreat. Yseult's views echo those which emerge from Alexis's spiritual quest: "J'adore dans le Christ sa naissance obscure, ses apôtres humbles et petits, sa pauvreté et son détachement de tout orgueil humain, tout le poème populaire et divin de sa vie couronnée par le martyre. Si je m'éloigne de

l'Eglise, c'est que les prêtres, en se faisant les ministres du pouvoir temporel et les serviteurs du despotisme, ont trahi la pensée de leur maître et altéré l'esprit de sa doctrine. Mais moi, je me sens prête à la pratiquer à la lettre" (339). Yseult herself embodies the ideals of Christ. The narrator even depicts her as a divine emissary, evoking the "feu mystique" in her eyes when she decides to marry Pierre the carpenter (375) and describes the "transfiguration divine" she undergoes when she tells Pierre of her matrimonial mission (441). Pierre will be her partner in this spiritual odyssey, as is brought out in a dream he has about Yseult: "Les cieux s'entr'ouvraient sur la tête de l'apôtre prolétaire, et son âme prenait son vol à travers les régions du monde idéal" (288). In the same dream Yseult tells him: "Aime, crois, travaille, et tu seras ange dans ce monde des anges" (289). This reflects *Spiridion*'s emphasis on the possibility of spiritual growth of mankind. Yseult functions as Pierre's inspiration to become better educated; her books supplied the means to that end. This parallels Edmée's role in Bernard's transformation in *Mauprat*. The elevated role of woman as the teacher of mankind recalls Saint-Simonian teachings. La Savinienne, as the devoted mother, also represents an ideal woman. Lucette Czyba has shown how the repeated comparisons to the Virgin Mary serve to idealize her maternity (21-22).[4]

Pierre, as representative of the working class, is convinced that "le Christ divin" is on their side. He is intended to provide evidence of the divine spark present in the working man. Given that belief, it then follows that the lower classes can provide their own path to enlightenment. As opposed to Achille Lefort, Pierre is convinced that it is so: "Sa règle, il la fera lui-même; ses guides, il les tirera de son propre sein; ses conseils, il les puisera dans l'esprit de Dieu qui descendra sur lui. Il faut bien un peu compter sur la Providence" (315). Characters such as the Count de Villepreux or the Carbonarist conspirator, Achille Lefort, who believe that the upper classes should provide the guiding lights, are discredited in the novel. Lefort becomes an object of ridicule for whom conspiracy is an adventure, not a serious effort to help mankind. The Count is unable to live up to the beliefs he mouths when his daughter suddenly asks his consent to marry Pierre. Although the Count

supposedly represents the most progressive among the aristocracy, his lack of commitment to social change is severely attacked: "Toute grande action avait ses sympathies: mais aucune doctrine ne le captivait au delà du temps qu'il lui avait fallu pour l'écouter et la connaître. Il lisait dans les hommes et dans les choses de son temps comme dans des livres d'agrément; et quand sa curiosité était rassasiée, il s'endormait en souriant sur la dernière page, consentant à ce que chacun eût sa façon de penser, pourvu que l'ordre social n'en fût point trop ébranlé et que les théories n'eussent pas la prétention de passer dans la pratique" (294). One of the most telling indictments of the Count is that he has neglected the education of his grandchildren, a clear signal of his lack of commitment to the future.

If help from the upper classes is not forthcoming, then the lower classes must help themselves. This is the role that the system of *compagnonnage* fulfills. It is imperfect, yet functions as an institution of solidarity and fraternity. Pierre sees the system as a potential model for the larger fellowship of man: "Il y a un Devoir plus noble, plus vrai que tous ceux des initiations et des mystères: c'est le devoir de la fraternité entre tous les hommes" (72). In Pierre's view, a feeling of fellowship between all men is a prerequisite for any new society. Liberating the lower classes without first establishing a sense of social solidarity would be pointless: "Je voudrais que tous les hommes vécussent ensemble comme des frères, répondit Pierre; voilà tout ce que je voudrais. Avec cela, bien des maux seraient supportables; sans cela, la liberté ne nous ferait aucun bien" (166). Fraternal love, highlighted in *Spiridion*, emerges as man's best and only recourse while awaiting the coming of the new age.

In many ways *Horace* is a quite different kind of novel from *Le Compagnon du tour de France*. The most obvious difference is its setting of Paris, it is the first of Sand's novels to take place entirely in the capital. Although the novel incorporates some scenes of the Parisian upper class, the emphasis is on student life in Paris. The working title was "L'Etudiant." The financial difficulties of students' lives are evoked in some detail. Urban poverty is depicted repeatedly through the households of Horace and Marthe and later of Marthe and Paul. Paris is also shown from the perspective of Paul's two sisters, who come to the capital to live with him. They see the city through naive, provincial eyes. What they miss in Parisian life highlights the inhumanity which the action of the novel demonstrates: "Quelle différence, en effet, avec leur existence provinciale! Plus d'air, plus de liberté, plus de causerie sur la porte avec les voisines; plus d'intimité avec tous les habitants de la rue; plus de promenade sur un petit rempart planté de marronniers" (97). There is a kind of reverse exoticism at work here, as Sand shows a different side to the world with which the reader is clearly expected to be familiar.

The principal character of *Horace* is far from representing the ideal embodied in Pierre Huguenin. This is partly seen as a reflection of the contrast between virtuous country life and the corruption of the city. While Pierre is a paragon of wisdom and selflessness, Horace is not interested in his fellow man but only in his personal pleasures. Work, which Pierre highly prizes, is unbearable in any form for Horace. The narration of the two novels is also strikingly different. *Horace* is told in the first person by Théophile, a friend of Horace. As a narrator Théophile is quite different from the third-person narrator of *Le Compagnon*. To a large extent he embodies values and voices expressions which are not those of the author. The narrative approach, bordering on the unreliable narrator, is a rarity among Sand's novels. Despite these essential distinctions, a common ground between the two novels does exist. They use irony in the narrator-reader relationship and point toward a similar, embodied idea: the pernicious effect of romantic illusion. Furthermore, each novel celebrates the altruistic renunciation by the male characters of their quest for fulfillment in love. Pierre Huguenin and Paul Arsène give up, even if temporarily, the women they love in heroic acts of self-denial.

Not all of Théophile's opinions are objectionable; a number of his views coincide with those of the author. Théophile's praise of friendship, his criticism of *l'art pour l'art* and his defense of republican beliefs represent the views of George Sand. There are also several passages in which Sand seems to bypass her first-person narrator altogether and slips into the omniscient narrative mode.[5] The narrative point of view is not kept as tightly under control here as it is in *Spiridion*, in which first-person narration also predominates. What makes the narrative approach in *Horace* of particular interest is the narrator's attitude toward the principal character. The first sentence establishes the context in which Théophile intends to present Horace to the reader: "Les êtres qui nous inspirent le plus d'affection ne sont pas toujours ceux que nous estimons le plus" (1). He admits from the outset that Horace has few admirable qualities, but, at the same time, he makes himself into Horace's advocate. This turns out to be a difficult task since Horace reveals how few redeeming traits he really possesses. Théophile admits that Horace has no principles, convictions, nor scruples. He is, in fact, at a loss to explain his interest in Horace: "Horace avait cela de particulier, qu'en le voyant et en l'écoutant, on était sous le charme de sa parole et de son geste. Quand on le quittait, on s'étonnait de ne pas lui avoir démontré son erreur; mais quand on le retrouvait, on subissait de nouveau le magnétisme de son paradoxe" (18-19). The reader, of course, has only Théophile's word for Horace's magnetic quality. The reactions of the other characters to Horace, however, provide little support for Théophile's enthusiastic interest. The most objective judgment about Horace comes from Jean Laravinière, the revolutionary and the friend of Paul Arsène, who for a time lives in the same hotel as Horace. After intimate contact between the two, Jean rejects Horace as "un hâbleur sentimental" (223), a view which Horace's actions amply justify.

Théophile is constantly trying to find positive aspects to Horace's ideas and actions. At one point Horace describes the type of mistress he is looking for—small feet, white hands "et beaucoup de dentelles blondes sur des cheveux blonds" (24). Théophile explains why his friend's absurdly romantic and snobbish views do not disturb him: "Horace m'inspirait le plus vif intérêt. Je n'étais pas absolument convaincu de cette force héroïque et de cet austère enthousiasme qu'il s'attribuait dans la sincérité de son cœur. Je voyais plutôt en lui un excellent enfant, généreux, candide, plus épris de beaux rêves que capable de les réaliser. Mais sa franchise et son aspiration continuelle vers les choses élevées me le faisaient aimer sans que j'eusse besoin de le regarder comme un héros. Cette fantaisie de sa part n'avait rien de déplaisant: elle témoignait de son amour pour le beau idéal" (25). Considering Horace's views on women as the search for an ideal is a far cry from what that search represented in *Le Compagnon du tour de France*. Horace takes no interest in women's real lives; he sees them only from the outside, in their physical appearance and role in society. Although he is attracted by Marthe's beauty, he cannot conceive of becoming the lover of a *limonadière* named Madame Poisson. His love must be heroic, preferably tragic: "Moi, si je me livre à l'amour, je veux qu'il me blesse profondément, qu'il m'électrise, qu'il me navre, ou qu'il m'exalte au troisième ciel et m'enivre de voluptés. Point de milieu: l'un ou l'autre, l'un et l'autre si l'on veut; mais pas de drame d'arrière-boutique, pas de triomphe d'estaminet. Je veux bien souffrir, je veux bien devenir fou, je veux bien m'empoisonner avec ma maîtresse ou me poignarder sur son cadavre" (23). External considerations are all that matter. Horace's conception of love differs sharply from the one Théophile expresses: "A celui qui est pénétré de la sainteté des engagements réciproques, de l'égalité des sexes devant Dieu, des injustices de l'ordre social et de l'opinion vulgaire à cet égard, l'amour peut se révéler dans toute sa grandeur et dans toute sa beauté; mais à celui qui est imbu des erreurs communes de l'infériorité de la femme, de la différence de ses devoirs avec les nôtres en fait de fidélité, à celui qui ne cherche que des émotions et non un idéal, l'amour ne se révélera pas" (105). The "idéal" contrasts with the one which Horace embraces since it is not predicated on removing women from all social contexts but rather on recognizing their equal status in society. Horace is no believer in equal rights for women, as his reaction to Eugénie's views on that topic illustrates. He even criticizes Théophile for allowing Eugénie to participate in meetings on women's rights. After having spent one night with Marthe, Horace asserts his right to be regarded as her "maître" (174). He clearly represents a retrograde position in Sand's view of male-female relations.

Théophile often finds himself in the position of having to defend Horace against the criticism of his common-law wife, Eugénie.

While her views coincide more closely with those of George Sand, Théophile does not give her a prominent role in his narration. Often, after Théophile defends his friend to Eugénie, Horace acts in a way which undercuts his argument. Théophile is not bothered, for example, by Horace's pursuit of Marthe, even though he knows of the prior claim of Paul Arsène and is familiar with Horace's views on women. One evening when Marthe runs off to spend the night at Horace's hotel, Eugénie is horrified at the consequences of Marthe's having compromised herself in that way; Théophile's attitude is altogether different: "Je ne pus me défendre de rire un peu de sa consternation" (167). Théophile later defends Horace's actions when the latter arrives. His overweening sense of personal triumph and utter disregard for Marthe's position demonstrate clearly his callous egotism and make Théophile's positive assessment seem hollow.

The fact that Théophile finds Horace's behavior excusable and even amusing causes the reader to view Théophile's evaluation of him with suspicion.[6] Théophile, for example, is not offended by Horace's degrading attitude toward Eugénie: "Eugénie, condamnée à subir cet étrange tête-à-tête, et n'ayant, du reste, pas à s'en plaindre personnellement, car il daignait à peine lui adresser la parole (le regardant plutôt comme un meuble que comme une personne), était indignée de cette paresse princière. Quant à moi, je commençais à sourire lorsque, les yeux encore appesantis par une rêverie somnolente, il reprenait ses divagations sur la gloire, la politique et la puissance" (50). Théophile is charmed even by Horace's idleness. Théophile is so naïve or blind as far as Horace is concerned that he believes he will be changed by Marthe's love: "Jusqu'ici, me dis-je, il y a eu dans son ambition quelque chose de trop personnel qui lui a montré l'avenir sous un jour d'égoïsme. A présent qu'il aime, son âme va s'ouvrir à des notions plus larges, plus vraies, plus généreuses. Le dévouement va se révéler, et, avec le dévouement, la nécessité et le courage de travailler" (141). By this point, the reader has distanced himself from the narrator's view of Horace—which is clearly at odds with the evidence presented—and thus sees the implausibility of Théophile's optimistic view of Horace. Théophile's remark, however, serves to awaken in the reader the notion that love can and should change individuals for the better, a thought dear to George Sand. Thus the unbelievable narrator serves the purpose of activating the reader.

The narrative strategy calls for the reader to have a similar reaction to the narrator's political stance. Although Théophile sides with those advocating political change, he refuses to play any active role: "Mon sort est celui d'un certain nombre de jeunes gens sincères qui ne peuvent désavouer du jour au lendemain la religion de leurs pères, et qui pourtant ont le cœur chaud et le bras solide. . . . Ils voudraient pouvoir arborer les couleurs nouvelles de l'égalité, qu'ils aiment et qu'ils pratiquent. Mais il y a là une question de convenances qu'on ne leur permet pas de violer, et que, de toutes parts, on sache aussi bien qu'eux qu'elle est arbitraire, vaine et injuste. Je suis donc forcé de m'abstraire de tout concours à l'action politique" (264). This is clearly an appeal to the reader to reject such passivity. What particularly brings that across to the reader is the portrayal of the politically active Paul Arsène and Jean Laravinière. Even though Théophile does not actively help in their armed revolt, his portrayal of their views and actions is essentially positive. The selfless heroism and utter devotion to the cause the two men display clearly invite admiration. In the process of depicting their beliefs, Sand introduces discussions of socialist theories, principally those of the Saint-Simonian school. As was the case in *Le Compagnon du tour de France,* this occasionally takes extratextual form, complete with footnotes, and thus is not effectively integrated into the flow of the text. Buloz refused to publish the novel because Sand was not willing to change or eliminate the political commentaries in the novel.[7]

The clearest negative example for the reader is not Théophile but Horace. Horace himself is a kind of victim. His parents have high ambitions for him; he is to rise from the lower middle class to a higher social and economic status. Like the parents of Athénaïs (*Valentine*) they do their job too well and Horace comes to feel far superior to his parents. Unlike Athénaïs and Bénédict, who retain a core of peasant virtue, Horace, as the son of a petit bourgeois, has no such cultural tradition on which he can draw. Partly as a result of his upbringing, Horace is obsessed with role-playing; he is always trying to appear to be something different from what he is. Théophile recognizes this as soon as he meets Horace, but finds nothing objectionable in it. Horace's affectations are all the more striking in that the other major characters, especially Paul and Marthe, are characterized above all by their authenticity, the sincerity and openness with which they portray themselves. Their actions speak louder than the claims and boasts Horace emits (and Théophile admires) and establish a sympathetic link between them and the reader which bypasses the narrator.

Horace incorporates many of the vices Sand attacks in other novels. Filled with ambition, he is convinced he has a glorious future: "Les grandes choses m'enivrent jusqu'au délire. Je n'en tire et n'en peux tirer aucune vanité, ce me semble; mais je le dis avec assurance, je me sens de la race des héros" (17-18). He has dreams of becoming a politician and sees the study of law as a means to that end. But he never attends classes and eventually abandons his studies altogether. He subsequently decides in his nonchalant way to become a writer. He sees this ambition too from the standpoint of playing a role; he buys "une robe de chambre, ou plutôt un manteau de théâtre" (99), seeing this dress as an essential part of being an author. All Horace has to show for his first efforts, however, are a number of draft titles for ambitious works he has started and then abandoned after a sentence or verse.[8] He has neither ideas nor genuine emotions on which to draw and thus is able only to imitate other authors. Horace's only finished literary works derive from the sole experience which resulted in any emotional involvement on his part, his relationship to Marthe. In his efforts to seduce the Viscountess de Chailly, Horace writes poetry based on that love and what he sees as its tragic end. The nature and use of these poems are egotistical and the effect on the Viscountess artificial: "Il déclama avec plus de talent encore qu'il ne m'en avait montré; les sanglots lui coupèrent la voix au dernier hémistiche. La vicomtesse faillit s'évanouir, tant elle se donna de peine pour pleurer! Elle en vint à son honneur, et versa des larmes . . . de véritables larmes. Hélas! Oui, on pleure par affectation aussi bien que par émotion vraie" (296-97). Horace eventually writes a short novel on the same topic and, according to Théophile, with a similar result: "L'on peut dire que son livre, s'il eût eu plus de retentissement, eût été un des plus pernicieux de l'époque romantique. C'était non seulement l'apologie, mais l'apothèse de l'égoïsme" (350). The attacks on romantic fiction, delivered in a vitriolic tone not typical of Théophile, demonstrate the distance Sand has traveled from her earliest fiction in which the exclusive rights of passion are celebrated.

Horace is far removed from the blind impulsiveness of the passions represented in Sand's earlier novels. For him love is something to try out, in the same way as other experiences. Théophile sees this as a violation of the sanctity of love: "Avec ces notions vagues et cette absence totale de dogme religieux et social, il voulait expérimenter l'amour, la plus religieuse des manifestations de notre vie morale, le plus important de nos actes individuels par rapport à la société!" (106). This is, in fact, the major indictment of Horace's attitude toward women, that he views male-female relationships from an exclusively personal point of view, ignoring the social ramifications. This was one of the important evolutions in Sand's discussion of the relationship between men and women since *Indiana* and *Valentine*. Love without an awareness of one's personal and social responsibility was in those novels a celebrated ideal. In *Le Compagnon du tour de France* and *Horace*, however, this kind of self-absorbing passion is ostracized. In fact, Horace's total disregard of *convenances* in his relationship with Marthe is also cast in a negative light; this is quite a break with the position in Sand's early novels that love has its own legitimacy regardless of social conventions and responsibilities. Horace is terribly irritated by Théophile and Eugénie's insistence that he recognize the responsibility he created by his relationship with Marthe. Horace is going through the motions of the kind of passion Indiana and Valentine deeply feel.

When Eugénie tells Horace that she believes he is incapable of treating Marthe as she deserves, Horace protests: "Sans rien affecter, sans rien jurer, je puis bien, ce me semble, pratiquer dans l'occasion le dévouement jusqu'au sacrifice" (146). Horace reveals here his incapacity for change, he can only play the role of being devoted. Love as a game, or as a sport, is carried even further in Horace's relationship with Léonie, the Viscountess of Chailly.[9]

Neither one is in love; the passionate feelings they profess for one another are purely artificial. Like Horace, Léonie is a dissembler; in fact, she is a kind of personification of artificiality. While she is neither beautiful nor intelligent, she is able to convince others that she possesses these qualities. As the daughter of a rich banker not even her nobility is genuine: "Enfin, elle avait une noblesse artificielle, comme tout le reste, comme ses dents, comme son sein, et comme son cœur" (124). The Viscountess's incapacity for love is demonstrated by her indifference to her own children. She and Horace engage in an activity described at one point as the "prostitution du cœur" (325). Their double game of duplicity also points to the hollowness of relationships in high society and to the emptiness of the lives of parvenus who attempt to lead that life.

Horace's love life is dictated above all by egotism. Théophile suspects that Horace acted out of calculated self-interest in enticing Marthe to spend the night with him at his hotel so that she would be compromised and have no choice but to become his mistress. Horace even admits that "la passion n'exclut point une certaine diplomatie" (175). As Théophile rightly remarks, Horace "aimait seulement en vue de son propre bonheur, et, si je puis m'exprimer ainsi, pour l'amour de lui-même" (172). His own feelings are of paramount importance. In his relationship with Marthe, Horace believes that he is always the injured party, the unfairly treated partner. On one occasion, Horace stays out all night, causing Marthe considerable anxiety; when Jean points that out to Horace later, the latter responds indignantly: "Parbleu! Et moi, croyez-vous que je sois sur des roses? . . . Est-ce que des souffrances puériles et injustes doivent être caressées, tandis que des souffrances poignantes et légitimes comme les miennes s'enveniment de jour en jour?" (218). Horace enjoys falling ill because then he is justly able to claim everyone's attention and sympathy.

Horace's love is very different from that of earlier characters such as Mauprat or Bénédicte (*Valentine*) in that he is very concerned with what others think of his actions. When he hears rumors concerning Marthe, he demands that she cease all contact with Paul Arsène, even insisting that she not shake his hand or smile at him. Horace's love does not uplift him, but instead drags Marthe down

to his level. She is forced to go along with his cruel and unreasonable requests and must even abandon her friends: "Elle repoussa même nos offres avec une sorte de hauteur qu'elle ne nous avait jamais témoignée" (181). As in the relationship of Amaury and Joséphine, "l'amour rend méchant" (178), a phrase which also applies to Horace and Marthe. They are not equal partners in the relationship; Marthe must always be subservient. In Sand's eyes no solid relationship can be built on such a foundation.

Through Horace Marthe's life is trivialized: "Il fallait que la modeste Marthe ne s'occupât que de lecture et de toilette, sous peine de perdre toute poésie aux yeux d'Horace, comme si la beauté perdait de son prix et de son lustre en remplissant les conditions d'une vie naïve et simple. Il fallut que pendant trois mois elle jouât le rôle de Marguerite devant ce Faust improvisé; qu'elle arrosât des fleurs sur sa fenêtre; qu'elle tressât plusieurs fois par jour ses longs cheveux d'ébène, vis-à-vis d'un miroir *gothique*" (187-88). As the reference to Goethe here suggests, Horace's treatment of Marthe and his view of women generally, is dictated in large part by literary models. Thus Marthe must become not only Faust's lover, but must transform herself into a variety of women from contemporary fiction, beginning with Musset: "Ce poëte enfant avait une immense influence sur le cerveau d'Horace. Quand celui-ci venait de lire *Portia* ou *la Camargo*, il voulait que la pauvre Marthe fût l'une ou l'autre. Le lendemain, après un feuilleton de Janin, il fallait qu'elle devînt à ses yeux une élégante et coquette patricienne. Enfin, après les chroniques romantiques d'Alexandre Dumas, c'était une tigresse qu'il fallait traiter en tigre; et après *la Peau de chagrin* de Balzac, c'était une mystérieuse beauté dont chaque regard et chaque mot recélait de profonds abîmes" (183-84). Ironically, the editors to whom Horace later tries to sell a manuscript tell him to give them a *feuilleton* novel, like those of Eugène Sue or Jules Janin. Long after his break-up with Marthe, Horace still thinks of the relationship in terms of fiction.

The image that Horace has of his mistress is thus far removed from reality. When their poverty becomes inescapable, Horace is horrified at the suggestion that Marthe go back to work: "A présent il faudra donc que je te voie courir dans la crotte,

marchander avec des bourgeoises pour quelques sous; faire la cuisine, balayer la poussière, gâter et empuantir tes jolis doigts, veiller, pâlir, porter des savates et rapiécer tes robes, être enfin comme tu voulais être au commencement de notre union? Pouah! Pouah! Tout cela me fait horreur, rien que d'y penser" (190). Horace can only love the imaginary figure he has created. What ends their relationship is a reality he cannot ignore, or accept: Marthe becomes pregnant. This completely destroys Horace's illusions: "Une femme en couches me représente l'idée la plus horrible" (244). When Horace discovers that Marthe has had his child he has no paternal stirrings. In fact, his first reaction in hearing about the baby is that he had not considered that possibility in finding a *dénouement* for his novel.

Théophile tries to tell Horace that he is too much under the influence of romantic literature: "Mon cher Horace, tu n'es pas, tu ne peux pas être le don Juan que décrit Hoffmann, encore moins celui de Byron. Ces créations poétiques occupent trop ton cerveau, et tu te manières pour les faire passer dans la réalité de ta vie" (320). Indeed, just as he plays Faust to Marthe's Gretchen, he attempts to play the role of Don Juan with Léonie. The absurdity of such a role becomes evident in the reaction of the Marquis de Vernes when Horace mistakenly tells him that Marthe committed suicide over him: "Ah! Voilà qui est bien, très bien, dit le marquis avec beaucoup de sérieux; je vous félicite. Cela ne m'est jamais arrivé. Un suicide! C'est superbe cela, mon cher, à votre âge" (299). He does not follow through on the cold-hearted lessons in the art of seduction the Marquis gives him; but this contact with the world of nobility leads him to take on the role of a young nobleman. Although he has neither the birthright nor the money, his skill at role-playing allows him to enter this world successfully until his indiscretion in bragging of his love with the Viscountess results in his ignominious expulsion from his new circle of friends.

The ludicrous side of Horace's romantic role-playing graphically emerges in the novel's ending. When Marthe falsely tells him that her son is not his child but Paul's, Horace pulls a dagger and vows to kill her: " 'Meurs donc, prostituée, et ton fils, et moi, avec toi!' Il avait son poignard à la main; et quoiqu'il n'eût certainement d'intention bien nette que de l'effrayer, elle reçut, en se jetant au-devant de son fils, non pas le coup de la mort, mais, hélas, puisqu'il faut le dire, au risque de dénouer platement la seule tragédie un peu sérieuse qu'Horace eût jouée dans sa vie—une légère égra-tignure" (404). We need to keep in mind that this is Théophile's per-spective on these events. From his point of view this represents a kind of absurd comedy, something to be treated lightly. From Marthe's perspective, concerned for her safety and that of her child, this event has an altogether different significance. In the vaguely Balzacian conclusion to the novel, the perspective is still that of a benevolent head-shaking over Horace's errant behavior: "Il a refait trois romans sur ses amours avec Marthe, et deux sur ses amours avec la vicomtesse. . . . Enfin, ayant moins de succès en littérature que de talent et de besoins, il a pris le parti d'achever courageuse-ment son droit; et maintenant il travaille à se faire une clientèle dans sa province, dont il sera bientôt, j'espère, l'avocat le plus brillant" (409). From the larger vantage point evoked here Marthe is no more than a minor episode in Horace's life.

Meanwhile in an ironic twist Marthe—not Horace—becomes a professional and successful actress. She makes her living doing successfully what Horace attempted to do. Whereas Horace is less than he seems, Marthe accomplishes much more. She is treated with contempt by polite society because she ran away from home with a man who did not marry her. She fled because of the inces-tuous attacks by her father. She discovers, however, that in running away with Poisson she had, like Indiana, simply "changé de tyran" (94). Jean Laravinière again acts as an objective judge in sensing the true virtue of Marthe while exposing the façade of Horace; he talks of the fact that "il y a des cœurs purs sous des robes souillées, et des cœurs corrompus sous des gilets magnifiques" (227). Marthe is a "pure woman" in the same sense as Hardy's Tess of the d'Urbervilles.

Paul Arsène, too, is a study in substance over appearance. Although born an artisan, he has such gifts as a painter that Dela-croix takes him on as a student. Despite his talent and love for painting, Paul is forced to give it up in order to get a job which will allow him to take care of his two sisters and to help Marthe surreptitiously. He gives up painting readily in order to serve others, observing "pourvu qu'on vive honnêtement, qu'importe qu'on soit artiste ou manœuvre?" (46). His love for Marthe is in utter contrast to that of Horace. Paul's devotion does not lead him to expect any rewards or any public recognition; he is content to love her and help her. Paul and Horace offer the two models for Théophile's abstract depiction of love: "Je crois qu'on doit définir passion noble celle qui nous élève et nous fortifie dans la beauté des sentiments et la grandeur des idées; passion mauvaise, celle qui nous ramène à l'égoïsme, à la crainte et à toutes les petitesses de l'instinct aveugle" (185). Paul's love is utterly selfless and his devotion to Marthe finds its compensation in the end only through one of those apparent chance twists of fate which abound in Sand's fiction. After participating in the attempted revolt of the Saint-Merry cloister (June 5, 1832), Paul is wounded and escapes by climbing up on a roof and falling though an attic window—and into Marthe's apartment.[10] This event is presented as an act of divine intervention. This is evident in the miraculous strength which suddenly surges into Marthe's arms and allows her to lift Paul onto the bed: "Elle tira le verrou de la porte, revint vers Arsène, joignit les mains, et demanda tout haut à Dieu, son seul refuge, ce qu'il fallait faire. Alors, obéissant à un instinct subit, elle essaya de soulever ce corps inerte. Deux fois elle tomba à côté de lui sans pouvoir le déranger; puis tout à coup, remplie d'une force sur-naturelle, elle l'enleva comme elle eût fait d'un enfant, et le déposa sur son lit de sangle" (303). God's intervention on behalf of the worthy was evoked earlier in Paul's conviction that God sanctions the lower classes' right to equality. Divine supervision of human affairs becomes more evident in *Consuelo*. The presence of this motif implies a justification of including events which stretch the limits of verisimilitude to the breaking-point. This is the case in *Horace* with the sudden reappearance at the end of the novel of Jean Lavinière, earlier declared dead, and with his miraculous cure by Théophile.

Paul's participation in the armed struggle to overthrow the government points to how completely he acts according to the values in which he believes. In this way he offers a contrast both to Horace and Théophile. His relationship with Marthe is also a victory of substance over appearance. They do not marry but rather live together in the kind of Saint-Simonian relationship advocated by Eugénie who denies the validity of civil marriage and places the primary emphasis on the vows between two people. Paul adopts Marthe's son in a similar vein. He and Marthe perform a kind of Saint-Simonian adoption: she solemnly gives him the child which he holds up to God. This is a realization of the principle, dear to George Sand, that "c'est l'amour, le dévouement et les soins qui constituent la vraie paternité" (339). These values are not only brought out in the novel through the positive examples of Marthe and Paul but to a greater degree through the negative example of Horace and, to a certain extent, Théophile. By giving her narrator this role, George Sand was in effect warning the reader: do not be so swept away in reading novels that you blindly adopt the views and attitudes embraced by the narrator (as the mouthpiece of the author) or by the principal characters. Thus, like *Le Compagnon du tour de France, Horace* is a novel with an anti-novel message.

5

Keepers of the Sacred Flame

Consuelo and *Jeanne*

*Un feu divin monta à ses joues, et la flamme sacrée jaillit de
ses grands yeux noirs, lorsqu'elle remplit la voûte de cette
voix sans égale.*

—*Consuelo* (74)

    After two novels with male central characters, George Sand
in her fiction written between 1842 and 1844 focused her attention
on women in the leading roles. Consuelo, the principal character of
the novel of the same name (1842) as well as of its sequel, *La
comtesse de Rudolstadt* (1843), and Jeanne, of the like-named novel
(1844), evince a number of similarities. They are visionary women
who transcend in one way or another their own time and place.
They have in common with Lélia that they do not fulfill the traditional domestic or social roles of women. In fact both are outside
the contemporary world of the intended reader, removed in time,
space and/or social station. Unlike Lélia, Consuelo and Jeanne do
not engage in protracted soul-searching; they are far removed from
the proudly self-centered and fiercely dominating character of
Lélia. Rather, like the Lélia of 1839 they have found and accepted
their role and strive to enlighten others while fulfilling a useful social and spiritual function. While Lélia acts superior but is really

floundering, Consuelo and Jeanne appear to be above the fray. The social vision evoked by the example of their lives is not as focused or insistent as it is in the previous novels—or will be in those of 1845. Yet George Sand was as engaged as ever in getting across her vision of a new society. The emphasis in the novels under question is less on the social and political aspects of a new order than on its religious and spiritual dimensions. This was after all an essential aspect of Pierre Leroux's thought, one that Sand had already treated in *Spiridion*.

Consuelo, *La comtesse de Rudolstadt*, and *Jeanne* are ambitious, complex works. George Sand writes in the 1852 introduction to *Jeanne* that the serial publication of the novel had its effect on its construction. This was in fact the period during which the popular novel in serial form was becoming a publishing sensation. The length of *Consuelo / La comtesse de Rudolstadt* is as much a sign of the influence of this phenomenon on George Sand as are the numerous elements of popular fiction of the gothic/adventure/sensational variety to be found there.[1] Sand called the completed work "cet interminable fatras de rêveries" (*Correspondance* 5: 736) and "un bavardage énorme" (*Correspondance* 5: 822). According to her what is worth anything in the novel comes from Leroux.[2] Critics then and now have proven to be kinder to the work than the author; the Consuelo novels are widely regarded today as Sand's greatest achievement.[3] Sand called *Jeanne* a "roman de contrastes" and this could equally well be applied to the Consuelo novels. For Sand the eighteenth century, which provides the time frame of the story, is the century which epitomized the notion of contrast with its worship of reason and delight in sentiment, its belief in logic and love of magic. Sand uses these contradictions as the basic framework for the novel. Voltaire appears alongside Cagliostro, Frederick the Great alongside Trismégiste. Consuelo's life with its radical ups and downs epitomizes these contrasts. She remarks, for instance, on the fact that in the same castle in which she begged as a child she later finds herself in the position of owner with the title of Countess.

George Sand effectively uses these oppositions for dramatic effect, while at the same time claiming she is being faithful to the

eighteenth-century world: "Que l'on fasse bon marché de l'intrigue et de l'invraisemblance de certaines situations; que l'on regarde autour de ces gens et de ces aventures de ma fantaisie, on verra un monde où je n'ai rien inventé, un monde qui a existé et qui a été beaucoup plus fantastique que mes personnages et leurs vicissitudes: de sorte que ce qu'il y a de plus impossible dans mon livre, est précisément ce qui s'est passé dans la réalité des choses" (1: 6). While this claim could be seen as substantiated in the first section of *Consuelo* in which Sand portrays Consuelo's youth in Venice—a city she knew first hand—it becomes more problematic as the novel progresses, particularly when Consuelo leaves Venice for the Bohemian woods, as foreign to Sand as they are to Consuelo. In fact, the novel changes character dramatically once Consuelo leaves Venice. In the first section of the novel the action unrolls against a backdrop of theater life and intrigue portrayed with a good deal of verisimilitude, even if there is no detailed depiction of the setting. The opening recalls that of *Le Compagnon du tour de France* in that action predominates and the characters' dialogue is used to set the atmosphere and give background information. As was the case in the earlier novel the opening scene is realistic and imbued with a considerable amount of humor, as in the depiction of the tug of war between the obstinate Porpora and the scheming Count Zustiniani. This is the role in fact that many of the minor characters play in the Consuelo novels, to set the mood and add humor to a fairly somber story.

Amélie de Rudolstadt plays this role in the second section of the novel; she also provides Consuelo—and the reader—with essential background information on the Rudolstadt family. But the world in which she is presented is far different from the Venetian world of love adventures. In fact, if the name of the castle Consuelo goes to in Bohemia, Riesenburg (Château des Géants) brings to mind the gothic novel, particularly Horace Walpole's *Castle of Otranto*, this is not surprising. The link to the gothic tradition becomes evident as soon as Consuelo arrives at the castle:

> Lorsque la voiture eut franchi lentement le pont-levis qui résonna sourdement sous les pieds des chevaux, et que la herse

retomba derrière elle avec un affreux grincement, il lui sembla qu'elle entrait dans l'enfer du Dante, et saisie de terreur, elle recommanda son âme à Dieu. Sa figure était donc bouleversée lorsqu'elle se présenta devant ses hôtes; et celle du comte Christian venant à la frapper tout d'un coup, cette longue figure blême, flétrie par l'âge et le chagrin, et ce grand corps maigre et raide sous son costume antique, elle crut voir le spectre d'un châtelain du moyen âge; et, prenant tout ce qui l'entourait pour une vision, elle recula en étouffant un cri d'effroi. (1: 175)

The appearances of the other members of the family—with the exception of Amélie—only serves to reinforce Consuelo's sense of dread. When given a welcome kiss by Amélie's hunchback aunt, she feels as if it were the kiss of death. Albert's ghostlike initial appearance is as well suggestive of a figure from beyond the grave. We soon receive other information about his family which seems to place the action smack in the middle of a gothic novel. There is an apparent curse hanging over the Rudolstadt family: the children all die before the age of thirty, the age Albert is just about to reach. Albert has had visions—he is gifted with "seconde vue"—of the arrival of an "angel of consolation" who will save him. In fact the arrival he anticipates is that of Consuelo. When Consuelo begins to sing Albert suddenly addresses her in Spanish, calling her by her real name which she has told no one at the castle. Such events are not restricted to this section of the work. They occur throughout the two novels, usually in connection with Albert.

Meanwhile Consuelo undergoes adventures worthy of a heroine of gothic fiction. She is constantly getting lost in corridors and underground passageways in castles, first in Riesenburg than at the castle of the Baron de Kreutz and finally at that of Frederick the Great. She is almost raped and nearly walled in alive. In Albert's grotto church, full of stalactites resembling ghosts, serpents and giants and overgrown with eerie vegetation, Consuelo has a vision in which Satan appears and speaks to her. In a trance she kisses Albert, then horrified, stumbles and falls into a pile of human remains. She tries to run away but again falls, this time on top of a freshly-dug grave. Later, suffering from deliria, she attempts to

throw herself out a high window of the castle; it is a scene of classic gothic:

> Elle bondit au milieu de la chambre, échevelée, les pieds nus, le corps enveloppé d'une légère robe de nuit blanche et froissée, qui lui donnait l'air d'un spectre échappé de la tombe; et au moment où on croyait la ressaisir, elle sauta par-dessus l'épinette qui se trouvait devant elle, avec l'agilité d'un chat sauvage, atteignit la fenêtre qu'elle prenait pour l'ouverture de la fatale citerne, y posa un pied, étendit les bras, et, criant de nouveau le nom d'Albert au milieu de la nuit orageuse et sinistre, elle allait se précipiter, lorsque Albert, encore plus agile et plus fort qu'elle, l'entoura de ses bras et la rapporta sur son lit. (1: 357)

The description of the setting for Consuelo's initiation into the ranks of the *Invisibles* is as well vintage gothic, as is her presence at the ruined castle during a violent storm where she overhears an important conversation.

All the gothic trappings are more than just a concession to popular taste. The pattern of death linked to passion is common-place in the gothic novel, but here it takes on new meaning from the fact that it is only after Albert's death that Consuelo begins to love him: "Depuis qu'Albert n'est plus, je l'aime, je ne pense qu'à lui, je ne puis aimer que lui" (3: 113). The fact that the gothic-inspired episodes are grouped around Consuelo and, even more, around Albert reinforces their spiritual, visionary nature and points to one of the ideas Sand hoped to convey in this work. That Albert is conscious of having lived other lives and, in fact, slips into the speech and mannerisms of some of his prior lives on occasion is a demonstration of the mystical view of time presented in the two novels. According to Albert "le temps n'existe pas" (3: 539), a view held by the *Invisibles* as well: "Nous vivons par l'esprit et par le cœur dans le passé, dans l'avenir et dans le présent tout à la fois. Nos prédécesseurs et nos successeurs sont aussi bien *nous* que nous-mêmes" (3: 366). This notion of time, embodying metempsychosis, is in accord with the belief that mankind, by continuously striving, will improve and eventually reach perfection.[4] This is the notion Albert presents at the end of *La comtesse de Rudolstadt*: "Nul ne vit en vain; rien n'est perdu. Aucun de nous n'est inutile" (3: 573). Albert's gift of "seconde vue" reinforces this idea, suggesting as it does that space too does not represent a physical reality but can be overcome. Albert's prediction of the time of Consuelo's arrival in Riesenburg as well as her "consoling" function serve to highlight the heroic role of Consuelo and the like function she comes to play for society in *La comtesse de Rudolstadt*. This sense of Consuelo's "coming" is dramatized in the passage at the end of *Consuelo* in which Albert's uncle waits on an appointed day, time, and place far from Riesenburg to pick up a person Albert has predicted will appear and who is none other than Consuelo.

Such occurrences are often presented as real and inexplicable. The narrator occasionally comments on such events but only to state his inability to judge them. After describing Albert's ability to read other's secrets, for example, the narrator comments: "Je n'expliquerai pas d'une manière naturelle ce don étrange qu'il possédait parfois. Certaines facultés (non approfondies et non définies par la science) restèrent chez lui incompréhensibles pour ses proches, comme elles le sont pour l'historien qui vous les raconte, et qui, à l'égard de ces sortes de choses, n'est pas plus avancé, après cent ans écoulés, que ne le sont les grands esprits de son siècle" (2: 77). Certainly the characters who claim to use only reason as their guide for understanding the universe are seen in a decidedly negative light. This is particularly the case with Frederick the Great. George Sand shows how cruelly and blindly he acts using reason as his guide, causing Consuelo to comment that "il y a décidément, dans ce royaume de la raison, une conspiration permanente contre la raison" (3: 128). In actuality Frederick does not base his actions on reason and logic but his pretense of doing so makes him act unjustly—and irrationally. He is unfavorably compared to Gottlieb, the mystical shoemaker and follower of Boehm, who is simpleminded but warm and generous.

Sand uses the gothic elements in the story to make other points as well. When Consuelo appears at Riesenburg her pupil Amélie insists upon viewing her as the heroine of a gothic romance, as "un enfant mystérieux de quelque famille de princes" (1: 220).

Consuelo's response holds a social significance: "Ainsi, dit-elle avec un peu de mécontentement, un honnête ouvrier, ou un pauvre artiste, n'aurait pas eu le droit de transmettre à son enfant quelque distinction naturelle? Il faut absolument que les enfants du peuple soient grossiers et difformes!" (1: 220). Consuelo, in refuting the oft-used gothic device of ratifying a hero's or heroine's worth by exposing their hidden high birth, suggests that birth is irrelevant , that a person's character and value are independent of social origins. Sand takes other opportunities as well to subvert traditional aspects of the gothic. In fact, in the extensive description of Count Hoditz's elaborate preparations for the festival in honor of his wife, Sand pokes fun at the gratuitous use of gothic effects. At one point a "shadow" leads the party into a dimly lit hall where they hear eerie music "qui était censée exécutée par les habitants du monde invisible" (2: 497). The ludicrousness of the Count's musical compositions serves by contrast to accentuate the greatness of real art, as represented by Consuelo and Porpora. The Count's whole estate has been transformed into artificiality; there is only one area which has been left natural; it represents for the Count "le désert, le chaos" (2: 488).

Given the popularity of Mrs. Radcliffe and her imitators, George Sand could be sure that her readers would be familiar with the gothic tradition. Thus she has her narrator speculate at one point as to what Mrs. Radcliffe would have done with the story:

> Si l'ingénieuse et féconde Anne Radcliffe se fût trouvée à la place du candide et maladroit narrateur de cette très véridique histoire, elle n'eût pas laissé échapper une si bonne occasion de vous promener, madame la lectrice, à travers les corridors, les trappes, les escaliers en spirale, les ténèbres et les souterrains pendant une demi-douzaine de beaux et attachants volumes, pour vous révéler, seulement au septième, tous les arcanes de son œuvre savante, mais la lectrice esprit fort que nous avons charge de divertir ne le prendrait peut-être pas aussi bien, au temps où nous sommes, l'innocent stratagème du romancier. (1: 253)

The self-conscious narration does not prevent Sand from preceding to send her heroine on as many hidden passageways and underground tunnels as the author of the *Mysteries of Udolpho* could have done herself. Of course once again the similarity only serves to accentuate the radically different type of heroine Consuelo represents. When at one point the chaplain and the Canoness speculate on which novels are the source of Consuelo's "idées romanesques" it demonstrates how natural and genuine her feelings and thoughts are. Sand in the Consuelo novels does not highlight the dangers of imaginative literature as she had in *Le Compagnon* and *Horace*, rather she uses literary conventions for her own purposes. Her modus operandi parallels that of the *Invisibles* in *La comtesse de Rudolstadt* who use magic and freemasonry as a veneer to camouflage their true activities.

What the *Invisibles* are about is in fact creating a new religion: "Nous ne voulons pas fonder seulement un empire universel sur un ordre nouveau et sur des bases équitables; c'est une religion que nous voulons reconstituer" (3: 368). The religious concepts highlighted in the Consuelo saga are largely those expressed by Albert and later echoed by the *Invisibles*. The religious initiation of Consuelo parallels that of Sand into the phlosophy of Pierre Leroux.[5] Albert feels he must personally atone for the crimes committed during the religious wars of the Reformation. His hideaway is the Schreckenstein where atrocities were committed, where "des supplices et des violences atroces ont consacré l'asile de ma prière et le sanctuaire de ma douleur" (2: 9). Albert creates there an altar made of bones to which he prays. He instructs Consuelo in his religious thought and in the process proposes a history of religion. Albert is convinced that the true religion has been stolen from the people. Priests have obfuscated the tenets of Christianity. The leader of the *Invisibles* predicts a time when the symbols which come between man and his religion will disappear: "Le temps est proche où le voile du temple sera déchiré pour jamais, et où la foule emportera d'assaut les sanctuaires et l'arche sainte. Alors les symboles disparaîtront, et les abords de la vérité ne seront plus gardés par les dragons du despotisme religieux et monarchiques" (3: 363).[6] This is to be the religion which eliminates barriers between men;

Consuelo considers this to be the essence of Albert's religious beliefs: "Cette religion est la mienne, puisqu'elle proclame la future égalité entre tous les hommes et la future manifestation de la justice et de la bonté de Dieu sur la terre" (3: 241). The model advocated here, as in *Spiridion*, is Saint John's gospel.[7] The similarity to that novel can also be seen in the fact that among the many titles Albert eventually acquires are "Docteur de l'Evangile éternel" and "Chevalier de Saint Jean" (3: 509).

While Albert's religious beliefs make him a heretic in the eyes of the Catholic Church, he is a leader in the new humanitarian church: "Cet homme bizarre, dont le délire avait consterné les âmes catholiques, devint un flambeau de sagesse pour des esprits d'un ordre supérieur. Il fut initié aux plus intimes confidences des Invisibles, et prit rang parmi les chefs et les pères de cette église nouvelle" (3: 436). The new religion is not meant to replace Christianity but to carry out its dictates in a way not done before. Christianity is seen here as dynamic, capable of growing and maturing; it is a viable religion if interpreted in the direction of equality and tolerance. A new form of Christianity is all the more necessary in that the Catholic Church is portrayed as equally responsible with the nobility for past injustice and inhumanity. One way of reviving Christianity is to fuse it with other religious doctrines. According to Sand this is, in fact, how Christianity originated.[8] Albert, for instance, expresses sympathy for the beliefs of the Lollards: "Une secte mystérieuse et singulière rêva, entre beaucoup d'autres, de réhabiliter la vie de la chair, et de réunir dans un seul principe divin ces deux principes arbitrairement divisés. Elle voulut sanctionner l'amour, l'égalité, la communauté de tous, les éléments de bonheur. C'était une idée juste et sainte" (2: 19). He sees them as celebrating Satan as the god of the people since the priests have claimed God as their own. He finds a great deal to admire in other heretical sects as well. He practices the Hussite form of communion, for example, with local peasants. Consuelo's religious beliefs develop in a similar way. She attaches a cypress branch, symbol of Albert's heretical grotto church, to her altar in order to practice "la religion unique, éternelle, absolue" (2: 461), thus combining Christianity and paganism. She also sees Albert's theory of the "transmission des âmes" (2: 532) as a logical development of Christianity, since it incorporates the idea of eternal life.

The official representatives of the Church do not fare well in the novels. The Jesuit who accompanies Albert on his travels is scheming and egotistical. The chaplain of the Rudolstadt family is obsessed with orthodoxy and family and personal interest to the exclusion of all else. Like other clerics in Sand's fiction he thrives on family troubles. Consuelo gains more strength from her belief than do the representatives of orthodox Christianity, the Rudolstadt family, from theirs. The traditional faith of the Rudolstadts leads to pride and egotism and results in the near fatal neglect of Albert. Consuelo's faith, on the other hand, is a fountain of love and strength. According to Albert, Consuelo knows instinctively God much better than he, despite his theological studies. She is, in fact, seen as a divine emissary, as evident from Albert's prophetic comment upon Consuelo's arrival at the castle: "La paix du Seigneur est descendue sur cette maison" (1: 230). She becomes for Albert "prêteresse de mon culte" (2: 12) and later, for all of mankind, "la déesse de la pauvreté," bringing love and "consolation" to all of mankind. Angels, according to Consuelo's own view, no longer intervene directly in human affairs, making it necessary for humans to help one another: "Dans un temps où l'on ne croit plus à la révélation directe et à la manifestation sensible de la Divinité, la protection et le secours du ciel se traduisent sous la forme d'assistance, d'affection et de dévouement de la part de nos semblables" (3: 265). Consuelo is a supreme example of this transfer of the divine role of care and love to man, or more accurately, to woman.

Women also play a central role in the other spiritual force celebrated in the novel: art, in particular music: "La musique et la poésie sont les plus hautes expressions de la foi, et la femme douée de génie et de beauté est prêteresse, sibylle et iniatiatrice" (1: 385). Music represents something more than the career Consuelo happens to embrace. She is predestined to become a great singer, as an integral part of her divine mission on earth. Music is seen as possessing a supreme spiritual, moral and even social significance. Music can be "le langage divin" (1: 378) according to Albert: "La musique dit tout ce que l'âme rêve et pressent de plus mystérieux et de plus élevé. C'est la manifestation d'un ordre d'idées et de sentiments supérieurs à ce que la parole humaine pourrait exprimer. C'est la révélation de l'infini" (1: 378). In the epilogue of *La comtesse de Rudolstadt*, Albert is asked to reveal to Adam Weishaupt the sum total of his accumulated wisdom; he does so by playing his violin. Listening to Albert play, Consuelo earlier had seen the whole history of Bohemia pass before her eyes. It would be impossible for Albert to play his violin if he weren't divinely inspired. Albert sees making music with Consuelo as a form of worship: "Si jamais le bonheur d'unir, dans une prière selon mon cœur, ta voix divine, Consuelo, aux accents de mon violon, sans aucun doute je m'élèverai plus haut que je n'ai jamais fait, et ma prière sera plus digne de la Divinité" (1: 383). When Albert plays his violin for Consuelo in the grotto she falls into a kind of trance. She imagines she is hearing an angel "venait offrir à leurs lèvres avides la coupe de bois, le calice du pardon, de la réhabilitation, et de la sainte égalité" (2: 28). This is the same *coupe* mentioned earlier which the priests have hidden from the people. Music is presented as a means of regaining lost spiritual values and of creating equality among people. Consuelo's natural talent and superior character make her into a keeper of the sacred flame of art. Her extraordinary voice is a manifestation of divinity: "Un feu divin monta à ses joues, et la flamme sacrée jaillit de ses grands yeux noirs, lorsqu'elle remplit la voûte de cette voix sans égale et de cet accent victorieux, pur, vraiment grandiose, qui ne peut sortir que d'une grande intelligence jointe à un grand cœur" (1: 74). Marcello, the composer, whose music she has just sung can only compare her voice to that he hopes to hear one day from angels. Consuelo is, in many ways, an angel on earth.

In practice the performance of music is a means of differentiating among the different characters. Consuelo's extraordinary singing is not just a natural gift; she works long and hard to train her voice and improve her technique. Anzoleto's lower level of achievement is a reflection of his weaker character. The same is true of Consuelo's pupil Amélie: "Elle avait le timbre flexible, et pouvait avoir reçu de bonnes leçons; mais son caractère était trop léger pour lui permettre d'étudier quoi que ce fût en conscience" (1: 225). Only inspired music holds the promise of spiritual fulfillment. In turn an inspired artist is elevated by his art, as Consuelo's master, Porpora tells her: "Quoi que tu fasses et où que tu sois, au théâtre comme dans le cloître, tu peux être une sainte, une vierge céleste, la fiancée de l'idéal sacré" (1: 146). Consuelo's divine gifts do not always translate into popular success; in fact, her professional career is more a martyrdom. Consuelo as a singer is both a saint and a fairy-tale princess. The Canon calls her "sainte Cécile revenue sur la terre" (2: 346) while Porpora tells her: "Le jour où tu te donneras à un mortel, tu perdras ta divinité" (1: 147). In a development which recalls E.T.A. Hoffmann, Consuelo in fact loses her voice at age thirty due to her fright over her husband's temporary imprisonment. The symbolic significance of Consuelo's loss of voice has been interpreted from a variety of points of view, demonstrating the considerable critical interest in the novel as well as the diversity of interpretations.[9]

As the epitome of the inspired artist Consuelo is frequently compared to political leaders. Her natural virtue and innate nobility, added to her tremendous talent make her into one of the select few, more so than the officially anointed rulers of the world. Porpora points out what Consuelo has already demonstrated: "Dieu t'a fait reine; il t'a mis au front un diadème de beauté, d'intelligence et de force" (2: 329). Her encounters with Maria Theresa and Frederick the Great show how superior she is to them in almost every way imaginable. Maria Theresa has been corrupted by power. For her, appearance and reputation are all that matter. Consuelo is not overawed in her presence, displaying her simple virtue and self-assurance to such an extent that Maria Theresa is offended: "C'était trop de présomption et d'outrecuidance de la part d'une petite bohémienne, que de vouloir être estimable et sage sans que l'impératrice s'en mêlât" (2: 377). The ironic view of Maria Theresa is reinforced by her judgment that the degenerate Corilla is morally superior to Consuelo. Consuelo is just as proud and virtuous in her relation to Frederick the Great who is revealed to be shallow and egotistical, concerned only with maintaining his personal control over Prussia.

Art can also play a potentially beneficial social role. This is what Joseph Haydn explains to Consuelo: "Si les malheureux

avaient tous le sentiment et l'amour de l'art pour poétiser la souffrance et embellir la misère, il n'y aurait plus ni malpropreté, ni dé-
couragement, ni oubli de soi-même, et alors les riches ne se permet-
traient plus de tant fouler et mépriser les misérables" (1: 138). In
this view art can not only embellish the lives of the poor, it can help
to create social solidarity. The merging of the social and spiritual
potentialities of music are dramatized in the passage near the end
of *La comtesse de Rudolstadt* in which Consuelo is initiated into the
Invisibles. Consuelo is in the process of telling the assembled *Invisibles* of her consciousness of her duty to help the downtrodden
when she stops: "L'enthousiasme de Consuelo était porté au
comble; les paroles ne lui suffisaient plus pour l'exprimer. Une
sorte de vertige s'empara d'elle, et, ainsi qu'il arrivait aux pytho-
nisses, dans le paroxysme de leurs crises divines, de se livrer à des
cris et à d'étranges fureurs, elle fut entraînée à manifester l'émotion
qui la débordait par l'expression qui lui était la plus naturelle. Elle
se mit à chanter d'une voix éclatante" (3: 477). It is not surprising
that Albert when he is giving his vision of the new social order is
constantly referred to as "le poète." There is no divorce in this
fictional world between poetry and politics, between a visionary
view of the future and efforts to bring about greater social equality
in the present.

One form of music which in itself is a manifestation of liberation is that of the common people: "Il y a une musique qu'on
pourrait appeler naturelle, parce qu'elle n'est point le produit de la
science et de la réflexion, mais celui d'une inspiration qui échappe à
la rigueur des règles et des conventions. C'est la musique populaire" (2: 23). As would later be the case of Josef in *Les Maîtres Sonneurs,* Consuelo's musical genius is in part revealed by her enthusiasm for this type of music. Although as an artist she belongs to a
separate social caste, Consuelo feels a strong empathy with the
common people and their music. She is proud of her origin as the
daughter of an itinerant singer. As Consuelo is walking to Vienna
with Haydn the sad living conditions of the peasants she sees gives
her a new appreciation for her life as an artist:

Elle ne vit plus dans tous ces bons cultivateurs que des sujets de la faim et de la nécessité; les mâles enchaînées à la terre, valets de charrue et de bestiaux; les femelles enchaînées au maître, c'est-à-dire à l'homme, cloîtrées à la maison, servantes à perpétuité, et condamnés à un travail sans relâches au milieu des souffrances et des embarras de la maternité. . . . Alors cette sérénité apparente ne sembla plus à Consuelo que l'abrutissement du malheur ou l'engourdissement de la fatigue; et elle se dit qu'il valait mieux être artiste ou bohémien, que seigneur ou paysan, puisqu'à la possession d'une terre comme à celle d'une gerbe de blé s'attachaient ou la tyrannie injuste, ou le morne assujettissement de la cupidité. (2: 132)

Consuelo cherishes freedom as an almost sacred commodity; peasants are not only poor and ignorant, they are tied down to their farms. Consuelo is constantly escaping from situations in which she fears the loss of her freedom. In fact the path she follows is set to a large extent by such events, running away from Venice and Anzoleto, fleeing him again in Bohemia, escaping from Frederick the Great and imprisonment. Consuelo's love for the open road is an expression of her yearning for freedom: "Qu'y a-t-il de plus beau qu'un chemin? pensait-elle . . . ce chemin, c'est le passage de l'humanité, c'est la route de l'univers. Il n'appartient pas à un maître qui puisse le fermer ou l'ouvrir à son gré. Ce n'est pas seulement le puissant et le riche qui ont le droit de fouler ses marges fleuries et de respirer ses sauvages parfums. . . . A droite, à gauche, les champs, les bois appartiennent à des maîtres; le chemin appartient à celui qui ne possède pas autre chose; aussi comme il l'aime" (1: 390). The passage—and the feeling—are reminiscent of Joseph von Eichendorff and German romanticism. But here the social consciousness is clearly in evidence. Walking becomes a protest against property ownership.

There are other aspects of Consuelo and Haydn which recall Eichendorff's *Good-for-Nothing* (*Aus dem Leben eines Taugenichts*) as well. In fact Haydn's poverty, naive and bubbling personality, and violin-playing make him very similar to Eichendorff's hero. Consuelo and Haydn are penniless but happy and, like the Good-for-

Nothing, jump carefreely from adventure to adventure; they, too, as poor artists are God's special children, under a kind of divine protection. The episode in which they save a town's music celebration is very reminiscent of the German *Dorfgeschichte* (village tale) with its easy humor and gentle satire. Consuelo also feels a close identification with nature on her journey. This is particularly the case in the Canon's garden in which, in a Hoffmanesque vision, she imagines she hears the flowers talking to her. More important than her relationship with flowers is that with birds. Images of Consuelo as a bird are to be found throughout the two novels. In leaving the Riesenburg castle surreptitiously she comments to herself: "L'oiseau qui ne peut se défendre a des ailes pour se sauver" (2: 102). Later the narrator describes Consuelo and Haydn on their travels as "deux oiseaux de passage" (2: 124). She and Haydn spare nightingales caught in traps they set "sous prétexte que ces oiseaux musiciens étaient des confrères" (2: 149). Subsequently, in a song in front of the Canon's house, they describe themselves as nightingales (2: 232). In leaving Vienna, Consuelo feels like "l'alouette qui monte en chantant dans le ciel" (2: 472).

Birds function here as symbols of freedom, able to soar away from problems and entanglements. They are, of course, musicians as well, who ply their art, as indicated of the lark here, flying toward the heavens. That birds—and through them artists—are go-betweens for man and God is shown most clearly in the robin which Consuelo tames while in Spandau prison. Gottlieb is convinced that both Consuelo and the robins are angels. Consuelo imagines that the robin has composed a note to her and almost believes he will talk to her. After Consuelo has been delivered from Spandau and is awaiting initiation in the pavilion of the *Invisibles* the robin returns, brought there by Gottlieb. He becomes for her a "consolateur" (3: 330), the role that she fulfills towards others.

The concept of freedom, so visually symbolized in the bird images, is prominent as well in the vision of a new society projected in the Consuelo novels. This is the case with the view of marriage expressed by Wanda, Albert's mother and the sibyl of the *Invisibles*: "Que le sacrement soit une permission religieuse, une autorisation paternelle et sociale, un encouragement et une exhortation à la

perpétuité de l'engagement; que ce ne soit jamais un commande-
ment, une obligation, une loi avec des menaces et des châtiments,
un esclavage imposé, avec du scandale, des prisons, et des chaînes
en cas d'infraction" (3: 491). The *Invisibles* call in fact for a whole
new approach to male-female relationships, one based on freedom
of choice: "Nous voulons inaugurer et sanctifier l'amour, perdu et
profané dans le monde, le libre choix du cœur, l'union sainte et
volontaire de deux êtres également épris" (3: 476). Thus the type of
union advocated in *Le Compagnon* and *Horace*, as well as in earlier
novels, receives a kind of official sanction through the *Invisibles*.
The totally subservient role women play in society and the dangers of their powerlessness are dramatically evoked through the
attempted rape of Consuelo by Trench the Austrian and by the
account of the rape of the Princess of Culmbach whose mother
hired a man to assault her daughter while she stands guard at the
door. But the *Invisibles* also recognize that because of their upbringing and lack of educational possibilities women are incapable of
playing the same roles in society as men; the full initiation into the
secrets of the organization that Consuelo receives represents a great
exception among women. This is a reflection of Sand's own views
on the role women could and should play in public life. The
relationship between Consuelo and Albert is exceptional and could
hardly be taken as a model. But the Liverani episode is introduced
into *La comtesse de Rudolstadt* as a means of dramatizing the need for
unions based on mutual attraction.

Equality is a central theme throughout the work, one which
is invested with religious approbation. It is also symbolically represented by the brotherhood of man in miniature which the secret
society of the *Invisibles* represents. The point is emphasized that at
the final get-together of the *Invisibles* all social classes mingle together. Albert carries out in his own life the principle of equality,
treating the hapless Zdenko as his equal and redistributing his
wealth to the poor. As in *Mauprat* there are characters in this work
who demonstrate that given equality of opportunity all men can
rise to the same intellectual height. This is demonstrated here
through the transformations of Karl and Gottlieb.

The ideals advocated in the Consuelo novels are brought out above all through the principal characters of Consuelo and Albert. Consuelo's devotion to others manifests itself most fundamentally as a lack of concern about her own welfare. Her lack of egotism is evident above all through the contrast with the characters which whom she successively lives—Anzoleto, Amélie, Frederick the Great. Her name indicates the function she fulfills for others, practically for Albert, symbolically for all of mankind. As Albert tells her, she is not really meant to belong to any one person: "Dieu t'a réservé une existence à part" (1: 333). At the same time the narrator projects a heroic aura around Consuelo, comparing her, for instance, to Joan of Arc. This is the case, too, when she goes in quest of the missing Albert:

> Elle marchait avec rapidité; aucun obstacle ne l'arrêtait. Le silence de ces grands bois ne portait plus la tristesse ni l'épouvante de son âme. Elle voyait la piste des loups sur le sable, et ne s'inquiétait pas de rencontrer leur troupe affamée. Il lui semblait qu'elle était poussée par une main divine qui la rendait invulnérable. Elle qui savait le Tasse par cœur, pour l'avoir chanté toutes les nuits sur les lagunes, elle s'imaginait marcher à l'abri de son talisman, comme le généreux Ubalde à la reconnaissance de Renaud à travers les embûches de la forêt enchantée. Elle marchait svelte et légère parmi les ronces et les rochers, le front rayonnant d'une secrète fierté, et les joues colorées d'une légère rougeur. Jamais elle n'avait été plus belle à la scène dans les rôles héroïques; et pourtant elle ne pensait pas plus à la scène en cet instant qu'elle n'avait pensé à elle-même en montant sur le théâtre. (1: 257)

The reference to Tasso's *Jerusalem Delivered* places Consuelo—one is tempted to say despite herself—in the epic, heroic tradition. In this novel celebrating the "resurgence of the feminine" (Frappier-Mazur), the normal pattern of the epic hero being transformed through abnegation and initiation is turned on its head; Consuelo ably plays that role as she does so many others—while still remaining decidedly a woman. Albert is not the only one Consuelo saves, she also rescues Frederick the Great from assassination. After carrying out the mission the *Invisibles* entrust her with—helping to prepare the way for the new society—Consuelo at the end of *La comtesse de Rudolstadt* becomes "la bonne déesse de la pauvreté," ministering to the wants and needs of the forgotten segments of society.

Consuelo is presented from the beginning of the novel as an exceptional being.[10] Her seriousness, Spanish background, and great talent result in her separation from the other girls in Porpora's charity school in Venice. Especially when she sings her uniqueness becomes manifest: "Quelle miraculeuse transformation s'était opérée dans cette jeune fille tout à l'heure si blême et si abattue, si effarée par la fatigue et la crainte! Son large front semblait nager dans un fluide céleste, une molle langueur baignait encore les plans doux et nobles de sa figure sereine et généreuse" (1: 73). Although generally modest and unpretentious, she has an iron will and great pride. She is not only an extraordinary individual, the situations in which she becomes involved are unique as well. Consuelo in Vienna puts her situation in dramatic terms: "J'ai par le monde un époux adoptif dont je ne puis être la femme sans tuer mon père adoptif; et réciproquement, si je remplis mes devoirs de fille, je tue mon époux" (2: 315). The narrator sounds a similar note when Consuelo is at Frederick's court: "C'était une singulière destinée, que la seule femme capable d'exercer sur Frédéric une sorte de prestige ressemblant à l'amour, fût peut-être la seule dans tout son royaume qui n'eût voulu à aucun prix encourager cette disposition" (3: 135). Like Pierre Huguenin (*Le Compagnon du tour de France*) Consuelo rises above others in her class and as a result is placed into situations which are out-of-the-ordinary. The fact that Consuelo is presented from the beginning of the work as a unique individual establishes a pattern for breaking the realist code established in the Venetian section of *Consuelo*. This allows for the subsequent introduction of characters who too are extraordinary in different ways, Albert, Haydn, Frederick the Great, Wanda. In *Le Compagnon* Pierre Huguenin seemed out of place; there was too great an expectation of realism built up by the narrator. But the reader expectations in *Consuelo* and *La comtesse de Rudolstadt* are quite different. This also makes the coincidental meetings and chance encounters not as jarring as they would seem in a work with realist pretensions.[11]

Yet if Consuelo is larger than life she is also a woman. She is no abstraction but a living, changing person, more so than Pierre, or certainly Albert.[12] In fact the narrator gives us deeper insight into the thoughts and feelings of Consuelo than is true of any previous character in Sand's fiction. Much of what goes on is seen through her eyes, generally with little or no commentary by the narrator. Occasionally the soul-searching that Consuelo undergoes is presented in a highly stylized and rhetorical language which does not ring true. Her monologue after Anzoleto arrives at Riesenburg is an example of this. But there are passages as well which draw the reader intensely into Consuelo's situation, as is the case, for instance, with her prison diary. That Consuelo is a flesh-and-blood woman is demonstrated in the very sensuous scene in which she kisses Liverani, her unknown rescuer from Spandau prison. Liverani is in reality Albert de Rudolstadt, but Consuelo does not learn this until much later. Her reaction to an event involving Liverani similar to one earlier with Albert reveals how different her relation to Liverani is. In *Consuelo* Albert has carried Consuelo over water at his grotto; her feelings at the time were dictated by her belief that Albert had killed Zdenko: "Il lui tendit la main pour l'aider, et la souleva quelquefois dans ses bras. Mais cette fois Consuelo eut peur, non du torrent qui fuyait silencieux et sombre sous ses pieds, mais de ce guide mystérieux vers lequel une sympathie irrésistible la portait, tandis qu'une répulsion indéfinissable l'en éloignait en même temps" (2: 8). When Liverani carries her across the river in *La comtesse de Rudolstadt* her reaction is quite different: "Consuelo se sentait fascinée et dominée. Elle traversait le vent et l'orage emportée par ce sombre cavalier, qui ressemblait à l'esprit de la nuit" (3: 274). Wearing a black mask and dressed all in black, Liverani clearly fills the role of "esprit de la nuit," awakening the "dark" side of Consuelo, her sensuality. The transformation that has taken place in Consuelo's relationship to Albert/Liverani has occurred through his presumed death and rebirth, as he himself had predicted: "Pour devenir amants, il faut que la mort passe encore une fois entre nous" (2: 528-29). Although Albert has changed

outwardly the transformation in their relationship is above all due to the different role that Consuelo takes on. Her function of "consoler" placed her more in the function of mother to Albert than lover. In the end, Consuelo becomes a real mother. Mothers play throughout the two novels an essential role. Consuelo's mother is as great an influence on her life, even in death, as Albert's mother is on him. Motherhood is even invested with mystical power.[13] When Consuelo is trapped and about to drown, she throws up her hands in prayer to her mother—and finds a staircase which allows her to escape. Wanda's role in Albert's life, appearing mysteriously at key moments in his development, is similar. She, in fact, is officially dead. It is revealing that Wanda reappears as Albert's mother only after Consuelo has given up this role for that of his lover.

The change in Consuelo's feelings does not come easily. She feels trapped in a terrible moral dilemma by her passion for Liverani, since she suspects Albert may still be alive. But the leader of the *Invisibles* explains that her passion is sanctified by a higher moral code than that of society at large: "L'affection soudainée, insurmontable, violente, qu'on appelle l'amour, est une conséquence des bons ou mauvais instincts que Dieu a mis ou laissé pénétrer dans les âmes pour leur perfectionnement ou pour leur punition en cette vie. Les mauvaises lois humaines qui contrarient presque en toutes choses le vœu de la nature et les desseins de la Providence font souvent un crime de ce que Dieu avait inspiré, et maudissent le sentiment qu'il avait béni, tandis qu'elles sanctionnent des unions infâmes, des instincts immondes" (3: 381). Consuelo's passion for Liverani is a prime example of the violent and irrational power of passion, since in her case it involves a man with whom she has never spoken, nor heard speak. The assurance by the *Invisibles* that pursuing one's passion is justified is not enough for Consuelo; she renounces her love in the name of her duty to mankind: "Quel être insensible et lâche me croyez-vous, si vous me jugez encore capable de rêver et de chercher des satisfactions personnelles après ce que j'ai vu, après ce que j'ai compris, après ce que je sais désormais de la vie des hommes, et de mes devoirs en ce monde? Non, non! Plus d'amour, plus d'hyménée, plus de liberté, plus de bonheur, plus de gloire, plus d'art, plus rien pour moi, si je dois faire souffrir le

dernier d'entre mes semblables!" (3: 476). Of course, the conflict is an artificial one, meant to test Consuelo. In the manner of the protagonist of the *Bildungsroman*, Consuelo ends by finding a socially useful role. Like so many German novels of the nineteenth century *Consuelo / La comtesse de Rudolstadt* represents an intertwining of the *Künstlerroman* and the *Entwicklungsroman*.

Consuelo and Albert educate and elevate each other through their love. Albert learns from Consuelo just as she does from him. Consuelo is not only the consolation in Albert's life, she is his salvation. When all others have given him up for insane she instinctively recognizes his true nature: "Non, Albert n'est pas fou; une voix me crie au fond de l'âme que c'est le plus beau type du juste et du saint qui soit sorti des mains de la nature" (1: 255). There is a message inherent in Albert's "insanity," namely that, as Consuelo speculates, "à force de vertu un homme deviendrait fou." Albert's ideals are in such utter contrast with the way of life of his family and of society as a whole that it is inevitable that he be thought mad. This is all the more the case in that Albert has an understanding for the continuity of time and an instinctive ability to place himself anywhere within this continuum. For "rational" society this is insanity; in the context of Sand's novels it is inspired genius.

Albert does undergo a significant change in the novels. This occurs not only through his contact with Consuelo but also through his "death" and rebirth. According to his mother this was a necessary step in Albert's development: "La vie réelle ne pouvait pas encore s'emparer de lui avant qu'il eût subi cette dernière crise dont j'étais sortie miraculeusement, cette mort apparente qui devait être en lui le dernier effort de la notion d'éternité luttant contre la notion du temps" (3: 411). It is an experience, in fact, which Wanda herself has undergone and which has allowed her to become the sibyl of the *Invisibles*. Similarly, Albert at the end of *La comtesse de Rudolstadt* has become a seer: "Il nous parut comme transfiguré. Son regard semblait lire dans un livre invisible, vaste comme le monde, écrit en traits de lumière à la voûte du ciel" (3: 575). In this last section of the novel the third-person omniscient narrator has given way to a first-person narrator who has come to record

Albert's words for posterity. This reinforces the image of Albert as prophet of humanity.

That the novel ends with the perspective of the first-person narrator is a culmination of the general movement of the text, narrowing down a multiplicity of viewpoints. Thus Albert is first introduced to the reader—and to Consuelo—through Amélie who provides a variety of possible ways to view him and his conduct, in this case his inexplicably detailed knowledge of past events:

> Ma tante était bien portée à attribuer cette puissance divinatoire à une faveur spéciale de la Providence. Mais Albert est si sombre, si tourmenté, et si malheureux, qu'on ne conçoit guère pourquoi la Providence lui aurait fait un don si funeste. Si je croyais au diable, je trouverais bien plus acceptable la supposition de notre chapelain, qui lui met toutes les hallucinations d'Albert sur le dos. Mon oncle Christian, qui est un homme plus sensé et plus ferme dans sa religion que nous tous, trouve à beaucoup de ces choses-là des éclaircissements fort vraisemblables. Il pense que malgré tous les soins qu'ont pris les jésuites de brûler, pendant et après la guerre de trente ans, tous les livres hérétiques de la Bohème . . . il doit être resté, dans quelque cachette ignorée de tout le monde, des documents historiques du temps des hussites, et qu'Albert les a retrouvés. (1: 239)

As the novel progresses, the alternate views are gradually eliminated to leave the reader with that of Consuelo. A similar multiplicity of perspectives can be seen in the various accounts of Albert's travels with the Jesuit. The first-person narrator at the end of *La comtesse de Rudolstadt* also highlights a shift toward immediacy. In fact, the third-person narrator begins *Consuelo* being quite chatty, addressing the reader directly on a number of occasions. After the Venetian episodes, however, the narrator becomes considerably less visible. Often he will validate and objectify information first supplied by the characters. Sand allows the characters to develop the ideas in the novel to a far greater extent than in *Le Compagnon*. At the same time Sand is not adverse to having the narrator mislead the reader for dramatic effect. Thus Consuelo's confessor among the *Invisibles* is repeatedly referred to in the masculine until it is dramatically revealed that it is a woman, Albert's mother. The narrator allows Consuelo and the reader to misinterpret the conversation between Albert and Trench near the end of *La comtesse de Rudolstadt*, inviting the reader to believe, along with Consuelo, that Albert had found another woman to love. The narrator manipulates the reader but remains largely in the background. There is a great deal more sophistication in the narration than in *Le Compagnon*. This is true as well in the handling of the multiple story lines used. The movement of the novel is from an astonishing array of intertwining events to a concentration on just Consuelo and Albert. Consuelo and Albert move from society at large to the more select *Invisibles* to their own family. This great historical canvas embracing Frederick the Great and Maria Theresa ends with one family, the stable element in a time of change and revolution, the time Albert foresees in his final vision.

Like the Consuelo novels, *Jeanne* is set in the past; it begins in 1816 and after the prologue jumps to 1820. But just as the Consuelo novels had as their temporal focus a more distant past than the eighteenth century, namely the Reformation, the same is true of *Jeanne*. In this case the time reference is to the pre-historic past. Like Albert, Jeanne appears as a reincarnation of an ancestor, in her case of a druidess. Jeanne is an out-of-the ordinary woman, one who, while remaining in her social class, rises above her peers as well as above those from higher social classes. Like Consuelo she is a consoler and a seer. Her identification with a druid priestess points to the religious significance of the story; here, too, it is a question of the "people's religion." The example of Jeanne's life is also of social significance as a representative of the peasant class. Jeanne's allegiance to the social class to which she belongs is stronger than that of Consuelo. In fact, the division of French society into distinct social and economic classes is emphasized in *Jeanne*, as is the fact that representatives of these classes are far apart in terms of education, language and culture. Indeed, these differences, leading to failed communication and misinterpretations of actions, are the basis of the novel's development.

Jeanne is not as optimistic as the Consuelo novels. In *La comtesse de Rudolstadt* the harmony of the different classes is shown at least in a momentary realization (the *Invisibles*) and as a promise for the future. In *Jeanne* the emphasis is instead on what keeps the various segments of society apart. There is a sense of inescapable destiny hanging over the action of the novel. While not as singularly negative as *Lélia* or *Jacques*, *Jeanne* also ends with the death of the protagonist. Unlike Consuelo, Jeanne never becomes a mother.[14] This is a result of a chain of events which enfolds from the light-hearted adventure of the three men, all members of the upper classes, who encounter Jeanne at the opening of the novel and each place a coin in the sleeping girl's hand. While *Consuelo* and *La comtesse de Rudolstadt* are a succession of events whose unity lies in their connection to the main character, *Jeanne*'s plot, like that of *Le Péché de M. Antoine*, revolves around a central mystery, Jeanne's adamant refusal to consider marriage with any of her suitors. As is revealed toward the end of the novel, this is in direct relation to the action of the three men. Convinced that the coins were put in her hand by fairies, Jeanne sees herself as under their special protection. Following her mother's advice, Jeanne makes vows of chastity, poverty, and humility. These vows are in direct opposition to the wishes the three men had made in placing the coins in her hand. The inverted fulfillment of the wishes is a demonstration of what havoc the upper echelons of society can sow when trying to direct the destinies of those beneath them.

The peasant world in which Jeanne lives is not seen in glowingly positive terms; in fact it is portrayed in a way which recalls that of Balzac in the *Paysans* published in the same year.[15] The setting, the Creuse mountains, is "le site le plus pauvre, le plus triste, le plus désert qui soit en France . . . ce lieu sinistre, sans grandeur, sans beauté, mais rempli d'un sentiment d'abandon et de désolation" (5-6). Jeanne stands out as different from the other peasants above all because she is chaste, modest, and selfless. She has no interest in money, believing, in fact, that gold brings bad luck. Her fellow peasants, in contrast, are "le plus âpre au gain qui soit au monde" (19). They perform services for others only for money. Like Balzac's peasants they also are ready to put on an act in front of a representative of the upper classes, as Léonard does for Guillaume. They are ignorant, superstitious, and suspicious. Some of them, like the Grand'Gothe and Raguet, are downright evil.

Other peasant characters are made to appear silly, as when Claudie is dressed up in fine clothes by the ladies of the castle. Sand also renders some peasant speech phonetically, particularly in the case of Cadet, as in the following example: "Alle a ce qu'il faut, et alle sait les paroles de la *chouse*. Faut la laisser; vous voyez ben que ça li ficherait malheur por el restant de ses jours, de laisser *consommer* les *ous* de sa mère. Alle saillera d'élà aussi nette qu'alle y entre, foi d'houme! Vous allez voére!" (98). This makes Cadet appear ludicrous, particularly when his speech is placed side by side with standard French.[16] There is even typical country bumpkin humor, as in Cadet's view of the town of Boussac: "Et moi, j'y demeurerais ben *arrié* (aussi)! dit le gros Cadet; c'est rudement joli la ville de Boussac! C'est la pu brave ville que j'asse pas connaissue" (131). Claudie's rejoinder is "Je crois bien, imbécile. . . . Tu n'en as jamais vu d'autre!" (131). After hearing the Englishman Arthur speak French with a British accent, Cadet assures Claudie that he is speaking English. This is far removed from the reverential tone in which peasants are depicted in Sand's rustic novels.

The upper-class characters, with the exception of Arthur, tend to view the peasants as one homogeneous, indistinguishable group. This is evident, for instance, in the reaction of two Frenchmen upon seeing Jeanne asleep. Guillaume de Boussac tells Léon Marsillat to put on gloves before touching her since peasant children tend to be very dirty. Léon refers to peasant girls as "Lisette" and views Jeanne as "une créature ruminante" (12). The narrator's view of the peasant is similar:

> Quelles pouvaient être les pensées d'un enfant de la nature, qui n'avait pas appris à lire, et dont l'intelligence (si tant est qu'elle en eût) n'avait reçu aucune espèce de culture? Guillaume se le demandait précisément. . . . Et nous nous sommes fait souvent la même question nous-mêmes. . . . A quoi pense le laboureur qui

creuse patiemment son sillon monotone? A quoi pense le bœuf
qui rumine couché dans l'herbe, et la cavale étonnée qui vous
examine par-dessus le buisson? Est-ce donc la même vie qui
circule lentement dans les veines de l'homme et dans celles de
l'animal attaché au travail de la terre? (67)

This is a view of peasants very different from that in the rustic
novels. The purpose of the unflattering portrait is to serve as a foil
for Jeanne, who rises above her class. Of course, the other social
classes do not fare better in the novel. The aristocracy's representative, Guillaume, and that of the upper middle class, Marsillat, are
far from representing ideal modes of conduct.

The narrator's willingness to voice his views on peasants is
in keeping with the narrative stance throughout the novel. The narrator of *Jeanne* tends to be talkative and intrusive and easily side-
tracked into areas which sometimes bear a tenuous connection to
the main story line. Thus there is, for instance, a discussion of the
relative merits of a number of different central French cities. In general, however, the commentaries are better integrated into the story
than is the case in *Le Compagnon du tour de France* which has a similar narrator. This is the case, for instance, with the narrator's explanation of the "viviers," the paths which hold dangers similar to
quicksand. The discussion occurs quite naturally in the context of
Guillaume's trying to find his way. One senses throughout Sand's
strong interest in the people and places which form the backbone of
the novel. In this first novel to deal with country life in a major, sus-
tained way, Sand felt compelled to include as much as possible of
the regional lore in which she was so intensely interested. There is a
long discussion of local history as well as the introduction of folk-
lore figures such as the "lavandière." The narrator at times is very
close to the voice of the author herself, whose enthusiasm for the
wealth of material to tap is obvious. The narrator notes in reference
to the tapestries of the Boussac château: "Je les crois d'Aubusson,
et j'ai toute une histoire là-dessus qui trouvera sa place ailleurs"
(137). The reference is to the *Dame à la Licorne* tapestries Sand was
instrumental in helping to save.[17] At another point the narrator
tells an anecdote that "j'ai appris l'an dernier d'un vieux mendiant"

(282). It is plain to see that Sand was tapping a vein in *Jeanne* which offered an abundance of possibilities for later extraction. At other times the narrator, as Michèle Hirsch has pointed out, shares the perspective of the upper class male characters.[18]

As was the case in *Le Compagnon du tour de France*, the narrator is not only very visible but also conspicuously above all the characters, as well as the reader. This is, of course, in keeping with the fact that the central plot involves a mystery which it is in the narrator's hands to reveal. Thus the narrator is privy to what fate has in store. This is brought out explicitly in pithy statements which appear occasionally at the end of chapter divisions. At the end of the prologue, for instance, the narrator comments that the three men gave the coins to Jeanne "ne se doutant guère que leurs aumônes allaient devenir dans sa petite main l'instrument de leurs destinées" (16). Sand's indebtedness to the *roman-feuilleton* is in evidence here. *Jeanne* was published in that form, a fact which Sand says affected the composition of the work.[19]

One of the means Sand used in stimulating interest in the story was to present the protagonist in an exotic light. The narrator gives the reader many indications of how Jeanne should be viewed, identifying her in the text variously as "la druidesse endormie," "la bergère d'Ep-Nell" or "la vierge d'Ep-Nell." At another point the narrator refers to her as "la beauté pour laquelle soupiraient un homme de mérite, un intéressant jeune homme et un brillant avocat" (260). The purpose of such a statement is to elevate Jeanne in the eyes of the intended (middle-class) reader, to demonstrate that she was desirable not only to her fellow peasants but to those socially superior to her. The narrator's desire to demonstrate that this uneducated peasant girl is worthy of the bourgeois reader's interest and sympathy leads him on occasion to justify aspects of Jeanne's character. After citing one speech by Jeanne, the narrator comments: "Son parler naïf, la vulgarité des images qu'elle retraçait n'avaient pas désenchanté le jeune baron de l'admiration qu'il avait conçue pour elle" (111). The underlying assumption here is that the reader would be disenchanted by Jeanne's "vulgarity." The narrator then goes on to justify his view of Jeanne's speech: "L'accent de Jeanne partait d'un cœur ardent et vrai, sa voix était douce comme celle du ruisseau qui murmurait sous la bruyère à deux pas d'elle; son accent rustique n'avait rien de grossier ni de trivial. On sentait la distinction naturelle de son être sous ces formes primitives" (111). Later on there is even a footnote (257) apologizing for Jeanne's incorrect French. This is a far cry from Sand's later attitude toward peasant speech in her novels.

Although Jeanne is presented as a simple peasant her actions demonstrate that she belongs to a higher sphere of existence. Like Consuelo, Jeanne stands out in her selflessness. Unlike Claudie, Jeanne feels no envy toward the rich. She is convinced that money brings evil; this is one of the principal reasons she gives for not wanting to marry the rich Arthur.[20] She is never concerned with her own welfare but with that of those around her. She is single-minded in her devotion to her mother, even after the latter's death. As with Consuelo that is her one strong family tie. She also parallels Consuelo in nursing back to health a male admirer, in her case Guillaume de Boussac. She is willing to give all to save Guillaume in his illness: "J'avais donné mon âme et mon corps à Dieu pour qu'il envoie la mort sur moi au lieu de l'envoyer sur vous" (185). Given Jeanne's capacity for selfless devotion Guillaume's sister Marie sees Jeanne as "une chrétienne des premiers temps. C'est une fille qui souffrirait le martyr en souriant, et que l'église canoniserait si elle savait ce que Dieu a mis de grâce dans son cœur" (177). In fact, after Jeanne injures herself in jumping from Marsillat's tower toward the end of the novel she does indeed suffer in silence.

The suggestion that Jeanne is something more than a simple shepherdess is made early in the novel. After depicting the site where according to the narrator human sacrifices were carried out, the narrator introduces the sleeping Jeanne on the very same rocks. This contrast emphasizes her innocence and purity. After Marsillat jokes about finding "la druidesse Velléda," he discovers Jeanne who seems to be in a kind of enchanted sleep. Her appearance is striking and exceptional: "C'était bien le plus frais visage humain qui eût jamais bravé sans voile et sans ombrelle les ardeurs du soleil de midi" (12-13). Her pure white skin, unusual in a peasant, is, the narrator explains, due to the fact that she has the undiluted blood of "une race gauloise primitive" (13). This aspect of her character connecting her to a primitive race is dramatically brought out in the scene in which she saves the body of her mother from the burning house: "Jeanne lui [Guillaume] parut belle et terrible comme une druidesse dans cet acte de piété farouche et sublime. Elle avait perdu sa coiffe de toile, et sa longue chevelure blonde tombait autour d'elle; ses yeux rougis par la fumée avaient l'égarement de l'ivresse, sa voix était forte, et sa parole, ordinairement lente et douce, était brève et accentuée" (99). Afterwards Jeanne places the corpse on the dolmen of Ep-Nell, just as a druidess might have done preparing for a human sacrifice. That the house collapses just after Jeanne emerges with her mother's body is a sign of providential favor. It comes as no surprise that Jeanne later in the novel is repeatedly compared to Joan of Arc. Marie evokes the possibility that Jeanne has Joan of Arc's soul through the process of metempsychosis which plays such a major role in the Consuelo novels. Just before she dies Jeanne orders that all the villagers be assembled, explaining, "ça m'est commandé d'en haut" (351). In dying Jeanne sees "la grand fade" (356) in a scene reminiscent of the ending of Flaubert's *Un cœur simple*.

There is an aura surrounding Jeanne that makes even ordinary, everyday actions she performs seem extraordinary. Doing housework, she gives the impression of being someone much more than a maid: "Il y avait dans sa physionomie une sorte de majesté angélique qui faisait disparaître la vulgarité de ses attributions. A la voir nouer lentement les cordons de ses oreillers, d'un air sérieux et pensif, on eût dit d'une grande-prêtresse occupée à quelque mystérieuse fonction dans les sacrifices" (199). Jeanne is clearly meant to be seen as someone with a special spiritual mission. Although she believes herself to be an orthodox Christian, her religious visions are a mixture of pagan beliefs and Christian dogma. Jeanne, for instance, calls the Virgin Mary "la reine de toutes les fades" (259). This is, in itself, not unusual with the peasants of the Creuse mountains, according to the local priest: "Ils croient tout, la vérité comme le mensonge, l'idolâtrie comme la religion, et le druidisme comme le polythéisme. Les bons et les mauvais esprits mêlent leurs attributions autour de leur existence. Les fades jouent ici un grand rôle" (83). On the one hand the peasants' beliefs are equated with superstition and seen as an unfortunate result of their lack of education. On the other hand, Arthur, who often functions in the novel as an authorial mouthpiece, has a more positive assessment of the peasants' spiritual life: "[Les paysans] ont l'esprit plus tourné à la poésie que nous, et, en cela, je ne sais trop si nous devons les plaindre ou les envier, les désabuser ou les admirer" (223). In the debate over how to educate peasants he advocates a more cautious approach than the radical elimination of peasant superstition advocated by Marsillat: "Leur laisser la poésie, et les aider à découvrir le symbole" (224). The deeper significance of Jeanne's views on gold is an illustration of what Arthur means. She is convinced that possessing gold brings bad luck and unhappiness. As she explains toward the end of the novel, Jeanne upon awakening and finding the coins in her hand had kept the smaller ones but had buried the gold coin. This belief is in keeping with Jeanne's vow of poverty as well as with her acceptance of the peasant way of life. It is also a reflection of the author's belief that riches are, in many ways, a misfortune. This becomes a central theme in Le Meunier d'Angibault. For Jeanne there is also a more down-to-earth proof that coveting gold brings unhappiness: "Toutes les fois qu'un bourgeois en a montré à une fille, elle a quasiment perdu l'esprit, et elle s'est rendue à lui, quand même il était vieux, méchant et vilain" (229). The reality of this danger is illustrated concretely through the figure of Léon Marsillat.[21]

When Jeanne learns the truth about the source of the three coins, this does not at all cause her to change her beliefs or to renounce her vows. She asserts that the fairies could have been in effect using the three men as the agents of their will. This is in accord with the belief highlighted in La comtesse de Rudolstadt that with the disappearance of transcendental intervention man has himself become a kind of angel, fulfilling a divine mission on earth. Jeanne simply fills this role in a more concentrated fashion than the vast majority of people. As Sand had shown in Consuelo this is what she sees as being the true and original role of priests, which has been lost in the Catholic Church. By making Jeanne a direct descendant of the druidess Tulla (79) Sand indicates that Jeanne possesses that primitive spiritual power.[22] In fact, Sand makes a point of stressing in a footnote her belief that druidism was a precursor of Christianity since it shared with the later faith a belief in a trinity and in a life after death. Jeanne's mythic and mystical view of time emphasizes the possibility of her being a reincarnation of a druidess/primitive Christian: "Jeanne ne connaissait ni les mots ni les époques auxquelles se rapportaient ces croyances vagues et profondes. Elle savait seulement, par sa mère, qu'il y avait eu autrefois des femmes saintes qui, vivant dans le célibat, avaient protégé le pays et initié le peuple aux choses divines. Ces prêtresses se confondaient dans son interprétation avec les fades" (281). At the same time Jeanne's belief can be taken back to a specific cult, that of Ep-Nell. As the local priest explains to Guillaume, this is the uncorrupted form of the place in which Jeanne's house is located, Epinelle, significantly, the only house located there. The Ep-Nell, meaning "no leader," was used, according to the priest, to designate a breakaway group which asserted its independence from the druids; thus it represented "le culte libre" versus "l'église officielle" (78). This is again a reflection of Sand's own religious beliefs—her distrust of Church authority—as well as of her democratic convictions. Jeanne in fact asserts to the priest her spiritual independence, declaring that no priest, nor even the Pope himself, could dictate to her any actions in contradiction to the dictates of her own conscience.

The tenets of Ep-Nell are evident in the vision Jeanne has just before she dies:

> Ecoutez, vous irez à Toull-Sainte-Croix, vous assemblerez tous les gens de l'endroit, et vous leur direz de ma part ce que je vas vous dire; il y a un trésor dans la terre. Il n'est à personne; il est à tout le monde. Tant qu'un chacun le cherchera pour le prendre et pour le garder à lui tout seul, aucun ne le trouvera. Ceux qui voudront le partager entre tout le monde, ceux-là le trouveront; et ceux qui feront cela seront plus riches que tout le monde, quand même ils n'auraient que cinq sous. (355)

The message combines Jeanne's distrust of riches with a vision of cooperation and selflessness which were for Sand the prerequisites for the transformation of society into a "new age." Jeanne's words are meant to be taken prophetically; their importance and validity derive from the fact that they are spoken on her deathbed. Yet the fact that Jeanne dies as the last of her line can hardly be taken as hopeful. That the upper-classes—through the actions of Léon Marsillat—are responsible for her death is a demonstration of their tendency not only to corrupt but to destroy the working classes and what they represent.

Although, as we have seen, peasants are not shown in an exclusively positive light in the novel, they are still seen, as a whole, as superior to the other classes enmeshed in egotism and cynicism. Their way of life has deep roots, something clearly lacking in that of Léon Marsillat. The traditional way of life is presented in Jeanne's case as a source of strength. Her identification with country life is so strong that she suffers when taken out of that environment: "Plante sauvage, attachée au sol inculte qui l'avait produite, elle n'avait fait que végéter depuis qu'elle s'était laissé transplanter dans une région cultivée. . . . Elle ne se disait pas qu'elle avait failli y [in the city] perdre sa poésie; mais elle se sentait vaguement redevenir poète, à mesure qu'elle s'enfonçait dans le désert" (284). Jeanne is a poet in the same sense as Albert at the end of *La comtesse de Rudolstadt*. She transcends conventional society, being able to perceive what lies hidden for the ordinary mortal. Her perception of reality is of a different nature from that of those around her: "Jeanne était restée à peu de chose près, ce qu'elle était à Ep-Nell, rêvant, priant, et aimant sans cesse, ne pensant presque jamais; une véritable organisation rustique, c'est-à-dire une âme poétique sans manifestation, un de ces types purs comme il s'en trouve encore aux champs, types admirables et mystérieux, qui semblent faits pour un âge d'or qui n'existe pas, et où la perfectibilité serait inutile, puisqu'on aurait la perfection. . . . Ils sont tout prêts pour la société idéale que le genre humain rêve, cherche et annonce, mais leur inquiétude ne le devance pas" (190). Having vowed never to marry, Jeanne removes herself from normal and full participation as a woman in the life of her community. But it is not just this and her lack of selflessness that set her apart: she is a "new woman" analogous to the new man that Albert's son represents. She lacks the vices—greed and egotism—typical of her age. Both are meant to live in a different, improved world.

While Jeanne is portrayed as a poet, priestess, and prophet, the role assigned to the principal male character, Guillaume is much less positive. If Jeanne's source of strength is her undiluted peasant stock, Guillaume's weak character is as well a product of his family background, the aristocracy. He and Jeanne, despite being wet-nursed by the same woman, are worlds apart in almost every conceivable way. This is emphasized in the description of Guillaume's trip into the Creuse mountains. He has resolved, the narrator writes, to endure stoically this "excursion poétique dans un pays inculte, dépeuplé et presque sauvage" (17). The peasant world with which Jeanne identifies so closely is for him a totally foreign culture. He, in fact, has considerable difficulty simply communicating with peasants. His conversations with Jeanne are full of misunderstandings because they don't understand in the same sense the expressions used. Whereas Jeanne's beliefs are firmly entrenched and derive from her own character, Guillaume's views are shaped by outside forces. He is described as "né avec un caractère assez faible, mais converti à l'envie d'être grand par le christianisme romantique de l'époque" (66). Jeanne is extraordinary without trying and without being conscious of the fact herself. Guillaume, on the other hand, with no justification, sees himself as fulfilling an out-of-the-ordinary destiny: "Il avait lu trop de beaux livres pour ne pas se faire de sa destinée une sorte d'idéal romantique propre à le maintenir dans le respect, même peut-être un peu exagéré, de soi-même" (18). He sees as a part of this destiny that he should be in the Creuse when Tulla his former nurse dies. But he only becomes conscious of his duty toward her upon reflecting on passages from Chateaubriand.

Guillaume has been adversely affected by reading novels. This aspect of *Jeanne* is a continuation of the theme introduced in *Horace* and *Le Compagnon du tour de France*. The narrator states early on that René and Werther had exercised a considerable influence on the young men of that generation. As youngsters Guillaume and Marie have devoured "les romans les plus vertueux et les plus incendiaires" (187). His view of peasants is conditioned by what he has read: "Il aimait la campagne et les paysans de loin, dans ses souvenirs. Il les rêvait alors, graves, simples, austères comme les Natchez de Chateaubriand. De près, il les trouvait rudes, mal-propres et cyniques" (26). When, however, he discovers that Jeanne, his "sœur de lait," has just been orphaned the situation is enough to place her as a peasant in a different light: "Déjà il rêvait tout un poème champêtre dans le goût de Goldsmith, et il n'était pas fâché d'en être le héros vertueux et désintéressé" (58). The narrator demonstrates the absurdity of Guillaume's attitude as well as of the down-to-earth nature of Jeanne in depicting her reaction: "Mais il manquait encore à ce poème une héroïne qui comprît son rôle et celui de son protecteur. Jeanne se croyait si peu menacée par les séductions du jeune avocat, qu'elle ne songeait à voir dans le jeune seigneur qu'un personnage respectable, étranger à sa desti-née. D'ailleurs, aucun de ces beaux messieurs n'occupait en ce moment les pensées de Jeanne" (58). Jeanne, unfortunately for Guillaume, has not read the same novels; she is utterly unaware of the role she is expected to play. Ironically, Guillaume, immersed in his fantasy world, is unable to conceive of the real extent of the innocence and virtue of the heroine he has imagined. When Jeanne leaves a flower in a cave to placate the fairies, Guillaume interprets this action in a different way: "En sortant de la grotte, Guillaume, ramené à de mauvaises pensées, se dit que cette fleur de serpolet était peut-être un signal, une promesse, un rendez-vous que Jeanne laissait là pour l'objet de son mystérieux amour" (74). The thought that Jeanne might love Marsillat gives a wholly different turn to Guillaume's thoughts, causing him to abandon his romance: "Son roman s'en alla en fumée, à son grand regret" (72). Guillaume views Jeanne from the perspective of his own class's conduct. In fact what he wants is for Jeanne to adopt the appearance and behavior of an aristocrat. This is evident in his joyful reaction when he sees Jeanne dressed up in Marie's clothes, mistakenly believing that his mother has "elevated" Jeanne to be his social equal.

Guillaume's sister has similar views concerning Jeanne. She is eager to help Sir Arthur in his quest for Jeanne's hand in mar-riage because it is for her such a wildly and marvelously romantic idea, a rich English lord marrying a poor, ignorant peasant girl.

Marie's extravagant romanticism is a product not only of reading novels, but also of her religious upbringing: "Cette jeune fille enthousiaste n'avait jamais vu le monde, elle ne le connaissait pas, elle le haïssait par un effort de divination. Livrée dans sa première jeunesse à une ardente dévotion, elle avait pris l'Evangile au sérieux. Elle était fanatique de droiture et de dévouement. Dans un corps très frêle, elle portait une âme de feu, et, sous des manières pleines de grâce et de douce sensibilité, elle cachait un caractère énergique, entreprenant, et amoureux des partis extrêmes" (187). Like her brother, Marie's character traits are by-products of a life of leisure. Her beliefs have much less basis in reality than those of the peasants in the novel. She even dreams of being herself a shepherdess like Jeanne, as she explains to her brother: "Croirais-tu que, malgré moi, je me surprenais à méditer le projet de quitter le monde, de dépouiller ce rang qui me pèse, de m'enfuir au désert, de chausser des sabots, et d'aller garder les chèvres avec Jeanne sur les bruyères d'Ep-Nell?" (340). She sees only the idyllic side of Jeanne's life as a peasant, ignoring the deprivations and missed opportunities.

On the other extreme is her mother's attitude toward Jeanne. She sees her as a good servant but one who should stay in her social station. When she tells her friend, Madame de Charmois, of how Guillaume found Jeanne, the latter exclaims, "Mais c'est tout un roman, cela" to which Madame de Boussac responds, "C'est un roman bien simple et qui se termine là. L'héroïne soigne mes poules et ma laiterie" (145). Madame de Charmois's suggestion that Guillaume should make Jeanne his mistress so he would not want to marry her is a demonstration of how cynically the upper classes deal with peasants. In contrast to the mythic presentation of Jeanne, both Madame de Boussac and Madame de Charmois are seen in the context of contemporary reality. Madame de Charmois's life is shaped by the fact that her husband has been appointed subprefect in Boussac while waiting for a prefecture in a larger city. Madame de Boussac is seen as a product of her age: "L'empire l'avait beaucoup moins corrompue que madame de Charmois; mais il en avait fait comme de toutes les femmes qui y ont joué un bout de rôle, un enfant gâté, une personne frivole, soumise à des besoins de luxe et de vanité, que le régime collet-monté de la restauration ne pouvait

pas corriger radicalement" (148). The only asset she has in the Restoration is her aristocratic name. The historical determination of the two noblewomen's characters serves to highlight the timelessness of Jeanne's virtue and beliefs, unaffected by historical forces.

Léon Marsillat has the least flattering role in the novel. For him Jeanne represents not a person, but a sexual object, to be seduced and abandoned. Marsillat as a bourgeois aspiring to an aristocratic life style—he is proud of the castle he has purchased—is seen in a more negative light than the genuinely aristocratic Guillaume de Boussac. He does at least have the virtue of having a firm, unvacillating character. But he lacks self-control and a basic moral code. The one male character who both sees the unique character and virtue of Jeanne and has the courage to ignore social strictures in order to propose marriage is the (inevitably) eccentric Englishman Sir Arthur. The fact that it should be an Englishman who plays this role is a demonstration of the decadence of polite French society. As in *Indiana* an Englishman is used to demonstrate the failings of French society. In fact, he is very similar to Ralph: "Un esprit sérieux, une âme passionnée, un caractère généreux, inébranlable dans sa fermeté" (175). He exhibits the failings of neither the French upper nor middle classes. He is not only free of prejudices, he, like Jeanne, has a natural tendency to do good. His enthusiasm for the virtuous Jeanne is a product of this firm moral character, not a result of a fevered imagination. In this sense his relation to Jeanne is quite different from that of his friends, Guillaume and Marie: "Il atteignait et embrassait sans cesse l'idéal sans effort, il n'avait pas besoin de s'échauffer la tête pour professer et observer ses croyances religieuses et philosophiques" (201). Jeanne's affinity for him is demonstrated in the feelings she admits she has had for him despite her distrust of the English.

In her final vision Jeanne orders Arthur to marry Marie. Their union is one hopeful sign for the future in an otherwise bleak ending. Guillaume, in fact, changes through his contact with Jeanne and the example his sister's marriage provides: "Il ne fit point d'actions éclatantes; il resta rêveur et amant de la solitude; mais il porta dans toutes ses relations avec les hommes que le préjugé lui rendait inférieurs une charité et une bienveillance à toute épreuve. Il ne fit

en cela qu'imiter sa sœur et son beau-frère, dont les idées et les actions généreuses semblèrent d'un siècle en avant du temps misérable et condamné où nous vivons" (358). It is above all, of course, in the figure of Jeanne that the social message of the novel resides. As was the case with the Consuelo novels, the point is made in a rather oblique fashion. Rather than expose the ills of her contemporary society, Sand was, in creating Consuelo and Jeanne, setting up signposts toward the new society she envisioned. The mystical treatment of time in the novels—somewhat paradoxical in works inspired at least in part by the example of Walter Scott—suggests the applicability of the virtues and ideas embodied in the two women not only to their own time but to all ages.

6

In This Day and Age

Love and Money in *Le Meunier d'Angibault* and *Le Péché de M. Antoine*

*Au jour d'aujourd'hui, mon vieux, monnaie fait tout, comme
dit l'autre, et puisque j'en ai, et que tu n'en as pas, nous ne
pouvons pas faire affaire ensemble.*
—*Le Meunier d'Angibault* (217)

Consuelo and *Jeanne* are explorations of the past. Each novel
is set in the recent past while referring back to a more distant age.
In the two major novels written in 1845, *Le Meunier d'Angibault* and
Le Péché de M. Antoine, George Sand turns her attention resolutely to
the present. Each is set in contemporary Berry and deals explicitly
with social issues of the day. The focus is on the role of money in
French society of the 1840s with an added emphasis in *Le Meunier
d'Angibault* on agriculture and in *Le Péché de M. Antoine* on manufacturing. The more solid grounding of these novels in contemporary reality compared to the fanciful visions of *Consuelo* or *Jeanne*
did not find favor with the critics or with the reading public. While
Sand's social and political beliefs had not changed, she altered her
strategy for imparting these values to the reader. In the novels
of 1845 she uses a more direct and tightly focused approach to

integrating her social beliefs into her fiction. In contrast to *Le Compagnon du tour de France*, the social message materializes in the conduct of the characters, and not in the commentary by the narrator. Sand had assured the publisher for *Le Meunier d'Angibault* that the work would be a *roman de mœurs* and that she would try "de ne pas fatiguer le lecteur par de longues dissertations, sur des matières abstraites" (*Correspondance* 6: 657). The novel nevertheless was rejected for publication: the ideology expressed was too clearly contrary to that prevailing in France at the time.[1] Sand had similar difficulties with *Le Péché de M. Antoine*.

Jeanne and Consuelo are exceptional women, endowed with qualities which elevate them above the normal position of women in society. Jeanne possesses purity and prophetic gifts while Consuelo surpasses others by her almost superhuman singing and her devotion to others. The heroines of *Le Meunier d'Angibault* and *Le Péché de M. Antoine* are more realistic. Marcelle de Blanchemont and Gilberte de Châteaubrun represent ideal women, yet they are solidly of this world. They face hard choices involving money and family, and despite their aristocratic family lineage, they share with the author a professed lack of interest in their social status. Indeed, they ignore social convention and end up marrying lovers from a lower social class. In their own way, they too escape from the conventional places society has assigned them, although not so radically as Jeanne or Consuelo.

Compared to the two visionary women of the previous novels, Marcelle and Gilberte are much more oriented toward domestic affairs and traditional male-female relationships. Both novels are fundamentally love stories. In these novels Sand clearly intended to present her characters in a context with which the contemporary reader could more readily identify. In this sense, at least, the novels are "realistic" in line with Susan Suleiman's definition of the *roman à thèse*.[2] The reader is to recognize the applicability of the lessons presented to his own life. The characters' attitudes show that they do not blindly accept the strictures of the society in which they live. The opening of *Le Meunier d'Angibault* offers a clear if largely implied contrast between the characters' views and those of the typical Frenchman of the period. The description of the relationship

between Marcelle and Henri Lémor conveys this contrast. The behavior of these two lovers is motivated "par un sentiment de pudeur," Henri being "craintif et respectueux" toward Marcelle. We learn that Marcelle's room "avait servi de retraite voluptueuse à quelque marquise du temps passé," but the next sentence emphasizes the contrast with Marcelle: "Leur descendante, la blonde Marcelle, était aussi chastement et aussi simplement mise que doit l'être une veuve pudique" (26). Her superiority to others in her class appears in the narrator's comparison between her and a *grisette*: "On eût pu d'ailleurs la prendre pour la compagne naturelle de l'homme qui était à genoux auprès d'elle, pour une grisette de Paris; car il est des grisettes qui ont au front une dignité de reine et une candeur de sainte" (26). Marcelle's elevation above the aristocracy is shown through this association with the working class. Marcelle herself sees no reason to be scornful of "filles entretenues": "Si l'on voulait bien comparer nos mariages indissolubles avec leurs unions passagères, verrait-on beaucoup plus de désintéressement chez les jeunes filles de notre classe?" (40). This idea had been put forth by Lélia, but here its intended shock value is heightened by being expressed by a virtuous aristocrat.

The novel clearly shows that male-female relationships in polite society are characterized by lust and cynicism. The purity of the love between Marcelle and Henri is offered as a model of opposing behavior. They are so chaste that they are afraid to get too close to one another. The narrator insists that it is not passion but religion which motivates Marcelle's love: "Sincèrement dévote dans son adolescence, elle était nécessairement devenue passionnée pour un amant qui respectait ses scrupules et adorait sa chasteté. La piété même l'avait poussée à s'exalter dans cet amour et à vouloir le consacrer par des liens indissolubles aussitôt qu'elle s'était vue libre" (35). Her love is granted spiritual sanctity. The description of their first meeting after Marcelle has been widowed resembles a religious service: "La jeune baronne de Blanchemont, tirant de sa poche une jolie et menue boîte de cuir de Russie, fit jaillir une étincelle, alluma une bougie placée et comme cachée d'avance dans un coin, et le jeune homme, craintif et respectueux, l'aida naïvement à éclairer l'intérieur du pavillon" (26). This echo of Sand's treatment

of love as a religion, so evident in her earlier works, is not fully developed in the rest of the novel. Although in its basic plot line a love story, the novel does not elevate love to the high status it enjoyed in previous works. It is not seen in isolation, as was the case in *Indiana* or *Valentine*, but in conjunction with theories on improving society.

Marcelle's morality differs from what one might expect from a woman in her position; she has never contemplated any relationship apart from that with her husband: "Écoutez, Henri, me voilà libre, je n'ai rien à me reprocher. J'ai si peu souhaité la mort de mon mari, que jamais je ne m'étais permis de penser à ce que je ferais de ma liberté si elle venait à m'être rendue. Vous le savez, nous n'avions jamais parlé de cela, vous n'ignoriez pas que je vous aimais avec passion, et pourtant voici la première fois que je vous le dis aussi hardiment!" (28). In contrast, her husband has been killed in a duel over another woman. The passage not only indicates the heavy-handedness and sanctimoniousness Sand uses to make her points, but also shows the artificiality of the dialogue between Marcelle and Henri. Their conversation and the direction their relationship takes do not ring true; they resemble marionettes being manipulated by the author. At the end of the first chapter, when Marcelle makes her decision to rid herself of her wealth in order to be able to marry Henri, the narrator comments that it was a resolution "qu'elle seule peut-être pouvait envisager sans sourire d'admiration ou de pitié" (37). This is an attempt to forestall possible reader skepticism and cynicism. On other occasions the narrator feels obliged to excuse or apologize for the behavior of the characters; he even feels obliged to justify the fact that he gives an account of the physical appearance of Marcelle.

The conflict which prevents Marcelle and Henri from marrying is of their own making. As with Chateaubriand's René, Henri's quandary is largely self-induced: he loves Marcelle too much to accept her love. The conflict is too clearly set up with the intent of converting Marcelle: "Eclairée tout à coup par l'effroi, la douleur et la résistance de Lémor, Marcelle repassait dans son esprit consterné tout ce qu'elle avait entrevu de la crise sociale où s'agite le siècle. . . . Elle savait donc bien, comme nous tous, que ce présent engourdi et malade est aux prises avec le passé qui le retient et l'avenir qui l'appelle" (36). As Marcelle's love becomes part of the larger social struggle, she and her lover become class enemies. One of her first acts in her new way of life designed to reconcile her and Henri is to part company with her "vie cachée," the private, comfortable sphere of life she has established: "Retraite de mon choix, ornements selon mon goût, je vous ai aimés, pensa-t-elle; mais je ne puis plus vous aimer, car vous êtes les consécrateurs de la richesse et de l'oisiveté" (41). The kind of retreat which offered Valentine the possibility of escaping the cruelty and lack of understanding of the outside world is no longer a viable solution. It no longer suffices to withdraw from society; one must actively strive to become part of the march toward a new age. This is a major element in the message of *Le Meunier d'Angibault* and *Le Péché de M. Antoine*.

Part of Marcelle's plan for changing her life involves leaving Paris for life in the country. Only the opening chapter—or "Journée" as the text divisions are labelled with no apparent logic—takes place in Paris; the rest of the novel shifts the setting to the country. There is a clear sense that by leaving Paris Marcelle is escaping corruption and contamination. She announces her intentions to her in-laws as if she were embarking on a voyage into the wilderness: "Je suis résolue à m'établir en province, au fond d'une campagne, où j'habituerai les premières années de mon fils à une vie laborieuse et simple" (117). Nevertheless, she—and the reader—soon find that the pernicious forces at work in French society have affected life in the country as well. The Bricolin family, who lease and operate a farm on Marcelle's estate, demonstrate the catastrophic result of the all-consuming concern with money, presented in the novel as the major force in French society. The lives of the Bricolin family revolve exclusively around money; it is all Bricolin talks about. When Marcelle unexpectedly arrives at their farm, they immediately think of her visit in financial terms: "Venait-on réclamer ou demander?" (88). The Bricolins judge and evaluate everything in this manner. They have no spiritual or intellectual interests. Bricolin is not even interested in technical advances in agriculture. He has no use for religion, but, if one were necessary, he has a clear notion of what he would want it to be: "J'en voudrais bien une comme ça qui empêcherait mes métayers de me voler mon blé la nuit, et mes journaliers de mettre trois heures par jour à manger leur soupe" (127). This creed of egotism and greed contrasts sharply with Marcelle's piety and generosity. Bricolin's constant repetition of "au jour d'aujourd'hui," Sand's original title for the work, indicates the extent to which he lives for the present, day by day, in contrast to Henri and Marcelle's concern for the future of mankind. Bricolin's immersion in the present constitutes a general trait of those who rise out of the peasant class financially and socially: "Tandis que le paysan est toujours maigre, bien proportionné et d'un teint basané qui a sa beauté, le bourgeois de campagne est toujours, dès l'âge de quarante ans, affligé d'un gros ventre, d'une démarche pesante et d'un coloris vineux qui vulgarisent et enlaidissent les plus belles organisations. . . . Toute idée de dévouement à l'humanité, toute notion religieuse, sont presque incompatibles avec cette transformation que le bien-être opère dans leur être physique et moral" (94-95). Money comes to control their whole being. Bricolin hopes to buy the Blanchemont estate from Marcelle so that he can become the "seigneur" of Blanchemont through "la noblesse des bons écus" (273). He represents a parodying double of the true aristocrat and a savage indictment of the urge to merge with higher social classes.

The way of life of such "bourgeois de campagne" demonstrates that wealth is perceived as an end in itself not as a means of improving their daily lives. In fact, Bricolin is so miserly in respect to household expenses, that the family lives no better than ordinary peasants. Paradoxically, the mania for riches destroys the well-being of Bricolin and those like him:

> Leurs facultés pour l'acquisition et la conservation de la richesse, très développées d'abord, s'éteignent vers le milieu de leur carrière, et, après avoir fait fortune avec une rapidité et une habileté remarquables, ils tombent de bonne heure dans l'apathie, le désordre et l'incapacité. Aucune idée sociale, aucun sentiment de progrès ne les soutient. La digestion devient l'affaire de leur vie, et leur richesse si vigoureusement acquise est, avant qu'ils l'aient consolidée, engagée dans mille embarras et compromise par

mille maladresses. . . . Sans parler de la vanité qui les précipite
dans des spéculations au-dessus de leur crédit; si bien que tous
ces riches sont presque toujours ruinés au moment où ils font le
plus d'envieux. (95)

The sense of inevitable doom evoked here and elsewhere in the
novel anticipates Zola. The downward path of the Bricolin family is
all the more striking since the novel highlights characters who are
moving up morally. In contrast to the portrait of peasants in *La
Terre* is the assertion that greed has all but eliminated passion. For
Zola the two were hardly mutually exclusive. On the other hand,
Sand expressly shows how single-minded the love of money can
become.

Bricolin lies clearly beyond redemption. The tragedy is that
he is leading his entire family down the same road to moral ruin.
He refuses to consider allowing Rose to marry the miller Grand-
Louis because he is not rich enough. His refusal comes despite the
tragic outcome of a similar denial of his elder daughter's request to
marry. "La Bricoline" has gone insane as a result and turned into a
kind of wild animal: she tears apart farm animals with her bare
hands and eats them raw. The message is clear: life without love en-
dangers our basic humanity, reducing us to the level of savages. At
the same time, one senses a poetic justice in la Bricoline's nonsense,
as witnessed by her comment on her family's wealth: "Tout le
monde a peur de moi, parce que je suis très riche, très riche, si riche
que l'on m'a défendu de vivre" (276). Her desire is to become rich
with tenderness, a quality she tells Rose, that her family has lacked:
"Cette nuit, pas plus tard que cette nuit, je trouverai la tendresse et
je t'en ferai part. C'est alors que nous serons riches! *Au jour d'aujourd'hui*, comme dit ce gendarme qu'on a mis ici pour nous garder,
nous sommes si pauvres que personne ne veut de nous" (307). Her
vengeance is that of the madwoman of *Jane Eyre*: she sets fire to the
farm. Her wild tirade recalls the gothic novel tradition as well.
Bricolin's fanatic desire to accumulate wealth—even at the expense
of his own family's welfare—becomes in the end the instrument of
his downfall. The fire engulfs his barn all the more rapidly because
it is filled with grain, the sign of his wealth. The fiery destruction of

the Bricolin farm represents a reprise of the fire motive from the tale of how Bricolin's father had lost his wealth, through the *chauffeurs* during the Revolution. Bricolin's daughter plays a similar role by redistributing wealth through fire.

In glaring contrast to the misery produced by Bricolin's wealth stand those lives of those who are actually blessed with the good fortune of being poor. The most prominent example is the poor cottager Piaulette, whose home Marcelle visits one day:

> L'intérieur de la maison était aussi misérable que l'entrée, et Marcelle fut touchée de voir par quelle excessive propreté le courage de la femme luttait là contre l'horreur du dénuement. Le sol inégal et raboteux n'avait pas un grain de poussière, les deux ou trois pauvres meubles étaient clairs et brillants comme s'ils eussent été vernis; la petite vaisselle de terre, dressée à la muraille et sur des planches, était lavée et rangée avec soin. Chez la plupart des paysans de la Vallée-Noire, la misère la plus réelle, la plus complète, se dissimule discrètement et noblement sous ces habitudes consciencieuses d'ordre et de propreté. La pauvreté rustique y est attendrissante et affectueuse. On vivrait de bon cœur avec ces indigents. Il n'inspirent pas le dégoût, mais l'intérêt et une sorte de respect. (291)

Although they never eat any meat or vegetables (even though she is nursing), the children enjoy robust health. Marcelle comments repeatedly on the good luck of her son Edouard in being forced to live the life of the poor.

Marcelle is equally aware that poverty, which can in one sense eliminate certain dangers and temptations, can also stifle personal growth. Marcelle sees the peasants as "vegetating" (156); they have no possibility of rising out of ignorance because of a lack of money and opportunity. Later in the novel she compares their existence to that of farm animals: "Elle se demanda quelle pouvait être l'existence intellectuelle de gens qui, trop pauvres pour avoir de la chandelle, étaient obligés, dès que la nuit venait, de se coucher en hiver, ou de se tenir le jour dans les ténèbres pour se préserver du froid. Je me disais, je me croyais ruinée, parce que j'étais forcée de quitter mon appartement doré, ouaté et tendu de soie; mais que de degrés encore à parcourir dans l'échelle des existences sociales avant d'en venir à cette vie du pauvre qui diffère si peu de celle des animaux" (295). This same comparison appeared in *Jeanne*, but it now strikes a sympathetic note. A certain contradiction is evident in Sand's portrayal of poverty. In depicting the poor in *Le Meunier d'Angibault*, Sand had to confront the difficulty of extolling the virtues of the poor while simultaneously eliciting sympathy and support. This duality produces an awkwardly sentimental portrait of the poor at odds with the more realistic depiction to be found in the essays of the same period.[3]

The essential problem is that in contemporary society human beings and their relationships tend to be reduced to their monetary value. It is against this characteristic of the modern world that the principal characters rebel. Their approach to a society based on money molds the social vision Sand was attempting to convey to the reader. In Grand-Louis's first encounter with Marcelle, he refuses payment for his services: "Je sais bien que dans les grandes villes tout se paie, jusqu'à un verre d'eau. C'est une vilaine coutume" (77). Marcelle is constantly trying to rid herself of her wealth. Independent of her desire to marry Henri, the narrator assures us, Marcelle has become aware of the justice of his ideas on wealth. When she learns that nearly all her fortune is gone, she writes to her lover: "Henri, quel bonheur! Quelle joie! Je suis ruinée" (118). Her dramatic formulation of this unconventional reaction is designed to attract the reader's attention. Indeed, the reader's admiration for her is pre-programmed in the enthusiastic reaction of Grand-Louis to Marcelle's equanimity on learning of the loss of her fortune. The loss of her wealth smoothes the way in her relationship with Henri and reinforces the adverse relationship between money and spiritual values. Marcelle's initial reaction to her economic status confirms this point: "Ainsi, se dit-elle, tout va être rompu entre moi et le passé. Richesse et noblesse s'éteignent de compagnie, *au jour d'aujourd'hui*, comme dit ce Bricolin. O mon Dieu! Que vous êtes bon d'avoir fait l'amour de tous les temps et immortel comme vous-même!" (105). The reference to nobility underscores the idea that money leads to class distinction and antagonism. Now free, Marcelle openly embraces the idea of entering a different social class: "Il y a longtemps que je me dis que c'est un malheur que de naître riche, et d'être destiné à l'oisiveté, à la haine des pauvres, à l'égoïsme et à l'impunité que donne la richesse. J'ai regretté bien souvent de n'être pas fille et mère d'ouvrier. A présent, Louis, je serai du peuple" (110). The impossibility of Marcelle's ever being "du peuple" is confirmed by Grand-Louis who often functions as the voice of common sense. A mild irony informs the depiction of Marcelle's enthusiastic embrace of poverty and the simple life.

Henri Lémor's views on money also run counter to those of French society as a whole. Upon inheriting his father's business he promptly gave away all his money to the workers. To earn a living he has become a mechanic, vowing never to accumulate more than one week's wages. Early in the novel Henri's merit is demonstrated, as is that of Marcelle, by how far removed he is from the average man of polite society: "Sa cravate assez mal nouée révélait une grande absence de coquetterie ou une habitude de préoccupation; ses gants bruns suffisaient à prouver que ce n'était pas là, comme se seraient exprimés les laquais de l'hôtel de Blanchemont, un homme fait pour être le mari ou l'amant de madame" (27). If they knew his views, it would serve to strengthen the lacquis' opinion. Henri's conviction that wealth is evil leads to his refusal to marry Marcelle until she divests herself of her wealth. He believes that no possible good can come of her money because it is tainted. Henri also has a keen awareness of his social class and of the social gulf which separates him from Marcelle. As happens so often in Sand's fiction, love triumphs over class struggle in the end. The marriage of Marcelle and Henri and of Emile Cardonnet and Gilberte de Châteaubrun in Le Péché de M. Antoine are symbolic unions, demonstrating the reconciliation of the social classes.

The work that Henri does in the course of the novel is largely symbolic as well. In order to be close to Marcelle, Henri becomes Grand-Louis's assistant at the mill, at least in name. When Henri realizes he will be helping Grand-Louis make flour that will be used to make the bread Marcelle eats, it puts his work in a new light: "Cette circonstance toute vulgaire dans les habitudes du

moulin prit une couleur romanesque et quasi poétique dans le cerveau du jeune Parisien, et il se mit à aider le meunier avec tant de zèle et d'attention, qu'au bout de deux heures il était parfaitement au courant du métier" (243-44). Henri's reacts enthusiastically to this situation: "Ami, s'écria-t-il, le travail est beau et saint par lui-même; vous aviez raison de le dire en commençant! Dieu l'impose et le bénit. Il m'a semblé doux de travailler pour nourrir ma maîtresse; oh qu'il serait doux encore de travailler en même temps pour alimenter la vie d'une famille d'égaux et de frères!" (244). Henri's "labor" allows him to integrate his love for Marcelle with his humanitarian beliefs.

The setting of the mill establishes further the idealized view of the work that goes on there. It is described as a "paradis terrestre" (64) and the area around it as "une forêt vierge" (63). It is above all untainted by monetary considerations. Marcelle upon visiting the prosperous Bricolin farm after being at the mill compares "cette grossière et repoussante opulence agricole, au poétique bien-être du meunier" (86). In fact, the productivity of the Bricolin farm is presented in a decidedly negative light: "Rien de plus triste et de plus déplaisant que cette demeure des riches fermiers. . . . Ces bâtiments sombres, et offrant des traces d'ancienne architecture, mais solides et bien entretenues, formaient un développement de granges et d'étables d'un seul tenant qui faisait l'orgueil des fermiers et l'admiration de tous les agriculteurs du pays. Mais cette enceinte, si utile à l'industrie agricole, et si commode pour l'emménagement du bétail et de la récolte, enfermait les regards et la pensée dans un espace triste, prosaïque et d'une saleté repoussante" (85). The "saleté" is in fact manure, which the narrator admits représents a "richesse" which increases agricultural production. This is one of the more obvious examples in the novel of the perception of reality being shaped to fit Sand's thesis.

No matter how "poetic" the site in which one lives and works, the problem remains that at the same time one must live in a society ruled by money. Since the new egalitarian society advocated by Henri will be long in coming, the question arises as to how one should live in the meantime.[4] One well-intentioned individual, such as Marcelle, can do little to change society, but at least can

lead her own life according to the principles in which she believes. This is the lesson she imparts to Rose: "Une seule personne bien intentionnée peut faire si peu de bien, même en donnant tout ce qu'elle possède, et alors elle est si tôt réduite à l'impuissance. . . . Avec nos bonnes intentions, nous autres qui ne savons pas comment la société pourrait apporter remède à de telles alternatives nous ne pouvons rien, sinon préférer pour nous-mêmes la médiocrité à la richesse et le travail à l'oisiveté. C'est un pas vers la vertu, mais quel pauvre mérite nous avons là, et combien peu il apporte remède aux misères sans nombre qui frappent nos yeux et contristent notre cœur" (136-37). In effect one can do little but wait for the new order to arrive, as she advises Rose to do. The time for sacrifice has not yet arrived.[5] In fact, in the existing state of society distributing money to the poor could have a pernicious effect according to Henri: "L'argent qu'on distribuerait à une poignée de misérables n'enfanterait chez eux que l'égoïsme et la paresse, si on ne cherchait à leur faire comprendre les devoirs de l'association" (197). It is this kind of "association" that Grand-Louis sets up at the end with a few poor families to work the mill with the few thousand francs he has received from the inheritance of the old beggar Cadoche (388). The new society may lie far in the future, but George Sand, the novelist, can create it in miniature with a stroke of her pen.

The professed inability of the individual to effect social change provides a ready-made justification for attitudes and actions on the part of Marcelle and Henri which would appear to clash with their views on equality and wealth. Thus Marcelle offers a rather lengthy justification for keeping enough money to prevent her son from being ignorant:

> Il y a quelque chose d'affreux à penser que la superstition est la seule religion accessible au paysan, que tout son culte se réduit à des pratiques qu'il ne comprend pas, dont il ne saura jamais ni le sens ni l'origine, et que Dieu n'est pour lui qu'une idole favorable aux moissons et aux troupeaux de celui qui lui voue un cierge ou une image. . . . Si mon fils est indigent, il faudra donc qu'il soit idolâtre, au rebours des premiers chrétiens qui embras-

saient la vraie religion avec la sainte pauvreté? Je sais bien que le
pauvre a le droit de me demander: Pourquoi ton fils plutôt que
le mien connaît-il Dieu et la vérité? Hélas! Je n'ai rien a répondre,
sinon que je ne puis sauver son fils qu'en sacrifiant le mien. . . .
Ainsi, les devoirs que nous impose la famille sont en contradiction avec ceux que nous impose l'humanité. Mais nous pouvons
encore quelque chose pour la famille, tandis que pour l'humanité, à moins d'être très riches, nous ne pouvons rien encore. (157)

Henri echoes this same sort of view at the end of the novel:
"Gardons ton fils à l'abri du mal autant que possible, enseignons-
lui l'amour du bien et le besoin de la lumière. Cette génération la
trouvera peut-être. Ce sera peut-être à elle de nous instruire un
jour. Garde ta richesse; comment pourrais-je te la reprocher, quand
je vois que ton cœur en est entièrement détaché et que tu la re-
gardes comme un dépôt dont le Ciel te demandera compte? Garde
ce peu d'or qui te reste" (299-300). Because her son represents the
future and the future is the new society, Marcelle and Henri see the
use of her remaining wealth on him as justified. Henri is also careful to justify his decision to marry Marcelle after all: their love is to
be an act of symbolic social importance: "Aimons-nous, non pour
être heureux dans *l'egoïsme à deux*, comme on appelle l'amour, mais
pour souffrir ensemble, pour prier ensemble, pour chercher ensemble ce qu'à nous deux, pauvres oiseaux égarés dans l'orage,
nous pouvons faire, jour par jour, pour conjurer ce fléau qui disperse notre race, et pour rassembler sous notre aile quelques fugi-
tifs brisés comme nous d'épouvante et de tristesse!" (298-99). We
are far removed in this closing vision of the novel from the ambitious ideals incorporated into *Le Compagnon du tour de France* and
the Consuelo novels of the individual striving alone or with others
to effect immediate changes in society. All hope in *Le Meunier
d'Angibault* is put in the future; for the present only symbolic acts
have value.

The temporary, individualistic solutions to the social and
economic issues raised in the novel do not help to make *Le Meunier
d'Angibault* a convincing *roman à thèse*. The shuttling back and forth
between realism and fantasy does not further this goal either. While

real issues are raised in the novel and seen in the context of actual characters facing difficult choices, the characters' positions are not carried through with consistency and the reader feels that in the end the socialist rhetoric is so much ballast. To a large extent, the basic plot involving Marcelle and Henri's temporary estrangement is an artificial conflict, one of the lovers' own making and too obviously tailored to the novelist's message. What is more disturbing is that those characters who devote their energy to losing their fortunes are in the end rewarded financially for their success. Grand-Louis serves as the *deus ex machina* of the author, using his sudden wealth to assure his own marriage with Rose as well as smoothing the path for Henri and Marcelle. In this final ironic reversal money, the root of all evil, brings blessing and happiness.

❖ ❖ ❖

A number of elements which are tangential or tentative in *Le Meunier d'Angibault* become more fully elaborated in the somewhat longer *Péché de M. Antoine*. The most important positive characters in *Le Meunier*—Marcelle, Henri and Grand-Louis—are associated with the untamed natural setting of the mill. *Le Péché* maintains this association and takes it a step farther, schematizing the characters' relationship to nature into a moral litmus test. The gathering place for the positive characters of the novel is the castle of Antoine de Châteaubrun. It is the home of Antoine's daughter, Gilberte, and the home away from home of their friend, the carpenter Jean Jappeloup. It also becomes the place toward which Emile Cardonnet gravitates increasingly in the course of the novel. The castle is no more than a shell; it has been pillaged by peasants and is overgrown with vegetation which Antoine and his daughter make a point of allowing to grow wild. They do not prune any vines or shrubs and Antoine refuses to cut down old fruit trees which bear almost no fruit. Like the Châteaubrun family, Jean Jappeloup is in tune with nature: he is able to interpret nature's signs to predict natural phenomena such as storms and floods.

That the Châteaubrun château is in harmony with nature is brought out by the effect of the big storm with which the novel

opens: "L'on eût dit que quelque fée géante avait lavé avec soin les sentiers et les vieux murs, épuré les sables et débarrassé le passage de tout le déchet de démolissement que le châtelain n'aurait jamais eu le moyen de faire enlever. L'inondation, qui avait gâté, souillé et détruit toute la beauté de la nouvelle maison Cardonnet, avait donc servi à nettoyer et à rajeunir le monument dévasté de Château-brun" (1: 88-89). The wind and rain which does so much damage to other property, including Cardonnet's factory, actually has a beneficial effect on the château. The closeness to nature of those associated with the château is brought out as well by contrast with other characters in the novel. The assistant of Emile's father, Galuchet, a pretentious simpleton who despises peasants, is manifestly out of place in these surroundings. His appearance prompts the narrator to comment on the dress of the middle-class male in general: "Au milieu de ce cadre austère et grandiose, qui transporte l'imagination aux temps de la poésie primitive, apparaisse cette mouche parasite, le *monsieur* aux habits noirs, au menton rasé, aux mains gantées, aux jambes maladroites, et ce roi de la société n'est plus qu'un accident ridicule, une tache importune dans le tableau" (2: 8-9). The fact that Galuchet does not belong in the natural setting in which the other characters feel so at home is graphically illustrated when he is thrown into the river by Jean Jappeloup. His skewed relationship to nature is demonstrated as well by his fishing. He fishes only to see how many fish he can catch; it is the same kind of senseless destruction of nature and endless urge to accumulate that can be seen in his employer, Cardonnet.

Cardonnet, the capitalist entrepreneur, has an actively hostile attitude towards nature. His factory depends on the river for power and after the flood damages it severely, he vows to conquer the river: "Maudit ruisseau. . . . Je saurai bien t'enchaîner et te contenir. . . . Le génie de l'homme doit rester ici vainqueur des aveugles révoltes de la nature. Vingt ouvrières de plus, et tu sentiras le frein. De l'argent, et toujours de l'argent! . . . Ou cette eau roulera mon cadavre, ou elle portera docilement les trésors de mon industrie!" (1: 149). For Cardonnet money is all powerful; nature, just like his fellow humans, must bow to its force. Cardonnet is a totally committed and ruthless entrepreneur. In setting up the factory his strategy, as explained by Jean Jappeloup, is to buy land at high price, pay workers at first above-average wages in order to circumvent the possible view that he is a dangerous competitor to other industrialists, and to gain the confidence of the community. Then once established he will exploit his workers and systematically eliminate all competitors. Yet Cardonnet defends the capitalist system and, in fact, views becoming rich as a public service: "Que l'industrie règne donc et triomphe; que tous les hommes travaillent: qui du bras, qui de la tête; c'est à celui qui a plus de tête que de bras à diriger les autres; il a le droit et le devoir de faire fortune. Sa richesse devient sacrée, puisqu'elle est destinée à s'accroître, afin d'accroître le travail et le salaire" (1: 164). His formula for improving society is to keep the lower classes working as hard as possible, thus teaching them the virtues of hard work and sobriety while preventing them from having time or energy to revolt.[6]

The opposing character to Cardonnet in the novel is Antoine. He is as bungling as Cardonnet is efficient and as unworldly as Cardonnet is practical. He is totally lacking in personal ambition and his disinterest in financial affairs is presented as a positive quality. Antoine's attempts to belittle himself only serve to accentuate his merit and the striking contrast with Cardonnet: "Il est bien certain que j'ai toujours été un peu prodigue, que je n'entends rien à l'économie domestique, aux affaires, et que j'eus moins de mérite qu'un autre à sacrifier ma fortune, puisque j'y eus moins de regrets" (1: 110). The event which has made him poor shows him in an almost heroic light: he has given up his family fortune to pay debts that he had little or no legal obligation to pay. He is far removed from showing Cardonnet's mania of continuous acquisition. Antoine is also oblivious to social distinctions, as evinced by his reception of Emile at the beginning of the novel: "Je n'ai pas de questions à vous faire, et je prétends remplir les devoirs de l'hospitalité sans vous faire décliner vos noms et qualités" (1: 24). Cardonnet is scornful of Antoine because he socializes with peasants. In fact Antoine works as a carpenter himself in order to keep the family going.

At the same time the narrator is careful to keep the reader reminded of the fact that this is an aristocratic family, especially through the proud comments of the family's housekeeper, Janille. Emile is keenly aware of the social origin of the family and of Gilberte in particular, even before he meets her: "Il se sentit pénétré de compassion en songeant qu'il y avait là une jeune fille dont l'aïeul avait eu des pages, des vassaux, des meutes, des chevaux de luxe, tandis que, désormais, cette héritière d'une ruine effrayante à voir, allait peut-être, comme la princesse Nausicaa, laver elle-même son linge à la fontaine" (1: 47-48). Gilberte's beauty and the fact that her speech has "une distinction remarquable" point to her identity as a kind of princess in rags. Like a fairy-tale princess in disguise she lives in forced separation from society—due to her illegitimacy and poverty—but is hardly burdened with a sense of loss. She has no regrets at being deprived of her "rightful" place in society. Society's loss is nature's gain: "La fille du châtelain, cet enfant du célibat, dont le nom maternel était resté un problème pour tout le voisinage, parut au détour d'un massif d'églantiers, belle comme la plus belle fleur inculte de ces gracieuses solitudes" (1: 97). Society may reject her, but in the natural world she is accepted and elevated. As was the case with Consuelo she is frequently compared to birds, with the emphasis here on innocence and freedom. Her harmony with nature is emphasized throughout the novel.

In fact her attitude and behavior can be characterized as "natural"; it is radically different from the artifice which is the hallmark of women's thoughts and actions in polite society. She feels no embarrassment in encountering for the first time the rich and handsome Emile, nor does she try to attract his attention in any way. Just after Emile has met her she is shown grafting branches of rose bushes. When her father tells her to wear gloves so the thorns won't prick her she responds: "Et qu'est-ce que cela fait, mon père, dit la jeune fille en souriant. Je ne suis pas une princesse, moi, et j'en suis bien aise. J'en suis plus libre et plus heureuse" (1: 99). She does not play out the normal role of women of her social rank, taking pleasure instead in her identity as child of nature. As was the case with Marcelle de Blanchemont, Gilberte de Châteaubrun is meant to be seen in vivid contrast to the materialistic and artificial bourgeois world of commerce and industry. Yet in this passage Gilberte by declaring herself not to be a princess, effectively draws attention to her aristocratic background. As was the case with Marcelle, Sand was intent in the portrayal of her heroines to emphasize their social superiority so as to elevate them in the eyes of the bourgeois reader and to highlight the fact that they willingly give up their place in a higher class.

One could interpret the rosebush passage also in a different way, namely as being an expression of Marcelle's sexual freedom and an assertion of her right to lose her virginity. When she later gives Emile a special rose from her garden as a "talisman," the symbolic meaning is clear. The sensual side of their relationship is stronger than was true of that of Marcelle and Henri. Emile's obsession with her hair is used here in the familiar Sandian way. There is in particular the scene by the ruins of the Crozant castle: "[Elle] se laissa tomber sur la mousse au bord de l'eau bondissante, jeta son chapeau sur le gazon, forcée de relever ses cheveux dénoués qui pendaient sur ses épaules" (1: 273). With the proximity of the water as a further aphrodisiac, Émile is unable to keep himself from kissing Gilberte's hair; he soon thereafter declares his love. The Crozant castle is an appropriate locale for this scene since it represents a heightened version of Châteaubrun; the narrator emphasizes the fact that it is impossible to tell where the castle stops and the natural rocks begin.

Like Marcelle, Gilberte is not so blindly in love that she insists on an immediate union with Emile. She is willing to wait indefinitely until Emile's father allows them to marry without the condition he has attached that Emile give up his socialist views. For Gilberte love is not an all-consuming passion but, as she tells Emile, a relationship based on a similarity of views on morality and justice: "Si je vous estime au point de vous dire sans méfiance et sans honte que je vous aime, Emile, c'est parce que je vous sais grand et de cœur et d'esprit; c'est parce que vous plaignez les malheureux et ne songez qu'à les secourir, parce que vous ne méprisez personne, parce que vous souffrez des peines d'autrui, parce qu'enfin vous voudriez donner tout ce qui est à vous, jusqu'à votre sang, pour soulager les pauvres et les abandonnés" (2: 55). She would no longer love him if he forsook his social ideals. It is the woman here, as so often in Sand's fiction, who has the inner strength to sustain her lover. Gilberte is a woman whose favor Emile must earn. Like Bernard Mauprat, he is described as being "un chevalier errant" (1: 202) carrying out the wishes of his lover. After one meeting with Gilberte, Emile "baisa l'herbe que ses pieds avait à peine foulée, l'arbre qu'elle avait effleuré de sa robe" (2: 60). The narrator describes Emile's feelings for Gilberte as being "une sainte ivresse" (1: 266). He sees his love in such ideal terms that he suffers when it becomes necessary to place it in some kind of social context: "Le monde et les lois de l'honneur, si froides en pareil cas, étaient donc là pour ôter à la virginité de sa passion ce qu'elle avait de plus pur et de plus idéal" (1: 266). Yet unlike Sandian lovers of the early 1840s, Emile's romantic passion does not derive from literature. He and Gilberte read a considerable amount, but their readings are in social theory, history and philosophy, not fiction. This fact is a reflection of Sand's obsession in the novel with conveying her socialist ideals and an indication of how far she was willing to drift from verisimilitude in order to achieve this goal.[7] This is evident throughout the novel, as in the passage in which Emile's care over her reading selections is evoked. Emile checks all the books he borrows for her in order to ascertain that there are no passages which might cause "une jeune vierge" to blush: "Une mère n'eût pas mieux agi en pareil cas que ne le fit le jeune amant de Gilberte, et plus l'incurie affectueuse du père et de la fille eût favorisé, sans le savoir, des tentatives de corruption, plus Emile se faisait un devoir cher et sacré de justifier l'abandon de ces âmes naïves" (1: 227). Such passages—which so awkwardly and unrealistically highlight the characters' virtues—abound and offer a vivid contrast to the simplicity and naturalness with which Sand was to portray her positive characters in her next novel, *La Mare au diable*.

Gilberte has arrived at similar views on society to those of Emile through her own intuition and through her interpretation of the Christian faith: "Je ne suis pas philosophe, moi, je suis trop ignorante! Mais je suis pieuse, je suis nourrie des préceptes de l'Evangile, et je ne puis les interpréter dans un sens opposé à ceux qu'Emile leur donne" (2: 112). In another example of high-handed artifice in the novel, all the positive characters in the novel share the same social vision. They have, however, arrived at their beliefs in different ways. Jean Jappeloup the carpenter has become a socialist through common sense and experience. He has learned that to become rich is in itself an immoral activity, as he explains in reference to Cardonnet: "Un homme parti peut-être d'aussi bas que moi-même, et qui a fait un pareil chemin, n'est pas un honnête homme" (1: 29). Jappeloup is proud of having been born poor; he also approves of Antoine, who was born rich but lost his fortune. He has used the same method in evaluating society that he uses in analyzing any phenomenon. He is able, for example, to prophecy the certain ruin of Cardonnet's factory, not from any scientific study but because, as Emile says, "il y a certaines natures privilégiées chez lesquelles l'observation et la logique remplacent le savoir" (2: 35). If Gilberte has a natural grace and beauty, Jean Jappeloup has a natural genius and authority. When Emile first meets him, "[il] ne pouvait se défendre de le trouver beau, et d'admirer, dans sa facilité à exprimer rudement ses pensées, une sorte d'éloquence naturelle empreinte de franchise et d'amour de la justice; car si ses paroles, dont nous n'avons pas rendu toute la rusticité, étaient simples et parfois vulgaires, son geste était énergique, et l'accent de sa voix commandait l'attention" (1: 42). As evident here, Jean Jappeloup is in many ways a reincarnation of Grand-Louis, possessing the same ability to rise above his apparent limitations. Both are variations on the "paysan illuminé" more dramatically portrayed in Jeanne or Patience (*Mauprat*). As was the case with peasant characters in previous novels, Sand in this passage felt the need to justify the elevation of such characters to the bourgeois reader.[8] This is, in fact, the perspective here as in *Le Meunier d'Angibault*, that of the urban middle class. There is even a footnote explaining to "nos lecteurs parisiens" how to sleep out-of-doors (1: 186). The different reader orientation is one of the major changes in the later rustic novels.

As was the case with the other characters of this type Jean Jappeloup does not fit comfortably into the society in which he lives. In fact at the beginning of the novel he is being sought by the police. His "crime" was having sent three bottles of wine to a friend who was ill, thus acting illegally as a "wine merchant." He is fined 500 francs, more than he earns in a year. Five hundred more francs are later added for having poached a rabbit. In a formulation recalling Hugo, Jappeloup tells Emile: "ça vous étonne, vous, jeune homme, qu'un pauvre diable qui a toujours obligé son prochain, au lieu de lui nuire, soit poursuivi comme un forçat évadé?" (1: 67). Jappeloup's need for freedom is demonstrated in his abhorrence of the idea of spending even one night in prison. While highlighting the inhumane system of justice, Jappeloup's persecution also reinforces his identification with another persecuted carpenter who incorporated the ideals of fraternity, equality, and charity. In fact Jappeloup refers to Jesus as a carpenter with socialist views. The title of chapter six, "Jean le Charpentier," defines him by his profession and its symbolic association. That association is as strong here as it was with the character of Pierre Huguenin in *Le Compagnon du tour de France*.

Like Pierre, Jean Jappeloup takes pride and pleasure in his work and treasures highly his personal freedom. He tells Cardonnet that he will not accept his offer of employment because it would mean that he would become "votre propriété et votre esclave" (1: 70). Working for Cardonnet would be spiritually stifling: "Je serais donc un manœuvre, travaillant à la corvée comme défunt mon père travaillait pour les abbés de Gargilesse? Non, Dieu me punisse! Je ne vendrai pas mon âme à un travail aussi ennuyeux et aussi bête" (1: 73). He opposes the idea that Cardonnet would have complete control over his time. In working independently he is able to structure his time according to his own desires. Jappeloup's views on working for Cardonnet constitute a condemnation of factory-style work conditions; in fact even Cardonnet complains that his workers act like machines and never think about what they are doing, not realizing that such is precisely the behavior he has trained them to have. Jappeloup's own work demonstrates the joy of freely chosen and performed labor, as when he is cutting trees with his ax: "Sa hache brillante tournoyait en éclairs autour de lui, et sa voix sonore stimulait les autres travailleurs, surpris de trouver si facile une tâche que l'intelligence et l'énergie d'un seul homme commandait, simplifiait et enlevait comme par miracle" (2: 74-75). Work here is fun and exhilarating—and also not for profit—since Jappeloup is doing this as a personal favor for the Marquis de Boisguilbault.

Emile's view of work is similar: "L'homme est né pour travailler toujours, mais conformément à ses aptitudes, et dans la
mesure du plaisir qu'il y trouve! Ah, que ne suis-je un habile charpentier! Avec quelle joie n'irais-je pas travailler avec Jean Jappeloup"
(1: 187). This is a view of labor difficult to reconcile with the realities of factory life. This aspect of Cardonnet's factory is kept decidedly vague: we never learn what he intends to produce there.[9]
Emile's chosen field is not manufacturing but agriculture. His attitude toward agriculture is very different from that of Bricolin in *Le
Meunier d'Angibault*. Emile is ready to make use of any new advances which will improve the lot of the peasant working the land.
At the same time Emile's view of agriculture has its idealistic side:
"J'aurais été heureux de me faire paysan, de travailler d'esprit et de
corps, d'être en contact perpétuel avec les hommes et les choses de
la nature. Je me serais instruit avec ardeur, j'aurais creusé plus
avant que d'autres peut-être le champ des découvertes! Et, un jour,
sur quelque lande déserte et nue transformée par mes soins, j'aurais
fondé une colonie d'hommes libres, vivant en frères et m'aimant
comme un frère" (1: 161). This is the same fusion of labor and social
vision we encountered in *Le Meunier d'Angibault* in the attitude of
Henri Lémor working at the mill. The idea of manual labor conjures
up here the image of fraternity and equality. Work, freely chosen
and its harshness alleviated by modern science, is seen as a liberating force. This is Jean Jappeloup's personal attitude developed into
a social system. It evinces similarities with Fourier's concept of the
phalanstère.[10]

Cardonnet rejects Emile's vision as hopelessly naive: "Voilà
l'utopie du frère Emile, frère morave, quaker, néo-chrétien, néo-pla-
tonicien, que sais-je? C'est superbe, mais c'est absurde" (1: 162). He
adopts instead the Saint-Simonian formula expressed in the slogan
"à chacun suivant sa capacité" (1: 164), a view which repulses
Emile: "Quoi! C'est là tout l'idéal de l'industrie, dit Emile, écrasé
sous cette conclusion. Le peuple n'a pas d'autre avenir que le travail incessant, au profit d'une classe qui ne travaillera jamais?" (1:
163). Imagining a society full of efficient, ruthless capitalists like his
father, Emile considers it as "une utopie plus effrayante que les

miennes" (1: 165). Emile embraces instead the idea of "à chacun suivant ses besoins":

> Puisque nous ne pouvons à nous seuls créer une société où tous seraient solidaires les uns les autres, soyons comme ouvriers de l'avenir, dévoués aux faibles et aux incapables d'à présent. . . . Associons tous nos travailleurs à tous nos bénéfices, que notre grande fortune ne soit pas votre propriété et mon héritage, mais la richesse de quiconque nous aura aidés suivant ses moyens et ses forces à la fonder; que le manœuvre qui apporte sa pierre soit mis à même de connaître autant de jouissances matérielles que vous qui apportez votre génie; qu'il puisse, lui aussi, habiter une belle maison, respirer un air pur, se nourrir d'aliments sains, se reposer après la fatigue, et donner l'éducation à ses enfants. (1: 167)

Emile is evoking here the same kind of worker association which Grand-Louis is planning to establish at the end of *Le Meunier d'Angibault*. In fact this is how *Le Péché de M. Antoine* concludes as well. With the money given by the Marquis de Boisguilbault, Emile and Gilberte plan to establish an agricultural cooperative. They have "earned" the estate by remaining true to their socialist principles even if that means giving up their love. In both novels these communal associations are offered as opposing models to the exploitive labor relationships depicted and represented as typical of those in society as a whole.

For Emile what is most important in his life are not just specific social or political theories but simply the fact of possessing a vision, a set of ideals: "S'il n'y a pas une vérité éternelle, une raison divine des choses, un idéal qu'on puisse porter dans l'âme, pour se soutenir et se diriger à travers les maux et les injustices du présent, je n'existe plus" (1: 156). It is just this sense of striving toward an ideal—even if unobtainable—goal that is lacking in Cardonnet: "Son caractère de fer était le résultat d'une âme absolument vide d'idéal" (1: 169). His philosophy is a version of that of Vigny: "Nous avons pour devoir religieux de travailler ici-bas sans relâche et de nous en aller sans murmure" (1: 155). It is not surprising that

he has no interest in literature or any other spiritual pursuits; he mocks Emile by telling him that he is suited only for being a poet. It was because Leroux's system took into account the spiritual aspect of social intercourse that Sand found it superior to the Saint-Simonian model or that of Fourier.

The father-son conflict becomes a battle of good versus evil. Cardonnet vows to do to Emile what he is trying to do to the river: "Il est de toi comme du torrent qui me fait la guerre: tous deux vous vous soumettrez quand vous sentirez la main du maître" (1: 234). When Cardonnet offers Emile the chance to marry Gilberte he is clearly playing the role of the figure with whom Antoine identifies him at the beginning of the novel, Mephistopheles: "Jure-moi que tu m'appartiens, que tu n'auras au monde d'autre pensée que celle de m'aider à t'enrichir; abandonne-m'en tous les moyens sans les discuter; et, en retour, je te jure, moi, que je donnerai à ton cœur et à tes sens toutes les satisfactions qui seront en mon pouvoir (2: 39). . . . Je veux que tu signes enfin, non sur du papier devant un notaire, mais sur ma tête et avec le sang de ton cœur, et devant Dieu, un contrat qui annihile tout ton passé de rêves et de chimères, et qui engage ta conviction, ta volonté, ta foi, ton avenir, ton dévouement, ta religion, à la réussite de mon œuvre" (2: 44). There are later references to Cardonnet's "génie infernal" (2: 46) and his "invention diabolique" (2: 51). What his father is trying to do to him, Emile tells the Marquis, is to transform him from a man into a "brute" (2: 52). His humanitarian beliefs are what define Emile's humility; take them away and all that is left are animal instincts of greed and egotism. Cardonnet is advocating that Emile develop in the opposite direction to Bernard Mauprat, to become uncivilized.

The problem being raised here is not just one of generational conflict but concerns the relationship between love on the one hand and moral and political convictions on the other: "Dans une société où tout serait en harmonie, l'amour deviendrait, à coup sûr, un stimulant au patriotisme et au dévouement social. Mais lorsque les intentions hardies et généreuses sont condamnées à une lutte pénible avec les hommes et les choses qui nous entourent, les affections personnelles nous captivent et nous dominent jusqu'à produire l'engourdissement des autres facultés" (1: 229). In fact the point is

made in the novel that it takes some one capable of having a set of ideals to experience strong, genuine love. Cardonnet is incapable of this: "Un grand amour était pour lui un idéal inaccessible" (1: 237). His relationship with his wife is a far cry from the mixture of love and idealism which characterizes Emile and Gilberte's love. She is stifled by their marriage: "Tout élan de cœur ou d'imagination avait toujours été refoulé en elle par l'ironie et une sorte de pitié dédaigneuse, et elle s'était habituée à n'avoir pas une pensée, pas une volonté en dehors du cercle tracé autour d'elle par une main rigide" (1: 171). It is a relationship that, unlike that of his son and Gilberte, allows for no spiritual growth or development of any kind.[11] Indeed, Cardonnet has succeeded in reducing her to a kind of animal state: "Rien n'efface et ne détruit rapidement l'intelligence comme la soumission aveugle. Madame Cardonnet en était un exemple. Son cerveau s'était amoindri dans l'esclavage, et son époux, ne comprenant pas que c'était là l'ouvrage de sa domination, en était venu à la dédaigner secrètement" (1: 172). Cardonnet's treatment of his wife's bouts of depression—caused by his treatment of her—is equally degrading: "Voyons, qu'y a-t-il? La pauvre petite femme a quelque ennui? Avez-vous envie d'un cachemire? Voulez-vous que je vous mène promener en voiture? Non? Alors ce sont les camélias qui ont gelé?" (1: 173). He does not view her as a human being. The inhumanity of his relationship with his wife mirrors that in the treatment of his workers. The two oppressed groups in society are shown as being equally at the mercy of the exploitive and inhumane capitalist system.

With his father playing the role of the tempter Emile finds a substitute father in the Marquis de Boisguilbault. The Marquis, like so many other persons and relationships in this novel, is not what he seems. He appears to be hard-hearted and misanthropic and Emile initially believes that he is "fort attaché à ses titres et antiques privilèges" (1: 133). But Emile later discovers that the Marquis had been misunderstood and also learns to his—and the reader's—surprise that the Marquis has the same socialist beliefs as Emile. He has arrived at his conviction through study; after happening upon a few Saint-Simonian brochures, he was led to pursue the subject:

> Je rappris les langues mortes que j'avais oubliées, je lus pour la
> première fois, dans les sources mêmes, l'histoire des religions et
> des philosophies, et, un jour enfin, les grands hommes, les saints,
> les prophètes, les poëtes, les martyrs, les hérétiques, les savants,
> les orthodoxes éclairés, les novateurs, les artistes, les réfor-
> mateurs de tous les temps, de tous les pays, de toutes les révolu-
> tions et de tous les cultes m'apparurent d'accord, proclamant,
> sous toutes les formes, et jusque par leurs contradictions appa-
> rentes, une vérité éternelle, une logique aussi claire que la
> lumière du jour: à savoir, l'égalité des droits et la nécessité in-
> évitable de l'égalité des jouissances, comme conséquence
> rigoureuse de la première. (1: 217)

The Marquis's exhaustive research results in precisely the same
conclusions that Emile has come to through his innate sense of justice, Gilberte through her innocence and closeness to nature, and
Jappeloup through his unerring instinct. Thus the Marquis serves
to ratify scientifically the beliefs already presented through the
other characters. The multiplicity of sources for the same social
views is designed to convince the reader of the inevitability of these
fundamental truths.

The Marquis sees the necessity of restructuring the way his
estate is run but does not believe it is possible at the present time:
"Les esprits ne sont pas mûrs, les cœurs ne sont pas disposés, je
vois bien de la terre et des bras, je ne vois pas une âme détachée du
moi qui gouverne le monde" (1: 262). He has a "fatalisme optimiste"
(1: 260), however, for the future; he is certain that socialism will win
out in the end. Like Albert de Rudolstadt and Jeanne, he is labelled
a poet; this is evoked as well in the speech which ends the novel:
"J'ai mis dans les arbres et dans les fleurs, dans les ruisseaux, dans
les rochers et dans les prairies toute la poésie de mes pensées" (2:
167). The Marquis becomes a kind of oracle for Emile and their improbable friendship develops to such an extent that it even leads to
a reconciliation between the Marquis and Antoine, who had been
estranged for years due to Antoine's affair with the Marquis's wife.
It is the Marquis de Boisguilbault's wealth that is bequeathed to
Emile and Gilberte to found an agricultural commune.[12] Gilberte

is, in fact, the daughter of the Marquise. As W. Karénine pointed out, the resolution of the novel follows a familiar pattern. Sand is indeed using fictional conventions to draw the reader in, but the ultimate purpose is not simply to show virtue rewarded but to bring together those characters who will serve to found the model for a new society.

Antoine's "sin" is kept as a mystery through much of the novel, just as is, at the beginning of the novel, the reason for Jean Jappeloup's not revealing his real name. These aspects of the plot, along with the comic minor characters such as Janille or Galuchet, are likely concessions to the reading public's passion for the popular novel. Numerous flashbacks are used to give background information on the characters and their situations. The story line is so contrived that it is sometimes painfully apparent how the narrator is manipulating the characters' actions in a certain direction. This is the case, for instance, with the elaborate explanations given by the narrator for the—unlikely—chain of events which result in Gilberte entering the Marquis's estate, penetrating into his sanctuary, and seeing the hidden portrait of her mother. There are also surprising twists such as the sudden revelation by Jean Jappeloup that his wife had been an adulteress in just the same way as the Marquis's wife. Such aspects of the story are troublesome, as is the improbable character of the Marquis de Boisguilbault. As in *Le Meunier d'Angibault* there is a constant interplay of realism and fantasy in the novel. But here the improbabilities are more disturbing because of the more concretely based fictional world established, particularly through the depiction of Cardonnet's factory. Contrasted with the description of the practical concerns of establishing a plant powered hydroelectrically are such statements as the assertion that none of the Marquis de Boisguilbault's tenant farmers have ever thought of cheating him even though he does not supervise his estate at all. Benevolent characters generate benevolent behavior. The characters in other Sandian novels are, of course, not paragons of believability either, but novels like *Consuelo* or *Jeanne* are not meant to take place in the real, contemporary world. The action of *Le Péché de M. Antoine* takes place "il y a quelques années" (1: 6) and the reader is led to expect a fictional world more closely resembling contemporary reality. At other times the narrator insists on revealing his presence through awkward or coy statements, as in the passage in which he refuses to reproduce Emile's declaration to Gilberte (1: 275). The ending of *Le Péché de M. Antoine* seems forced as well, with even Cardonnet being included in the grand "fête de famille" at the castle of the Marquis de Boisguilbault. Here once again Sand was sacrificing believability to her message, in this case a symbolic image of social harmony. It is on a small scale a picture of the society which Emile—and George Sand—believed would come about in the future.

7

Friendship Transformed

La Mare au diable and *François le champi*

*Quand même que mon amitié se serait tournée en amour,
quel mal le bon Dieu trouverait-il, au jour d'aujourd'hui
qu'elle est veuve et maîtresse de se marier?*
— *François le champi* (380-81)

"Le public était resté froid devant les premiers chapitres du roman si pompeusement annoncé; il ne se gênait pas pour dire que *le Péché de M. Antoine* était un *Péché de George Sand*."[1] This contemporary judgment largely characterizes the public and critical reaction to George Sand's social novels published in the first half of the 1840s.[2] In fact, *Le Péché de M. Antoine* (1845) was received somewhat more favorably than *Le Meunier d'Angibault* (1845) or *Le Compagnon du Tour de France* (1840), but all were viewed as evidence of a serious decline in Sand's writing. What critics, and presumably ordinary readers, found objectionable in the novels was above all the large dose of socialist theorizing and argumentation they contain. Sand does not hesitate to convert these novels into polemical forums for her ideas; her characters discuss her theories, often at considerable length, and the narrator is always ready to add appropriate commentary. *Le Compagnon* caused a rupture between

Sand and the *Revue des Deux Mondes* which refused to publish the work. Véron, in turn, refused to accept *Le Meunier d'Angibault* for publication in *Le Constitutionnel*. The objection was not that George Sand was using her novels to serve a serious social purpose; indeed the use of the novel as "an instrument for social betterment" was an important consideration in the novel's rise to legitimacy in the 1830s (Iknayan 61). The unfavorable reaction arose not in response to the intent of the novelist but to her method. Part of the problem lay in the fact that the openings of these novels often lead the reader to expect a novel of manners which, however, develops into a *roman à thèse*.[3]

The three novels cited above are set in the country. The same is true of the famous series of *romans champêtres* of the second half of the 1840s, *La Mare au diable* (1846), *François le champi* (1847) and *La petite Fadette* (1848), but the difference in their reception was phenomenal. The rustic novels were greeted with acclaim and became some of Sand's most popular and enduring works. Their stature as classics dates back to at least the time of Proust. Contemporary critics looked with favor on what they considered to be a modern updating of the pastoral tradition; they praised, sometimes in extravagant terms, the idyllic setting and simple and virtuous characters. Moreover, the stories were not marred, as were in the critics' eyes the earlier social novels, by the presence of obvious devices to steer reader reception. Armand de Pontmartin writing in the *Revue des Deux Mondes* can be taken as representative of critical opinion:

> N'est-ce pas une des surprises, des rares bonnes fortunes de notre triste époque littéraire d'avoir vu fleurir sur les gouffres révolutionnaires, au milieu des secousses d'une âme égarée par les passions et les sophismes de son temps, ces trois gracieuses et naïves fleurs des champs, *La Mare au diable, François le Champi* et *La petite Fadette*? Ces trois fraîches pastorales, qu'on dirait écloses, sous un sourire de printemps, dans une imagination calme et recueillie, sont venues fort à propos remplir la lacune que menaçaient d'établir dans le talent et la renommée de Mme Sand ses romans socialistes. (909-10)

Most reviewers echoed this view, often declaring that George Sand had seen the error of her ways and had returned to the fold. Indeed, reading the rustic novels confirms that Sand was using a very different strategy to convey her socialist beliefs. The main characters do not embody the views of the author; there is no talk in these novels of the necessity of establishing an "association" of workers as a model for a new society. Gone too are the multiple story lines; each of the novels discussed in this chapter focuses on just two characters. The action in which they are involved is simple and straight-forward, leading to substantially shorter works.

While the socialist theories are still present, they have been removed from discussion by the characters and are set forth instead in fairly lengthy introductions.[4] These longer introductions play a more important role in directing reader reception than in any of Sand's previous novels. In *La Mare au diable* the action does not begin until the third chapter (Germain's discussion with Père Maurice); the first two chapters center on Sand's theory of art and society and on the condition of the peasants. The first edition of the novel also contained Sand's essay on "Socialisme et Communisme" in the form of an afterword, thus enclosing the unpretentious tale of Germain and Marie in a heavy, theoretical framework. At the end of the first chapter "George Sand" asks the reader's indulgence for her remarks: "Lecteur, pardonnez-moi ces réflexions, et veuillez les accepter en manière de préface. Il n'y en aura point dans l'historiette que je vais vous raconter, et elle sera si courte et si simple que j'avais besoin de m'en excuser d'avance" (12). However, the reader who expects the story to begin at this point must still exercise patience. The second chapter introduces Germain from afar but deals principally with Sand's view of the French peasant. The elaborate prefatory material, introducing such a short, simple story, betrays Sand's consciousness, despite her later claims to the contrary, that she was trying something new in this novel. Her comment on the simplicity of the story cited above is an indication of this awareness as well. At the end of the second chapter there is a similar remark: "Quoique paysan et simple laboureur, Germain s'était rendu compte de ses devoirs et de ses affections. Il me les avait racontés naïvement, clairement, et je l'avais écouté avec intérêt. Quand je l'eus regardé labourer assez longtemps, je me demandai pourquoi son histoire ne serait pas écrite, quoique ce fût une histoire aussi simple, aussi droite et aussi peu ornée que le sillon qu'il traçait avec sa charrue" (24-25). As we shall see, the repeated references to the simplicity and morality of the story were directed at readers and critics looking for an alternative to the long and scandalous popular novels of the day. Sand's relation to the *roman-feuilleton*, however, was typically ambiguous: while opposing most aspects of this type of fiction, she at the same time employed a number of its most characteristic devices. This resembles her use of the *roman intime* in her first novels and of the *roman noir* in the late 1830s.

George Sand was not only reducing the novel to an absolute minimum but also introducing peasant characters into her fiction in a new way. Peasants instead of being simply part of the landscape, functioning as vehicles for establishing the country setting, carry the action. The story is built around events which arise naturally from their lives, not from their connections to characters from higher social classes. Furthermore, the story is told from the point of view of the peasant. This is particularly evident in *François le Champi* and *La petite Fadette* in which actual peasant storytellers relate the tales. *La Mare au Diable*, too, is presented as being "George Sand's" retelling of a story she has heard, as she explains at the end of the novel: "Ici finit l'histoire du mariage de Germain, telle qu'il me l'a raconté lui-même. . . . Je te demande pardon, lecteur ami, de n'avoir pas su te la traduire mieux" (131). While in earlier novels the narrator had assumed the task of "translating" the speech of certain characters; here the narrator frames the whole story in terms the intended reader will be able to understand. The frame narrator of the rustic novels differs from that of Sand's other novels of the 1840s. She ("George Sand") no longer makes her presence known by comments on the characters and digressions on history or society. Rather, after providing the initial orientation in the opening chapters, she allows the story to emerge through the words of the peasant narrator.

The guidance given the reader in the first two chapters relates in large part to the lives of French peasants. It begins with a description and discussion of a Holbein engraving which shows a farmer plowing a field with Death walking alongside. Although the frame narrator uses this image as an example of the negative approach to depicting reality in art, she also sees it as suggesting aspects of the real situation of the peasantry: "Je venais de regarder longtemps et avec une profonde mélancolie le laboureur d'Holbein, et je me promenais dans la campagne, rêvant à la vie des champs et à la destinée du cultivateur. Ces richesses qui couvrent le sol, ces moissons, ces fruits, ces bestiaux orgueilleux qui s'engraissent dans les longues herbes, sont la propriété de quelques-uns et les instruments de la fatigue et de l'esclavage du plus grand nombre" (13). The enslaved condition of the peasant precludes the enjoyment of the beauty of the landscape in which he lives. A distinction is drawn between the peasant who must see living off the land in economic terms and the bourgeois who choose to see everything, including nature, in monetary terms.

The initial perspective is that of the peasant to whom farming means long, back-breaking labor for a small return. In the second chapter ("Le Labour") another perspective emerges in the narrator's reaction to the scene of the farmer (Germain) plowing the field with his son: "Tout cela était beau de force ou de grâce: le paysage, l'homme, l'enfant, les taureaux sous le joug; et malgré cette lutte puissante où la terre était vaincue, il y avait un sentiment de douceur et de calme profond qui planait sur toutes choses" (20). The point of view shifts from the peasant to the artist who finds a poetic beauty in this scene and subsequently in the song Germain sings while plowing. This change in perspective allows the narrator to contrast the situation of the peasant with that of the educated classes:

En voyant ce couple si beau, l'homme et l'enfant, accomplir dans des conditions si poétiques, et avec tant de grâce unie à la force, un travail plein de grandeur et de solennité, je sentis une pitié profonde mêlée à un regret involontaire. Heureux le laboureur! Oui, sans doute, je le serais à sa place, si mon bras, devenu tout d'un coup robuste, et ma poitrine devenue puissante, pouvaient ainsi féconder et chanter la nature, sans que mes yeux cessassent de voir et mon cerveau de comprendre l'harmonie des couleurs

> et des sons, la finesse des tons et la grâce des contours, en un mot
> la beauté mystérieuse des choses! . . . Mais, hélas, cet homme n'a
> jamais compris le mystère du beau, cet enfant ne le comprendra
> jamais! (22-23)

By introducing this double perspective on the peasant's lot, Sand is able to make the reader aware, before the story begins, of real aspects of the peasant's life and of the fact that the educated reader's views on peasants are quite different from those of the peasants themselves. Concurrently, by introducing Germain in the context of Holbein and Virgil, both discussed in the second chapter, she endows her story with a legitimacy based on tradition. This also suggests that Germain is a figure worthy of serious consideration and literary treatment.

Despite the glorification of the peasant in the story of Germain and Marie, he still may seem inferior to the educated classes: "Il manque à cet homme une partie des jouissances que je possède, jouissances immatérielles qui lui seraient bien dues à lui, l'ouvrier du vaste temple que le ciel est assez vaste pour embrasser. Il lui [à cet homme] manque la connaissance de son sentiment. Ceux qui l'ont condamné à la servitude dès le ventre de sa mère, ne pouvant lui ôter la rêverie, lui ont ôté la réflexion" (23-24). According to the Leroux system, the peasant has "sentiment" but lacks "connaissance." For George Sand, however, this still constitutes a condition superior to that of the educated classes; his feelings have not been vitiated by education. Like the eighteenth-century "natural man," Sand's peasants live closer to nature and their feelings are stronger and more authentic. This results in a powerful poetic potential which, however, remains largely dormant: "Un jour viendra où le laboureur pourra être aussi un artiste, sinon pour exprimer (ce qui importera assez peu alors), du moins pour sentir le beau. Croit-on que cette mystérieuse intuition de la poésie ne soit pas en lui déjà à l'état d'instinct et de vague rêverie?" (15-16). The unconscious beauty of Germain's singing embodies this ideal that will be more fully developed in Les Maîtres Sonneurs. Sand could point as well to the proletarian poets she was encouraging as concrete examples of the poetic soul of the working classes.

Once the story starts in the third chapter Sand allows the action to proceed without commentary. Most of the text is dialogue; descriptive passages are short and succinct. The story opens *in media res*: "Germain, lui dit un jour son beau-père, il faut pourtant te décider à reprendre femme" (26). Unlike the socialist novels, the story is no longer filtered through a narrator, but presented directly to the reader by the characters. This adds an immediacy lacking in *Le Péché de M. Antoine*. The openings of both *Le Meunier d'Angibault* and *Le Péché de M. Antoine* use a technique borrowed from the popular novel. The principal characters are not initially identified, being referred to rather as "une forme noire," "le personnage," or "le voyageur." In *La Mare au diable* and the other rustic novels, the characters are immediately and specifically identified. These novels do not contain any mysteries to be solved or "sins" to be revealed; the reader is told everything up front. The opening speech of Père Maurice details Germain's initial situation of being a widower with three children who needs to remarry. For Père Maurice to provide this background information, necessary for the reader, is in keeping with the kind of formal, ritualistic tone of the conversation which recalls earlier forms of literary discourse (the Bible, fairy tales, the pastoral). In that sense, Père Maurice's speech aligns itself more closely with the literary code of the novel than is the case with a similar speech by Marcelle near the beginning of *Le Meunier d'Angibault*. The reader's reception of Père Maurice's speech has been programmed in the first two chapters. In addition to Virgil, the narrator mentions approvingly Goldsmith's *Vicar of Wakefield*. The reader is to expect not a realistic *roman de mœurs* but a kind of apologue. The desired reader reaction—admiration of the character's actions—is also established through this reference.

The story gives ample evidence of the "mission de sentiment et d'amour" Sand is advocating, and it exhibits considerably more overt sentimentalism than the 1845 novels. Its principal source is the role played by Germain's son Pierre in bringing together Germain and Marie. The characters shed a lot of tears in the novel, including Germain. The closing scene of the novel, rejoining once again Germain, Marie and Pierre, calls to mind the eighteenth-century family art of Diderot and Greuze. The reader is invited to enter this world of sentiment, thereby developing an emotional attachment to Germain, a peasant. The language of the story aids the reader's imaginative entry into the peasant world. As the opening sentence shows, Sand makes rich use of the peasant idiom and Berrichon expressions.

The quiet dignity and respect in the patriarchal scene with which the novel opens remain constant throughout the novel. The opening sentence reveals the family link of the two characters. This early reference to family indicates the key role of the family in the series of rustic novels. Family considerations strongly influence Germain and Marie's decisions concerning marriage.[5] If love in the socialist novels was seen in its relation to the lovers' social convictions, here love is placed in the context of the family. We are in either case far from the view of love as an exclusive concern—and right—of the individual, as a powerful force ignoring social groups and conventions. The importance of marriage as the foundation of family life emerges in *Les Noces de campagne*, appended to the end of the novel. Sand generalizes this descriptive piece by stating she is portraying a peasant marriage, "celle de Germain, par exemple" (132). Therefore, the general view of the peasant with which the novel began reappears at the end. The sanctity of the family is evoked as well in the second chapter through the reverential depiction of the plowman (Germain) and his son (Pierre). The depiction of the family places emphasis on the maintenance of harmony and stability. This idea dominates the relationship of Père Maurice's family in which a large number of children and grand-children live and work together with no hint of conflict. This peasant world remains far removed from that of the novels of Balzac and Zola. It was important to Sand to establish the existence of a peasant culture separate from that of the mainstream (middle-class) culture in France because it would provide the basis for future social emancipation. The new society would originate in the common people, not in the middle class.[6]

In Sand's earlier novels only peasants exceptional in some way or who were involved in a love affair with an aristocrat received much attention. In *La Mare au Diable* the whole peasant world constitutes an entity worthy of serious interest. This society embraces the poor as well as the prosperous: "La mère Guillette habitait une chaumière fort pauvre à deux portées de fusil de la ferme. Mais c'était une femme d'ordre et de volonté. Sa pauvre maison était propre et bien tenue, et ses vêtements rapiécés avec soin annonçaient le respect de soi-même au milieu de la détresse" (38). The dignity extended to the entire peasant world in this novel makes such a description seem not as jarring as the similar depiction of Piaulette in *Le Meunier d'Angibault*. The dignified tone of *La Mare au Diable* precludes inclusion of such buffoon types as Cadet in *Jeanne*. Instead there is a gentle humor in the depiction of Germain, which surfaces principally in his relation to his son and in his reaction to being lost in the woods. The humor derives from the images of this burly farmer being ruled by his young son and being shown how to live in the wilderness by the diminutive Marie.

The aspects of the novel we have examined to this point contrast sharply with Sand's previous fiction. In fact, *La Mare au diable*, was written under the influence of Sand's distaste for current literary fashion in France. In a letter Sand wrote to Eugène Delacroix as she was finishing *Le Péché* (September, 1845) and shortly before she was to write *La Mare au diable* (October, 1845) she confessed that she had not read any contemporary novels for quite some time and had recently decided to see what she had been missing. Her reaction was not favorable: "Quel style, quelle grossièreté, quelle emphase ridicule, quelle langue, quels caractères faux, quelle boursouflure de froide passion, de sensiblerie guindée, quelle littérature de fanfarons et de casseurs d'assiettes! Quels héros! . . . *O sancta simplicitas*, où t'es-tu réfugiée!" (*Correspondance* 7: 100). The authors she mentions include Dumas, Sue and Frédéric Soulié, the most successful of the serial novelists.

In the first chapter of *La Mare au diable* ("L'auteur au lecteur") Sand again takes up the subject of popular fiction in explaining her purpose in writing the novel: "Certains artistes de notre temps, jetant un regard sérieux sur ce qui les entoure, s'attachent à peindre la douleur, l'abjection de la misère, le fumier de Lazare. Ceci peut être du domaine de l'art et de la philosophie;

mais, en peignant la misère si laide, si avilie, parfois si vicieuse et si criminelle, leur but est-il atteint, et l'effet en est-il salutaire, comme ils le voudraient?" (8). Sand's remarks are often taken to refer to Balzac's *Paysans* (1844-45), which Sand later claimed was the initial inspiration for her rustic novels, written as an attempt to rectify the negative portrait of the peasant made in Balzac's novels. However, the reference is also to novels by Dumas and Sue, particularly when she speaks of the undesirability of portraying such characters as "le forçat évadé" and "le rôdeur de nuit" (9). This criticism should come as no surprise, considering the reaction Sand expressed to her recent reading of these authors. Sand concedes a serious moral intent to the popular novelists, but she castigates their approach: "Dans cette littérature de mystères d'iniquité, que le talent et l'imagination ont mise à la mode, nous aimons mieux les figures douces et suaves que les scélérats à effet dramatique. Celles-là peuvent entreprendre et amener des conversions, les autres font peur, et la peur ne guérit pas l'égoïsme, elle l'augmente" (9). This is an unmistakable reference to Sue's *Mystères de Paris* and other "mystery" novels.

It is immediately following this last passage that Sand presents the familiar exposition of her own approach, namely that the artist's mission was one "de sentiment et d'amour," that his goal should be "de faire aimer les objets de sa sollicitude" and that art "n'est pas une étude de la réalité positive; c'est une recherche de la vérité idéale" (10-11). The fact that this statement of purpose arises directly from considerations on the popular novel indicates to what degree this confrontation shaped the narrative strategy of *La Mare au diable*. Sand subsequently denied any intent to establish a new kind of novel: "Quand j'ai commencé, par *La Mare au diable*, une série de romans champêtres . . . je n'ai eu aucun système, aucune prétention révolutionnaire en littérature" (1-2). The speed with which she wrote *La Mare au diable*—she claimed it took her four days—points not to the fulfillment of any analytical plan for a new approach to the novel but rather to a sudden burst of creative energy.

George Sand was an instinctive writer who did not engage in extended theorizing about the novel. I thus find it unlikely that, as critics have claimed, Sand was so chagrined by the disappointing reception of her social novels that she consciously developed a new theory of reader activation which resulted in La Mare au diable and the other rustic novels.[7] This is not to say that Sand was unaware that she was striking out in new directions in writing La Mare au diable; the length of the first two chapters which act as a preface confirm that. The approach Sand used in writing La Mare au diable was, I believe, the fruit of a spontaneous, instinctive reaction to the roman-feuilleton. Her own distaste for the excesses and banality of many serial novels, and her own failure to achieve success in this field surely contributed to her reaction. She was also responding to the contemporary discussion in the press on the nature of the novel.

In attacking the roman-feuilleton, George Sand was echoing the opinion of the majority of literary critics. Although critics granted the novel as a new genre a good deal of liberty, they believed the serial novel had abused its privileges and had led to a form of fiction characterized by coarseness and immorality. Critics also accused Sand of jumping onto the roman-feuilleton bandwagon.[8] Concurrently, no one could agree on what direction the French novel should take. Many critics called for novels with the opposite orientation of the serial novel; Marguerite Iknayan found in her study that there were "increasing recommendations for simplicity and naturalness" in the late 1830s (172). In a representative article in Le National in 1844, E. D. Forgues wrote that the tendency he wished to encourage was "celle qui consiste à chercher l'attrait du récit dans sa simplicité même, et à donner au roman toute l'utilité qu'il peut avoir, en lui conservant son caractère de conte moral" (qtd. in Iknayan 124). Other critics advocated a return to older models. In her rediscovery of the pastoral, Sand was thus directing her efforts in the direction favored by critics.

George Sand clearly indicates in her prefatory remarks to La Mare au diable that the story will differ from what the reader is likely to expect, namely shorter and simpler. Indeed, if one compares La Mare au diable to Le Péché de M. Antoine, the simplicity of the story is inescapable. The plot revolves around a handful of characters and the events that surround a short trip taken by the two principal characters. Critics who reviewed the novel favorably were so dumbfounded by the powerful impact of such a simple and straightforward story that they found it impossible to describe what made the novel so riveting. One wrote: "Le charmant roman dont je parle, il échappe par la nature même à l'analyse, car l'imbroglio n'y joue aucun rôle et l'intrigue en est insaisissable" (*Revue indépendante* 338). By contrast, Sand had difficulty finding a title for *Le Péché* because of her indecision as to who the principal character was—Emile Cardonnet, his father, Jean Jappeloup, the Marquis de Boisguilbault or M. Antoine. While *La Mare au diable* only presents characters from farming communities, a variety of social and economic classes are represented in the much longer *Péché*. The story in which these and other characters are involved is much more elaborate, with a complicated interplay of characters and numerous plot twists surrounding a central mystery.

The novel offers an even sharper contrast to such popular blockbusters as *Le Juif Errant* (1844-45) or *Le Comte de Monte-Cristo*. This is the point most reviewers stressed in discussing the novel. The critic of *La Quotidienne* compared *La Mare au diable* to other novels of 1845-46:

> Il n'y a pas d'époque où le dévergondage d'idées, où le mépris de la langue et du goût n'ait été poussés plus loin que dans celle-ci. En 1845, quelques romans obscènes, mauvais livres et mauvaises actions, s'étaient impudemment étalés au bas de quelques journaux, la curiosité publique s'en était emparée et leur avait fait une réputation de scandale. Cette année, l'impudeur et l'immoralité ont été plus loin encore, comme si le roman avait accepté la triste mission de pousser encore à la dissolution et à la dépravation des mœurs. Il semblait qu'après les *Mémoires du Diable*, après les *Mystères de Paris* et après le *Juif-Errant*, il n'y avait plus rien à tenter; des écrivains ont eu le courage d'aller au-delà; le cynisme éhonté de ces livres monstrueux a été dépassé. . . . Parmi les romans qui ont paru cette année, il en est un cependant qui mérite une mention spéciale. . . . *La Mare au diable*, par George Sand, est un petit roman tout simple, sans imprévu, sans intrigue nouée et compliquée. . . . Il y a dans la

lecture de ce petit roman de quoi consoler de bien des mauvais
livres. (*La Quotidienne* 2)

The critic of *La Revue indépendante* proclaimed in a similar vein: "*La Mare au diable* a donc été pour moi une oasis, où je me suis reposé avec d'autant plus de plaisir que je revenais de *Monte-Cristo*, et que j'allais à *Piquillo alliaga*. Un des grands charmes de *La Mare au diable* c'est qu'il n'y a ni aventures ni surprises" (567). It is revealing that both critics describe the novel essentially in terms of what it is not; this is a constant refrain in contemporary reviews.

Critics placed this simple tale of virtuous country life in direct opposition to popular bestsellers which regaled the reader with sex, crime, and adventure. However, a closer reading of the novel reveals a number of similarities.[9] It comes as no surprise that *La Mare au diable* is essentially a love story chronicling the awakening feelings of Germain for Marie. I differ, however, with the view that the centrality of the love intrigue completely overshadows other aspects of the story, reducing them to insignificance.[10] One major theme of popular fiction of the July Monarchy—the corrupting power of money—is clearly in evidence in *La Mare au diable*. This theme manifests itself in the repugnant behavior of the rich widow Catherine Guèrin and her father, which is savagely ridiculed, and, in particular, in the rich Ormeaux farmer's attempted seduction of Marie. The contrast between these immoral "semi-bourgeois" and the impoverished but virtuous Marie is one of the major aspects of the story; the economic disparity adds dramatic interest to the climax of the story, namely the confrontation between the Belair characters and those of Fourche.

In the first chapter Sand had already discussed the corrupting influence that money had on the enjoyment of life in the country: "L'homme de loisir n'aime en général pour eux-mêmes, ni les champs, ni les prairies, ni le spectacle de la nature, ni les animaux superbes qui doivent se convertir en pièces d'or pour son usage. L'homme de loisir vient chercher un peu d'air et de santé dans le séjour de la campagne, puis il retourne dépenser dans les grandes villes le fruit du travail de ses vassaux" (12). The economic structure of agriculture forces the peasant to have the same overriding concern with money: "De son côté, l'homme du travail est trop accablé, trop malheureux, et trop effrayé de l'avenir, pour jouir de la beauté des campagnes et des charmes de la vie rustique. Pour lui aussi les champs dorés, les belles prairies, les animaux superbes, représentent des sacs d'écus dont il n'aura qu'une faible part, insuffisante à ses besoins, et que, pourtant, il faut remplir, chaque année, ces sacs maudits, pour satisfaire le maître et payer le droit de vivre parcimonieusement et misérablement sur son domaine" (13). It is in this economic context that nature is viewed in the rustic novels, namely as a place which offers escape from this plague of modern civilization. This is the sense in which Sand's view of nature—which immediately follows the passage above—should be viewed: "La nature est éternellement jeune, et généreuse. Elle verse la poésie et la beauté à tous les êtres, à toutes les plantes, qu'on laisse s'y développer à souhait. Elle possède le secret du bonheur, et nul n'a su le lui ravir" (13). Nature's generosity thus stands in contrast to the greed characterizing French society as a whole.

The character in the novel who most clearly embodies this idea is Marie, the shepherdess. When Marie and Germain are trapped in the forest by the pond Germain remains virtually helpless while Marie knows how to use nature to supply their needs. Her utter selflessness also reveals the closeness to nature; she goes so far as to offer to take care of Germain's children after he is married should his new wife have no interest in children. Not surprisingly, Marie is also poor. She makes quite clear to Germain the socioeconomic gulf between them: "Je ne suis pas habituée, comme vous, à faire quatre repas, et j'ai été tant de fois me coucher sans souper, qu'une fois de plus ne m'étonne guère" (72). She even mocks his semi-bourgeois habits: "Vous voudriez du vin, pas vrai? Il vous faudrait peut-être du café? Vous vous croyez à la foire sous la ramée! Appelez l'aubergiste: de la liqueur au fin laboureur de Belair" (74). While Marie tells Germain that she can not think of marrying because she has no money, this does not cause her any concern. Quite clearly we have here a concept complimentary to that of money's corruption, namely the purifying effect of indifference to money. This does not mean, however, that all the well-to-do characters in Sand's novel are corrupt. One need only point to

Germain's father-in-law; he wants Germain to remarry rich if possible but is easily persuaded to allow him to marry the penniless Marie. Money corrupts if the individual allows it to play a central role in his life and to influence moral choices. As in popular fiction, greed is the root of much evil.

One of the principal aspects of popular fiction which dismayed critics was the treatment of sexual mores. While this is not evoked as melodramatically and openly in *La Mare au diable* as it is, for example, in *Les Mystères de Paris*, it nevertheless contains a strong sexual undercurrent. This is most evident in the events which occur at the "mare au diable," the name hinting at the possibility of infernal temptation. The narrator had previously alerted the reader to the potential for a sexual encounter between the two by providing a long justification of the propriety of Germain taking a young unmarried girl on a trip. Germain finds it very difficult to control his sudden passion for Marie while he watches her sleep. After trying to kiss her as she sleeps, he vows to control his urges: "Germain passa de l'autre côté du feu, et jura à Dieu qu'il n'en bougerait jusqu'à ce qu'elle fût réveillée. Il tint parole, mais ce ne fut pas sans peine. Il crut qu'il en deviendrait fou" (92). Marie faces more imminent danger from the Ormeaux farmer who immediately tries to seduce her when she starts to work for him. While running away from him she tears her clothes to shreds.

The fight between the Ormeaux farmer and Germain—itself a fixture of popular fiction—is more than a chivalrous act on Germain's part: it is a bitter struggle between sexual rivals.[11] Sand even adds a symbolic act of sexual victory: Germain "ramassa le bâton de houx du fermier, le brisa sur son genou pour lui montrer la force de ses poignets, et en jeta les morceaux au loin avec mépris" (131). Germain asks Marie afterwards if he has not sufficiently demonstrated his virility: "Je te prierai de te demander à toi-même si, quand il s'agit de défendre une femme et de punir un insolent, un homme de vingt-huit ans n'est pas trop vieux?" (134-35). The age difference and Marie's view of Germain as "un oncle ou un parrain" (99) also add a hint of incest which then becomes quite distinct in *François le champi*.[12]

Contemporary critics found this to be the one objectionable aspect of the novel. Indeed, most refused to acknowledge the presence of these scenes, as in the following resumé of the story from *La Revue indépendante*: "Devant le feu où Marie échauffe le petit Pierre, Germain devient insensiblement amoureux de la jeune fille, et finit, avant que le jour paraisse, par l'aimer comme un fou. Il va, pour l'acquit de sa conscience, faire une visite au père de la veuve à marier, lui achète une paire de bœufs, s'en revient libre comme devant, et fait enfin consentir la petite Marie à l'épouser" (339). Sainte-Beuve omits the all-important scenes in Fourche as well in his review in *Le Constitutionnel*.

Reviewers preferred to dwell on Germain's marriage proposal. In fact the wedding receives considerable attention in the appendix "Noces de campagne." This adds further and final emphasis to the value of family life which the narrator continually evokes in the novel, particularly in the scenes in which Germain's seven-year-old son plays a role. The trip with Germain and Pierre allows Marie to prove herself as a potential wife and mother by demonstrating her love of children, her instinctive ability to deal with them lovingly but effectively, her resourcefulness and her generous dose of common sense. Here, too, Sand is following in the footsteps of the popular novelists who typically espoused traditional moral values. Critics have recognized, however, that what in effect was signaled to the reader was not the final message but the dangers that placed moral and sexual purity in doubt (Neuschäfer 26). The popularity of these novels rests not on the domesticating conclusions but on the liberating expositions. It is in this sense that Sand's rustic novels offered, like popular fiction, a form of escapism, a chance for the reader to live momentarily a different life. This was one of the aspects that contemporary critics stressed as a reason for the novel's success. These critics were thinking above all of the rustic setting which offered as exotic a setting to the bourgeois Parisian reader as the criminal underworld of Sue's novels or the adventurous exploits of Dumas's characters.

George Sand intended her rustic novels to convey a social message to the reader, and she makes this abundantly clear in her prefaces. In this respect, too, Sand resembles the popular novelists like Sue who often incorporated their own social visions into their novels. A recent study of serial novels of 1844 shows how frequently these novels end with a typically Sandian scene: social harmony established, or re-established, between different social groups (Neuschäfer *et al* 123). This is of course an important element in *La Mare au diable* and in *La petite Fadette*.

Yet George Sand herself saw her approach to enlightening the public as diametrically opposed to that of popular novelists. Instead of jolting the reader into recognition of the problems of the poor by graphically depicting their miserable existence, she prefers to convert the hard-hearted by showing the superior moral existence of simple peasants. Although Germain may be ignorant by Parisian standards, Sand asserts in the second chapter, he still rises above the fictional bourgeois reader she portrays: "Eh bien! tel qu'il est, incomplet et condamné à une éternelle enfance, il est encore plus beau que celui chez qui la science a étouffé le sentiment. Ne vous élevez pas au-dessus de lui, vous autres qui vous croyez investis du droit légitime et imprescriptible de lui commander, car cette erreur effroyable où vous êtes prouve que votre esprit a tué votre cœur, et que vous êtes les plus incomplets et les plus aveugles des hommes!" (24). The story of Germain and Marie is designed to bring out this truth of the heart pointing to the importance of "sentiment" in Pierre Leroux's theory of man's progression towards perfection.

This message—in contrast to earlier novels like *Le Péché*—must emerge from the story itself since there is no longer a narrator commenting on the action and putting forth social and economic theories. The reader, after being given an initial orientation in the preface, is left to his own devices. Sand engages in the practice of popular novelists who, instead of introducing didactic passages, as Sand had done in her social novels, simply added dialogue to fill the quota of words for the next installment. She was also following the guidelines laid down by critics in the literary *feuilletons* of the day. Critics generally agreed that the novel should have a serious purpose but should not display it too openly. In fact, one major reason why critics praised *La Mare au diable* so enthusiastically was that they largely ignored the preface and afterword and did not acknowledge any social message emerging from the novel. The sole critics to discuss the socialist intention of the author were Sainte-Beuve and the critic of the socialist *Le Populaire*. The latter virtually ignored the novel and concentrated instead on a discussion of "Socialisme et Communisme." The former lamented the presence of the preface and did not see any connection between it and the novel proper. It was only after all three rustic novels appeared that critics like Sainte-Beuve began to see a pattern and voiced reservations about the socialist implications of the novel.

George Sand's rustic novels were received so favorably in the press because they followed the recommendations of the majority of critics and because they offered a viable alternative to the serial novel. Sand conveyed legitimacy on her literary experiment by evoking an older tradition, that of the pastoral. She cites pastoral works and authors freely in her prefaces to demonstrate her link to the genre. This was favorably viewed by critics who were searching for a new foundation for the novel to try to wrench away the hold the serial novel had taken on the readers' taste.

However, these factors could hardly have been telling with the general public. It was in considerable part precisely the incorporation of aspects of popular fiction that fed the taste of the public. The very title of *La Mare au diable*, as one critic objected, led to reader expectations centering on the *roman-feuilleton* (*Le National* 1). In fact, Sand's novel let readers have it both ways. They could pat themselves on the back in enjoying this simple, pastoral tale with its naive-virtuous characters, thus demonstrating their own moral stance and in the process joining in the critics' condemnation of the *roman-feuilleton*. At the same time they could indulge themselves in what the novel offered in the way of sexual innuendo, in the promise of freedom from economic tyranny and in escape from the pressures of modern society.

❖   ❖   ❖

Many of the ideas set forth in the first two chapters of *La Mare au diable* reappear in the "avant-propos" to the *François le champi*. The prefatory material takes the form of a dialogue between

"George Sand" and R., representing François Rollinat, and peasant life once again provides the principal focus. The praise of the instinctive life of the peasants is carried further than in *La Mare au Diable*. R. even expresses the desire to be a peasant: "Je voudrais être paysan; le paysan qui ne sait pas lire, celui à qui Dieu a donné de bons instincts, une organisation paisible, une conscience droite; et je m'imagine que, dans cet engourdissement des facultés inutiles, dans cette ignorance des goûts dépravés, je serais aussi heureux que l'homme primitif rêvé par Jean-Jacques" (210). Less emphasis is placed on the notion that the peasant's life is incomplete and needs to be supplemented by "connaissance." For R. the peasant's ability to experience reality directly and intuitively is a distinct advantage: "Je voudrais . . . ne jamais penser à la musique quand j'écoute le vent, à la poésie quand j'admire et goûte l'ensemble. Je voudrais jouir de tout par l'instinct, parce que ce grillon me paraît plus joyeux et plus enivré que moi" (210). R.'s education forces him to have what Schiller called a sentimental relationship to reality: "J'essaie de me placer au sein de ce mystère de la vie rustique et naturelle, moi civilisé, qui ne sais pas jouir par l'instinct seul, et qui suis toujours tourmenté du désir de rendre compte aux autres et à moi-même de ma contemplation ou de ma méditation" (206). While the peasant experiences life directly and instinctively, R. and others of the educated classes encounter it vicariously by filtering their perceptions through their need to analyze and communicate.

The coloring of country life through the eyes of urban civilization is the origin of the pastoral which is seen as "le rêve, l'idéal de tous les hommes et de tous les temps" (212). Folk art surpasses this artificial literature: "Il y a certaines complaintes bretonnes, faites par des mendiants, qui valent tout Goethe et tout Byron, en trois couplets, et qui prouvent que l'appréciation du vrai et du beau a été plus spontanée et plus complète dans ces âmes simples que dans celles des plus illustres poètes" (211). As she had done in the first two chapters of *La Mare au diable*, Sand is tailoring her theory of art in this introduction to prepare the reader for the tale that is to follow. On the one hand, the principal characters of this novel incorporate to a greater extent than those of *La Mare au Diable* the instinctive side of the peasant character. François, the *champi*, embodies this idea because of his total lack of education; he grows up in an isolated environment largely untouched by society. On the other hand, the elevation of folk art prepares the reader for the folk tale that follows. It is a story about peasants told by peasants. The interruptions in the narration keep calling the reader's attention to this fact. For instance, at one point an extended discussion over the use of the word "secousse" serves to underscore the oral nature of the tale as well as the picturesqueness of the language.

The use of peasant narrators is intended to overcome a problem that R. points to in *Jeanne*: "Tu peins une fille des champs, tu l'appelles *Jeanne*, et tu mets dans sa bouche des paroles qu'à la rigueur elle peut dire. Mais toi, romancier, qui veux faire partager à tes lecteurs l'attrait que tu éprouves à peindre ce type, tu la compares à une druidesse, à Jeanne d'Arc, que sais-je? Ton sentiment et ton langage font avec les siens un effet disparate comme la rencontre de tons criards dans un tableau; et ce n'est pas ainsi que je peux entrer tout à fait dans la nature, même en l'idéalisant" (215-16). While *La Mare au Diable* resolves this problem to a certain extent, there are still occasional clashes between the peasant world and that of the narrator. The use of peasant narrators avoids this conflict while allowing deeper penetration into authentic peasant culture. In this case two perspectives are given since the story is told first by the servant of the local priest and then by the *chanvreur* (hemp-breaker): "Le chanvreur a conté des histoires jusqu'à deux heures du matin. La servante du curé l'aidait ou le reprenait; c'était une paysanne un peu cultivée; lui, un paysan inculte, mais heureusement doué et fort éloquent à sa manière" (216-17). The *chanvreur* figures more prominently in Sand's peasant world as a storyteller; she intended to combine the three rustic novels under the title "Les Veillées du chanvreur." That they are presented as *veillées*, tales orally transmitted, emphasizes their character as folk literature.

Nevertheless, the author still had to resolve the problem of making the novel's language authentic yet understandable. R. suggests a compromise: "Raconte-moi l'histoire du *Champi*, non pas telle que je l'ai entendue avec toi. C'était un chef-d'œuvre de narration pour nos esprits et pour nos oreilles du terroir. Mais raconte-la-moi comme si tu avais à ta droite un Parisien parlant la langue moderne, et à ta gauche un paysan devant lequel tu ne voudrais pas dire une phrase, un mot où il ne pourrait pas pénétrer. Ainsi tu dois parler clairement pour le Parisien, naïvement pour le paysan" (217). *François le champi* contains a greater number of dialectal forms than *La Mare au Diable* but, in contrast to the use of such expressions in earlier works, in this novel they are not footnoted.[13] Sand wanted the reader to take part in the world of the characters as fully as possible and she eliminated any aspects of the work which could detract from that goal. The same formal, ritualistic language employed by the characters in *La Mare au diable* also appears in this novel. Set phrases and formulae are repeated, such as the resuming statement, "il fit comme il disait" (363). While the style introduces an exotic element, it also creates the impression that this is a kind of sacerdotal text which is being passed on to successive generations. The fact that there are two narrators who are able to tell the same story indicates that it is to be seen as a fundamental text of peasant culture. The story of the *champi* marrying his "mother" thus assumes an exemplary character.

George Sand succeeded more in creating a believable language for her narrator than for her characters. The conversations between François and Madeleine tend to exhibit sentimental and rhetorical excesses. Occasionally, it is clearly the author's language that the characters are speaking. François's language level frequently exceeds what one might reasonably expect from an uneducated foundling. He initially says very little and is thought to be a simpleton. Shortly thereafter, however, he gives a long speech in reaction to la Zabelle's attempt to take him away to the orphanage: "Tu veux donc que je meure du chagrin de ne plus te voir? Qu'est-ce que je t'ai fait pour que tu ne m'aimes plus? Est-ce que je ne t'ai pas toujours obéi dans tout ce que tu m'as commandé? Est-ce que j'ai fait du mal? . . . Garde-moi, je t'en prie comme on prie le bon Dieu! J'aurai toujours soin de toi; je travaillerai toujours pour toi; si tu n'es pas contente de moi, tu me battras et je ne dirai rien; mais attends pour me renvoyer que j'aie fait quelque chose de mal" (245-46). This is excerpted from a larger speech. Unexpected are both François's language and the length of his speech, which require the reader to assume that François possesses a kind of natural gift for language.

Besides his simplicity, François also possesses certain natural insights and abilities. When Madeleine tells him not to let her son Jeannie pull his hair, François responds with precocious wisdom: "J'aime mieux souffrir le mal que de le rendre" (238). There is something more to this than Sand's inability to portray realistically a child's thoughts and words. She is clearly out to make a point with this portrait. François as a "champi"—his last name is Fraise— is presented literally as a child of nature and as such is free from the contaminating forces of society. Rousseau's influence looms large in this novel. François is in the innocent state before the fall: "François était le garçon le plus innocent de la terre. . . . Il arriva donc en âge de quinze ans sans connaître la moindre malice, sans avoir l'idée du mal, sans que sa bouche eût jamais répété un vilain mot, et sans que ses oreilles l'eussent compris" (262-63). François is also superior to his peers in other ways: "Il était clair pour tout le monde que le champi était bon sujet, très laborieux, très serviable, plus fort, plus dispos et plus raisonnable que tous les enfants de son âge" (254). He also has the special gift shared by the "paysans illuminés" of earlier novels: he is able to sense what the future will bring. He thus anticipates shortly before it happens the forced separation between himself and Madeleine. Like Patience (*Mauprat*), François learns to read and evinces a keen interest in learning.

The point Sand is making with François, however, is different from that she makes in portraying characters such as Patience or Jeanne. François is not a prophet pointing the way for the lower classes to a new society. In her rustic novels Sand is more concerned with the here and now and with problems of social interaction and acceptance. Larger questions relating to the structure of society and the kind of social units which the future will bring, concerns which provided the central focus of her socialist novels, are not directly addressed. Specific issues are raised, as is here the problem of orphans or that of property ownership through the account of the land speculations surrounding Blanchet's death. The root cause of these problems is greed, which Sand considers as the plague of every stratum of nineteenth-century French society. It comes as no surprise that, as in previous novels, the largest share of blame accrues to the rich. According to Madeleine they are responsible for the precarious situation of *champis*: "S'il y a des gens assez malheureux pour ne pouvoir pas élever leurs enfants eux-mêmes, c'est la faute aux riches qui ne les assistent pas" (261). The poor themselves are not responsible; it is rather the injustice of the social system and the egotism of the rich which are at fault.

The point is made repeatedly that, if François is more virtuous and harder-working than other "champis," it is because he has not been mistreated. Having had the good fortune of falling into the hands of two caring women, François has been able to develop his innate qualities and abilities. Unlike Jeanne, François is not really endowed with special gifts or powers, he is simply an uncorrupted "natural man." Given this, it is not surprising that François feels uncomfortable in the company of other children: "Il n'était pas pressé d'aller courir avec ceux qui le traitaient bien vite de champi, puisque avec eux il se trouvait tout d'un coup, et sans savoir pourquoi, comme un étranger" (263). Nurtured in nature, François is rejected by the blind prejudice of society. *Champis* are viewed by the other characters as thieves (Catherine) or the offspring of the devil (Blanchet). François himself takes pride in his origin; he later tells Madeleine's sister-in-law that he will always be a *champi* and does not hesitate to let others know it. In the novels of the 1840s Sand insisted on showing characters with low social origins who were proud of their class and its culture. The overwhelmingly positive portrait of François is a celebration of the virtues and potentials of the lowest rungs of society and a critique of those who, born with all possible material advantages, do not measure up to the model conduct of this unabashed *champi*. François's rejection by others only strengthens his love for the women who bring him up.

François reserves his deepest love for Madeleine, and this bond develops and evolves in the course of the novel. As Anne Bergen has pointed out, Sand was depicting in this relationship what she considered the ideal form of love, that between son and mother. For Madeleine, too, love represents a commodity more precious than life itself. When she rescues François from being sent away she exclaims: "On me tuera si l'on veut, j'achète cet enfant-là,

il est à moi, il n'est plus à vous. Vous ne méritez pas de garder un enfant d'un aussi grand cœur, et qui vous aime tant. C'est moi qui serai sa mère, et il faudra bien qu'on le souffre. On peut tout souffrir pour ses enfants" (247).

As in previous novels, such "adoptions" are taken seriously by Sand. The fact that she "buys" François from la Zabelle demonstrates, as do François's actions after his inheritance, that in the right hands and spent in the right spirit money can do good. Like François's, Madeleine's good deeds are second nature. The narrator tells us in this instance that "Madeleine disait ces paroles-là sans trop savoir ce qu'elle disait" (247). Under the inspiration of the moment she experiences a sudden surge of strength: "Elle se mit à marcher vers le moulin avec autant de courage qu'un soldat qui va au feu. Et, sans songer que l'enfant était lourd et qu'elle était si faible qu'à peine pouvait-elle porter son petit Jeannie, elle traversa le petit pont" (248). The quasi-supernatural aura surrounding this act recalls Consuelo.

Mysticism here takes a different form, however, as the conclusion of this episode shows: "L'enfant devenait si pesant qu'elle fléchissait et que la sueur lui coulait du front. Elle se sentit comme si elle allait tomber dans faiblesse, et tout d'un coup il lui revint à l'esprit une belle et merveilleuse histoire qu'elle avait lue, la veille, dans son vieux livre de la Vie des Saints; c'était l'histoire de saint Christophe portant l'enfant Jésus pour lui faire traverser la rivière et le trouvant si lourd, que la crainte l'arrêtait" (248). Madeleine's inspired actions are not only innate, they derive from her profound religious beliefs. It is not a religion based on church attendance and adherence to Catholic dogma, it is a highly personal and naive religious belief, rooted in folk beliefs. Indeed, Sand advocated this kind of religion in Consuelo and La comtesse de Rudolstadt. Not only does Madeleine's faith give her strength, but it also has endowed her with at least the symbolic ability to bestow life; after fainting, François is revived by Madeleine: "Madeleine, réchauffant sa tête contre son cœur, lui soufflait sur le visage et dans la bouche comme on fait aux noyés" (249). While Madeleine is not responsible for François's birth, she is the source of his rebirth.

Although much of Madeleine's piety is natural, it is also, as with François, seen in its social context. The context is, however, not that of society as a whole, but that of the marital relationship. As in the other rustic novels, Sand shows very little of French society beyond the family. As Josef Mayr points out, the rustic novels relinquish all claim to represent the totality of French society; this affords the reader considerable freedom to incorporate this partial reality into a broader social world (10). Madeleine is married to a brutal, unfeeling man who, like Indiana's husband, suddenly loses interest in his wife. Her piety is a reaction to this situation: "Madeleine avait remis son âme à Dieu, et, trouvant inutile de se plaindre, elle souffrait comme si cela lui était dû. Elle avait retiré son cœur de la terre, et rêvait souvent du paradis comme une personne qui serait bien aise de mourir" (236). She subsequently becomes "meilleure chrétienne peut-être qu'une religieuse" (252). Her actions come to resemble those of a saint: "Madeleine pouvait . . . se priver de ses propres aises, et donner à ceux qu'elle savait malheureux autour d'elle, un jour un peu de bois, un autre jour une partie de son repas, et un autre jour encore quelques légumes, du linge, des œufs, que sais-je? Elle venait à bout d'assister son prochain, et quand les moyens lui manquaient, elle faisait de ses mains l'ouvrage des pauvres gens, et empêchait que la maladie ou la fatigue ne les fît mourir" (267). Rejected by her husband, Madeleine discovers that her faith enables her to find a useful role to play in society. She is able to undo some of the evil caused by her husband's actions. Unlike Indiana, Madeleine does not take refuge in a life of complete isolation and relative self-indulgence but devotes herself to the service of others. This resembles the depiction of Marcelle in *Le Meunier d'Angibault*.

François freely accepts Madeleine's self-sacrifices and devotion to her fellow man: "Le champi voyait tout cela, et le trouvait tout simple; car, par son naturel aussi bien que par l'éducation qu'il recevait de Madeleine, il se sentait porté au même goût et au même devoir" (268). The "education" that François receives from Madeleine not only focuses on practical matters, but it also derives from their reading of the Bible and the Lives of the Saints. They continuously read the same works, share their thoughts and feelings, and

often focus on the same idea, but "elle est si retournée, si bien goûtée et digérée, que l'esprit qui la tient est mieux nourri et mieux portant, à lui tout seul, que trente mille cervelles remplies de vents et de fadaises" (265). This statement clearly praises Sand's own novel and parodies the popular novel. The result of their readings has a bearing on the process of reading *François le champi*: "Or donc, ces deux personnes-là vivaient contentes de ce qu'elles avaient à consommer en fait de savoir, et elles le consommaient tout douce-ment, s'aidant l'une l'autre à comprendre et à aimer ce qui fait qu'on est juste et bon. Il leur venait par là une grande religion et un grand courage, et il n'y avait pas de plus grand bonheur pour elles que de se sentir bien disposées pour tout le monde, et d'être d'accord en tout temps et en tout lieu, sur l'article de la vérité et la volonté de bien agir" (266). Their reading serves as an intratextual justification of Sand's simple story and as a model for the reader's reception of the novel. Flashy events and characters (resulting in "trente mille cervelles remplies de vents et de fadaises") quickly fade in comparison with a few and simple elements which encour-age the love of justice and virtue. *François le champi* is a modern version of the *Lives of the Saints*.

If religion is Madeleine's refuge from her unhappy marriage, it also strengthens her love for François. The romantic code of love was, after all, intertwined with religion.[14] Their reading of the lives of the saints brings them closer together by inspiring them with the same thoughts. Madeleine's feelings toward François soon become intertwined with her religious faith, as evident in her reaction to her husband's order that François leave the mill:

> Elle s'en fut au bout de l'écluse du moulin, dans un recoin de terrain que la course des eaux avait mangé tout autour, et où il avait poussé tant de rejets et de branchages sur les vieilles souches d'arbres, qu'on ne s'y voyait point à deux pas. C'était là qu'elle allait souvent dire ses raisons au bon Dieu, parce qu'elle n'y était pas dérangée et qu'elle pouvait s'y tenir cachée derrière les grandes herbes folles, comme une poule d'eau dans son nid de vertes brindilles. Sitôt qu'elle y fut, elle se mit à deux genoux pour faire une bonne prière, dont elle espérait grand confort;

mais elle ne put songer à autre chose qu'au pauvre champi qu'il
fallait renvoyer et qui l'aimait tant qu'il en mourrait de chagrin.
Si bien qu'elle ne put rien dire au bon Dieu, sinon qu'elle était
trop malheureuse de perdre son seul soutien et de se départir de
l'enfant de son cœur. (289)

The proximity to the water—which so often in Sand has erotic over-
tones—also relates to Madeleine's praying to God. As in *Valentine*
religious feelings and love reinforce one another. François and
Madeleine initially meet by the fountain near the mill and this spot
becomes a kind of shrine to their relationship to which they return
at the end of the novel, when their love has changed character. In
François's thoughts, too, religious images become enmeshed with
his sudden passion for Madeleine: "Voilà que tout d'un coup François la vit toute jeune et la trouva belle comme la bonne dame, et
que le cœur lui sauta comme s'il avait monté au faîte d'un clocher.
Et il s'en alla coucher dans son moulin. . . . Quand il fut là tout seul,
il se mit à trembler et à étouffer comme de fièvre. Et si, il n'était
malade que d'amour, car il venait de se sentir brûlé pour la première fois par une grande bouffée de flamme, ayant toute sa vie
chauffée doucement sous la cendre" (392). The "bonne dame" is the
Virgin Mary.

It is not surprising that Madeleine finds solace in nature
when she is troubled; the novel makes it clear that François and
Madeleine are in tune with nature and out of step with society. It is,
of course, their piety and virtue which set them apart from others.
While society censures Madeleine's relation with François, God
blesses it: "Madeleine embrassa le champi dans le même esprit de
religion que quand il était petit enfant. Pourtant si le monde l'eût
vu, on aurait donné raison à M. Blanchet de sa fâcherie, et on aurait
critiqué cette honnête femme qui ne pensait point à mal, et à qui la
vierge Marie ne fit point péché de son action" (297-98). There is a
clear division in the novel into two groups of characters. Opposed
to François and Madeleine are her husband Cadet Blanchet and
his mistress La Sévère, who represent completely different values.
As Madeleine becomes more saintly, he becomes more corrupt:
"Comme il engraissait, qu'il devenait dérangé et n'aimait plus le

travail, il chercha son aubaine dans des marchés de peu de foi et dans un petit maquignonnage d'affaires qui l'aurait enrichi s'il ne se fût mis à dépenser d'un côté ce qu'il gagnait de l'autre. Sa concubine prit chaque jour plus de maîtrise sur lui" (251). La Sévère plays the role of an evil witch; having destroyed Blanchet, she endeavors to ruin Madeleine as well. She was responsible for persuading Blanchet to force François to leave the mill, after he had rebuffed her attempts to seduce him. As in the previous novels, the good characters group together naturally, as do those representing evil. Here, for example, Madeleine and Jeannette, the daughter of François's second master, instantly become good friends and mutual confidantes as soon as they meet.

Jeannette, in fact, plays an important role at the end of the novel, breaking the news to Madeleine of François's desire to marry her. Madeleine has a surprisingly easy time changing her relationship with François from mother to lover. While Consuelo undergoes a similar transformation, her case involved a long process capped by a formal initiation ceremony. Madeleine's transformation only requires a brief conversation with Jeannette. The shift is all the more sudden in that, shortly before, Madeleine had rejected the idea of that kind of relationship between her and François as the devil's work. Although she initially believes François wants to marry her only out of a sense of duty, she quickly accepts the fact that he passionately loves her.

Once the idea of transformation in François's love is raised—in typical Sandian fashion—through an overheard conversation, it is equally swift: "Quand même que mon amitié se serait tournée en amour, quel mal le bon Dieu y trouverait-il, au jour d'aujourd'hui qu'elle est veuve et maîtresse de se marier?" (380). The reference to God's approbation corresponds to the important role religion plays in the relationship between François and Madeleine. Sand's insistence on the piousness of the principal characters derived from a desire to forestall a possible adverse reaction to the marriage. She has the narrator prepare the reader for what is coming through the inserted comment of one of the "listeners" of the story: "ça va donc tourner en histoire d'amour" (273). Sand did not hesitate either to blur the characters' ages to make their union less unseemly;

Madeleine ages more slowly than François. There is also the sense that François "earns" the right to marry Madeleine, in a similar fashion to Bernard Mauprat or Emile Cardonnet. After Blanchet's death François appears at the mill just in time to save Madeleine from the clutches of the evil la Sévère. He literally saves her life, nursing her back to health, before he successfully saves her property. Marrying Madeleine—and saving her reputation—can be seen as a logical extension of his role.

As in *Le Péché de M. Antoine* and *Le Meunier d'Angibault*, virtue is financially rewarded. François inherits 4000 francs, making him a wealthy man. François the *champi* as astute businessman raises further the question of *vraisemblance* in the novel. The preface brings up the question of realism in connection with the portrayal of rural life in literature:

> On n'arrive pas au vrai encore. Il n'est pas plus dans le réel enlaidi que dans l'idéal pomponné; mais on le cherche, cela est évident, et, si on le cherche mal, on n'en est que plus avide de le trouver. Voyons: le théâtre, la poésie et le roman ont quitté la houlette pour prendre le poignard, et quand ils mettent en scène la vie rustique, ils lui donnent un certain caractère de réalité qui manquait aux bergeries du temps passé. Mais la poésie n'y est guère, et je m'en plains; et je ne vois pas encore le moyen de relever l'idéal champêtre sans le farder ou le noircir. (215)

Sand wanted to give a reasonably faithful portrait of rural life, which meant including the negative aspects as well as the positive, hence the presence of Blanchet and la Sévère. She rejected the kind of treatment of peasant life to be found in Balzac's *Paysans* as exaggerating the negative: "Nous ne nous sommes pas tellement passionnés pour le vrai dans ces derniers temps, que nos arts et notre littérature soient en droit de mépriser ces types de convention plutôt que ceux que la mode inaugure. Nous sommes aujourd'hui à l'énergie et à l'atrocité, et nous brodons sur le canevas de ces passions des ornements qui seraient d'un terrible à faire dresser les cheveux sur la tête, si nous pouvions les prendre au sérieux" (214). The decidedly negative vision of Balzac's rural novel and of the

roman-feuilleton are for Sand simply a literary fashion or convention, having no more intrinsic value or justification than any other approach, such as the pastoral. Emphasizing the positive is as realistic as its opposite. When asked at the end of the novel if the story is true, the *chanvreur* replies: "Si elle ne l'est pas, elle le pourrait être" (403). This is an affirmation of the universal truth of the story. While the events may be staged and the characters almost caricatures, Sand affirms that the fundamental message of the characters' lives is valid.

The approach Sand embraced in writing *François le champi* was aimed at achieving a specific effect on the reader. The lack of realism and the sentimentality in *François le champi* relate closely to Sand's specific narrative strategy for her rustic novels. In the preface Sand expresses admiration for Nodier's precise and realistic narrative skill but explains that she does not have the technical skill ("science") of Nodier and therefore "il faut que j'invoque le sentiment" (219). The characters in *François le champi* and *La Mare au diable* express their feelings openly and freely; a number of scenes in *François le champi* (la Zabelle's attempt to send François away, his homecoming, Madeleine's attempt to marry him to Madeleinette) are structured to reach an emotional climax. The display of feelings not only "humanizes" these peasants but also draws the reader emotionally into the fictional world. The genre represented here is not the realistic novel but the pastoral. It is within this tradition that George Sand's rustic novels are best understood and appreciated.

8

Other Winds Blowing

Celebrating Change in *La petite Fadette* and *Les Maîtres Sonneurs*

*Elle a des goûts et des idées qui ne sont pas du terrain où elle
a fleuri, et il faut qu'un autre vent la secoue.*
—*Les Maîtres Sonneurs* (316)

In the aftermath of the 1848 revolution, Sand's discouragement was accompanied by bitterness: "J'ai du chagrin de ce qui
s'est passé, de ce qui se passera peut-être, *je boude*. Je boude contre
le peuple, contre le parti, contre ma cause, contre moi-même si vous
voulez" (*Correspondance* 9: 801). Sand's letters to Mazzini in 1850
show profound discouragement with the state of society and pessimism concerning the future. Given the current state of affairs she
no longer exhibited any desire to write fiction; if the public did not
react to real events, how could she expect her fiction to have any effect.[1] In the 1850s her attention was directed increasingly to the
theater, especially after the great success of the stage adaption of
François le champi in 1849. Her energy was also directed toward
completion of her autobiography. Her attitude toward her fiction
became almost flippant. She expresses surprise over the popularity
of *François le champi* (the novel) which, she claims, bored her

(*Correspondance* 8: 269). About *La petite Fadette*, she commented: "Ces sortes de *fadaises* me coûtent peu de fatigue morale, mais seulement une certaine fatigue physique quand il faut se presser" (*Correspondance* 8: 257). Nevertheless, that work and *Les Maîtres Sonneurs*, the last of the rustic novels, enjoyed considerable critical and popular success.

La petite Fadette and *Les Maîtres Sonneurs* are somewhat longer and more complex than the earlier rustic novels. The range of characters is greater, although, as in the previous novels, there are no middle or upper class characters. The action is set entirely in the peasant world and is narrated by peasants, *La petite Fadette* by the *chanvreur* and *Les Maîtres Sonneurs* by Etienne Depardieu, one of the principal characters. The peasant narrators do more than introduce picturesque local expressions into the stories; the tales they tell are shaped so as to reflect peasant folk beliefs and superstitions. Many of these beliefs are centered around characters from outside the Berrichon peasant world, Fadette and her family and Huriel and the forest people. These "foreigners" become involved in love affairs with representatives of the "safe," traditional peasant world. In the process the latter learn that their world is not as perfect and complete as they had believed. The plot lines point to a frontal attack on bourgeois complacency and materialism.[2]

The original preface to *La petite Fadette* gives little indication of this tendency. Like the preface to *François le champi*, it assumes the form of a dialogue between Sand and François Rollinat. "George Sand" expresses her desire to forget the social turmoil, strife and disappointment of the 1848 revolution in which she had played such an active role just a few months earlier. To this end, she evokes, as in the preface to *La Mare au diable*, the beauty of the plowman's song: "J'écoutai le récitatif du laboureur, entrecoupé de longs silences, j'admirai la variété infinie que le grave caprice de son improvisation imposait au vieux thème sacramentel. C'était comme une rêverie de la nature elle-même, ou comme une mystérieuse formule par laquelle la terre proclamait chaque phase de l'union de sa force avec le travail de l'homme" (8). This mystical union of man and nature, celebrated in song, is precisely what Sand is striving for in writing her pastoral novels. The healing, "consoling" power of nature is more urgently needed than ever: "Célébrons tout doucement cette poésie si douce; exprimons-le, comme le suc d'une plante bienfaisante, sur les blessures de l'humanité" (10). Her novel is to resemble "la musique de la nature" (10) to which the two friends listen.

Songs, however beautiful, still can not match the music of nature:

> Il y aura toujours dans le souffle de l'air que la voix humaine fait vibrer, une harmonie bienfaisante qui pénétrera vos âmes d'un religieux soulagement. Il n'en faut même pas tant; le chant de l'oiseau, le bruissement de l'insecte, le murmure de la brise, le silence même de la nature, toujours entrecoupé de quelques mystérieux sons d'une indicible éloquence. Si ce langage furtif peut arriver jusqu'à votre oreille, ne fût-ce qu'un instant, vous échappez par la pensée au joug cruel de l'homme, et votre âme plane librement dans la création. C'est là que règne ce charme souverain qui est véritablement la possession commune, dont le pauvre jouit souvent plus que le riche. (9)

The escape to nature has another appeal besides its beauty and tranquillity: it is freely available to the poor as well as to the rich. Nature is not a neutral commodity in Sand's rustic fiction; its beauty is seen in relationship to the social and economic situation of those who live in its midst. Peasants are considered here, in contrast to the first chapter of La Mare au diable, as being capable of enjoying the charms of nature. The evolution of Sand's attitude toward peasants in her fiction in the 1840's reveals a tendency to portray the peasant's condition in an ever more positive light. In the case of La petite Fadette the disappointment that Sand had just suffered at the hands of the civilized world no doubt led her to glorify the simpler, rougher but unchanging and reliable peasant world.

Sand explicitly contrasts in her preface the beauty and tranquility of her world with the cruelty and injustice of society at large: "Tandis que nous respirons le parfum des plantes sauvages et que la nature chante autour de nous son éternelle idylle, on étouffe, on languit, on pleure, on râle, on expire dans les mansardes et dans les cachots" (7). The novel in fact is dedicated to Armand Barbès, the imprisoned revolutionary. This does not mean, however, that Sand had in mind a politically slanted novel. In fact, as the preface emphasizes, Sand is highlighting nature's healing powers as an alternative to political turmoil. In electing to portray man in nature, Sand is choosing not to portray man in society, thus avoiding dealing directly with social problems. Other writers can be expected to fulfill that mission: "Sans doute, il y aurait dans la recherche des vérités applicables à son salut matériel, bien d'autres remèdes à trouver. Mais d'autres que nous s'en occuperont mieux que nous" (10). Her goal, as in the previous novel, is not to give a complete and realistic portrait of French country life but to present, as did the pastoral, "un certain idéal de la vie champêtre" (10) opposed to the somber brutality of the real world. Having the story told by a habitual storyteller is another way of putting distance between the tale and reality. This is the third, and last, of the rustic novels which Sand proposed to collect under the title "Les Veillées du Chanvreur."

The *chanvreur* narrates the story in such a way that the reader believes that what he is experiencing is not reality but a kind of fairy-tale world which resembles our own in certain ways but differs in others. The opening chapter of the novel introduces the Barbeau family and their situation in several broad strokes. Place names are given, but few other details are provided. Instead we are placed rapidly into the action, namely the birth of the twins: "Le père Barbeau était un homme de bon courage, pas méchant, et très porté pour sa famille, sans être injuste à ses voisins et paroissiens. Il avait déjà trois enfants, quand la mère Barbeau, voyant sans doute qu'elle avait assez de bien pour cinq, et qu'il fallait se dépêcher, parce que l'âge lui venait, s'avisa de lui en donner deux à la fois, deux beaux garçons" (20). Imputing the conscious decision to have twins to Mère Barbeau is characteristic of the mildly ironic attitude toward the characters, in particular the members of the Barbeau family. Barbeau has a matter-of-fact, self-assured way of viewing things at which the narrator occasionally pokes fun. He takes the news of his wife's delivery of twins very calmly, simply commenting that he will have to enlarge the cradle. Their conversation in its simplicity and directness recalls folk literature, as does the depiction of the protagonists' birth as an out-of-the-ordinary event. The characters of Barbeau and his wife emerge effectively from their conversation; the narrator adds little in the way of description or commentary. The preference for the larger picture applies to the treatment of time as well. As in fairy tales, time is telescoped. Only selected events from the twins' childhood are presented.

The peasant background of the *chanvreur* as narrator has another determining influence on the way the story is told, the incorporation of his belief in superstitions and in the predictions of peasant wise women. The first of the latter, Mère Sagette, is presented to the reader as a voice of authority and experience. Through the narrator's attitude and that of the characters, the reader is led to accept her "wisdom" (note her name) as genuine in the context of the story. The special emphasis she gives to her advice and warning, that the twins be separated as much as possible, alerts the reader to the danger the twins' relationship poses: "Mais écoutez ce qu'une femme d'expérience va vous dire. . . . Ne le mettez pas en oubliance. . . . Ce que je vous dis là, j'ai grand-peur que vous ne le mettiez pas dans l'oreille du chat; mais si vous ne le faites pas, vous vous en repentirez grandement un jour" (23-24). The repetition of this solemn, emphatic warning builds the expectation that, in fact, the advice will be ignored and that tragedy will result. Other superstitions concerning twins shape the direction of the narrative as well. Père Barbeau worries since he has heard that twins become so attached to one another that if they are separated one will die. This is what appears to be happening to Sylvinet in much of the novel. Also the last sentence of the novel is a reminder of the fulfillment of the prophecy of another wise woman, la Baigneuse de Clavières, who had predicted that Sylvinet would fall in love only once and with an extremely strong attachment.

While in several important ways the story is tailored to fit the peasant superstitions presented, there is, in fact, a great deal of ambiguity in the narrator's attitude toward superstitious beliefs. Initially, he expresses no doubt as to the validity of what he presents, allowing the reader to enter as completely as possible the peasant world he is projecting. This is the case, for instance, in the episode of the *feu follet*. At the beginning of the incident, the narrator speaks about autumn as being "une saison où les sorciers et les follets commencent à se donner du bon temps, à cause des brouillards qui les aident à cacher leurs malices et maléfices" (103). Landry walked fast singing, he tells the reader, "car on sait que le chant de l'homme dérange et écarte les mauvaises bêtes et les mauvais gens" (104). Here, and later when Landry sees the *feu follet*, the reader is not invited to doubt the reality of this seemingly supernatural phenomenon: "On sait qu'il s'obstine à courir après ceux qui courent, et qu'il se met en travers de leur chemin jusqu'à ce qu'il les ait rendus fous et fait tomber dans quelque mauvaise passe" (107). Only after Fadette has conjured the spirit does the narrator offer a rational explanation of the *feu follet*, the schoolmaster's scientific definition. Subsequently, the narrator also explains that Landry was so afraid because by chance he had never encountered the phenomenon before, while Fadette's courage derived from frequent encounters with such plays of light and from her grandmother having told her what it really was.

A similar double perspective is evident in the description of the Fadet family. The narrator lists a number of skills Fadette's grandmother is reputed to have then expresses doubt as to the truth of the beliefs. When Landry is searching for his brother, Fadette seems to know by some mysterious means where to find him. After teasing him she agrees to help. Landry is amazed to find Sylvinet just where and when Fadette had told him: "Landry fut si aise qu'il commença par remercier le bon Dieu dans son cœur, sans songer à lui demander pardon d'avoir eu recours à la science du diable pour avoir ce bonheur-là" (83). Once again, the narrator after the fact gives possible rational explanations using expressions such as "pouvait bien avoir vu . . . quelqu'un avait pu en parler . . . cette petite pouvait avoir écouté" (88-89). The ambiguity results from the desire to guide the reader as thoroughly as possible into the peasant culture. The desired dramatic effect in the use of seemingly supernatural occurrences depends on the reader's initial perception that they are real. Also, the *chanvreur* in this novel is not, as in

François le champi, telling the story to a group of peasants, a gathering at which "George Sand" and R. happen to be present. Rather the *chanvreur* is telling the story directly to those two educated listeners. The narrator, would then, logically tailor his tale to his listeners. In line with this orientation the chanvreur frequently offers explanations of dialectic expressions.

Ambiguity also characterizes the portrayal of Fadette and her family. Fadette with her nicknames and anti-social behavior clearly inhabits a world apart from that of the Barbeau family. Since she comes from a family "qui n'avait ni terre ni avoir autre que son petit jardin et sa petite maison" (69), she is also economically far removed from the class of farmers. The peasant community holds her in low esteem in part because of her perceived pattern of behavior and in part because her mother had left her family and run off with another man. But the narrator gives indications early on that the reader's view of Fadette is likely to change, as in speaking of her name: "Mais tous ces noms et surnoms me feraient bien oublier celui qu'elle avait reçu au baptême et que vous auriez peut-être plus tard envie de savoir" (74). This points to the possibility of Fadette's leaving the fairy-tale world of sorcery in which she is introduced for the real world in which people are not called Fadette (little fairy) or *grelet* (cricket). Fadette's transformation is also hinted at in such details as the fact that she wore a "mauvais jupon tout cendreux" (78-79), casting her in the role of *Cendrillon*.

For the Barbeau family, Fadette's background establishes her character once and for all. According to Sylvinet it is inevitable that she follow in her disreputable mother's footsteps: "Il évitait ce méchant grelet, qui, disait-il, suivrait tôt ou tard l'exemple de sa mère, laquelle avait mené une mauvaise conduite, quitté son mari et finalement suivi les soldats" (99-100). Clearly this is not a family with which the Barbeau clan would want to become connected. Even when there is evidence of a change in Fadette, Barbeau remains skeptical: "Cela ne me suffit pas pour croire qu'une enfant qui a été si mal élevée puisse jamais faire une honnête femme, et connaissant la grand-mère comme je l'ai connue, j'ai tout lieu de craindre qu'il n'y ait là une intrigue montée pour te soutirer des promesses et te causer de la honte et de l'embarras. On m'a même

dit que la petite était enceinte" (204). If she is pregnant, this is, of course, not the fault of Landry, but is a result, in this view, of Fadette's inherited licentiousness. Landry contends that Fadette should be given all the more credit for overcoming her adverse family background. This is what Landry tells Sylvinet at one point as a lesson he could apply to himself: "Ce n'est pas comme ça chez nous, répondit Landry. Jamais nous n'avons reçu de père ni de mère le moindre coup, et mêmement quand on nous grondait de nos malices d'enfant, c'était avec tant de douceur et d'honnêteté, que les voisins ne l'entendaient point. Il y en a comme ça qui sont trop heureux, et pourtant, la petite Fadette, qui est l'enfant le plus malheureux et le plus maltraité de la terre, rit toujours et ne se plaint jamais de rien" (90). That the individual is free to develop morally independent of his family or social origin is a point emphasized by Sand in the novel. It is formulated succinctly by Fadette in telling Sylvinet that he should not believe that he, as a twin, is a victim of fate: "Dieu n'est pas si injuste que de nous marquer pour un mauvais sort dans le ventre de nos mères" (260). As often occurs in the novel, Fadette functions as the voice of the author.

Fadette is acutely aware of her low place on the social and economic scale. Yet she is proud of herself and her family and does not accept the idea that the Barbeau family is superior to hers. She rejects Landry's offer of money for the service she had provided in helping to find Sylvinet, castigating Landry for being overly proud and thinking money can buy anything: "Je ne vous estime point . . . ni vous, ni votre besson, ni vos père et mère, qui sont fiers parce qu'ils sont riches, et qui croient qu'on ne fait que son devoir en leur rendant service" (111). She makes her position clear in commenting on Landry's remark that the spot where they have accidentally met is not well suited for conversation:

> Tu ne trouves point l'endroit agréable, reprit-elle, parce que vous autres riches vous êtes difficiles. Il vous faut du beau gazon pour vous asseoir dehors, et vous pouvez choisir dans vos prés et dans vos jardins les plus belles places et le meilleur ombrage. Mais ceux qui n'ont rien à eux n'en demandent pas si long au bon Dieu, et ils s'accommodent de la première pierre venue pour

poser leur tête. Les épines ne blessent point leurs pieds, et là où ils se trouvent, ils observent tout ce qui est joli et avenant au ciel et sur la terre. Il n'y a point de vilain endroit, Landry, pour ceux qui connaissent la vertu et la douceur de toutes les choses que Dieu a faites. (139-40)

Once again Fadette expresses ideas important to George Sand, as evinced by the fact that Fadette's speech takes on the language of the author. Fadette opposes her world of nature to that of money and ease which Landry represents. Her extensive knowledge of herbal medicine and of how to deal with such natural phenomena as the *feu follet* testify to her close connection to nature.[3] Her separation from the world of money in which Landry operates is shown in the fact that she gives away her herbal medicines rather than selling them. The message is clear: just as herbs' effectiveness can not be judged by their appearance, the same is true of a person's moral qualities. Attacking prejudice toward the less fortunate in society remains one of Sand's fundamental goals in this novel.

Rejected by society, Fadette finds acceptance in a different sphere: "En voyant combien les gens sont durs et méprisants pour ceux que le bon Dieu a mal partagés, je me suis fait un plaisir de leur déplaire, me consolant par l'idée que ma figure n'avait rien de repoussant pour le bon Dieu et pour mon ange gardien, lesquels ne me la reprocheraient pas" (144). Indeed, Fadette is more pious than anyone else in the community. She arrives early at church on Sundays in order to say extra prayers. But here once again she is misjudged by the community. Many claim her piety is not genuine, but a mask to hide her evil ways. Until Fadette and Landry meet after the dance the reader is left in the dark as to Fadette's true character. There are a number of comments which suggest she is in league with the devil and receives special powers from this relationship. This is brought out in particular in her early meetings with Landry. Landry initially feels the same mistrust and distaste for Fadette that the rest of his family exhibits. He is weary of having any dealings with the little sorceress and is constantly on his guard against evil spells she may cast.

Fadette's use of language indicates that her world is very different from that of Landry. The first sentence she speaks in the novel shows to what extent her speech differs from that of the Barbeau class: "Au loup! Au loup! Le vilain besson, moitié de gars qui a perdu son autre moitié!" (76). She uses language as a kind of weapon: "Elle aimait à provoquer les injures et les moqueries, tant elle se sentait la langue bien affilée pour y répondre" (99). This is one of the only possible means at her disposal to fight against the prejudices she endures. Not only is she scornful and taunting in what she says, how she speaks is different as well. She uses repetitions, alliteration and rhyme for effect and emphasis. The song Landry hears her sing when he's trying to cross the river seems to be evidence of her connection with the *feu follet*:

> Fadet, Fadet, petit fadet,
> Prends ta chandelle et ton cornet;
> J'ai pris ma cape et mon capet;
> Toute follette a son follet. (107)

Fadette's speech and song have a hypnotic effect on Landry. He dreams that Fadette talks to him in rhyme. Even after she reveals her true character to Landry, he is enchanted by her speech: "Jamais il n'avait entendu une voix si douce et des paroles si bien dites que les paroles et la voix de la Fadette dans ce moment-là" (140). From this point on, however, Fadette's speech changes its character, becoming closer to that of the peasant community. This reflects the changes she undergoes that make her acceptable in Landry's world. It also signals to the reader the change from fairy tale to love story, as Fadette, the *grelet*, becomes Fanchon Fadet.

The transformation Fadette undergoes remains external only and in the perception that others have of her.[4] Landry tells her that she ought to be "un peu plus comme les autres" (139) and this is what she does, dressing better and behaving in a more polite, civilized manner. Her appearance changes to such an extent that Landry does not even recognize her at first in church. The change extends to her skin color: "Je ne sais pas avec quelle mixture de fleurs ou d'herbes elle avait lavé pendant huit jours son visage et ses mains, mais sa figure pâle et ses mains mignonnes avaient l'air aussi net et aussi doux que la blanche épine du printemps" (169-70). Going from brown to white is evidence of her beginning social change, from a kind of gypsy world to that of the well-to-do peasants. She becomes, like Brunette in *Les Maîtres Sonneurs*, the queen of her region: "Enfin elle était non pas la plus jolie fille du monde, comme Landry se l'imaginait, mais la plus avenante, la mieux faite, la plus fraîche et peut-être la plus désirable qu'il y eût dans le pays" (230). Her improved appearance, the narrator is careful to point out, is not just the result of better care but is a product of better food, better lodging and a happier life. Fadette's brother, Jeanet, improves in similar fashion. He is initially dirty and nasty, but Landry finds that his disposition is a result of his environment. With Landry's help and the benefit of better food and treatment, Jeanet the "grasshopper" becomes "un gars fort mignon, tout plein de petites idées drôles et aimables, et ne pouvant plus déplaire à personne" (240).

Fadette's appearance may have changed, but her fundamental beliefs have not. She had always been profoundly religious but her true beliefs had been obscured by her grandmother's reputation of working with the devil. Now it becomes clear that Fadette had "plus de religion que de diablerie dans ses charmes" (246). Instead of now being considered a disciple of the devil she is described in positive terms as having "un esprit du diable" (230). Her piety is such that she gives Landry religious instruction. Far from being pregnant, as Barbeau had suspected, she keeps Landry's mind off sex by educating him: "Pour le distraire de l'idée qu'elle ne voulait point encourager, elle l'instruisait dans les choses qu'elle savait" (185). She uses her intuitive knowledge of medicine and psychology to cure Sylvinet. After breaking his fever, by doing nothing more than laying her hand on his brow, she seems almost a Christ figure: "Je vais sortir, et vous vous lèverez, Sylvinet, car vous n'avez plus la fièvre" (263). After Barbeau has verified that Fadette has indeed been misjudged, he accepts her into his family. Of course, Fadette has in the meantime also become rich. She inherits so much that she is richer than the Barbeau and Caillaud families put together. This allows Sand to introduce a scene both ironic and sentimental in which Père Barbeau's pride is taken down a peg upon discovering the extent of Fadette's wealth. Fadette, however, finds a different use for her wealth: she opens a home for children of the poor.

The changes Fadette undergoes are largely superficial. Her social acceptance is based on external factors and rumor. Fadette does not have to modify her views in order to enter Landry's world. This is not true of Landry; he changes in significant ways. He is the twin who early on is more closely linked to the Barbeau way of life. In difficult situations, as when Sylvinet is lost, Landry always tries to determine what his father would have done. He has the same intense interest in agriculture as his father. When he is forced to leave home and his twin in order to be a farm hand at the Caillaud farm, he is depressed until he sees the farmer's cattle: "Aussitôt que l'enfant vit les grands bœufs du père Caillaud, qui étaient les mieux tenus, les mieux nourris et les plus forts de tout le pays, il se sentit chatouillé dans son orgueil d'avoir une si belle aumaille au bout de son aiguillon. Et puis il était content de montrer qu'il n'était ni maladroit ni lâche" (45). Landry is a complete farm boy whereas Sylvinet has "le cœur d'une fille" (42). In keeping with his father's values it is thus not out of character when he offers Fadette a cash payment for her service to him. Nor is it surprising that his initial view of Fadette, in keeping with the opinion of the community at large, is decidedly negative. Interestingly, as he falls in love with Fadette his interest in agriculture abates. Sand's rustic novels offer this contrast with other examples of that genre that love becomes for the peasants an all-consuming passion. A similar pattern is evident in Germain (*La Mare au diable*) and Etienne (*Les Maîtres Sonneurs*).

Fadette's love produces major changes in Landry's world view. Initially his relationship to nature is largely antagonistic, as shown in his comments on the river when looking for his brother: "Cette méchante rivière qui ne me dit mot, pensait-il, et qui me laisserait bien pleurer un an sans me rendre mon frère, est justement là au plus creux, et il y est tombé tant de cosses d'arbres depuis le temps qu'elle ruine le pré, que si on y entrait on ne pourrait jamais s'en retirer" (69). Similarly, later on he is tricked by the *feu follet* so that he almost drowns. After becoming friends with Fadette, Landry is no longer afraid of the *feu follet*. More significantly, he learns from Fadette how to use nature in beneficial ways other than farming. In fact he becomes adept at using herbal cures on animals. Thus, while Fadette at the end of the novel enters the Barbeau family, it is not really she who changes her fundamental nature but rather Landry. He becomes part of the natural world of Fadette. Of course the point Sand is making is once again that of social harmony, which is eased artificially in this novel as well through the sudden wealth of Fadette.

The other plot line in the novel also results in the opening up a perspective which is too narrow. This involves the relationship between the twins. Sand had planned to entitle the novel "Les Bessons," highlighting their relationship. This forms the primary focus of the first part of the novel, before Fadette appears. Of course the two plots intertwine, as Sylvinet becomes ill from jealousy over Landry's love for Fadette and Fadette cures Sylvinet. Indeed, her cure takes too well. In the improbable ending, Sylvinet becomes a decorated army officer, having left the farm because he, too, had fallen in love with Fadette. What also links the two subplots is the prominent role played by superstitious beliefs. This, however, is not the major focus of interest in the chronicle of the twins' relationship. The emphasis is on the factors which can drive family members apart. In the case of the Barbeau family, there is initially a strong sense of peace and harmony in the extended family. The twins, too, are initially shown in this light: "En fait, l'un valait l'autre, et si Landry avait une idée de gaieté et de courage de plus que son aîné, Sylvinet était si amiteux et si fin d'esprit qu'on ne pouvait pas l'aimer moins que son cadet" (29-30). They become inseparable, sharing identical views on every subject.

When they are forced to choose which twin will become the farm hand at the Caillaud farm, they face a conflict of family duty versus affection. Landry is able to overcome his emotions—as he is in other situations—and carry the burden of leaving his family. He is in fact the one who accommodates himself to his twin, sacrificing his pleasures for his brother. However, Sylvinet is not able to appreciate his brother's sacrifices. He demands an exclusive attention and love. Sylvinet's love for his brother is so intense that it makes him fiercely egotistical and jealous, in Sand's view, two unpardonable sins. His feelings for Landry are such that when he sees his twin kiss a girl at the end of a dance he is beside himself: "Il avait été si en colère de le voir embrasser une des filles du père Caillaud, qu'il avait pleuré de jalousie et trouvé la chose tout à fait indécente et malchrétienne" (63). It is also Fadette who brings about the transformation in this twin. She is able to see through his illness, judging that he is only seeking attention. According to Fadette, Sylvinet would have been quite different if he had been brought up as she had been: "Je vais vous dire ce qui vous a manqué pour être un bon et sage garçon, Sylvain. C'est d'avoir eu des parents bien rudes, beaucoup de misère, pas de pain tous les jours et des coups bien souvent. Si vous aviez été élevé à la même école que moi et mon frère Jeanet, au lieu d'être ingrat, vous seriez reconnaissant de la moindre chose. Tenez, Sylvain, ne vous retranchez pas sur votre bessonnerie. Je sais qu'on a beaucoup trop dit autour de vous que cette amitié bessonnière était une loi de nature qui devait vous faire mourir si on la contrariait, et vous avez cru obéir à votre sort en portant cette amitié à l'excès; mais Dieu n'est pas si injuste que de nous marquer pour un mauvais sort dans le ventre de nos mères" (259-60). Thus this subplot carries a similar message, namely that we are not "marked" at birth to lead a certain kind of life. Any person has the potential for change and improvement.

❖ ❖ ❖

At the end of *La petite Fadette* Sylvinet goes off to join the army, eventually to win glory and the rank of colonel. Sylvinet evinces a number of similarities in character and fate to Joseph of *Les Maîtres Sonneurs*. The latter also leaves his friends and family. But his fate is not so illustrious; although he gains some repute as a bagpiper, in the end he is killed, apparently the victim of a brutal murder. Sylvinet and Joseph leave their peasant community and lead very different lives from those of the same social background. They possess a more delicate organization and are more finely attuned to their surroundings and to other people. Like Sylvinet,

Joseph is mediocre as a farm worker; he is frail and absent-minded. He suffers from the same failings, egotism and jealousy. It is in fact Joseph's stubborn insistence on his superiority as a musician which most likely leads to his death. Thus Joseph presents a more dramatic illustration of the dangers of egotism. Both characters are ruled by their emotions, not their intellects. As a result their behavior is often irrational and contradictory. They have not achieved the balance evident in characters like Landry or Huriel, who represent ideal modes of conduct.

There is, however, another side to Joseph, a dimension that is not present in Sylvinet. Joseph is a musician of genius. His moroseness and self-inflicted isolation as a child derive from an inability to communicate. It is only when he discovers music that he is able to fill the void. He uses the primitive flute he has made to speak to Brulette, the girl he loves. She understands Joseph's passion for music as a need to express himself. When Joseph realizes he will never win Brulette's love, he expresses his feelings not in words but in the playing of his bagpipes, the only language he knows. His ability to play music is a kind of divine gift; for Brulette this was already evident in Joseph as a child: "Je sais que tu as dans les oreilles, ou dans la cervelle, ou dans le cœur, une vraie musique du bon Dieu parce que j'ai vu ça dans tes yeux quand j'étais petite" (112). The view of music here is close to that expressed in the Consuelo novels. As in those works music is a powerful force, one that is capable of changing dramatically those who know its secrets. After playing on his flute, it seems to Etienne that Joseph has undergone a transformation: "De chétif et pâlot, il paraissait grandi et amendé, comme je l'avais vu dans la forêt. Il avait de la mine; ses yeux étaient dans sa tête comme deux rayons d'étoile, et quelqu'un qui l'aurait jugé le plus beau garçon du monde ne se serait point trompé sur le moment" (119). For Joseph music is his one chance to show himself equal, even superior, to others: "A présent, Joset le fou, Joset l'innocent, Joset l'ébervigé, tu peux bien retomber dans ton imbécillité; tu es aussi fort, aussi savant, aussi heureux qu'un autre!" (118). He is a kind of albatross, awkward on land but soaring upwards on the wings of song. Music allows him to escape reality.

Eventually Joseph becomes an accomplished bagpiper, "un vrai maître sonneur des anciens temps" (389). He is able to move his listeners to tears with his music and is especially adept at improvising and playing variations on popular tunes. As he becomes a more proficient bagpiper he changes in other ways as well. He becomes stronger and more self-assured. He actively pursues his love for Brulette. But the inconsistencies in his behavior remain. He asks Huriel's sister, Thérence, to marry him and upon her refusal immediately turns his attention to Brulette; he defends against Huriel and Etienne his behavior as being beyond what reason could grasp: "Oui, vous avez raison dans le raisonnement, dit-il. Vous y êtes tous deux plus forts que moi, et j'ai parlé et agi comme un homme qui ne sait pas bien ce qu'il veut; mais vous êtes plus fous que moi si vous ne savez pas que, sans être fou, on peut vouloir deux choses contraires. Laissez-moi pour ce que je suis, et je vous laisserai pour ce que vous voudrez être" (406-07). His self-confidence eventually turns to arrogance, especially in matters of music. When the other bagpipers propose that he go through the initiation ceremony he responds scornfully. Even before becoming a member of the guild, Joseph acts as though he were the master and the other bagpipers the novices. His musical ability is a natural gift but his talent has been broadened by leaving his native Berry and learning from Huriel's father, in Bourbonnais. One of the sources of Joseph's superiority as a musician over other bagpipers in Berry is his ability to play in the manner of more than just his own region. The importance of broadening one's perspectives is stressed in the novel.

The close association between music and nature runs throughout the novel. Huriel describes music as a "herbe sauvage" which does not grow well in Berry. The reason is, according to Huriel, that music needs to be totally free and untamed, like the wild woods of Bourbonnais: "La chanson, la liberté, les beaux pays sauvages, la vivacité des esprits, et si tu veux aussi, l'art de faire fortune sans devenir bête, tout ça se tient comme les doigts de la main" (141-42). The necessity for a musician to be free is in part what leads Joseph to disdain membership in the bagpipers' guild and to mock the initiation rites. In fact, in contrast to the secret society of *La Comtesse de Rudolstadt*, the bagpipers' guild here is characterized by petty jealousy and maliciousness. Also in contrast to the musical genius of the novel, Consuelo, Joseph's interests are exclusively devoted to music, even to the exclusion of a genuine love for a woman, as Brulette recognizes. Thus, although on the one hand, Joseph represents the genius of the common people expressed in popular music, he does not project the kind of ideal that Consuelo represented. The lesson to be learned from his life, that according to "le grand bûcheux" music is "une trop rude maîtresse pour des gens comme nous autres" (496), expresses the idea that music should not be allowed to take absolute control of all a person's time and energy. That is simply another form of egotism.

Joseph is reported to have sold his soul to the devil for his mastery of music. This is the interpretation that Etienne initially has of Joseph's mysterious meetings with a man dressed in black who one day brings him a bagpipe. It is only later that we learn that this is Huriel, the *muletier*, whose appearance is connected with his profession of carrying and selling coal. Etienne himself, as an old man, is the narrator of the story, and therefore the peasant beliefs and superstitions in the novel are presented from a peasant perspective, as if they might be true. In fact, Etienne sees Joseph as fated not to have an easy life since Etienne's grandmother who "se piquait de connaissances sur l'avenir, disait qu'il avait le malheur écrit sur la figure" (91). At the end of the novel Etienne is struck with the prophetic value of his grandmother's remark. The popular interpretation of Joseph's death is in keeping with the sense of inevitable doom since the people are convinced "qu'on ne peut devenir musicien sans vendre son âme à l'enfer, et qu'un jour ou l'autre, Satan arrache la musette des mains du sonneur et la lui brise sur le dos, ce qui l'égare, le rend fou et le pousse à se détruire" (496). In fact, his death is foreshadowed in the initiation ceremony when a figure representing the devil, "le roi des musiqueux," and dressed as a wild beast demands Joseph's soul. When Joseph fights him he is almost killed since the figure's costume is covered with spikes and nails. There is, however, not the same sense of inevitable fulfillment of folk prophecies in this novel as in *La petite Fadette*.

There is a stronger sense in this novel that Joseph's downfall is of his own doing.

In general the story is told, from the beginning on, in a considerably more realistic vein than the previous novel. Exact dates and places are given at the outset; there is not the same feeling of traversing a fairy-tale landscape. Etienne's account of events is in general sober and neutral. He acts as an objective observer, providing the perspective from which the reader is to view the story. The initiation ceremony, for instance, comes across here very differently from Consuelo's initiation into the "Invisibles." This is due to the factual account that Etienne gives of the proceedings as a non-involved spectator. From this viewpoint the ceremony is simply ridiculous and cruel. This perspective offered the reader leads to a considerably greater sense of realism in the novel. This is also a reflection of the fact that although told by a peasant the story is not narrated by an habitual storyteller like the *chanvreur*, prone to exaggeration and dramatic effect. On the contrary, it is Etienne telling his own life story to "George Sand," as she writes in her dedication of the novel. The negative portrait of the initiation into the bagpipers' guild also betrays a change in Sand's attitude toward social change. After the 1848 revolution she no longer saw herself as one of a select group working toward a new society. The failure of the revolution led her to concentrate her attention on improving personal relationships through better mutual understanding and tolerance, qualities lacking in and after the revolution. The elevation in *La petite Fadette* and *Les Maîtres Sonneurs* of the family as an ideal toward which to aspire is a reflection of this change. Given these beliefs, it is not surprising that there is a change in Sand's attitude toward secret and exclusive societies.

As in *La petite Fadette*, the narrator of *Les Maîtres Sonneurs* initially gives the impression that some of the characters are emissaries of the devil. This happens when Etienne first encounters Huriel: "Je reconnus, au moyen de la clarté qui sortait de la maison, Joset à côté d'un homme bien vilain à voir, car il était noir de la tête aux pieds, mêmement sa figure et ses mains, et il avait, derrière lui, deux grands chiens noirs comme lui" (122). The initial impression is strengthened when Etienne discovers that the two dogs are named Louveteau and Satan. Children run when they see him coming, crying "Le diable!, le diable!" (172). He, too, plays the bagpipes so well and is able to play for so long that it does not seem within the range of mortal man's abilities. As a *muletier*, Huriel belongs to a group which is seen by the Berrichon peasants as lawless savages: "Ce sont gens sauvages, méchants et mal appris, qui vous tuent un homme dans un bois, avec aussi peu de conscience qu'un lapin; qui se prétendent le droit de ne nourrir leurs bêtes qu'aux dépens du paysan, et qui, si on le trouve malséant, et qu'ils ne soient pas les plus forts pour résister, reviennent plus tard ou envoient leurs compagnons faire périr vos bœufs par maléfice, brûler vos bâtiments, ou pis encore" (133). This impression seems to be confirmed by the fact that Huriel allows his animals to eat Etienne's grain, and he himself enters Etienne's house when he's not there.

But like Fadette, this outsider in the peasant community actually possesses higher moral and spiritual values than the peasants themselves. Showing how much the ostracized group differs from popular conception is a part of the narrative strategy here; it creates a dramatic, albeit artificial, conflict and highlights the folly of uninformed prejudice. As with Fadette, Huriel's apparent association with the devil serves to mask his piety. After a night of dancing, he calls on the others to stop and pray. He points out to Etienne that the Berrichon farmers who find him immoral are the same ones who send their sheep to graze on their neighbors' land and engage in other questionable practices. He accuses the Berrichons of being avaricious and materialistic: "Voilà des dressoirs, des tables, des chaises, de la belle crémaillère, des pots à soupe, que sais-je? Il vous faut tout cela pour être contents. . . . Pour trop chérir vos aises, vous vous faites trop de besoins, et pour trop bien vivre, vous ne vivez pas" (143). Huriel offers in place of this way of life the benefits of living free and travelling: "Croyez-vous que l'homme soit fait pour nicher toute l'année? M'est avis, au contraire, que son destin est de courir, et qu'il serait cent fois plus fort, plus gai, plus sain d'esprit et de corps, s'il n'avait pas tant cherché ses aises, qui l'ont rendu mol, craintif et sujet aux maladies" (194-95). This is another expression of the love of the open road and living free idealized in the

Consuelo novels. In *Les Maîtres Sonneurs* this way of life sharply contrasts with bourgeois self-satisfaction and materialism.

The character who most completely incorporates the ideals of the way of life in Bourbonnais is Huriel's father, père Bastien, "le grand bûcheux." Like his son, père Bastien prefers to sleep outdoors and is constantly traveling from one forest to another. He is a tree cutter who, however, regrets having to destroy nature as his profession. His way of life, like that of Fadette, is closely identified with nature. Although advanced in age, he works hard and joyously: "De ma vie, je n'ai vu travail de main d'homme dépêché d'une si rude et si gaillarde façon. Je pense bien qu'il eût pu faire, sans se gêner, l'œuvre de quatre des plus forts chrétiens en sa journée, et cela, toujours riant et causant et sifflant quand il était seul" (216). He is another example—added to those of Grand-Louis (*Le Meunier d'Angibault*) and Jean Jappeloup (*Le Péché de M. Antoine*)—of the joys of work for those who live free. Work under such circumstances is easy and invigorating. But "le grand bûcheux" is something more than a hard worker. He is a master musician who passes on his skills to Joseph. He has not come by his knowledge through formal study; Etienne describes him as "un homme comme j'en ai peu vu de pareils, croyez-moi, et qui, sans avoir étudié, avait une grande connaissance et un esprit qui n'eût point gâté un plus riche et mieux connu" (211). He is naturally enlightened and divinely inspired, like Jeanne or Patience (*Mauprat*). He has insights into thoughts and feelings that others do not. He is the only major character in the novel who does not change; he is a source of stability and inspiration for the others.

His son, on the other hand, does undergo a transformation, one which, like that of Fadette, allows him to fit into the peasant community which had initially rejected him. This involves in his case, too, a change in appearance: "Au lieu de son sarrau encharbonné, de ses vieilles guêtres de cuir, de son chapeau cabossé et de sa figure noire, il avait un habillement neuf, tout en fin droguet blanc jaspé de bleu, du beau linge, un chapeau de paille enrubanné de trente-six couleurs, la barbe faite, la face bien lavée et rose comme une pêche: enfin, c'était le plus bel homme que j'aie vu de ma vie" (154). Huriel goes even further than just giving up the

appearance of being a *muletier*, he gives up the profession as well. He is prompted to do so through the accidental killing of a man who had insulted Brulette and the realization that the profession is ill-suited to someone planning to start a family. This clears the way for his marriage to Brulette and, at the end of the novel, to his entrance into a kind of communal relationship with Etienne and Thérence.

Like Etienne, Brulette has a decidedly negative opinion of *muletiers* such as Huriel. But even more serious obstacles to her union with him exist. Huriel is someone who demands an exclusive love from his chosen partner. Brulette, however, is fond of dancing and flirting. Etienne portrays her initially as lazy and vain: "Ma cousine ne travaillait pas beaucoup, ne sortait guère par les mauvais temps, avait soin de s'ombrager du soleil, ne lavait guère de lessives et ne faisait point œuvre de ses quatre membres pour la fatigue" (81). However, she is so pretty and such a good dancer that she is treated like a queen. Her obsession with cleanliness makes the contrast with Huriel, often covered with dirt and coal dust, all the more vivid. Despite the fact that, as Etienne's father comments, Brulette is "trop pauvre pour être si demoiselle" (82) she has a flock of would-be suitors, including all three major male characters of the novel, Etienne, Joseph, and Huriel. In contrast to Jeanne who was in the same situation, Brulette does not reject out of hand any of her admirers. She is not in any hurry to make her choice. It is only when she goes to Bourbonnais to help care for Joseph and is treated by Huriel's sister, Thérence, as a heartless tease that she begins to see her behavior in a new light.

The event which dramatically changes Brulette, however, occurs when she is asked to take care of an infant who has apparently been abandoned. It is only later that we learn that the boy, Charlot, is really the son of Joseph's mother, who had secretly remarried. The child is dirty and unruly and learning to take care of him becomes an important maturing experience for Brulette. When she discovers that Charlot is not being properly cared for when she is away, she vows never to leave him alone again: "De ce jour-là, il se fit en elle un changement tel, qu'on ne la reconnaissait point. Elle ne quittait plus la maison que pour faire pâturer ses ouailles et sa chèvre, toujours en compagnie de Charlot; et, quand elle l'avait couché le soir, elle prenait son ouvrage et veillait au dedans. Elle n'alla plus à aucune danse et n'acheta plus de belles nippes, n'ayant plus occasion de s'en attifer" (323). In fact, her devotion to Charlot becomes so intense that rumors arise of her being the child's real mother. This is kind of penance she must undergo for her light-hearted youth, as she herself is forced to admit. In striking evidence of the change in her character, Etienne upon seeing a monk enter Brulette's home with a basket assumes it contains "des dentelles ou des rubans à vendre," since Brulette is known as "la plus pimpante de l'endroit" (307). The fact that it is a baby not ribbons illustrates the wrenching break from carefree self-indulgence to a life of responsibility and care for others. Eventually Brulette becomes so involved in caring for Charlot that she loses her interest in attending dances, as shown by her reaction after having gone to one: "Voici la dernière fête où j'irai tant que j'aurai Charlot; car si tu veux que je te le dise, je ne me suis pas divertie une miette. J'ai fait bon visage pour te contenter, et je suis aise, à présent, d'avoir soutenu l'épreuve; mais, tout le temps que j'ai été là, je n'ai pensé qu'à mon pauvre gars" (330-31). It shows how far Brulette has come that now she speaks of going to a dance as a "trial," which is how she had originally seen the task of caring for Charlot. It is revelatory of Sand's state of mind at this time that the demonstration of Brulette's changed and improved character is made through her ability to be a good mother. Brulette herself sees that before she did not deserve motherhood: "J'avais peut-être la tête un peu trop éventée pour mériter d'entrer en famille de bonne heure" (331). The family has become the ideal toward which the characters strive.[5]

Through Brulette's care, Charlot's character improves dramatically; originally he is described as an animal with neither thoughts nor feelings. But Brulette's love effects a dramatic change: "L'enfant n'était pas tant laid que bourri, et quand la douceur et l'amitié de Brulette l'eurent, à fine force, apprivoisé, on s'aperçut que ses gros yeux noirs ne manquaient pas d'esprit, et que, quand sa grande bouche voulait rire, elle était plus drôle que vilaine. Il avait passé par une gourme dont Brulette, autrefois si dégoûtée, l'avait pansé et soigné si bravement qu'il était devenu l'enfant le plus sain, le plus ragoûtant et le plus proprement tenu qu'il y eût dans le bourg" (335-36). Having become well-behaved and loving, Charlot offers another version of the message inherent in François the *champi* and Fadette. Brulette changes radically as well, shedding a great deal of her vanity and frivolousness. Her desire to change, to improve herself actually grew out of her love for Huriel, as she explains to her father: "Je savais bien qu'on m'avait reproché une humeur légère et des goûts de coquetterie. . . . Aussi, voyant qu'Huriel avait tant de courage pour me quitter sans me demander rien, j'avais fait de grandes réflexions. Le bon Dieu m'y avait aidée en m'envoyant la charge de ce petit enfant, qui ne me plaisait pas d'abord et que j'aurais peut-être refusé, si, à mon devoir, ne se fût mêlée l'idée que, par un peu de souffrance et de vertu, je serais plus digne d'être aimée, que par mon babillage et mes toilettes" (425). As in *Mauprat* or *Consuelo*, love here is a powerful force which leads to personal growth and improvement. Brulette also comes to see her home in a different light. Returning to Berry from Bourbonnais, she no longer regards her region as the only place she could live: "C'est chose étrange, me disait-elle, comme je trouve, à mesure que nous approchons de chez nous, que les arbres sont petits, les herbes jaunes, les eaux endormies. Avant d'avoir jamais quitté nos plaines, je m'imaginais ne pas pouvoir me supporter trois jours dans ces bois; et, à cette heure, il me semble que j'y passerais ma vie aussi bien que Thérence" (301-2). The changes Brulette and Huriel undergo also allow for a coming together of the two ways of life they represent, Berry and the established peasant culture and Bourbonnais and life in nature.

This kind of reconciliation is also symbolized by the eventual union of Etienne and Thérence. Etienne represents the typical peasant, attached to his land and his routine and deeply suspicious of anything or anyone from the outside. However, as a child he had, one day, on the way home from market with his father, encountered a father and his daughter. In a repetition of the early encounter between Consuelo and Albert, Etienne carries the daughter who is ill. This seemingly insignificant event changes Etienne's life. It marks the beginning of his association with the Bourbonnais culture which opens him up to different ways of viewing the world. It also represents the end of his efforts to woo Brulette, since he is forced to admit to her that she is not the only girl with whom he has been taken, even if that meeting with Thérence was of short duration. When he later meets Thérence he recognizes her as the same "fille des bois." This is another example of the tendency in the social and rustic novels for the good characters to come together, sometimes in improbable ways. Here three weddings on the same day cap the celebration of the virtuous. As her nickname indicates, Thérence is closely associated with nature. In fact, she initially appears to be rather wild and savage and to behave in a less than civilized fashion to Brulette. But in fact she was acting out of devotion to her brother. Like Huriel, she is devout, as Etienne sees when he observes her unseen:

> Je m'avançais bien doucement, et, regardant à travers le feuillage de la petite croisée, qui n'avait ni vitrage ni boisure, je vis la belle fille des bois disant sa prière, à genoux auprès de son lit. . . . Je vivrais bien cent ans que je n'oublierais point la figure qu'elle avait dans ce moment-là. C'était comme une image de sainte, aussi tranquille que celles que l'on taille en pierre pour les églises. . . . Thérence était là, seule, et contente, aussi blanche que la lune dans la nuit claire du printemps. On entendait au loin la musique des noceux; mais cela ne disait rien à l'oreille de la fille des bois, et je pense qu'elle écoutait le rossignol qui lui chantait un plus beau cantique dans le buisson voisin. Je ne sais point ce qui se fit en moi; mais voilà que, tout d'un coup, je pensai à Dieu. . . . Ne me demandez point quelle prière je fis aux bons anges du ciel. Je ne m'entendais pas moi-même. Je n'eusse pas encore osé demander à Dieu de me donner Thérence, mais je crois que je le requis de me rendre mieux méritant pour un si grand honneur. (384-85)

As in *François le champi*, there is a close interrelationship here of love, nature, and religion. The final test for Thérence is her relationship to Charlot. As soon as she meets him she knows how to gain his trust and affection. As was the case with Brulette, the measure of her worth is her capacity to be a mother.

If Etienne thinks of evoking God's help in his love for Thérence, he is also ready to do battle with God's enemy: "Je n'étais point du tout curieux de me mesurer avec *Georgeon*, comme chez nous on l'appelle. Je ne me sentais peut-être pas plus rassuré que les autres; mais, pour Thérence, je me serais jeté en la propre gueule du diable" (466). He earns her love by helping in the process to save the lives of Huriel and her father, thus rescuing the highest values in Thérence's life, her family. Etienne's devotion to Thérence is so great that it leads him to change his way of life: "Pour marquer à Thérence que je n'étais pas si câlin qu'elle le pensait peut-être, je m'exerçais à coucher sur la dure, à vivre sobrement, et à devenir un forestier aussi solide que ceux qui l'entouraient" (435). He has come to realize that there is more to life than material comfort and more to experience than can be seen within the confines of Berry. Upon returning to Berry his sensations are similar to those of Brulette, seeing that everything was not as perfect as he had imagined. In fact, he comes to the point that he is prepared to follow Thérence into Bourbonnais. But in the end, her father's advice prevails: "Quand on veut que la pêche mûrisse, il ne faut point arracher le noyau. Le noyau, c'est la terre que possède Tiennet. Nous allons l'arrondir et y bâtir une bonne maison pour nous tous. Je serai content de faire pousser le blé, de ne plus abattre les beaux ombrages du bon Dieu, et de composer mes petites chansons à l'ancienne mode, le soir, sur ma porte, au milieu des miens" (497). Thus, as in *La petite Fadette*, the outsiders—Huriel's family—are integrated into the Berrichon peasant community. It is not the case, however, that they are surrendering their identities or values in doing so. Rather, as did Landry, both Brulette and Etienne have been transformed by their contact with the "foreign" culture, and the way of life they will lead will be a hybrid of Berry and Bourbonnais. In fact, all the major characters have flaws of one type or another which are corrected by contact with those from a different way of life. The point being made here is one of tolerance and open-mindedness; the advantages of not shutting out what is different are palpably clear—what initially may appear base and worthless is worth a closer examination and may prove to be, like Fadette or Huriel, a diamond in the rough.

9

Helping Sweet Providence

Sacrifice and Reward in *La Ville noire* and *Le Marquis de Villemer*

*Dieu n'abandonne pas ceux qui comptent sur lui et qui font
leur possible pour aider sa douce providence.*
—*Le Marquis de Villemer* (1)

Sand's novels of the late fifties and sixties tend to be full of
action. There is considerably less exploration of ideas through conversation between the characters or narrator commentary. Jacques
Langlade sees the influence of Sand's increased interest in the theater as leading to "un roman plus chargé d'événements."[1] He also
sees this as leading to greater psychological coherence in the depiction of the characters. Certainly Sand was also following the formula of the best-selling novels of the day through the use of
complex plots, dramatic turns of events, noble heroes and happy
ending (Langlade 55). But many of these elements are already
present in her earlier works. There are several other factors that led
to a more streamlined kind of fiction, less concerned with direct
reader conversion to specific social and political ideas. As we have
seen, Sand was disillusioned with politics after the 1848 revolution.
She would never again play the active role she had played in the

events of 1848. As she became a grandmother her attention shifted increasingly from the public arena to the family circle.[2] This evolution was, in part, dictated by the historical situation. Under the Second Empire "la question politique semblait résolue, la question sociale indéfiniment ajournée" (Langlade 33). The press was effectively muzzled through strict censorship.

One of Sand's major sources of inspiration for her novels after 1848 was the trips she took to various parts of France. *La Ville noire*, *Le Marquis de Villemer* and *Jean de la Roche* (1859) were inspired by Sand's travels to Auvergne and the town of Thiers in 1859. In Thiers she was able to see for herself the condition of factory workers, which led her to deal with a problem that according to the government did not exist.[3] Louis Napoléon had taken measures to eliminate worker unrest by creating "sociétés de secours mutuel" and banning autonomous worker organizations.[4] *La Ville noire*, at least, does not justify the critic who stated that Sand's novels of the 1850's represented the revenge of Cardonnet (*Le Péché de M. Antoine*) over his son.[5] At the same time, the modern reader—conditioned by familiarity with *Germinal* and other works of modern realism—may likely find that Sand's brand of "réalisme discret" (Langlade 5) or "réalisme sympathique" (Courrier xxvi) does not adequately come to terms with the problems it raises. This is, of course, imposing on George Sand a standard which did not come into being until twenty years later. Her purpose in *La Ville noire* and other works of the sixties was different from that of Zola and her approach to mimesis is consistent with her vision. She was not incapable of "realism," she simply chose a different path.[6]

The two novels Sand published in 1860, *La Ville noire* and *Le Marquis de Villemer*, have divergent settings yet exhibit a number of similarities. The plot lines of each work revolve around a strong, self-reliant woman who in a supreme act of selflessness voluntarily gives up the man she loves. The women's sacrifice turns out to be unnecessary, as the usual Sandian resolution brings the lovers together. But these works are quite different from the earlier novels following similar story lines. The women here play a deciding role; it is they who determine the nature of the relationships. Although quite different in tone, the two novels evince some similarities with

French realist fiction of the 1850s. The third-person narrator disappears behind the scenes; no judgmental commentary is offered on the characters or the action. The direction in which both love stories move is determined in large part by considerations such as wealth and ambition. In *La Ville noire* the characters are more firmly embedded in the world of labor and wages than was the case with the earlier industrial novel, *Le Péché de M. Antoine*.[7] The world in which the characters of *Le Marquis de Villemer* move, although it is more rarefied, is realistically based as well. The characters' situations are in large part dictated by historical forces and monetary considerations. But in both novels the realism is in the end undercut by Sand's refusal to give up some typically romantic features of her narrative vision. Confrontation becomes conciliation, poverty turns to wealth.

One of the themes the two novels have in common and share with such works of realism as *Madame Bovary* (1857) is the vanity of dreams. In *La Ville noire* this is illustrated through the experiences of Étienne Lavout, always called by his nickname, Sept-Epées. Not only is Sept-Epées an orphan—not surprising for a Sandian protagonist—he is also "pas du pays" (1) and thus is an even more precarious position. But he has a number of qualities which set him apart from other workers: he is educated, being able to read, write and do figures and is "le plus joli homme de la ville" (1-2). At the opening of the novel he is a metal manufacturing worker with dreams of becoming a rich and successful factory owner. He has begun to accumulate some money, which has led him to want more. He nourishes dreams of rising socially, to the extent that he would, as Tonine mockingly tells him, live the life of a bourgeois: "Je ne suis pas, disiez-vous, pour rester enterré dans la Ville noire. J'y suis entré petit apprenti, j'en veux sortir maître et propriétaire; moi aussi j'aurai quelque jour là-haut ma maison peinte et mon jardin fleuri; ma femme portera des robes de soie, et mes enfants iront au collège" (39-40). Sept-Epées is, however, far removed from such characters as Bricolin in *Le Meunier d'Angibault* or Blanchet in *François le champi* whose goal is riches for riches' sake. Sept-Epées scorns "la vanité du luxe bourgeois": "Mon but est plus élevé que cela. Je ne suis pas de ceux qui peuvent accepter un travail de machine pendant toute leur vie, car tout esprit un peu noble a horreur de l'esclavage; la tâche de l'atelier est abrutissante" (46). He dreams of putting his inventive imagination to use in constructing new types of machinery and establishing profitable factories.[8]

He sees his chance when, on a walk, he happens to come across a small factory which his resources just suffice to buy. He takes it as only the first step in his climb to prosperity: "Il me faudrait bien peu de temps pour faire prospérer ce petit établissement; je le revendrais alors le double, peut-être le triple de ce qu'il m'aurait coûté, ce qui me permettrait d'en acheter un plus considérable, et ainsi de degré en degré, en me rapprochant du centre de nos industries, c'est-à-dire en descendant le cours de la rivière, je remonterais celui de la fortune" (51). The narrator, however, dampens Sept-Epées's ambitious vision in the next passage: "Cette métaphore charma les esprits de l'armurier. Quand on s'est trouvé aux prises avec de grandes perplexités de la conscience, on prend quelquefois avec plaisir une formule quelconque, un simple jeu de mots qui se présente, pour une solution triomphante. Les gens simples et enthousiastes sont volontiers fatalistes. Le jeune artisan s'imagina que sa destinée l'avait amené en ce lieu sauvage pour y mettre la main sur l'instrument de sa richesse." (51-52). This serves to place Sept-Epées's subsequent acts in an ironic light, since the reader now expects Sept-Epées's eventual disappointment. When Sept-Epées unexpectedly sees a light on in the factory, he sees it as an omen: "C'est comme un fait exprès! Il y là du monde et de la clarté! Je ne suis pas superstitieux, sans quoi je me persuaderais bien que quelque bon ou mauvais esprit me conduit à mon salut ou à ma perte!" (56). It is a series of such seemingly fateful occurrences which persuade Sept-Epées that he is destined to buy the factory and make it profitable. The more enthusiastic he becomes, however, the more distance is created between his expectations and those of the reader.

This reader expectation is reinforced through the story of Audebert, the previous owner of the factory. In another apparent stroke of fate, Sept-Epées, drawn by the light, enters the factory just in time to prevent Audebert from committing suicide. Audebert subsequently tells Sept-Epées of his experiences. Like Sept-Epées,

Audebert's goal was not simply to make money. His purpose was to help his fellow man. He considered a variety of enterprises that might help others before he decided to buy a factory. He had such confidence in his vision of the future that he did not bother with accurate book-keeping: "Je me suis cru un homme au-dessus des autres, et je n'ai pas voulu calculer, tant j'avais la foi qu'une providence faite exprès pour moi viendrait à mon secours" (66). He recognizes in retrospect that "j'ai trop compté sur ma destinée, et elle-même s'est plu à me tromper" (66). The first year of his initial project brings profits so great that he is lulled into thinking that he cannot fail. He even buys land to set up a model farm. Soon the business begins to lose money: "Cependant mes affaires allaient de mal en pis. Je les négligeais chaque jour davantage. M'en occuper me navrait d'ennui et de dégoût. Je n'avais de répit qu'en les oubliant pour rêver encore au salut du genre humain" (70). Audebert presents a clear case of idealism confronted with reality. His dreams of helping others are dashed by his inattention to practical matters.

His removal from the working world is carried to its furthest point when Audebert finds his true vocation, poet. But this improbable transformation does not prevent Audebert from still helping his working colleagues, as Gaucher points out: "C'est de la morale qui nous vient toute mâchée, et qui nous entre dans la tête sans que nous nous en apercevions" (135). At first Audebert works in a factory while still pursuing his poetic ambitions. In fact, he derives inspiration from factory work: "On ne travailla guère ce jour-là; mais le lendemain Audebert, jaloux de prouver qu'un poëte n'est pas nécessairement un paresseux, se mit à l'ouvrage avec ardeur, et en sortit le soir plein d'idées poétiques qu'il lui tardait d'écrire" (135). In the wedding cantata at the end of the novel—of which the narrator provides a ten-page transcription—Audebert is able to combine images of labor and love. In fact at several points in the poem, all the machines in the factory are turned on to join in the celebration. There could hardly be a clearer case of industrial conflict being poeticized away.

Sept-Epées too finds that his own dreams are not as easily fulfilled as he had thought: "Au bout de peu de temps, Sept-Epées

sentit que plus on complique son existence, plus on y fait entrer de soucis et de périls. Il s'effraya de ne pas se trouver aussi positif qu'il faut l'être pour marcher à coup sûr et rapidement à la richesse. Il n'était pas avare; il ne savait pas marchander avec âpreté. Il avait pitié de ses ouvriers malades ou serrés de trop près par la misère. . . . Il trouvait tout le monde exigeant, et comme il était intelligent et réfléchi, il se sentait avec effroi devenir exigeant lui-même" (81-82). He also finds that the factory absorbs completely his time and energy. He spends all his time there, quickly discovering that he can not rely on others for supervision. The factory does not allow time either for thoughts of love or friendship; he sees his friends and family less and less often. Sept-Epées runs up against another difficulty as well: his knowledge and training are not sufficient to his needs.[9]

When he discovers that he simply does not know enough to construct the labor-saving devices he envisions, he decides to leave the factory in the hands of his assistant and become, in effect, an artisan journeyman: "Il s'arrêta donc dans la première ville qu'il rencontra, y travailla quelques semaines, et repartit pour une autre grande ville, curieux d'étudier son état sur une plus vaste échelle qu'il n'avait encore pu le faire, et de s'y perfectionner par l'essai de diverses pratiques" (183). Through his travels in France and Germany, he gains practical knowledge and skills and a more realistic view of his own efforts. He begins to see himself in a less romantic light: "Il cessa de mépriser les petits efforts et de se croire appelé à de hautes destinées. Il avait, comme Audebert, quoique dans un autre genre, subi la maladie du siècle. Il en guérit par la raison qu'il était jeune et clairvoyant" (190). The event that demonstrates his changed perspective occurs upon his return. He learns that his factory has been completely swept away by a storm. When his assistant offers as a possible explanation that it was "un endroit maudit et que le diable s'y était embusqué" (206)—indicated by its name, le Creux-Perdu—Sept-Epées responds: "Le diable qui s'était embusqué là, c'est l'amour du gain qui pousse les ambitieux jusque dans des précipices où la terre manque sous leurs pieds" (206).[10] He has come to a recognition that it is not fate, but his own actions, which are the determining factors in his life.

Sept-Epées also comes to realize through his travels that he is in love with Tonine Gaucher. He had earlier considered proposing marriage but had decided this would spell the end of his ambitious dreams. He has also considered another possible marriage, one that would have furthered his ambitions, with the daughter of a rich factory owner. But he can not keep his thoughts off Tonine. It is Tonine, as well, however, who rejects the idea of a union with Sept-Epées because of his ambition: "Je veux épouser mon pareil, et jamais un compagnon qui pense à la ville haute ne sera mon mari" (41). Her distaste for the bourgeois *ville haute* is largely a result of her sister's experience. She had married a rich factory owner, a former worker, who came to own the largest factory in town. He soon tired of his wife, however, and his neglect was a contributing factor in her sister's death. This experience has determined her attitude toward the *ville haute*, particularly since she had lived with her sister there: "Elle avait vécu à contre-cœur dans la richesse, elle n'y avait connu que le chagrin, l'indignation, la pitié" (20). While her sister came under the influence of life in the *ville haute*, trying to imitate her bourgeois neighbors, Tonine remained true to herself. In contrast she feels at home in the *Ville noire*, where all the factories are located and where the working people live: "Elle aimait sa Ville noire, la blanche fille de l'atelier; elle y respirait à l'aise et voltigeait sur la sombre pouzzolane des ruelles et des galeries, aussi proprette et aussi tranquille que les bergeronnettes le long des remous de la rivière" (130). There is no hint here of the air Tonine breathes in the *Ville noire* not being clean. The image evoked is that of pastoral calm and purity. When Tonine is asked by the doctor from the *ville haute* to marry him, her initial rejection is based on her insistence on remaining in the *Ville noire*. But it is precisely her pride in being from the *Ville noire* that leads her to consider his proposal seriously: "Tonine était femme, et son légitime orgueil de citadine de la Ville noire était flatté de l'avenir honorable et relativement très-brillant qui s'ouvrait devant elle. Elle était heureuse d'amener le secours d'un médecin instruit et dévoué à ses concitoyens, c'était même peut-être un devoir pour elle" (171). In rejecting the doctor, Tonine chooses love over the positive benefit of helping others as the

doctor's wife. Of course, in Sand's fictional world desires can come true in other ways, as is the case with Tonine.

Even as an inhabitant of the *Ville noire*, Tonine is depicted as possessing a kind of innate nobility—Sept-Epées calls it "une es-pèce de royauté morale" (225)—which allows her morally to rise above others in the community. Her nickname is the princess and even when she is devoting herself to the down-to-earth business of helping others in practical ways, this aura remains: "Il [Sept-Epées] la trouvait raccommodant son linge ou préparant son souper, à la fois servante et maîtresse dans la maison qu'ils habitaient, comme dans toutes les maisons où elle daignait apporter l'ordre ou le secours, l'aumône de ses bras, de son cœur ou de son esprit, tout cela sans épargner ses mains blanches, que, par je ne sais quel miracle d'adresse ou de coquetterie, elle conservait si belles qu'il en était parlé jusque dans la ville haute, et que bien des dames en étaient jalouses" (142). Her white hands symbolize her moral purity, not leisure and social superiority. She dedicates her life to helping others: "Elle avait des soins et de la bonté pour tous ceux qu'elle voyait souffrir autour d'elle, que c'était son plaisir d'obliger, et qu'adroite à consoler, elle s'en faisait un devoir. Chaque jour, ce caractère d'obligeance et de charité se développait chez elle, et après une enfance mélancolique et réservée elle devenait expansive et encourageante aux malheureux, comme si elle eût renoncé tout d'un coup à vivre pour elle-même" (139). Her life becomes a model of selfless devotion. In Audebert's wedding poem, with which the novel closes, Tonine is presented as a saint:

> Toi qui fus bénie en devenant sainte, Tonine aux mains secou-rables, souviens-toi du jour où tu donnas à boire au pauvre voyageur et ton pain à la pauvre mendiante, et du jour où tu fermas les yeux du voleur abandonné de tous, après avoir fait entrer le repentir dans son âme coupable, et du jour où tu soignas le pauvre paralytique, objet de dégoût pour sa propre famille, et du jour où tu donnas ta mante, et de celui où tu donnas ta chaussure, et de celui, où, n'ayant plus rien à donner, tu donnas tes larmes, et de tous les jours de ta vie qui furent

marqués par des bienfaits, des dévouements, des sacrifices; de
tous ces jours-là, Tonine aux belles mains, souviens-toi! (255)

She is clearly a sister to Sand's Jeanne and to Consuelo, the "déesse
de la pauvreté."

Unlike Jeanne, however, Tonine has an opportunity to help
her fellow man on a large scale. In a *coup de théâtre* she inherits the
factory of her brother-in-law. When Sept-Epées returns from his
travels he finds it transformed into a model operation: "C'est à présent un atelier-modèle qui rapporte gros, et dont tous les profits
sont employés à donner l'apprentissage et l'éducation gratis aux
enfants de la Ville noire, des soins aux malades, des lectures et des
cours aux ouvriers, des secours et des avances à ceux qui ont eu des
accidents" (219). Given Sand's continued interest in education it is
not surprising that she has Tonine improve the educational opportunities for the children of the *Ville noire*. What is less convincing is
that while Sept-Epées has to travel widely and work for a number
of different masters to gain the knowledge and skills he brings back
home, Tonine acquires the knowledge she needs to run a factory
without ever leaving: "Elle avait voulu entendre de son mieux la
science et les arts de l'industrie qu'elle avait à gouverner, et, sans
être sortie de son Val-d'Enfer, elle s'était mise au courant du mouvement industriel et commercial de la France" (243). Toward the
end of the novel, the author tends to subvert the novel's realism.
The betrothal of Tonine and Sept-Epées illustrates this tendency.
The whole *Ville noire* turns into a kind of family festival for the two.
There is also a game played out between Tonine and Sept-Epées.
She does not at first reveal to him that she is the mysterious bene-
factor who has made all the improvements to the town and factory.
This sets up the sentimental dinner scene in which she finally reveals the truth. The supposed purpose of the masquerade is to convince Sept-Epées to marry Tonine when he thinks she is still poor
and to forestall any hesitations he might have in marrying an
heiress. But this issue never really arises. In fact, the money Tonine
has inherited smooths the path for their marriage, since one of
Tonine's reasons for not wanting to marry was her desire to continue to help others. Thus the novel's resolution runs counter to

that of *Le Meunier d'Angibault* since money is no longer seen as a source of evil.[11]

In fact, there are indications from the beginning that whereas Sept-Epées is to give up his dreams and adapt a more realistic, practical way of viewing the commercial-industrial world and his place in it, George Sand is not willing to do the same with her own romantic vision. In beginning to read the novel, one might expect, given the title, that, as in *Le Péché de M. Antoine*, Sand would pay some attention to the plight of the industrial workers, trapped in a dark, unhealthy environment. In fact, the name of the industrial center is the *Trou d'Enfer*. In the opening dialogue of the novel, Sept-Epées's friend Gaucher talks of the "enfer où nous sommes et le paradis qui nous invite" (5), namely the *ville haute*, which, in contrast to the *ville basse* or *Ville noire*, is colorful, manicured and full of architectural improvements. It is so loud where Sept-Epées and Gaucher work that they have to shout to each other in order to converse. Yet Gaucher is far from being bitter or even unhappy over his situation. For him there is no class conflict; he has no hatred for those living in the *ville haute*: "Tous ces gens riches qui, de là-haut, nous regardent suer, en lisant leurs journaux ou en taillant leurs rosiers, sont, ou d'anciens camarades, ou les enfants d'anciens maîtres ouvriers, qui ont bien gagné ce qu'ils ont et qui ne méprisent pas nos figures barbouillées et nos tabliers de cuir. Nous pouvons leur porter envie sans les haïr, puisqu'il dépend de nous, ou du moins de quelques-uns de nous, de monter où ils sont montés" (5). Gaucher admits that not all workers will be able to make the climb out of the *Ville noire*. Gaucher in fact does not see the position of the factory worker as undesirable:

> J'aime la rude musique du travail, et si par hasard j'ai une idée triste, en frappant mon enclume, je n'ai qu'à sortir un peu, à venir ici, et à regarder rire l'eau et le soleil pour me sentir fier et content! Oui, fier! car, au bout du compte, nous vivons là dans un endroit que le diable n'eût pas choisi pour en faire sa demeure, et nous y avons conquis la nôtre; nous avons cassé les reins à une montagne, forcé une rivière folle à travailler pour nous mieux que ne le feraient trente mille chevaux, enfin posé

nos chambres, nos lits et nos tables sur des précipices que nos
enfants regardent et côtoient sans broncher, et sur des chutes
d'eau dont le tremblement les berce mieux que le chant de leurs
mères! (8)

As in *Le Péché de M. Antoine*, the struggle between nature and industrial development is evoked here, but in contrast to the earlier
novel, it is not seen in a negative light—as the rape of the land by a
ruthless factory owner—but as a communal effort by the workers.

In this opening dialogue with Gaucher, Sept-Epées is rather
reserved in his comments, and it is not at all unlikely that the
reader would begin to presume he has different views from those
of Gaucher and does not see his situation in the *Ville noire* in nearly
as positive a light. In fact, Sept-Epées describes his first visit to his
godfather's home in the *Ville noire* as a descent into hell: "Je de-
scendis à travers les jardins, puis le long du roc, et enfin dans les
petites rues où l'on marche à tâtons, et je me hasardai à demander
mon parrain, le père Laguerre. Descends encore, me fut-il répondu;
descends jusqu'au Trou-d'Enfer, et là tu verras à ta gauche l'atelier
où il travaille" (11). But, as we have seen, this impression is soon
corrected; in fact, Sept-Epées is even more convinced than Gaucher
of the likelihood of rising up into the society of the *ville haute*. Thus
after playing lip service to the horrors of factory life, Sand changes
the reader's perspective to such an extent that it represents a complete reversal. The reader sees the action largely from the perspective of the factory-owner that Sept-Epées becomes. In the end
Sept-Epées's life story tells the reader that hard work, honesty, and
fidelity lead to happiness and prosperity.

Not all the characters in the novel, however, represent the
vantage point of the factory owner. There are two characters who
feel some antagonism toward those in the other part of the city,
namely Tonine and Sept-Epées's godfather, Laguerre. We have
seen that Tonine's opposition is nullified by having her enter the
ranks of the factory-owners, although it is made clear that she
will take a markedly different approach in her position. Laguerre,
on the other hand, maintains a steady distrust of the *ville haute*:
"Travailleur austère, cœur dévoué, cerveau étroit, ce vieux ne

faisait aucune merci aux parvenus, raillait leur luxe, et, du fond de sa Ville noire, blâmait les plus simples jouissances du bien-être comme des vices, comme des attentats à la dignité de la race ouvrière" (26). He ridicules Sept-Epées's ambition of being a factory owner. At one point he tells his godson that if he's looking for women of easy virtue he should look to the *ville haute*. But the marriage of Tonine and Sept-Epées at the end of the novel signals, in its bringing together of the two cities, the end of Laguerre's hostility: "En ce jour-là, on vit donc, sur la pelouse qui bordait un des côtés du bassin, et qui était comme le péristyle entre le ravin et la plaine, les deux villes rivales, mais toujours sœurs, se mêler cordialement dans une fête improvisée. Bien des susceptibilités, bien des rancunes, bien des méfiances, s'effacèrent. D'anciennes amitiés furent renouées, des griefs s'envolèrent aux sons des violons, et le vieux parrain de Sept-Epées, flatté de plusieurs politesses sur lesquelles il ne comptait pas, déclara que si la Ville noire était le sanctuaire de toute sagesse et de toute vertu, la ville peinte avait aussi du bon" (258-59). Even Morino, Tonine's brother-in-law is rehabilitated; he leaves Tonine his factory upon the condition that she improve the quality of life of the workers. Not only are the two parts of the city brought together, there is also a kind of reconciliation of nature and industry. Tonine's factory is "une maison de plaisance traversée par les flots de la rivière," half in the country: "Cette noble fabrique touchait à la campagne, et au pied d'un immense rocher bien assis par la nature, les reins en arrière et le front renversé comme pour recevoir les orages, dont il préservait sa base tranquille, on voyait s'ouvrir l'immense vallée avec ses noyers plantureux et des jeunes blés inondés de lumière" (226). Now industry is working with rather than against nature.[12]

All conflicts in the novel are resolved in the peace and harmony evoked in the conclusion. This brings the work close to being a utopian novel.[13] Courrier sees in the ending "une mise en relief du caractère encore utopique des aspirations généreuses" (xxviii). There is a sense in which the ending incorporates elements of many of the ideas of the utopian socialists Sand admired. The harmonious cooperation of man and nature in a communal effort recalls both Lamennais and Fourier. The idea of progressive and enlightened industrial development reflects the Saint-Simonian doctrine and, the closest of Sand's socialist doctrinaires, Pierre Leroux, is reflected in the character of Sept-Epées.[14] In this novel which returns to the social concerns of the 1840s Sand was perhaps paying homage to those thinkers who most influenced her view of man and society. On the other hand, the relentlessly utopian nature of the conclusion seems to express an awareness on the part of Sand that the ideas these men put forward on how to redefine society were in fact utopian, possible to put into effect in a novel, but not in the real world. Her on-site study of factory conditions in Thiers, as well as her general awareness of social and economic developments in France, could well have led her to see that the state of French society had evolved to such an extent that the often simple solutions of Leroux and company were not going to be able to deal with the complexity of an advanced industrial society.

George Sand was aware that she was dealing with exceptional cases—Tonine's situation can not be representative even for those few workers who do make it into the class of masters since they would achieve that goal through hard work and perseverance. In fact, Sand is not really looking at individuals in this novel, but at the whole. This becomes evident from a passage in which the narrator discusses the nature of manufacturing:

> Les détails de la vie manufacturière sont souvent rebutants à voir. Rien de triste comme un atelier sombre où chaque homme rivé, comme une pièce de mécanique, à un instrument de fatigue fonctionne, exilé du jour et du soleil, au sein du bruit et de la fumée; mais quand l'ensemble formidable du puissant levier de la production se présente aux regards, quand une population active et industrieuse résume son cri de guerre contre l'inertie et son cri de victoire sur les éléments par les mille voix de ses machines obéissantes, la pensée s'élève, le cœur bat comme au spectacle d'une grande lutte, et l'on sent bien que toutes ces forces matérielles, mises en jeu par l'intelligence, sont une gloire pour l'humanité, une fête pour le ciel. (129-30)

Inside the factory it is dark and oppressive, the workers are "exiles," but this is subordinated to the larger epic view of the majesty of man conquering nature. This perspective may strike many modern readers as disappointing; it may well have been understandable in the early days of the industrial revolution—when the power of the machine seemed awesome and wondrous —but it seems less palatable when we remember that *The Communist Manifesto* had already been published. However, it is precisely because society had become so much more complex and social problems so overwhelming—despite the government's position—that Sand tended to prefer looking at the larger picture.

❖ ❖ ❖

Le Marquis de Villemer was published in the same year as *La Ville noire*, but the subject matter could hardly have been more different. While the first novel focuses on the factory workers and their interrelationships, the second novel takes the reader into the world of the leisured classes. Although George Sand's choice of subjects for fiction in the last two decades of her life was eclectic, certain patterns emerge nonetheless, and this is evident in some of the similarities between these two apparently disparate novels.[15]

The principal character of the novel is not, as the title suggests, the Marquis de Villemer, but is rather the woman he eventually marries, Caroline de Saint-Geneix. Although Caroline comes from a noble family, it is of the lesser nobility and, more importantly, has suffered complete financial ruin. This is the reason she must hire herself out as a reader to the Marquise de Villemer. This initial situation is given the reader through the letter Caroline writes to her sister. This places the reader immediately into the perspective which Caroline has on the events of the story; this is maintained through virtually the entire novel.

Like Tonine, Caroline is intelligent and self-assured. She is also, like her, sensible and unsentimental. In some ways she recalls Henry James's heroines. She tells the Marquise with no hesitation—or tears—her own unhappy love story, her fiancé having deserted her when her family lost its fortune. Both women are a far cry from the heroines of the early novels, who experienced emotional roller-coaster rides and wore their hearts on their sleeves. Tonine has learned from the tragedy of her sister's life, just as Caroline has from her own experiences. Both women have matured and lost any illusions they might have had. They see more clearly and act more responsibly than the men. In fact they take decisive action to forestall becoming involved in love affairs with men they love because they see imperative moral reasons for doing so. It is they who are level-headed and self-sacrificing, not the men. Both women are proud and confident. They do not feel socially inferior to those around them and express no desire to rise to a higher social or economic class. Caroline is not impressed with the world of high nobility with which she comes in contact through the Marquise: "Je t'assure qu'avec de meilleures manières et un certain air de supériorité, on est généralement ici aussi nul que possible. On n'a plus d'opinions sur rien, on se plaint de tout et on ne sait le remède à rien. On dit du mal de tout le monde et on n'en est pas moins bien avec tout le monde" (27). She is not impressed by riches either: wealth has interest for her only in that it is needed to fulfill practical needs. This parallels closely the attitude of Tonine who had at one point considered marrying a wealthy physician from the *ville haute* but only because it would have supplied her with funds she could have used to help others. Like Tonine, as well, Caroline maintains a high degree of personal freedom and independence. This extends even to her position with the Marquise: "Je suis une esclave; mais je le suis de par ma volonté, et dès lors je me sens libre comme l'air dans ma conscience. Qu'y -t-il de plus libre que l'esprit d'un captif ou d'un proscrit pour sa foi" (36-37). She takes every opportunity to assert her own convictions and never changes her views to please the Marquise or anyone else.

Like Tonine, Caroline has a strong faith in God and a belief that he is watching over her. This is in fact evoked in the opening sentences of the letter to her sister: "Dieu n'abandonne pas ceux qui comptent sur lui et qui font leur possible pour aider sa douce providence" (1). She does not have an attitude of resignation, however; she is clear-headed about her situation, yet always maintains high spirits: "Je suis naturellement gaie, et j'ai conservé ma force au milieu des plus cruelles épreuves. Je n'ai aucun rêve d'amour dans la cervelle, je ne suis pas romanesque" (9). She expresses complete satisfaction with her position and rejects all suggestions that she marry. She is concerned first and foremost with others, not herself. Caroline's strength of character is revealed most clearly in her relation to her sister's family. After the family's bankruptcy she remains with them and soon becomes the family's sole support: "Sentant que sa sœur manquait d'ordre et d'activité, voyant d'ailleurs qu'elle subissait d'année en année les labeurs et les préoccupations de la maternité, elle se fit la gouvernante de sa maison, la bonne de ses enfants, la première servante en un mot du jeune ménage, et dans cette austère fonction du dévouement elle sut mettre tant de grâce, de bon sens et de cordialité que tout fut heureux autour d'elle" (22). When her brother-in-law dies, this devotion to her sister's family becomes her life's mission.

Caroline's merit in sacrificing her own life for others is highlighted through contrasts with other women in the novel. Her patron, the Marquise, bemoans the fact that, because of her elder son's profligate ways, she is not able to live at her accustomed level; she is convinced that her current life is "une vie de privations, celle du marquis un purgatoire, enfin que l'on ne peut pas être heureux quand, avec beaucoup d'honneur et l'orgueil d'une conscience sans tâche, on n'a pas au moins deux cent mille livres de rente" (148). She tells Caroline at one point that she would have died had she had to face Caroline's fate of utter destitution; the Marquise feels this would have been more honorable than finding the courage, as Caroline had done, "de travailler pour vivre, et d'accepter une sorte de domesticité" (262). The Marquise is moved by the sacrifice Diane de Xaintrailles, a rich heiress, is making in marrying her eldest son, the Duke. The praise of this "sacrifice" causes Caroline some bitterness: "Eh quoi, se disait-elle, ma vie de misère, de dévouement, de courage et de gaieté quand même, mon renoncement volontaire à toutes les joies de la vie, ne seraient rien auprès de l'héroïsme d'une Xaintrailles qui admet l'idée de se contenter de deux cent mille livres de rente pour épouser un homme accompli!" (151). These comparisons place into a telling light the true extent of Caroline's devotion and selflessness. Such outbursts on her part are rare;

she does not hold a grudge against the Marquise for making her into the equivalent of a servant; in fact she feels genuine affection for her.

Caroline's strength of will emerges most clearly in her relationship with the Marquis. One incident in particular highlights her courage and determination. Late one night she hears glass break in the Marquis's room. She is convinced that the noise has been caused by robbers or murderers but doesn't hesitate to go herself to supply help: "Nul autre qu'elle ne pouvait arriver aussi vite, et sa seule approche pouvait faire lâcher prise aux égorgeurs. Dans la tourelle du Griffon se trouvait d'ailleurs la corde d'un petit beffroi. Elle se dit tout cela en courant" (186). As it turns out, the Marquis is in no danger from outside; he is just going through a severe emotional and physical crisis and has inadvertently broken the window in his room. Providence has directed Caroline to him just at the moment of crisis. It does not take long for it to become evident that she and the Marquis are kindred souls. This extends beyond personal attraction to similarities in ideas, intellectual interests and even work habits: "Elle était pour lui, non une autre personne agissant à ses côtés, mais son propre esprit, qu'il sentait vivre en face de lui" (247). Caroline is moved to sympathetic tears by the Marquis's account, in the book he is writing, of the injustices in past French society. Their relationship becomes closer when Caroline helps to nurse him through a serious illness, a development not unexpected in a George Sand novel. Caroline believes, however, that to allow herself to fall in love with the Marquis would be a betrayal of the Marquise's trust. When Caroline learns that the Marquis is intending to propose marriage, despite his mother's disapproval, she decides to disguise herself and run away. She is resolved to steel herself against giving in to the temptation of accepting the Marquis: "Il faut qu'à toute heure, n'importe où, je sois prête à le rencontrer et à lui dire: Souffrez en vain, mourez s'il le faut, je ne vous aime pas!" (286). She goes to the mountains to live with her former wet nurse, Justine Peyraque, thus completing the image the Duke had of her initially as "une reine et une bergère dans la même personne" (74). In fact Caroline feels completely at home in the mountains and, far from pining away, leads a full, active life.

At the same time she comes to realize that she really does love the Marquis, and she begins to reflect on the wisdom of her course of action, wondering if she were not acting out of hurt pride. She writes to her sister to tell her the legend she has heard of a mountain girl who had performed a miracle and then out of pride had tried to repeat it, dying in the process. Caroline clearly is affected by the story, seeing its relevance to her situation. Justine's husband, a fervent Protestant, tells her to stand firm, that God wants her to maintain her courage in not giving in to the Marquis. She does so until the dramatic events which lead to their union. In an unlikely turn of events, Caroline has unknowingly come into contact with the Marquis's natural son, Didier, who is being secretly brought up in the mountains. Through his son, the Marquis, who has been searching frantically for Caroline, finally finds her and follows her as she is driving in a carriage with Peyraque. But it begins to snow and the Marquis, already ill, succumbs to the cold. Caroline had been able to keep up her resolve not to have any contact with the Marquis until she discovers he has been lost in the snow. She saves him from certain death, allowing Caroline once more to nurse him back to health.

Just after he has been found, Caroline's love suddenly bursts through the protective wall:

> Je vous aime plus que ma fierté et plus que mon honneur! J'ai nié cela longtemps en moi-même, je l'ai nié à Dieu dans mes prières, et je mentais à Dieu et à moi. . . . J'ai été assez orgueilleuse, assez cruelle, et vous avez trop souffert par ma faute! Je vous aime, entendez-vous? Je ne veux pas être votre femme, parce que ce serait vous plonger dans des remords poignants, dans d'irrémédiables douleurs; mais je serai votre amie, votre servante, la mère de votre enfant, votre compagne cachée et fidèle. Je passerai pour votre maîtresse, pour la mère véritable de Didier, peut-être! Eh bien, j'y consens, j'accepte le mépris que j'ai tant redouté. (361-62)

Thus Caroline has decided to disregard the inevitable social disapproval in being the Marquis's "companion." She claims for herself a different moral code and a different interpretation of Christianity: "Il n'y a pas d'autre honneur en ce monde, il n'y a pas d'autre vertu devant Dieu que de t'aimer, de te servir et de te consoler" (366). It is not Peyraque's unyielding and conventional moral and religious values which win out, but rather the power of love.

This is not a surprising outcome in a George Sand novel. Caroline is being in a sense rewarded for her virtue. Yet in contrast to past female characters, this does not seem to be an absolutely necessary solution. Caroline is such a strong character that one can conceive of her living by her own devices quite successfully. It does not strike me as an abandonment of feminism when Sand portrays such a female character who eventually marries. I would disagree with Langlade, who sees the "feminist dream" as dead in Sand's late novels (18). Marriage, redefined as a union of equals, had always been presented in Sand's fiction as a desirable outcome. What she was fighting against in her "feminist" novels was a conventional view of marriage in which the husband was the lord and master. Here Caroline is the one who sets the terms for the relationship. Indeed, without Caroline the Marquis would not be the man he has become. He admits that Caroline has had a determining effect on his life: "Vous m'avez ordonné de vivre, et j'ai vécu, de me calmer, et je me suis calmé, de croire en Dieu et en moi-même, et j'ai cru" (213). Caroline not only nurses him back to health she also effects other changes in him: "Le marquis n'avait pas su jusque-là révéler toutes les séductions de son intelligence et de sa personne; il avait été contraint, troublé, malade. Caroline ne vit pas tout d'un coup le changement qui si fit en lui d'une manière insensible, lorsqu'il devint éloquent, jeune et beau, en recouvrant jour par jour, heure par heure, la santé, la confiance en lui-même, la certitude de sa puissance et le charme que donne le bonheur aux nobles physionomies longtemps voilées par le doute" (217-18). Caroline plays a similar role to that of Edmée or Fadette; she elevates and transforms her lover.

The Marquis is, like Caroline, a selfless person ready to give all to help others. He gives up not only his wealth to pay his brother's debts and to allow him to lead the life he is accustomed to, but he is willing to sacrifice what is most valuable in his own life in the process. For his brother's welfare he is ready to give up his health and even to sacrifice accessibility to the research materials he needs. The book he is writing, *Histoire des titres*, has becomes his life's passion. Its theme is a reflection of the Marquis's sense of justice and charity: "Ce fils d'une grande maison longtemps privilégiée, nourri dans l'orgueil de race et le dédain de la plèbe, apportait devant la moderne civilisation l'acte d'accusation du patriciat, les pièces du procès, les preuves d'usurpation, d'indignité ou de forfaiture, et prononçait la déchéance au nom de la logique et de l'équité, au nom de la conscience humaine, mais surtout au nom de l'idée chrétienne évangélique" (215). Thus the Marquis shares the ideas and concerns of the principal characters of Sand's socialist novels. But in his case it is all theory; in fact he keeps his views to himself and does not even plan to publish his work during his lifetime.

No real conflict with his mother over his marriage to Caroline arises. The crisis is artificially brought on by Madame d'Arglade, who convinces the Marquise that Caroline has been the Duke's mistress. It is for this reason that the Marquise has opposed the marriage, not, as Caroline had thought, because she was too poor and insignificant. Thus, as so often in Sand's fiction, what separates the lovers is not real obstacles but misperceptions and misunderstandings. The impediment to the idea of marrying Caroline that the Marquis's poverty represents is also cleared away. He becomes, through the Duke's marriage with an heiress, even richer than he was before. He no longer has a family duty to marry rich.

While in comparison with Caroline the Marquis appears weak and oscillating, he gains in stature when seen alongside his brother, the Duke. A notorious womanizer, the Duke has spent not only his fortune but those of his brother and mother as well. He is repeatedly compared to Richardson's Lovelace, which seems not inappropriate given the eighteenth-century flavor of this novel. He is mindful of the sacrifice his brother is making for his sake, but his gratitude does not lead to a fundamental change in outlook or behavior: "Il voulait, en vivant sur le pied le plus modeste chez son frère, durant six mois tous les ans, refuser tous les ans six mille francs sur sa pension, et si le marquis repoussait ce sacrifice, il emploierait la somme en réparations et en améliorations au manoir fraternel; mais il fallait une amourette pour couronner toute cette vertu, et là s'arrêtait la vertu du brave duc" (128). In another of the novel's unlikely developments, the unrepentant Don Juan is in the end won over by the sixteen-year-old Diane fresh from convent school. Despite his reputation, the Duke has no difficulty in being accepted as Diane's suitor by her family nor in being accepted by polite society as a whole. The Duke himself has an easy time of it explaining his past sins: "Ce qui m'a rendu mauvais, c'est le doute, c'est l'expérience, ce sont les coquettes et les ambitieuses" (242). Thus the women themselves—the victims—are to blame.[16]

That George Sand lets this go by without commentary on the cynicism or immorality of the leisured classes is in part a reflection of the softening of Sand's view. With the exception of the Marquis's book—dealing with past, not contemporary French society—there is no finger-pointing in the novel, or in *La Ville noire*. The Duke is brought into the fold at the end, just as everyone is at the end of the industrial novel. The reconciliation in *La petite Fadette* between rich and poor, outsiders and the peasant community is extended in *Les Maîtres Sonneurs* to embrace different regions and ways of life. It is carried further in the final vision of *La Ville noire* to embrace nature and industry and different social and economic classes and in *Le Marquis de Villemer* even the immoral and egotistical are included. It should be noted that in contrast to the marriages in the novels of the 1840s, the matches in the two novels of 1860 are safe. Tonine and Sept-Epées are both orphans from working-class families. Caroline and the Marquis are both from the aristocracy. In each case the unions are between social equals. Thus the respective marriages represent no threat to the social order.

The Duke's acceptance signals the different perspective from which individuals and their actions are viewed in these two novels. This was clear in the narrator's comments on factories in *La Ville noire*: the individual disappears behind the significance of the whole. In *Le Marquis de Villemer* Caroline's view of history—which inspires the Marquis to finish his book—also speaks in favor of the larger picture:

> Elle convint que l'historien est plus enchaîné que l'artiste à l'exactitude du fait, mais elle nia qu'on pût procéder par des principes différents dans l'une ou l'autre voie. Le passé et même le présent d'une vie individuelle ou collective n'avaient, selon elle, de signification et de couleur que dans leur ensemble et dans leurs effets. Les petits accidents, les irrésolutions, les déviations même rentraient dans le domaine de la fatalité, c'est-à-dire de la loi des choses finies. Pour comprendre une âme, un peuple, une époque, il fallait les voir éclairés par l'événement comme la campagne par le soleil. (204)

It is from this larger perspective that the Duke's behavior can appear excusable. If it is society as a whole that counts, then the women whose lives the Duke has ruined diminish in importance. A similar view emerges from the narrator's statement on landscape: "La grandeur est partout pour ceux qui portent cette faculté en eux-mêmes, et ce n'est pas une illusion qu'ils nourrissent, c'est une révélation de ce qui est en réalité dans la nature d'une manière plus ou moins exprimée" (210). It is not deception to overlay an individual, harmonizing perspective over observed reality; rather what results is a generalized and idealized truth. The narrator even at one point makes the argument that historical truth is relative, dependent on the perspective he uses. There is a tendency toward moderation in Sand's late novels, to see in shades of grey, rather than in black or white. Absolute villains are rare. There is a kind of moderation and tolerance (except in religious matters) that is quite different from earlier novels.[17]

The perspective in favor of the wider, general view of things, is evident in *Le Marquis de Villemer* also in the way in which the story is presented. The narrator mentions several times that he is reproducing selected letters of Caroline's and even that the letters are being edited: "Le reste de la lettre de Caroline avait trait à d'autres personnes et à d'autres circonstances qui l'avaient plus ou moins frappée. Comme ces détails ne se rattachent pas directement à notre récit, nous les supprimons en attendant que ce récit nous y ramène" (46). The story is not told in chronological order and the narrator is careful to inform the reader of how the pieces of narrative fit together. Short flashbacks give information on the past lives of Caroline and the Marquise. Each time the narrator comments on where he is going and why. The narrator in both novels is clearly placed above the action and the characters. In *Le Marquis de Villemer* he makes general statements inspired by the characters' conduct.[18] We are far removed indeed from the narrator being swept up by the emotion of the characters, as in earlier novels. Yet it is of course the individual fates of Caroline and the Marquis and of Tonine and Sept-Epées which interest the reader. While particularly the character of Caroline is engaging and convincing, the reader's relationship with the narrator is not as satisfactory. One almost has the sense that Caroline emerges as an individual despite the narrator. Could it have been the desire to downplay the importance of the individual which led George Sand to entitle the novel as she did, when Caroline is so obviously the central character?

10

The Freedom to Love

Revolt and Renewal in *Mademoiselle La Quintinie* and *Nanon*

Elevez-la chrétiennement, rien de plus! Pas d'exagérations,
pas de couvent, peu de prêtres, la liberté d'aimer.
                    —*Mademoiselle La Quintinie* (331)

Out of the mixed bag of George Sand's late novels I will discuss two which are representative of her enduring concern with coming to terms through her fiction with serious social issues. *Mademoiselle La Quintinie* (1863) and *Nanon* (1872) feature extensive exchanges of ideas involving religious, social, and political concerns. The characters' lives are directly and deeply affected by such concerns; both novels highlight characters with "missions" and wills strong enough to carry them out. These novels involve a struggle against extremists out to destroy the basic moral fabric of society. In the process some of the values always dear to George Sand—charity, sincerity, love, and freedom—are championed. Neither novel leaves the reader in doubt as to Sand's views on the questions she raises. This is particularly the case with *Mademoiselle La Quintinie*, a classic *roman à thèse*. There is a certain aggressiveness and intolerance to the novel which is lacking in the novels of the 1840s which, too, were explicit in their social messages.[1]

As so often in George Sand's fiction the ideas are enmeshed in a story of two lovers who must overcome serious obstacles to their unions. In *Mademoiselle La Quintinie* that obstacle is the Catholic Church. Lucie la Quintinie and Emile Lemontier meet and immediately fall in love. They do not, however, rush head-long into matrimony. They are singularly level-headed and unsentimental lovers. The directness and simplicity with which they express their love and the fact that this occurs in the first few pages of the novel indicate to the reader that the love intrigue will not involve, as in earlier Sand novels, two lovers tentatively groping toward each other. There are no social or financial barriers to overcome. Nor are there any prior commitments to contend with. Rather the obstacles come from outside; forces are at work within the Church, which for pernicious reasons is intent on keeping them apart. Thus the situation is quite different from the love intrigues in earlier novels in which the blind forces of society at large are to blame. Here the finger-pointing is direct and uncompromising.

Lucie and Emile soon discover that although they agree in almost all areas they have very different religious backgrounds and beliefs. Lucie is a firm believer in the Catholic Church and has seriously considered becoming a nun. Emile is the son of a well-known free-thinker whose views he has adopted. Emile is not willing to consider the possibility of marrying Lucie and letting each partner go his own way in the area of religion. This is presented not as intolerance but as a justifiable fear of having his wife's priest become an unwelcome third marriage partner. According to Lucie's grandfather, who has no love for the Catholics, "la dévotion rompt sans façon tous les liens du cœur et de la famille" (57). In fact he tells Emile that his own marriage was destroyed by a priest who insinuated himself into the marriage. Encouraged by his father, Emile nonetheless hopes for an eventual solution. But although Lucie is willing to listen to his arguments she is surrounded by friends and family who are adamantly opposed to her accepting Emile as her husband. Especially troublesome for Emile is the arrival on the scene of a mysterious Italian who has an unfathomable hold on

Lucie. We later learn this is Moreali, alias Abbe Févart, the priest who was Lucie's "director of conscience" in her convent school and before that her mother's platonic lover. It soon becomes apparent that Moreali is working behind the scene to frustrate the marriage by persuading Lucie's father to oppose it. The fact that Moreali is likable and intelligent makes him an all the more formidable adversary for Emile. His father warns him of the difficulty he faces in changing Lucie's beliefs and offers as an alternative the comfortable life of living together ignoring any difference in religion. He summarizes his son's choice: "Sois eunuque et engraisse, ou sois homme et lutte" (70). This is typical of the emotionally charged way in which religion is discussed in the novel. Alternatives to the author's viewpoint which are raised in the novel, as here, are immediately undercut by the terms in which they are put forward. The position of Emile and his father is always expressed in a direct, confident manner, as if it were a matter of course that any one without preconceived ideas would accept it without question. For the reader to be thus "coopted" from the beginning of the novel into the side of the protagonist, is a familiar pattern in the *roman à thèse*.[2]

The picture Emile's father paints of what Emile is likely to suffer from Catholic persecution shows a vast conspiracy at work: "Epoux et père, il [le prêtre] te disputera la confiance de ta femme et le respect de tes enfants, car il est partout! De tout temps, il a ourdi une vaste conspiration au sein des civilisations les plus florissantes, il traite avec les souverains, il les menace, il les effraye. Il a pénétré dans tous les conseils, il a mis le pied dans tous les foyers domestiques; il est dans les armées, dans les magistratures, dans les corps savants, dans les académies, sur la place publique, sur le navire en plein mer, dans la campagne, à tous les carrefours, dans le cabaret de village, dans le couvent, dans l'alcôve conjugale" (69). Lemontier offers this and other pieces of advice to his son in a long letter. But Emile has already heard it all since Lemontier is simply recording, for Emile's later study, a summary of their conversation. Sand does not use the epistolary form here nearly as adeptly as in *Jacques*. The letters, like this one, often seem superfluous. The long discussions of religious beliefs contained in many of the letters are offset by occasional letters from Emile's friend, Henri, an aspiring author, whose light-hearted view of the actions and actors serves as a comic counterweight to the seriousness of the novel. But they are hardly enough to change the tone of the novel. Lemontier's conversation with Emile and subsequent letter have the effect of charging Emile with a kind of crusade against the Church. He sees Emile's chances as at best uncertain: "Nous nous sommes embrassés, et je t'ai laissé retourner à ton jardin des Oliviers, où l'isolement, la douleur et l'effroi t'attendent. Tu vas beaucoup lutter et beaucoup souffrir: vaincras-tu? Je l'ignore. Tu es seul contre un million d'ennemis" (71). This is meant to be a reflection of the seriousness of the threat posed by the Church. But the obstacles which Emile will have to overcome only serve to fill him with a new determination; he now has a mission to fulfill. In the process he is ready to suffer to reach his goal: "Je subirai toutes les persécutions, j'accepterai l'effet de toutes les vengeances: il faut que toute initiation ait ses martyrs" (74). In striving to conquer Lucie's Catholic faith, Emile casts himself in the mold of the martyred saints. Here, as in the reference earlier to the olive garden, the secular religion of the Lemontiers is given equal weight with the Church through evocation of familiar reference points in that very tradition. In contrast to Henri, Emile takes himself very seriously, in fact, to the point of appearing over-zealous, even somewhat priggish. His refusal to tell a lie is so strong a conviction that, to Lucie's exasperation, he is unwilling to allow Lucie to use as an excuse for their being together the possibility that he be converted to Catholicism. Even Emile's father warns his son against being too rigid. He, in fact, resembles in this respect his namesake in *Le Péché de M. Antoine*.

The epistolary form (used in the first two thirds of the novel) is designed to create the impression of objectivity; the characters are presenting their own views not filtered through the narrator. But as we have seen, the Catholic viewpoint is hardly given a fair hearing. This is due in part to the juxtaposition of letters. Directly after the exchange of letters between Lemontier and Emile just referred to, the narrator inserts the first letter from Moreali to Lucie, thus giving the Catholic viewpoint. But whereas Lemontier's letter deals with questions of mankind's welfare and is full of noble sentiments and high ideals, Moreali's missive speaks in mysterious terms of his

enemies, of the alias he wants to use and of other subterfuges he is planning. The forces of good fight above-board and with the weapons of truth and sincerity; the forces of evil (the Church) use lies and trickery. The denouement of the novel is an illustration of this. Moreali, losing the fight for Lucie's soul, turns one of Lucie's servants into a spy and then when the house is empty sneaks in to try a find a mysterious letter. But Henri and Lucie foil his efforts by finding the letter first. This puts Moreali's back to the wall and leads to his confession and the eventual happy resolution of the novel. The confession is a perfect "set-up" for Lemontier who offers to Moreali—and the reader—an interpreting "résumé" of it. He is able to use the admissions he has forced out of Moreali as weapons against him and the Church.

An even more damning force for the Church comes from an unexpected source, Lucie. Lucie is described as "née sainte" (310). Her deep religious beliefs have not prevented her from becoming accomplished in a number of areas; like so many of Sand's highly spiritual women, she is an outstanding musician. In her conversations with Emile she demonstrates both intelligence and open-mindedness. It is these qualities which have led her to begin to have doubts about various aspects of the Catholic Church, even before her contact with Emile and his father. Her insight into abuses are an effective weapon in Sand's indictment of the Church in that she can be presumed to be at the outset favorably disposed toward that institution.

She had intended to be a teacher in a Catholic school, she writes to Moreali, but a closer acquaintance with these schools caused her to change her mind: "Ces établissements ne peuvent se soutenir qu'à l'aide de spéculations et de calculs dont le côté matériel me répugne, et puis ils sont bien plus institués par l'esprit de parti du dehors que par l'esprit de charité du dedans. L'hostilité déclarée, ardente, sans cesse en mouvement de cette lutte contre le siècle a quelque chose qui m'effraye et me consterne" (99). As if this weren't enough Lucie begins to see that a similar spirit reigns elsewhere in the Church: "J'ai vu un esprit de lucre et de domination poussé et soutenu par un esprit de conspiration, je ne dirai pas contre tel ou tel gouvernement, mais contre toute espèce

d'institutions ayant la liberté pour base" (100). Her dream of brotherhood and charity created by the Church has been destroyed in the face of the reality she has experienced. She had seen the ideal of the Church as being that of creating a "vaste fraternité religieuse" (101) which would bring spiritual and practical benefits to the masses. Instead the corruption she sees points to two of Sand's cardinal sins, selfishness and insincerity. Lucie lists in her catalog of grievances some of the same complaints Sand had evoked in *Mauprat* and *Consuelo*, that priests are home-wreckers, that hypocrisy is rampant within the Church, and that members of religious orders use the Church as a secure place to practice their sins. Finally, Lucie tells Moreali, she had as her last refuge of faith in the Church the Carmelite Convent but even that proves to be unworthy: "J'y ai reconnu, à mon dernier examen, un esprit étroit et sombre, un ascétisme sans chaleur, un sauvage mépris de l'humanité, une protestation sincère, mais sauvage et stupide, contre la civilisation et contre l'avenir de la société" (103). One note that Lucie sounds repeatedly in her criticism of the Church is that it is contrary to the spirit of the age. George Sand felt she was living in an age of progress and great scientific achievement and clearly believed that "en plein 19e siècle," as she writes several times in the novel, the Catholic Church was trying to turn the clock back. In fact, in the first letter of the novel, Emile celebrates the progress represented by the railroad and contrasts the ease of communication it represents with the medieval towers which represent the will to stop all communication.

Although Lucie loses her desire to teach in a Catholic school, she still maintains a deep interest in children. This is strengthened by an experience she has quite similar to that of Brulette in *Les Maîtres Sonneurs*. She adopts a child who is at first disagreeable and unloving, but she and the child slowly grow to love and need each other. She learns from this experience, she later tells Emile, the nature of her mission on earth: "Tous mes raisonnements exaltés sont tombés devant le fait éprouvé. L'état le plus sublime et le plus religieux, c'est l'état le plus naturel" (161). Being a wife and mother has become in her eyes a more exalted position than that of being a nun. She gradually comes to realize that if her love for Lucette brought her closer to a viable relationship to God, her love for Emile can do the same. She tells Emile, in fact, that she has heard a voice from heaven, telling her it's right to marry him: "J'ai reconnu que mon affection pour vous avait grandi et éclairé ma foi" (163). She sees that God is not to be found in solitude and contemplation but in the active life men and women were intended to lead.

As Lucie's beliefs begin to evolve in this direction, her attitude toward the practices of the Church changes: she sees them as "une gêne entre Dieu et moi" (197). She condemns as well the activities of the priests and monks which have nothing to do with religion. She rejects the subterfuges which Moreali uses. As she drifts farther from her Catholic faith she begins to embrace the concepts of tolerance, humanity, and freedom of choice which lie at the heart of Emile and his father's beliefs. Finally, she writes a letter to Emile's father acknowledging her understanding of his doctrine: "Il y a donc au-dessus de tous les cultes un culte suprême, celui de l'humanité, c'est-à-dire de la vraie charité chrétienne, qui respecte jusqu'aux portes du tombeau, jusqu'au delà, la liberté de la conscience" (230). She has come to a recognition, she tells him, that her love for God must coalesce with her love for an eventual husband: "J'ai le devoir de comprendre et de servir Dieu selon les vues de l'homme à qui je consacrai volontairement ma vie tout entière" (230). The priest has been replaced in his position of primacy by the husband. That it is the woman who conforms to the man offers a distinct departure from the pattern of Sand's novels of the 1830s and forties. The formal break with the Church occurs when Lucie attends a service in which the priest makes a fierce personal attack on a fellow priest; she declares she can have nothing more to do with an institution which condones such a breach of basic respect for one's fellow man. The ultimate judgment is based on relations between people not with God.

In her letter to Moreali outlining her views on the abuses of the Church, Lucie also tells Moreali that he seems to have changed his religious views as well. In his response Moreali acknowledges that this has indeed occurred. He no longer favors tolerance and mutual good-will but believes a more radical approach is necessary in modern society. He has come to believe in the teachings of Father

Onorio, a radical Italian priest whose basic position he summarizes for Lucie: "La religion est perdue. Tout est à recommencer. Il faut la reconstituer sur une base inébranlable, l'orthodoxie. En fait de religion, il n'y a pas de moyen terme, c'est tout ou rien. La discipline est devenue un fardeau à l'homme, parce que l'homme a marché dans la voie des prospérités matérielles et qu'il ne s'est plus soucié des choses de l'autre vie. La mort de l'âme, c'est ce que les hommes du siècle appellent le progrès" (109). Following his insistence on discarding all that is not faith, Onorio rails against modern science and modern thought and in fact advocates the destruction of modern civilization: "Les idées ont fait leur temps, elles n'ont servi qu'à égarer l'homme. Il faut que le règne du sentiment revienne, il faut que la foi purifie tout; mais c'est à la condition de détruire ce bel édifice humain qu'on appelle la civilisation" (111). He has given Moreali the mission of finding the few true believers left and with them beginning anew: "Cherche par le monde le petit nombre des vrais fidèles et porte-leur la vraie parole. Dégage-les de tous les liens du siècle et de la famille, qui sont des liens de chair et de sang" (111-12). This is the secret mission what has led Moreali to seek out Lucie. He plans to become the director of the new monastery which is to include Lucie. In contrast to the orthodox Catholics Onorio has at least the merit of being sincere in his beliefs. But what he advocates is the destruction of the family and of society. In his belief there is no room for human love or forgiveness: "Je me moque bien de votre nouvelle idole, de cette bête de l'Apocalypse que vous appelez l'humanité, c'est-à-dire la race humaine corrompue et vouée au culte de la matière! Jésus est venu pour la racheter, et elle s'est de nouveau vendue à Satan. Que Dieu l'abandonne, puisqu'elle a abandonné Dieu" (112). Clearly this branch of the Catholic Church is no more acceptable than that denounced by Lucie. In the process George Sand is indicting a kind of fundamental evangelicalism.

Sand employed still another strategy in denouncing the Church; exposing the true nature of a priest's life. This is accomplished through the portrayal of the mysterious figure of Moreali. He first appears when Emile happens to see him making a secret night visit to an altar Lucie has set up along the banks of a lake. He remains for much of the novel a shadowy and sometimes sinister figure, whose very identify is uncertain. He is compared at one point to Tartuffe. But he is not a totally evil character; he and Emile even become friends. His problems derive from the impossibility of controlling his passions. Lucie's mother had developed such a strong emotional attachment to him that she was never able to love her husband. In the act of conceiving Lucie, she had imagined she was making love to Moreali. Moreali had so influenced her that when dying she had told him to keep Lucie from marrying: "Préservez-la du mariage, qui est une honte et un abrutissement" (306). It was in part in fulfillment of this request and in part in the belief that Lucie was ideally suited for a convent that Moreali had engaged in the elaborate intrigue he set up to thwart the marriage of Lucie.

Moreali tells his tale to Lemontier who deduces from Moreali's experiences a need for two specific reforms in the lives and functions of Catholic priests: the abolition of priests' celibacy vows and of confession. Preventing priests from marrying is equated to robbing them of their humanity, making them into lower animals, even vegetables (320). Thus priests are being asked not to evolve into angels but to degenerate into beasts. His arguments are supported by the account Moreali gives of his ambiguous relationship with the beautiful women he has confessed. The relationship with Lucie's mother had wrought havoc on Moreali's life. He even took to following young girls on the streets of Paris with the thought of attacking them. By the end of the novel Moreali too has seen that the Church erred in prohibiting priests from marrying. The fact that the Church is not infallible after all leads him to a profound spiritual crisis. Moreali in the end decides to use the fortune he has inherited, like François the *champi* from an anonymous parent, to help the poor he encounters on his travels. His conversion is the final triumph of Lemontier's cause and that of the novel's *thèse*. But as so much else in the novel, it does not ring true. Especially troublesome in this respect is the General's willingness to forgive Moreali and become his friend and advisee after the priest has not only destroyed his marriage but had earlier contributed largely to the death of his wife.

George Sand's primary goal in writing *Mademoiselle La Quintinie* was to attack the Catholic Church. We have seen that the abuses of the Church surface in several different ways—through the efforts to stop Lucie and Henri's marriage, through Lucie's letters to Moreali, and through the actions and words of Moreali and Onorio. The multiple approaches, all showing the same results, are designed to leave the reader with no "way out"; no room for doubt remains as to the evil of the Church.[3] Yet there are also positive spiritual beliefs introduced in the novel which Sand wanted to transmit to the reader. These are embodied above all in Emile's father. Unlike Moreali he has maintained his intellectual independence: "Mon père a travaillé quarante ans, cherchant à travers les profondeurs du passé non pas tant les curiosités de l'érudition que les vérités de l'histoire philosophique. Il n'a été ni professeur ni fonctionnaire sous aucun gouvernement. Il n'a voulu appartenir à aucun corps de la science officielle. Sa fortune et son peu d'ambition directe lui ont permis de conserver une indépendance absolue" (29). This suggests impartiality and fairness on his part. He does not actually make his appearance on the scene until two thirds of the way through the novel. But his presence is felt through the letters Emile writes him and the responses Lucie gives. In the process Emile builds his father into a larger-than-life figure, as is indicated in this account of his father's service to mankind:

> Tes idées sont simples, concises et nettes; tu les as dégagées d'une suite d'études et de travaux qui se présentent à mes yeux comme une puissante chaîne de montagnes, et à présent tu t'es assis au faîte de la plus haute cime, tu as regardé la terre étendue sous tes pieds, et puis, élevant tes mains vers la Divinité, tu lui as dit: 'Non, le mal n'est pas ton œuvre! . . . L'erreur doit se dévorer elle-même comme ces volcans déchaînés, qui, aux premiers âges du globe, ont servi à constituer l'écorce terrestre, berceau fécond de la vie. En toi est la source du bien, la loi du vrai, et l'homme y boira de plus en plus à mesure qu'il te connaîtra.' Consolé par la foi, tu t'es relevé, mon père, et, le front baigné de lumière, tu as souri à ces hommes qui te criaient: 'Nous avons la vérité; Dieu ne se révèle qu'à nous et pour nous! . . .' (73)

As in earlier examples, Emile uses Biblical images to invoke the holy mission with which his father has been entrusted. Lemontier becomes in this perspective a divinely inspired prophet—of secular humanism. When the fight for Lucie becomes desperate Lemontier arrives and battles for control of Lucie's soul almost like an exorcist. As soon as Lemontier appears Moreali sends for Onorio and the siege begins.

Lemontier wins through the weaknesses of his combatants and of their cause but also through the strength of his own faith. In the process of presenting his arguments designed to "save" Lucie, Sand was, of course, introducing her own ideas to the reader. For Lemontier "la base de tout principe [est] la sainte liberté" (179). He is in favor of tolerance and progress: "Toutes les idées, toutes les actions humaines se rattachent désormais à l'un de ces principes éternellement en guerre: la négation du progrès, qui est un principe de mort; la *perfectibilité*, mot nouveau, encore incomplet, mais qui s'efforce d'exprimer le développement de la vie sous toutes ses faces divines et humaines" (65). As is typical for a *roman à thèse*, the opposing sets of values are shown in black and white, there is no room for uncertainty or hesitation. Lemontier fears in his time the arrival of a new era of intolerance and a return to Restoration era conditions, caused in part by the lack of freedom of press in the Second Empire: "Il y a une chose certaine, c'est que, si l'interdiction de la presse libre se prolonge beaucoup et si nos contemporains s'endorment sous certaines influences cléricales, avant dix ans le faux christianisme, l'hypocrisie, l'esprit persécuteur en un mot sera debout" (68). Sand implies throughout the novel that the Church's campaign against its opponents is being tacitly supported by the government.

Lemontier's religious beliefs revolve above all around worshiping God through developing to the maximum extent one's potential as a human being: "L'homme doit être l'homme autant que possible, c'est-à-dire se tenir aussi près de la Divinité que ses forces le lui permettent. C'est par là seulement qu'il se place au-dessus des animaux. . . . C'est par cette constante aspiration vers l'idéal que l'homme s'affirme lui-même, rend hommage à Dieu, prouve sa foi et fait acte de religion réelle" (64). An important part of being

human is love. The absence of love for another human being necessarily distorts the relationship to God: "Dieu ne veut donc pas être
aimé avec le même esprit et avec le même cœur qu'il nous a donnés
pour aimer notre semblable, et, du moment que nous croyons en
lui, nous avons nécessairement pour lui le sentiment qu'il réclame
de nous; mais ce sentiment n'existe pas dans une âme que l'ascétisme dérobe à l'amour humain, car il s'y dénature et devient
amour humain lui-même, ce qui est une idolâtrie, un délire et un
blasphème" (48-49). This not only casts priests—and Catholic
saints—in a negative light, it also raises marriage to a new spiritual
height. This is what Emile explains to Moreali: "Je crois lui [à Dieu]
obéir de la manière la plus intelligente et la plus sainte en aimant de
toutes les puissances de mon être la femme qu'il me donnera pour
associée dans la tâche sacrée de mettre des enfants au monde"
(121). When Moreali wonders then if any love will be left for God,
Emile responds: "Ces mêmes puissances, renouvelées, ravivées et
centuplées par l'amour, remonteront vers Dieu comme la flamme
de l'autel allumée par lui" (121). Thus marriage becomes the highest form of worship. After attacking the injustice of unequal marriages in her earliest novels, Sand at the end of her writing career
celebrates the beauty and sanctity of a marriage based on equality.

Although the bulk of the novel is in the form of letters ex-
changed among the characters, Sand still manages to have her narrator express explicitly views the author espouses. The narrator
speaks, for example, of "la moderne philosophie spiritualiste, con-
fuse encore à bien des égards, mais éclairée d'en haut, née du divin
principe de la liberté, nourrie de la notion du progrès et en pleine
route déjà vers les vastes horizons de l'avenir" (240). The narrator's
view of Lemontier is equally positive: "C'était un de ces persévé-
rants chercheurs de lumière que le vulgaire de tous les temps dis-
cute, raille, critique ou injure, mais qui, plus ou moins d'accord
entre eux, creusent en chaque siècle plus profondément le sentier
dont l'avenir fait de larges voies" (244). Of course, anyone who had
read Sand's preface would have had no doubt as to the novelist's
views on the Catholic Church. She discusses the genesis of the
novel as a reaction to the pious novel of Octave Feuillet, *Histoire de
Sibylle*, and claims she is simply trying to raise issues, not to attack

the Church. As we have seen, while Sand provides a veneer of neutrality in the novel through the epistolary form, she clearly stacks
the cards against her adversary. For instance, she introduces the
figure of Lucie's grandfather, a fervent atheist who is in opposition
to Moreali and the Church. Thus Emile and Lemontier are seen as
in the middle between the two extremes—the logical, common
sense alternative. The structure of the *roman à thèse* necessitates
providing the opposing party with an opportunity to air its views,
but this is no guarantee of impartiality or fairness, as this novel illustrates. As we have seen, the reader's role in the novel is highly
restrictive. It assumes from the beginning a sympathy for Sand's
views on the Church. When the novel appeared, judging by the reaction, many young Frenchmen were ready to adopt that role as
real readers. Reading the novel today is bound to be more problematic; the modern reader is not likely to play along so completely.
This is not surprising for a *roman à thèse* which by its nature tends to
be perishable.[4] Sand did not succeed here as well as she had earlier
in grafting her own identity onto a fictional form and thereby trans-
forming it into a personal and viable instrument for communication
of her thoughts and feelings.

Even in her preface, Sand was not able to maintain the pretense of neutrality. She speaks of a plot of the "parti clérical" to take
over the government and—in a passage Baudelaire found distaste-
ful—she questions the infallibility of a church which admits the existence of the devil. According to her view modern society has
made blind acceptance of church teachings particularly tempting:
"L'idée d'une doctrine arrêtée et formulée est quelque chose de si
tentant aux époques de doute et de transition, que les esprits fa-
tigués de luttes et paresseux devant tout examen—c'est le grand
nombre—se groupent autour du drapeau qui flotte au vent et se
déclarent enrégimentés, à la condition qu'on ne leur demandera
plus de comprendre leur devoir et d'étudier leur droit. Cet état de
quiétisme religieux et social est fort commode, mais profondément
immoral et malsain, surtout quand, au lieu de se former autour
d'un principe, il s'agglomère autour d'une ombre. C'est cette ombre
qu'il faut démasquer" (viii-ix). This "unmasking" was in fact the
real purpose of *Mademoiselle La Quintinie*. That Sand, in attacking

the Church, did not demonstrate in her own right the tolerance she advocates reveals how black her image of the Catholic Church had become. While in all other areas her late novels show evidence of a mellowing of views and a tendency toward incorporation of opposing points of vision into the larger view of the protagonists this does not occur here. In that sense it is not as representative of the mature Sand as is *Nanon*.

Nanon is one of the last novels George Sand completed. The strident combativeness of *Mademoiselle La Quintinie* has been replaced with a gentler, more conciliatory tone. *Mademoiselle La Quintinie* was written to come to terms with certain aspects of the Catholic Church. *Nanon* has a less direct purpose; it reflects Sand's concerns over the revolutionary events of 1871, but it does not offer a program as did the earlier novel. It is a historical romance, not a contemporary *roman à thèse*. Nevertheless there are a number of points the two works have in common. George Sand was concerned in both works with fighting extremism—whether in religion or in politics. Through her characters and the action of the novels she advocates the same values which appeared at the beginning of her career: respect for others, unselfishness, love and friendship, the full development of one's potential. Both novels show the triumph of these values brought about by characters who conceive of a mission and then carry it out with energy and perseverance.

Nanon is told in the first person by the title character, born in 1775 and writing in 1850. The events she principally addresses take place more than fifty years earlier during the French Revolution, an event which has a dramatic effect on the lives of the characters. The historical aspect of the novel, however, should be seen in the context of its having been written soon after the dramatic events surrounding the Franco-Prussian war and the furor over the Commune. The values which Nanon comes to incorporate must be taken as valid in other ages as well.

One of the constant preoccupations that George Sand addressed in this way was the Catholic Church. The diatribes are absent from *Nanon*—they would in any event be out of character for the narrator—but certain aspects of the Church appear in such an unfavorable light as to indict the Church as an ongoing institution. The reader's insight into the Church derives from the depiction of the monastery at Valcreux. The peasants living there are "serfs mainmortables de l'abbaye" (33). They do not have a great deal of love or respect for the monks and from what we see of the latter this is not surprising. They are aloof and tyrannical and take from the peasants without giving anything back. The exception is the novice monk, Emilien de Franqueville. As the younger son of a noble family he has been sent to take orders as a matter of course. Emilien is good-natured and terribly naive and it is from his inter-action with the other monks and with the peasants that we gain insight into the nature of the monks' way of life and religious prac-tices. When one day he sees Nanon worried and upset because her one sheep has trespassed on to the monastery's land to graze, he hastens to reassure her, telling her that "le bien des moines est à tout le monde . . . tu demandes tous les matins à Dieu ton pain quo-tidien, et l'église, qui est riche, doit donner à ceux qui demandent au nom du Seigneur. Elle ne servirait à rien si elle ne servait à ré-pandre la charité" (15-16). He explains to her that the grass belongs to God since he made it grow. He is naïve enough to feel that his allegiance is to God, not to the Church. The perspective the reader has on Emilien is, of course, that of Nanon; she presents him from the beginning very sympathetically and highlights his remarks in such a way that it is clear that the reader is to understand that wis-dom is being spoken from the mouth of a simpleton.

In contrast to the other monks, Emilien has strong personal beliefs which have little to do with official Church dogma. He sees the Church's functions essentially as ministering to the poor and af-flicted, not as dictating personal belief. It is inevitable that eventu-ally Emilien recognize the gulf which separates him from the other monks. He begins to realize that being a monk does not mean ful-filling a useful role in society: "Les moines . . . ça a pu servir dans les temps anciens; mais, du jour où ils ont été riches et tranquilles, il n'ont plus compté pour rien devant Dieu et devant les hommes" (48). This view is expanded by Father Fructueux, the monk who af-

ter the outbreak of the Revolution becomes the prior: "Il y a longtemps que la foi est morte, que l'Eglise s'est donnée aux intérêts de
ce monde et qu'elle n'a plus de raison d'être. . . . Les prélats et les
membres privilégiés, à nos dépens, des grosses abbayes se jetaient
dans les jouissances du siècle, dans le luxe et même dans la débauche. Nous ne voulûmes pas être si simples que de faire pénitence à leur place, et n'étant pas d'assez gros seigneurs pour nous
livrer impunément au scandale, nous nous renfermâmes dans le
bien-être et l'indifférence qui nous étaient permis" (121-22). After
the monastery is disbanded, it is no coincidence that the peasants
are portrayed as being more religious than before. Emilien is no
longer able to remain a monk after he has experienced the "souffle
de la liberté" (70).

Emilien differs from the other monks also in that he is not
content to live the easy, restful monastery life but is motivated to
improve himself and to help others. A large part of his inspiration
comes from Nanon, but the negative example of the monks' lives
also plays a role: "Ils ne m'ont appris ni latin ni grec; mais il m'ont
laissé voir leur mauvaise volonté pour le bonheur de ces pauvres
dont ils se disent les pères et les tuteurs. En les voyant rire de l'é-
pargne et du travail, encourager la fainéantisme et dire que cela ne
peut pas changer, j'ai résolu de me changer moi-même et j'ai rougi
d'être un fainéant" (69). Emilien also begins to serve the peasant
community and becomes affectionately known as "le petit frère."
He is the one who reassures the peasants during the *grand-peur* and
who reconciles peasants and monks during the difficult time at the
beginning of the Revolution. Playing an active role in the community is for Emilien a fulfillment of a duty to God. In contrast to the
other monks for Emilien there is no divorce between serving God
and serving his fellow man.

This is demonstrated in the altar Emilien prepares for the
first anniversary of the fall of the Bastille. It is constructed out of
fruits, flowers, grain, and farm tools and is topped by a cross made
from ears of wheat. He tells the peasants it is "l'autel de la pauvreté
reconnaissante dont le travail, béni au ciel, sera récompensé sur la
terre" (61). He then places Nanon at the base of the altar as "une
figure d'ange en prière pour les pauvres" (62). That it is Nanon

whom he chooses to be the angel he explains to the peasants in these terms:

> Mes amis, je me demande avec vous ce qui, dans une âme chrêtienne, est le plus digne de plaire à Dieu, et je crois que c'est le courage, la douceur, le respect pour les parents et la grande amitié du cœur. Cette petite que j'ai mise là est la plus pauvre de votre commune; elle n'a jamais rien demandé à personne. Elle n'a pas quatorze ans et elle travaille comme une femme. Elle a soigné et pleuré son grand-père avec une tendresse au-dessus de son âge; et ce n'est pas tout, elle a pour elle quelque chose qui est aussi très agréable à Dieu quand on l'emploie bien. Elle a beaucoup d'esprit et elle apprend vite et bien tout ce qu'elle peut apprendre. Ce qu'elle sait, elle ne le garde pas pour elle, elle est pressée de l'enseigner; elle l'enseigne et elle ne choisit pas celles qui peuvent l'en récompenser, elle donne autant de soins aux plus pauvres qu'aux plus riches. (63)

The depiction of Nanon here recalls the image of the "déesse de la pauvreté" at the end of *La comtesse de Rudolstadt*. It is interesting to note how different a significance the altar has here than in *Valentine*. There Valentine's altar represented the religion of passion, here the emphasis is on devotion to others, especially to the family.

By the time the scene described here takes place Nanon has already had a dramatic effect on the life of Emilien. He had been discouraged by his parents, his tutors and the monks from learning, and he had acquiesced by taking scant interest in learning to read or write. Nanon, however, tells him it is shameful not to take advantage of opportunities to learn. In fact, she insists that he learn as much as he can so he can pass it on to her. Thus Nanon is educated by Emilien during their walks together: "Tous les jours, je le trouvai sur mon chemin, et c'est à travers champs qu'il m'apprit à lire si vite et si bien, que tout le monde s'en étonnait et qu'on parlait de moi dans la paroisse comme d'une petite merveille" (51). Nanon is being educated in the fields emphasizes the "natural" quality of education—it is, or should be, as much a fundamental aspect of his life as the grain field is to the farmer. Nanon also illustrates the importance of taking every opportunity to learn and not restricting education to formal classroom instruction.[5] Nanon is soon in a position to teach other peasants the basics of reading and writing. She feels it is not enough simply for her to learn to read and write; she feels a compelling need to pass that knowledge on to others. The fact that she learns to read in the midst of the *grand-peur* highlights the principal thrust of Sand's juxtaposition of historical forces and individual lives, namely the importance of continuing life in the face of adverse outside forces. The novel is a celebration of domestic life over larger social issues.

Nanon's willingness to help her fellow man is a trait evident early in her character. She learns from the care she must take of the sheep her great-uncle gives her to raise: "J'étais née pour soigner, c'est-à-dire pour servir et protéger quelqu'un, quelque chose" (8). This aspect of her character anticipates Flaubert's portrait of Félicité in *Un cœur simple*, a tale written for George Sand and clearly with her characters and setting in mind. Her affectionate nature is evident in her violent reaction to her grand-uncle's death as well as in the fierce devotion she develops for Emilien. Their relationship grows slowly but steadily. They grow closer after both help to rescue Father Fructueux from being tortured by the other monks. When the monastery is sold to the ardent revolutionary, Costejoux, he invites Emilien, Nanon, and Fructueux to stay on at the monastery and run the farm. They found, together with Nanon's two cousins, what is in effect the agricultural commune advocated in Sand's socialist novels. The only disruptive force is Emilien's sister, a horribly spoiled aristocrat whose snobbishness provides a caricature of upper class arrogance and selfishness. She serves above all to set off more clearly the selflessness and sincerity of Nanon.

At first this communal life goes on despite the Revolution: "Toutes choses ainsi réglées, nous eûmes l'innocent égoïsme de goûter, au milieu de ces temps qui devenaient de plus en plus malheureux et menaçants pour la France, un bonheur extraordinaire" (101). But eventually the course of the Revolution puts an end to this idyllic life. When Emilien goes to Limoges to volunteer for the revolutionary army, he is arrested, suspected of planning to defect to the emigré forces; he is a victim of a false accusation by his father's estate manager and a former monk. When Nanon learns of his fate she immediately vows to rescue him despite the seemingly insurmountable odds. The novel becomes at this point an adventure/suspense story and in the process other aspects of Nanon's character are revealed. She is resolute, daring, and cunning in her efforts, a kind of irresistible natural force. She accumulates and uses any information she happens to acquire, is willing to take on false identities, and even flirts to advance her purpose. She is the embodiment of true loyalty. Indeed, she tells Costejoux she would have done the same for him or for Louise.[6]

Even after Emilien is rescued—with the help of Costejoux—the danger of his being retaken continues. Nanon, Emilien, and the latter's former servant Dumont decide, therefore, to go to the depths of Berry and live clandestinely. They live isolated in a hut made of *dolmens*: "Nous nous arrangions pour vivre en anachorètes. Nous sûmes plus tard que, dans les premiers temps du christianisme, il y en avait eu plusieurs dans les rochers que nous habitions, et même la tradition disait que notre *aire aux fées*, qu'on appelait le *trou aux fades*, après avoir été occupée par les *femmes sauvages* (les druidesses), avait servi d'ermitage à des saints et à des saintes" (207). The area around the hut, bordered by two rivers, is called the *île aux Fades* (214). This paradise is splendidly isolated; there are in fact no bridges across the rivers. They compare their life there to that of Robinson Crusoe. This natural isolation is increased by the fact that the local inhabitants are convinced the place is haunted and stay away. The peasants believe that Nanon and Emilien must be under the protection of the fairies. There is, in fact, a strong sense that, in their Berry hideaway, Emilien and Nanon are leading a charmed existence. This consists in simply living a normal, retired life dependent on the land. Everything they need is provided there, mushrooms, chestnuts, game, even wine (from plums). All the details of their day-to-day life are given, how Nanon, for instance, makes their spoons, forks, and salt shaker. Nanon's care for Emilien and Dupont is a celebration of domestic life and devotion to others: "Le temps se passait pour moi à m'occuper de la vie matérielle. Je voulais que mes compagnons fussent bien portants et soignés comme il faut. J'y mettais mon amour-propre et mon plaisir. Ils ne manquèrent de rien, grâce à moi. Je pensais à tout. Je lavais, je raccommodais le linge et les habits, je faisais les repas, je tenais la maison propre, je tendais et relevais les nasses, je coupais la fougère et la bruyère pour les fagots" (217-18). This life of simplicity and absolute equality (shared by an aristocrat, a peasant and a former servant) leads to a quiet happiness which is clearly the ideal the novel projects. The rapprochement of Sand's late novels to the spirit of German "poetic realism"—celebrating the quiet, sober virtues of home life, blessed by God and undisturbed by historical change—is very evident here. Earlier in the novel Emilien had told Nanon that he understood the language of the birds; his interpretation of what one bird is saying is revealing: "Elle dit qu'elle a des ailes, qu'elle est heureuse, et que Dieu est bon pour les oiseaux" (50). This is far removed from the mystical relationship Consuelo has with the robin at Spandau prison. Here the bird is happy simply to be alive, by the grace of God; there is no need to elevate that life by making the bird a go-between for man and God.

This life of idyllic isolation is evoked in contrast to the reign of terror which is described in some detail in the novel. In this respect *Nanon's* perspective on the Revolution is very different from that of *Spiridion* and *Mauprat*, which highlighted the time just prior to its onset and emphasized its benefits. In evoking here the negative aspects of the Revolution, Sand was certainly addressing herself to the Commune. The two earlier novels were both written before 1848 and Sand's bitter disappointment over the course and result of that revolution. That event must necessarily have effected Sand's perspective on the French Revolution as well. If Emilien and Nanon in Berry are living incorporations of brotherhood and self-lessness, the Revolution invokes in contrast the bestiality of man to man.[7] The very fact that the Revolution destroys their idyllic life condemns it. Costejoux, too, sees his dream of domestic bliss shattered by the Revolution. The negative view of the extremes of the Revolution is revealed through the comparison made between the Jacobins and the Catholic clergy: "Vous me demandez ce que c'est que les jacobins. Autant que je peux le savoir et en juger, ce sont des hommes qui mettent la Révolution au-dessus de tout et de leur propre conscience, comme les prêtres mettaient l'église au-dessus de Dieu même. En torturant et brûlant des hérétiques, le clergé disait: 'C'est pour le salut de la chrétienté.' En persécutant les modérés, les jacobins disent: 'C'est pour le salut de la cause,' et les plus exaltés croient peut-être sincèrement que c'est pour le bien de l'humanité" (122). This is a point emphasized by Sand throughout the novel; the Revolution (the Commune) is condemned because it results in the same kind of blind extremism which characterizes the Catholic Church: "On ne bâtit pas une nouvelle Eglise avec ce qui a fait écrouler l'ancienne" (123). According to Emilien the answer of how to undo the evils of society lies not in the extremes, in either submission or vengeance, but rather is to be achieved through free discussion and education: "C'est la discussion libre qui éclaire les esprits, c'est la force de l'opinion qui déjoue les complots fratricides, c'est la sagesse et la justice qui règnent au fond du cœur de l'homme et qu'une bonne éducation développerait, tandis que l'ignorance et la passion les étouffent" (223). This position recalls the emphasis on *Mademoiselle La Quintinie* as well as highlighting Sand's continued commitment to the importance of education. The validity of this position is communicated to the reader through the insight Emilien shows in the same passage into the future course of the Revolution, an insight whose accuracy the reader is in a position to appreciate. This same position is echoed later in Nanon's condemnation of Costejoux's revolutionary jacobinism; he has been tricked (like the leaders of the Commune) into thinking that the end justifies the means and that violence is the only way to solve the problems of society. Nanon, like Sand, advocates moderation.[8]

It is clear that for Nanon, as Emilien's sister tells her, "aimer est ta religion" (310). Her strong feelings for Emilien are evident throughout. It is thus rather unexpected that she declares herself shocked when Emilien eventually lets his true feelings be known. While the reader may be willing to enter into the spirit of the novel and accept the idyllic portrait of Nanon's character, her reaction in this instance seems beyond the realm of what the reader can be expected to accept. In her effort to make Nanon appear spotlessly virtuous and self-effacing, George Sand in this instance only appears to make her seem lifeless or prudish. Once Nanon is able emotionally to accept the possibility of a union with Emilien, she is nevertheless hesitant because of the difference in social and economic backgrounds. She even offers to become Emilien's servant should he want to marry an aristocrat. Despite the Revolution, Nanon feels that she as a peasant cannot marry the son of a Marquis. This problem becomes all the more acute when both Emilien's father and his older brother die, leaving him as the actual Marquis de Franqueville.

The solution Nanon finds to this dilemma demonstrates that there is another side to her, showing determination and practicality. She resolves to make herself rich enough to be on equal terms with Emilien. Her first thoughts of prosperity had actually begun much earlier, after the community had volunteered to buy for her her grand-uncle's property following the Bastille Day celebration, a property worth some hundred francs: "Cent francs! Cela me paraissait énorme. J'étais donc riche? Je fis deux ou trois fois en une minute le tour du jardin. Je regardai la bergerie de Rosette; elle m'avait donné un agneau au printemps; il était déjà fort et très beau, je l'avais si bien soigné! En le vendant, j'aurais le moyen de faire une vraie bâtisse à côté de celle que mon grand-oncle avait construite lui-même et que je voulais garder en respect de lui. J'aurais aussi le moyen d'avoir deux ou trois poules, et qui sait si plus tard, en achetant un petit chevreau, je ne l'amènerais pas à être une bonne chèvre?" (67). When the Revolution removes the necessity of paying rent to the monastery, Nanon begins to prosper: "N'ayant plus de loyer à payer aux moines et gagnant quelque chose, car je commençais à aller en journées et je travaillais à la lingerie du couvent, je n'étais plus dans la misère. Mes élèves me rapportaient, car ce fut la mode chez nous d'apprendre à lire jusqu'à ce que la vente des biens nationaux fût faite; après on n'y songea plus. Mais j'avais un second agneau et je vendis la seconde brebis; on me donna deux poules qui, étant bien soignées, furent bonnes pondeuses. Je fus toute étonnée, au bout de l'année, d'avoir économisé cinquante livres" (84). Sand continues to depict Nanon's rags-to-riches story in some detail up to the point when she first conceives of her plan to "earn" Emilien: "C'est alors qu'une idée singulière, sans doute une inspiration de l'amour, s'empara de moi. Ne pouvais-je pas devenir, sinon riche, du moins pourvue d'une petite fortune qui me permettrait d'accepter sans scrupule et sans humiliation la condition bonne ou mauvaise d'Emilien? . . . Je me mis à faire des calculs et je reconnus qu'au prix où l'on avait la terre dans ce moment-là, on pouvait, en peu d'années, se faire un revenu qui triplerait la valeur du capital" (263). Nanon describes how much she makes from various projects; she does so well that she negotiates to buy the property from Costejoux. Nanon describes in detail how she reclaims the land of the monastery farm which has been ravaged by the Revolution. The steady determinism and optimism with which she transforms the farm anticipates Jean Giono's *Regain*. There is another side to the depiction of Nanon's gradual rise to prosperity. It illustrates the approach Sand advocated to social change as well—not violent revolution but change by "petits pas."[9]

However, the realistic treatment of her climb to prosperity ends in a typically Sandian conclusion: when Father Fructueux dies he leaves her a considerable fortune he had inherited from his family. With this money she speculates, buying and selling land. Nanon at the same time condemns the speculation that leads to wide-spread famine. She (and Sand) seem not to see any inconsistency here. Certainly, Sand is far removed in *Nanon* from condemning wealth or the capitalist process.[10] Nanon eventually sees herself at a level which could be seen as the equal of that Emilien holds by virtue of his family. Her acceptance of this match is also made possible by her realization of the pride she has in her peasant background. She resolves to remain a peasant and in fact wears peasant dress for the rest of her life. At the conclusion of Nanon's narrative a third-person narrator adds a note on Nanon's later life: "Elle avait acquis, par son intelligente gestion et celle de son mari et de ses fils, une fortune assez considérable dont ils avaient toujours fait le plus noble usage et dont elle se plaisait à dire qu'elle l'avait commencée avec un mouton" (352). It seems not inappropriate that one of George Sand's last novels return to a major well-spring of her fiction, the incorruptible pride and virtue of the peasant. But there is another "equalizing" factor in the marriage of Nanon and Emilien. He comes home from the war with only one arm. His service to the country, symbolized by his amputation, has earned him the right to be a normal citizen: "J'ai expié ma noblesse" (332). Thus the match in the end is quite different from that of peasant and aristocrat in Sand's novels of the 1840s. There is in *Nanon* another marriage, that of Costejoux and Louise, whose failure is an indication of the fact that bourgeois and nobility are not as promising a combination as peasant and nobility. Yet the future holds hope, as always in Sand's world, through the intermarriage of the grandchildren; Nanon's son marries Costejoux's daughter, while his other daughter marries the son of Nanon's cousin. Optimism was a trait that Sand never lost and which runs as a leitmotif through almost all her fiction.[11] *Nanon* is fundamentally an uplifting story about turbulent times.

Conclusion: Seeking out the Truth

George Sand's Vision

Je n'ai jamais eu la prétention d'écrire une solution de quoi que ce soit. Ce rôle ne m'appartient pas. Ma vie entière se consumera peut-être à chercher la vérité, sans que je sache en formuler une seule face.

—*Correspondance* (5: 826-27)

George Sand's best fiction was written under the sway of fervently held beliefs. Her most representative novels sprang from a desire to pass on to others what portion of the "truth"—what ideals to live by, what improvements to society—she felt she had perceived. The general decline in the quality of Sand's novels after mid-century is largely a reflection of growing timidity in expressing her views in her writing. The novels of the 1850s and 60s lack the spark of conviction and enthusiasm to be found in the earlier works. On occasion these latter novels contradict aspects of the novels of the 1830s and 40s. It is to those works before 1848 that one must look for an appreciation of Sand's commitment to using her voice to support social and humanitarian causes. It is also during that period that the greatest variety of narrative approaches and voices was used, in an attempt to reach as wide a spectrum of the population as possible.[1]

One should note at this juncture that, of course, no absolute link exists between a writer's engagement in a cause and the quality of her writing. Of the novels dealing with spiritual and religious themes, for instance, *Mademoiselle La Quintinie* is clearly the work which best embodies Sand's views on the Catholic Church and suggestions for a new form of Christianity. But as a novel it is not as satisfying as *Spiridion* or *Consuelo,* which are less direct and explicit in their treatment of similar themes. *Mademoiselle La Quintinie* is too exclusively a *roman à thèse;* the characters embody principles and religious beliefs too one-sidedly. The deck is stacked so heavily in favor of Emile and his father that the course of the novel is a foregone conclusion. The passivity of the reading experience tends not to draw the reader into the action.[2] The epistolary form does not help the process either. The situation is quite different in *Spiridion* where the complex intertwining narrators and first-person narrative immediacy lead the reader to share the viewpoints of the characters and to become engaged in a great spiritual quest. The skillful use of gothic devices in that novel furthers that process as well. Of course the evil monks—a staple of the gothic tradition—give Sand an opportunity here as well as in *Mauprat, Lélia,* and *Nanon* to denounce the abuses of the Catholic Church. In *Spiridion* and *Consuelo,* however, the gothic does more; it serves as a reminder of the reality of a spiritual world beyond our sensory perception. This sets the stage for the spiritual odyssey chronicled in those novels. The characters use Christianity as a springboard for finding their own spiritual values which at the same time are proposed as prophetic models for mankind.

Spiridion concludes with Alexis crying out on his deathbed: "Je suis libre" (422). This is the ultimate stage he has reached in his spiritual journey and represents the highest value championed in the novel. Throughout Sand's fiction, but especially in her early novels, freedom of choice represents a core issue. Women above all are not free in their course of action. This is what Indiana and Valentine seek and Lélia finds, but not in a satisfactory way.[3] Jacques chooses to die, but this is not really a freely made decision; that it is forced on him by society is evident in his final cry of "Justice!" Sand's rejection of the Catholic Church derives to a large extent from her love of freedom and respect for personal choice. In her eyes the Church was so restrictive that it strangled possibilities for personal growth through individual spiritual insights. Sand typically shows monks and priests degenerating into an animal state; the Church encourages cultivation of their baser instincts. For Sand this is the worst sin imaginable, the perversion of the divine spark in each human being. Napoléon comments in *Spiridion*: "Chaque être et chaque chose porte en soi les éléments de la production et de la destruction" (386). It is our most fundamental responsibility— our debt to our creator—to cultivate and develop the superior instincts we have. Forces which further this goal are celebrated; institutions which fight it—first and foremost orthodox Christianity— are condemned. The primacy of education in Sand's fiction derives from this belief. Women have a special role to play in the educational process. Lying outside the mainstream of the male-dominated, capitalist society, they incorporate values which can lead to more compassionate, less egotistical individuals and through these new men to a more just and equal society.

The other, more down-to-earth side of male-female relations is, of course, not neglected in Sand's fiction. Sand's women in particular have difficulty coming to terms with their sexuality. This is a major concern of the female protagonists in *Indiana* and *Valentine* and of central importance in *Lélia*. The later heroines tend to strike a better balance between the physical and emotional aspects of love. They are the ones who control the sexual side of the relationship. Men, too, are seen as suffering from the dichotomy of body and spirit. If Jacques marries—resulting in disaster—it is because it is his only hope of "possessing" Fernande. Both Bénédict (*Valentine*) and Bernard Mauprat suffer from unfulfilled sexual desire. This theme tends to lose importance in the socialist novels but reappears in somewhat stylized form in the rustic novels.

Of particular interest are novels such as *François le champi* or *Valentine* in which passionate love receives religious approbation. Valentine prays to an altar containing a handkerchief soaked in the blood of her lover; François's and Madeleine's mutual passion is strengthened through their study of the Bible and other religious works together. Lélia offers an interesting variation on this theme.

Like Valentine she too has a special altar to which she prays. But in Lélia's case it is the skeleton of a monk which she actually worships, demonstrating both her incapacity for human love and her spiritual emptiness. In Sand's later novels love and religion are no longer intertwined in this way. It is a particularly romantic vision of religion, customized to personal taste and made to serve the protagonists' love interest. It is a theme which George Sand inherited from Rousseau and Chateaubriand but also from the German romantics represented, for example, by the Gretchen tragedy in *Faust*, a work much admired by Sand. In Sand's fiction there is an element missing in Goethe, namely the sense that women make of love a sacred cause because society has excluded them from active participation in other spheres of human activity and pre-defined for them their role as subservient to men. This is clearly evoked in novels as different as *Indiana* and *La petite Fadette*.[4]

Like many other aspects of Sand's vision, her view of male-female relations is seen above all from the standpoint of personal freedom. Her condemnation of traditional marriage is based on the wife's lack of freedom.[5] Sand's original treatment of this theme is evident from comments by reviewers who strongly objected to her advocacy of a union based on mutual attraction and respect.[6] The novels of the 1840s show that Sand did not reject marriage outright. In fact, marriage and maternity became high ideals toward which the characters of the late novels strive. The characters must prove they are worthy of marriage and motherhood.[7] Consuelo, Gilberte (*Le Péché de M. Antoine*), Tonine (*La ville noire*), Caroline (*Le Marquis de Villemer*) and Nanon all must be willing to sacrifice their love to a higher cause before being granted the right to marry. There is even a kind of apprenticeship to motherhood undergone by several women; Fadette, Brulette (*Les Maîtres Sonneurs*) and Lucie (*Mademoiselle La Quintinie*) care lovingly for children thrust upon them, showing they are ready for children of their own. Madeleine (*François le champi*) represents a special case: she shows her worth by caring for a *champi* and after educating him crowns the process by becoming his wife; her spiritual level is so high she earns the right to marry her own child.

What these women undergo is a kind of initiation, a frequent pattern for the consruction of Sand's novels.[8] This sometimes took the form of the literal initiation into a secret society (*Le Compagnon du tour de France*, *Consuelo*, *Les Maîtres Sonneurs*) but more often it is seen as an initiation into a set of values and beliefs. In the second version of *Lélia* (1839), Lélia offers Sténio a way of earning her love, through an initiation of this kind, dedicating his life to helping mankind. This indicates the growing acceptance of the gospel of Leroux as George Sand's personal credo. In works such as *Le Compagnon du tour de France* and *Horace* she demonstrates the dangers of reading and believing the wrong authorities, even though they might seem as harmless as Walter Scott. The one Christian text which Sand continued to promote throughout her life—in works as diverse as *Spiridion* and *Mademoiselle La Quintinie*—was the gospel according to St. John, the only interpretation of the life of Jesus with which she felt comfortable. But overshadowing Jesus and all others in the 1840s was the inspired typesetter. It is the belief in the values and ideas championed by Leroux which becomes the touchstone in characters' relations with one another. George Sand had already demonstrated in *Mauprat* and *Le Compagnon du tour de France* the power of love to transform radically the lives of those concerned. Bernard Mauprat is made into a new man by Edmée while Pierre achieves a higher level of knowledge and awareness through Yseult de Villepreux. There is even the negative example of Horace whose love causes Marthe to sink to his own low level of moral behavior.

In the novels of the mid-forties George Sand goes farther. She portrays her couples as striving hard to improve society. Not only do they uplift one another, their unions—inevitably representing different social classes—are themselves a step in the right direction. In the conclusions of both *Le Meunier d'Angibault* and *Le Péché de M. Antoine* there is talk of broadening the union symbolized by the marriages in both works to embrace others, creating a commune or "association." *Consuelo* and *La comtesse de Rudolstadt* rise to an even higher level, involving attempts to transform completely the structure of society. These novels demonstrate the positive role that art can play in the attempt to reform society. Consuelo's role it not just to entertain; her singing is of such a level that it is spiritually moving, capable of inspiring the listeners and guiding them to improve themselves in some way. The Consuelo novels combine so many different aspects of Sand's social and spiritual beliefs that they represent a pinnacle in Sand's incorporation of such themes into her fiction.

One of the characteristically romantic elements of the Consuelo novels is the treatment of time. The importance of palengenesis and similar mystical concepts in the novels point to the timelessness of the spiritual quest. This is an important part of *Spiridion* and *Jeanne*. In *Consuelo* the treatment of time also serves to create the impression that the values advocated are not restricted to any one period but are universally valid. In *Jeanne* the heroine's dual role as a reincarnation of a druid priestess and a simple peasant girl of the 1820s places her ideas and actions in a similar light. With *Jeanne*, however, the setting of the action, in contrast to the Consuelo novels, is much more restricted. The subsequent novels, *Le Meunier d'Angibault* and *Le Péché de M. Antoine*, also bring the reader into the present. The message loses its abstract, mystical quality to become focused and practical. Money, which played only a symbolic role in *Jeanne* and none at all in *Consuelo*, becomes a central element in these novels. This was a concern with which contemporary readers could clearly identify. In fact Sand was to a certain extent following literary fashion here, since the corrupting power of wealth was a major theme in French romanticism from Balzac to the lesser lights of the *roman-feuilleton*.

This did not help to make these novels popular, however. Readers apparently found the actions and characterizations were dictated too exclusively by Sand's desire to portray as clearly and completely as possible her social and political beliefs, resulting in such unfortunate creations as Emile Cardonnet and the Marquis de Boisguilbault (*Le Péché de M. Antoine*). Sand had hoped to effect change in the reader through bringing the action into the reader's realm of experience. But this was not logically carried through; the love intrigues and their denouements are too artificially contrived, even by standards of French romantic fiction.

Typically the characters in the "socialist novels" are grouped into two distinct groups, one characterized by the love of money, the others by the love of nature. With the rustic novels life in nature becomes the primary focus. It is perhaps appropriate to state once again that those works did not represent a total break with what Sand had been writing up to that point. They simply continued what Sand had been doing since *Le Compagnon du tour de France*, using a succession of narrative strategies and fictional models in an attempt to get her message across. What is new is that Sand in writing *La Mare au diable* and the other novels was not following a literary fashion as she had done in the past ("women's novel," gothic novel, *roman-feuilleton*, mystical novel, realist-Balzacian novel) but creating something new in French literature, the pastoral novel. Its chief innovation lay in fact that the narrative perspective is that of the peasant community. This led to a certain exotic element for middle-class urban readers which proved to be very successful in creating interest in the novels. But peasant themes—such as superstitions—do not only provide local color, they are skillfully manipulated by Sand to provide varying perspectives on the characters and events in an attempt to jolt the reader out of his complacency and prejudices. The message continues to be that of social justice through equality and understanding among different social and economic classes. Harmony and reconciliation play an increasingly important role in these novels, culminating in the all-embracing conclusion of *Les Maîtres Sonneurs*.

What stands in the way of harmonious human relationships in George Sand's novels is most often prejudice and egotism. The sympathetic portrayal of Berrichon peasants is a strategy for overcoming reader prejudice toward the lower classes; it was not an attempt at a realistic depiction of French country life. The pastoral novels are the last version of Sand's romantic vision. Her subsequent novels are not really guided by a coherent narrative vision. Although like the earlier novels they continue to fight false pride and egotism (*La ville noire, Le Marquis de Villemer*), one rarely feels the passionate commitment so palpable in the novels of the 1840s. The romantic emphasis on the individual tended to give way to the larger view of the realists. This was not, perhaps, as appropriate a model for a subjective, personal, and committed novelist like George Sand. Even in such a late work as *Nanon*, however, there is an element which recalls the earlier Sand, the indictment of egotism combined with a moving portrait of the dignity and resourcefulness of women. As in *Indiana* and *Valentine*, Sand insists on the importance of allowing love to follow its natural course. Neither distinctions of social class nor the disapprobation of society or family should be allowed to stand in the way. Unions based on foundations other than love—power, money, social status—are not only inevitably unhappy, they are immoral. Bénédict qualifies the consummation of Valentine's marriage as rape.

This view of love is of course an integral part of George Sand's social program. Without freedom and equality in personal relationships for women as well as men, there would be no basis for the creation of a just and classless society. What could be more appropriate for this representative of French romanticism than a vision at once particular and global, both literary and humanitarian, unifying all in a vision of future harmony and happiness. It was from the perspective of today a naïve vision. But the society which George Sand had in view was quite different from ours. Hers was a time of transition; France was just entering the industrial age. It was a time before French society splintered into a complex array of different economic interests and social concerns. It was a time when it appeared simpler solutions might suffice. George Sand's fiction represents a sincere and passionate attempt to provide some possible solutions.

Notes

Introduction: Speaking to the Heart

[1] Albert Sonnenfeld, for instance, writes of Sand's "uncritical fervor for Leroux, Lamennais and others incorporated into her novels of the 1840s" (318).

[2] See the remarks in her correspondence, such as 5: 535-6 and 6: 68.

[3] See the article by Françoise van Rossum-Guyon on the prefaces to *Indiana*.

[4] This is something George Sand herself had pointed out to her publisher: "Née *romancier* je fais des romans, c'est-à-dire que je cherche par les voies d'un certain art à provoquer l'émotion, à remuer, à agiter, à ébranler même les cœurs de ceux de mes contemporains qui sont susceptibles d'émotion et qui ont besoin d'être agités" (V 826).

[5] For a compilation of Sand's ideas on a variety of subjects, see Vermeylen's study as well as Karénine's classic work. The question of sources has been dealt with by a variety of writers but treated most thoroughly in the modern French critical editions of Sand's novels, such as those of Pierre Reboul (*Lélia*) or Léon Cellier (*Consuelo*).

[6] The term narratee could also be used here, but has not gained wide acceptance in Anglo-American criticism. I use as a basis for my approach Wolfgang Iser and Hans Robert Jauss.

[7] I disagree with Isabelle Naginski's equation of the characterized reader and the "ideal reader" (225). In Sand's case the characterized reader is often a caricature. See Béatrice Didier's discussion of the distinction between the characterized and real reader in Sand's fiction.

[8] See Shor 65 and Michel 36. Isabelle Naginski, once again, formulates succinctly this aspect of Sand's fiction in describing the central unifying factor in Sand's fiction as her "idealist outlook and her allegiance to the abstract" (9).

[9] According to Wolfgang Iser, "The literary text has its reality not in the world of objects but in the imagination of its reader" (*Prospecting* 29).

Chapter 1: Chaste Volupty

[1] See Kujaw and Naginski (55).

[2] *La Quotidienne* 26 Sept. 1832

[3] Reviewers were bowled over by the persuasive power of George Sand's prose, an aspect of the novel analyzed by Nancy Rogers (*Persuasive Style*, especially 258-68). I am not convinced by Kristina Wingard's assertion that Sand got away with the social criticism in the novel due to her male pseudonym (*Socialité* 26); I believe the factors Salomon cites played a more important role.

[4] While most studies have centered on the characters of Indiana and Valentine, other critics, especially Nancy Rogers and Kristina Wingard, have offered insights into the narrative strategies of the early novels.

[5] Sainte-Beuve's comments can be taken as representative: "Dès qu'en ouvrant le livre on s'est vu introduit dans un monde vrai, vivant, 'nôtre' . . . quand on a trouvé des mœurs, des personnages comme il en existe autour de nous, un langage naturel, des scènes d'un encadrement familier, des passions violentes, non communes, mais sincèrement éprouvées ou observées . . . alors on s'est laissé aller à aimer le livre . . . toute cette analyse vivante d'une vérité, d'une observation profonde et irrécusable, qu'on ne saurait assez louer," *Le National* 5 Oct. 1832: 3-4. For additional examples of this reaction see the survey of reviews in Salomon's edition (xlvii-xlix). See also Iknayan 61. Sand herself described *Indiana* as "de la vraisemblance bourgeoise" (*Correspondance* 2: 46-47)

[6] Béatrice Didier sees the narrator of *Indiana* as being identifiable not with the author but with "George Sand," the male pseudonym (248).

[7] Pierrette Daly points out that the narrator ressembles Raymon ("The Problems of Language" 24). But I would disagree with her contention that through Sand's use of this male narrator "her voice is suppressed" (26). Sand's views are expressed in the novel, despite the male narrator. As Crecelius puts it, Sand uses "a male voice but a female perspective" (59).

[8] An example is the balancing off of Delmare and Indiana in the following passage: "Elle était cruelle par vertu, comme il était bon par faiblesse; elle avait de trop la patience qu'il n'avait pas assez; elle avait les défauts de ses qualités, et lui les qualités de ses défauts" (191).

[9] She also points out the role the choice and use of names in the novel play in Sand's narrative strategy, particularly how the realistic "Madame Delmare" in the early part of the novel yields to the exotic "Indiana" (64). Names and titles are rejected along with the social system they represent.

[10] The same is true even of the physical description of Indiana, which is not given in a complete, systematic way. Françoise Massardier-Kenney points out that "by not framing her, Sand succeeds in enhancing and liberating her influence on the text" (118).

[11] The reviewer in the *Revue encylopédique* praised Sand's departure from the gothic: "Si nous louons tant M. Sand, c'est que nous le remercions beaucoup; il nous a vivement ému. . . . Nous sommes avides de productions simples, qui touchent sans briser, qui marchent sans moyens de coulisses, qui n'appellent à leur aide ni l'engeance infernale, ni les fées avec leur baguette surannée, ni le fantasque, ni le hurlé, ni le boursouflé. Ce roman ne s'adresse donc véritablement qu'à ceux qui gardent leurs loisirs et leurs larmes pour le pathétique simple et naturel" (215).

[12] For this reason I agree with Béatrice Didier's preference for the original version of the novel (242). I do not see, however, the direct appeals to the reader in the first edition, as Didier does, as "des moments d'embarras" (246) which are designed to mask the autobiographical nature of the novel.

[13] Recent critics have, however, seen the ending—and Ralph's transformation—in a different, more positive light. James Vest points out that the ending continues the same pattern of imagery to be found earlier in the text (38); Kristina Wingard justifies the transformation of Ralph as having been prepared by hints in the text as to Ralph's feelings for Indiana (*Socialité* 59). Crecelius views the novel as being based on the model of the romance; from that perspective the ending is not problematic (61). Isabelle Naginski sees Ralph's voice as androgynous (65) and his sudden transformation into poet as a mirror of Sand's sudden emergence as a writer with the publication of *Indiana* (67).

[14] I agree with Wingard that this passage is a veiled reference to a sexual encounter between Indiana and Ralph (*Socialité* 43-4). Lucy Schwartz points to the important role nature played in the *roman intime*, which served in many ways as a model for Sand's early novels (221).

[15] The shift in perspective is problematic in several ways. Are we to understand that this is the same narrator who has told the story in the third person? This is what virtually all critics have assumed; the exception is Pierrette Daly who postulates two different narrators ("The Problem of Language" 27). But how does one then account for the fact that the third-person narrator's account reveals a very different attitude toward the characters—especially Ralph—than does the first-person narrator? If we assume this is the same person we must take the novel to be his version of the story as he had heard it from Ralph and Indiana; in other words he is reporting the story *after* his meeting with the two lovers and after he has become their friend. Should we view then the way in which the third-person narrator tells the story as a strategy on his part to keep the ending (the "real" Ralph and his union with Indiana) in suspense? Or should we assume that, as W. Karénine claimed, Sand tacked on the conclusion (with its first-person narrator) at the last minute to come up with the requisite number of pages for her publisher? I would argue that these ambiguities are solved by viewing the first-person and third-person narrators as distinct; there is no evidence in the text that they are necessarily one and the same. This avoids the unsatisfactory interpreta-

tion of Crecelius that the narrator's "tentative comments" derive from the fact that he is uninformed (62).

[16] This aspect of Raymon's character was identified by Pierre Salomon as being derived from the pamphleteer Narcisse Achille de Salvandy (*Indiana* 114).

[17] Pierre Salomon finds the political discussions in the novel inappropriate (*Indiana* xlii). I disagree and concur with Wingard who stresses the importance and integral role of politics in the novel.

[18] George Sand commented in her 1853 preface to *Valentine*: "La partie descriptive de mon roman fut goûtée" (2).

[19] The exception is the Countess, whose life has been embittered by the fall of Napoleon. Wingard points out (*Socialité* 118) the interesting chronology of the novel, which begins during the Restoration and ends in 1837 or 1838, after the novel was written; no mention is made, significantly, of the 1830 revolution.

[20] Louise has a large dose of responsibility for the relationship, as Wingard points out (*Socialité* 82). The relationship of Valentine and Bénédict is fundamentally, however, as Crecelius points out one of "fatal love" following the pattern of *Tristan and Yseult* (81).

[21] For some contemporary critics George Sand did not go far enough in this direction, claiming that her novels represented an invitation to commit adultery (Kujaw 85).

[22] The reviewer in *Le Temps* noted: "C'est une épouvantable et déchirante satire de tout ce galimatias barbare qui forme le code de la morale bourgeoise" (qtd. in Kujaw 14); in the *Revue de Paris* a similar tone was struck: "George Sand a voulu . . . dévoiler les déplorables mystères d'égoïsme, de lâcheté, de perfidie que la morale bourgeoise, indulgente pour tout ce qui s'abrite derrière le code, a couvert de sa honteuse protection" (qtd. in Kujaw 64).

[23] This seems to me the implication that follows from the ending and from what Crecelius rightly describes as the "unfocused" nature of the novel (92). I would agree with her that the novel does not offer as clear an argument against bourgeois marriage as does *Indiana*.

[24] Reviewers of the novel emphasized the psychological realism of the characters. The *Revue des deux mondes* praised "le naturel et l'exquise vraisemblance de la figure principale" (15 December 1832, 697). The *Journal des débats* commented: "Bénédict . . . est toujours simple et naturel et vrai" (11 July 1833, 3). In an interesting review article in *La Chronique de Paris* on March 12, 1852, the reviewer discusses George Sand's output up to that point, finding much to praise but complaining that George Sand's works also represented "un assemblage de monstrueuses invraisemblances, de repoussantes impossibilités. Dans ses livres, la nature extérieure resplendit sous la magie du style; mais l'homme ne s'y montre pas vivant" (163). The one exception to this depiction? *Valentine*.

Chapter 2:   Escape from a World Vile and Odious

[1] For an appreciation of *Lélia*'s place in French romanticism, see Wingard 140.

[2] See Wingard 124-38.

[3] Wingard offers a catalog of gothic devices in the novel: "suicides (1 accompli, 1 raté), crimes, débauche, prostitution, 1 meurtre, 2 scènes de folie furieuse, 1 scène d'orgie, le tout relevé d'un soupçon de nécrophilie et couronné d'une scène d'amour au-delà du tombeau" (210).

[4] Isabelle Naginski comments: "*Lélia* presents a baffling enigma to the reader" (119).

[5] Interestingly, critics were divided over whether women as readers would be receptive to the message of *Lélia*. According to the *Revue de Paris* women would not be interested; Gustave Planche in *Revue des deux mondes* thought differently: "Les femmes surtout, qui excellent dans l'observation et l'analyse des sentiments, ne consulteront pas, pour décider leurs sympathies, les systèmes littéraires ou philosophiques. Elles noteront d'une main attentive tous les passages où elles auront trouvé l'expression et le souvenir de leur vie passée, le tableau de leurs souffrances. Elles auront des larmes et de la vénération pour l'impuissance qui se proclame, et qui révèle toutes ses misères" (qtd. in *Lélia* 588).

[6] See the table reproduced in *Lélia* xxvii.

[7] Crecelius points out that the non-judgmental treatment of Pulchérie as a prostitute represented something new in French fiction (102).

[8] See letters, for example, *Correspondance* 2: 741.

[9] *La Chronique de Paris* wrote in 1845: "L'auteur . . . s'élève à la philosophie, à la théologie, à la discussion des lois divines et humaines, et il invente, pour blasphémer Dieu . . . *Lélia*" (qtd. in Kujaw 109).

[10] See Beyerle (119). *Jacques* was also very popular among writers in Russia.

[11] Arlette Michel comments: "Par son indifférence même à la réalité sociale, Sand va plus loin que Balzac dans sa protestation contre l'institution du mariage et les mentalités collectives qui en règlent les rites" (36).

[12] Wingard writes that Clémence and Madame de Theurson, as examples of society women, incorporate what is degraded and destructive in society (275). I do not see Clémence's role as being so negative. I would agree with Wingard (281) that the Borels represent a successful effort to compromise with society. But their role is too minor to offer any kind of model.

[13] Arlette Michel argues that the subtext in *Jacques* is *La nouvelle Héloïse* (35). There are indeed a number of points in common but Rousseau's novel is not nearly as close as model as that of Goethe.

[14] Unlike other solitary romantic figures like Chateaubriand's René or Goethe's Werther, Jacques finds no solace in nature.

15 Wingard sees the change in the depiction of Jacques as a result of the serial publication of the novel; it was published as it was being written, allowing Sand no chance to revise (291).

16 Crecelius sees the tragic love of Jacques and Sylvia as "the hidden plot of *Jacques*" (136). She sees the ending with the union of Fernande and Octave as "productive, joyous incest" (139).

Chapter 3: Rising Up from Ignorance and Imposture

1 See *Correspondance* 3:10.

2 See the summary of reactions in Wingard 417.

3 Crecelius's judgment is representative: "Masterfully narrated, well, if somewhat overtly, plotted, *Mauprat* keeps the reader in suspense right up until the end" (154).

4 Crecelius sees the story, appropriately, as a version of "Beauty and the Beast" (149).

5 Wingard points out that Bernard's behavior in Paris demonstrates the vanity his education has led to; he needs the social education which America gives him. He is able through it to reach an equilibrium between society and nature (439).

6 Crecelius comments: "Having lulled men into a false security with a conspiriational wink, Sand is then free to tell them exactly what she thinks of their laws and their society" (155).

7 It fulfills the criteria for that genre established by Susan Suleiman including the requirement for "the presence of a doctrinal intertext" (56).

8 It should be pointed out that the emphatic moral lessons included in the final few pages of *Mauprat* were added by Sand in 1851.

9 Crecelius points out that the revolutionary setting points to what the Revolution could have done but did not, namely emancipate women (152). Wingard points out that placing the union of common people and women in the past shows Sand's awareness of the impossibility of that happening at the time the novel was written (414, 454).

10 I differ here from Wingard who sees Edmée too as being tamed in the course of the novel (425). I don't see any fundamental change in Edmée; she remains throughout a captive of Sand's view of woman as myth, as Wingard discusses, an incarnation of the values lacking in the male-dominated world (409).

11 This may in part be a product of the long period over which the novel was written.

12 Sand's letters offer a similar view of Christ, *Correspondance* 5: 826.

[13] In the original version, published in *Revue des deux mondes*, there was only one manuscript. There has been some speculation that the ending was rewritten by Leroux (Karénine 230).

[14] Even multiples of three come into play. As Spiridion's second disciple Alexis studies for two times three (six) years and waits until he is thirty to try to recover the manuscript.

Chapter 4: The Illusive Ideal

[1] See introduction.

[2] Cyzba, appropriately, sees Joséphine's role as an indictment of the bourgeois; she believes her wealth entitles her to a noble husband (24).

[3] Lucette Czyba writes that in effect Yseult has no body, and sees this as a reflection of repressive bourgeois morality (29).

[4] Czyba also points out that la Savinienne is endowed with all the qualities of the traditional romantic heroine so as to raise the status of the female proletariat in the eyes of the bourgeois reader (22). Her situation also illustrates the economic dependence of women (23).

[5] This is the case, for example, in the description of Marthe's leaving Horace's lodging after their first night spent together: "A l'aube naissante, la porte de l'hôtel de Narbonne s'ouvrit et se referma plus doucement encore après avoir laissé passer une femme qui couvrait sa tête d'un châle rouge" (167).

[6] W. Karénine points, I believe, to this aspect of the novel when she writes of the "malaise" the reader feels in how the story is told; she considers the narration an "erreur de forme" (291). She expresses irritation with Théophile and imagines a reader asking, if you're so advanced in your ideas, then why don't you marry your *grisette*? (290).

[7] See *Correspondance* 5: 418-423; Sand's letter to Buloz not only passionately defends *Horace*, it also offers interesting insights into Sand's views on politics in fiction.

[8] This has been seen as a portrait of Jules Sandeau; see Karénine 271.

[9] The Viscountess is generally seen as a thinly-disguised portrait of Marie d'Agoult (Courrier 12).

[10] According to Karénine, Sand heard a report from a student involved in the Saint-Merry massacre that resembled the story of Paul's escape (277).

Chapter 5: Keepers of the Sacred Flame

[1] Mireille Bossis has studied the similarities and differences between *Consuelo* and *Les Mystères de Paris*. She points out that Sand uses aspects of the

popular novel but tones them down. The darker side of the popular novel is missing in *Consuelo* (319).

[2] This is stated in a letter of February 14, 1844: "G[eorge] Sand n'est qu'un pâle reflet de P[ierre] Leroux, un disciple fanatique du même Idéal, mais un disciple muet et ravi devant sa parole, toujours prêt à jeter au feu toute ses œuvres, pour écrire, parler, penser, prier et agir sous son inspiration; avez-vous lu *Consuelo*? Il y a de bien ennuyeux chapitres, ils sont de moi. Il y a aussi des pages magnifiques, elles sont de lui. Je ne suis que le vulgarisateur à la plume diligente et au cœur impressionnable qui cherche à traduire dans des romans la philosophie du maître. Otez-vous donc de l'esprit que je suis un grand talent. Je ne suis rien du tout qu'un croyant docile et pénétré" (*Correspondance* 6: 431).

[3] See, for example, Wolfenzettel 39-41.

[4] This is what Sand wrote to the proletarian poet Poncy: "Le genre humain est soumis à une longue et pénible éducation. Le temps ne paraît long qu'à nous. Aux yeux de Dieu il n'existe pas. Nos siècles ne comptent pas dans l'éternité, et nous sommes vivants et agissants avec Dieu dans l'éternité, car nous mourons pour renaître et progresser" (*Correspondance* 6: 329-30)

[5] Note her letter of February 26, 1843: "Comme c'est la seule philosophie qui soit claire comme le jour et qui parle au cœur comme l'évangile, je m'y suis plongée et je m'y suis transformée. J'y ai trouvé le calme, la force, la foi, l'espérance et l'amour patient et persévérant de l'humanité, trésors de mon enfance que j'avais rêvé dans le catholicisme, mais qui avaient été détruits par l'examen du catholicisme, par l'insuffisance d'un culte vieilli, par le doute et le chagrin qui dévorent, dans notre temps, ceux que l'égoïsme et le bien-être n'ont pas abrutis ou faussés." (*Correspondance* 6: 68).

[6] Sand saw the Catholic Church's use of symbols as idolatry as evinced in a letter concerning her daughter's religious upbringing: "Je vous prie donc de la tenir à la maison pendant toutes ces dévotions; je ne veux pas qu'on lui mette de la cendre au front, ni qu'on lui fasse baiser des images. Je ne l'ai pas élevée pour l'idolâtrie, et si elle est destinée un jour à faire quelque emploi de son intelligence, ce sera probablement pour travailler selon la mesure de ses forces, à la destruction de l'idolâtrie" (*Correspondance* 5: 618).

[7] Saint John was frequently evoked in French romanticism; he became in Wingard's words "un symbole du poète philosophique prophétisant sur le monde et son avenir" (188).

[8] Note the following statement of religious faith from a letter of 1844: "Ne dites pas que je veux édifier une *religion nouvelle*. Vous n'êtes pas juste envers moi. Quand donc m'avez-vous vu prendre ce ton doctoral? Je ne crois même pas m'être servi jamais de cette expression, et si je l'ai fait, c'était dans la même acception que *religion de l'avenir*, ce n'est pas la même chose, songez-y. La religion de l'avenir ne sera pas une religion absolument nouvelle; celle de Jésus ne l'était pas non plus, vous le savez. Elle sortait de Pythagore, elle avait passé par Socrate et Platon; elle n'était qu'une transformation, une épuration, une formule nouvelle

de l'éternelle et unique religion de l'humanité. Si par religion nouvelle vous entendez une religion qui abjurerait le Christ et son esprit, vous me supposez une pensée folle et criminelle; mais je crois fermement que la génération qui nous suit n'adorera plus le Christ comme une idole et ne se prosternera plus devant ses prêtres." (*Correspondance* 6: 772).

[9] I will summarize some of the most recent views. Bozon-Scalzitti sees Consuelo's loss of voice as a result of her marriage; marriage has taken away "la jouissance de la voix féminine" (152). Daly, on the other hand, interprets the fact that Consuelo continues to sing after she is married as forging "un nouveau mythe de l'héroïne"; losing her voice is an indication that "tout n'est pas pour le mieux dans le monde de l'écriture au féminin" (26). Others have seen the loss of voice in the context of Consuelo's social mission. Eve Sourian, for example, writes: "Elle a perdu sa voix parce qu'elle n'est plus la fiancée de l'idéal; perdant ses extases avec l'infini, elle se dévoue au genre humain" (135). Annabelle Rea, however, speaks of the "ultimate failure of Consuelo, the woman of sky and sea, a failure symbolized by the loss of voice. Time was not ripe for Consuelo's mission to break down the barriers between the social classes" (235). Finally, Simone Vierne sees the loss of voice in connection to Consuelo's final role as priestess: "Elle a perdu sa voix de cantatrice, la seule chose en somme qui la rattachait au monde profane. Mais elle a gagné le don suprême, celui de ceux qui sont habités des dieux: elle compose de la musique" (293-94).

[10] According to Daly, Consuelo is first presented as a kind of fairy tale princess in disguise. The generous use of superlatives is typical of the fairy tale (22).

[11] Bossis points to the fact that these are "clichés sémantiques habituels du roman populaire" (326).

[12] Karénine views Albert as "horriblement ennuyeux, extraordinairement prolixe, nébuleux . . . et parle dans le style des lettres intimes et des articles de Leroux" (358).

[13] This is an example of the "exaltation de la maternité" typical of the romantic period (Kniehierhler 174).

[14] Simone Vierne points out that Jeanne's options are more limited than those of Consuelo, largely because she is an uneducated peasant living in the nineteenth century (23). In the simpler society of pre-revolutionary France, Consuelo was able to live a full life as a wife and mother *and* work to change society at the same time.

[15] I disagree with Vierne who sees the portrayal of peasants in the novel as "totally" different (5).

[16] Vierne points out that a longer speech by Cadet was edited out (not by Sand) when the novel was published (20).

[17] See Vierne 18; she discusses numerous other examples of the incorporation of Sand's experiences into the novel.

[18] The narrator, for instance, labels Jeanne's insistence on maintaining her vows "poésie populaire" (123).

[19] See *Jeanne* 1 and Vierne 11.

[20] Michèle Hirsch points out that Jeanne's refusal to marry is the "reconnaissance du fait qu'on ne peut vivre qu'à condition d'obéir à la loi de l'argent: Jeanne, refusant d'être achetée, refuse de vivre" (126).

[21] Hirsch sees that the desire to educate Jeanne, i.e., cure her of her superstitions, is linked to the sexual desire of the three men (120).

[22] Hirsch details the ways in which Jeanne exhibits the typical traits of a witch (119).

Chapter 6: In This Day and Age

[1] Sand in writing about the novel to Hetzel, after Véron's rejection, tries to reassure him that the book is not dangerous: "Je ne pousse pas à l'émeute et aux violences, bien convaincue que le peuple arrivant par la colère et la vengeance ferait pis que ce qui est. Seulement mon âme et mon cœur demandent sans cesse la révision des institutions sociales et la *solution* du problème économique, révision et solution inévitables dans l'avenir, et que les gouvernants feraient mieux de laisser discuter librement et pacifiquement, que d'abandonner aux sombres élucubrations des fanatiques silencieux. Au reste, mon roman ne contient pas de théories dogmatiques." (*Correspondance* 6: 661).

[2] Suleiman 11. Sand considered *Le Meunier d'Angibault* to be a *roman de mœurs* and in the same genre as *Valentine* (*Correspondance* 6: 653).

[3] See Godwin-Jones, "The Representation of Economic Reality."

[4] In a letter to Hippolyte Fortoul, Sand evokes the slow change she anticipated in the system of property ownership: "L'amour sauvage de la propriété domine les hommes petits et grands. Mais ce que nous sommes peut-être destinés à voir, si le peuple s'éclaire, c'est une gestion nouvelle de la propriété, et une succession de formes par lesquelles nous la ferons passer avant le siècle éclairé, où les lois règleront l'héritage, et restreindra [*sic*] le droit de l'individu, tout en le lui conservant dans de justes limites. Ceci est un idéal. Il faut l'avoir devant les yeux, et s'y laisser porter tout doucement par l'intérêt et le bon sens des masses. Ce sera bien long sans doute, et je répète que nous n'en verrons peut-être que des préludes." (*Correspondance* 5: 188-89).

[5] This echoes the advice Sand gives friends in her correspondence, to keep and use their wealth: "Si l'expropriation qui vous menace n'est pas détournée, si le secours que je vous rêve n'arrive pas à temps, il n'y aura rien d'irréparable. Pourquoi la perte de votre fortune serait-elle pour vous un mal si affreux? Tant qu'il y aura chance de la sauver et tant que vous y pourrez quelque chose, je vous prêcherai de le faire: parce que la richesse crée des devoirs et que

ceux qui le sentent étant très rares, il est à désirer qu'ils disputent cette richesse à l'heure qu'il est, à ceux qui ne le sentent pas et qui n'en savent pas faire bon usage. Mais tout ceci n'est qu'une moralité très secondaire et tout à fait provisoire à cause de l'état faux et misérable de la société." (*Correspondance* 5: 494-95).

6 As Courrier and Donnard point out there is an element of Saint-Simonian enthusiasm for the captains of industry in the portrayal of Cardonnet (24) but his ruthlessness carries him away from this ideal.

7 Sand stated in her correspondence that her concern with making her position as clear as possible in *Le Péché de M. Antoine* was a result of its not being published in *L'Époque*: "Dans un temps où il n'y aurait que deux partis et deux idées en présence, il faudrait développer et ne pas nommer l'idée qu'on sert. Mais, dans notre époque de nuances et d'écarts sans nombre, nommer, c'est précisément éviter les longs développements que vous craignez. C'est empêcher aussi que des sectes dont on n'est point n'accaparent à leur profit les efforts qu'on fait en sens contraire. Et puis quand on écrit dans *l'Epoque*, il faut peut-être signer ce qu'on est, autrement les gens pensent que 12.000 f. vous ont adouci le caractère et vous savez bien que ni vous ni moi ne sommes de cette humeur-là." (*Correspondance* 7: 72).

8 Sand in her correspondence often evinces a very negative view of the average reader of her time: "La mode, le prétendu *art pour l'art* (qui n'a jamais existé et qui eût fait rire les grands maîtres du passé, Goethe tout le premier, s'ils eussent vu comme nous l'entendons ici,) enfin la susceptibilité des lecteurs, et la *terreur* que *l'abonné bête* inspire aux entrepreneurs de journaux, ont voulu proscrire toute tendance à un intérêt *social* dans les romans *d'actualité*, n'est-ce pas absurde et *impossible*? Je vous demande ce que seraient les scènes de la vie intime au 19ème siècle si elles n'étaient le reflet de la scène générale et ce qui resterait de tout notre papier noirci dans vingt ans, si les lecteurs futurs n'y trouvaient que des costumes et des décors?" (*Correspondance* 7: 55-6).

9 This is one of the aspects of the novel Latouche urged Sand to change. He also felt uncomfortable with the character of the Marquis and with the ending of the novel (Courrier and Donnard 8).

10 There are references to Fourier in Sand's correspondence in his period, but Sand was critical of his system as a whole, believing it did not take into account the spiritual side of man; see *Correspondance* 6: 449,457.

11 Courrier and Donnard see here a similarity with the Saint-Simonian concept of women (23).

12 W. Karénine comments: "La fable du roman est donc passablement naïve et se ressent du bon vieux temps, où les auteurs aimaient tous à toucher les lecteurs sensibles, en leur contant les amours de deux jeunes gens opprimés par de méchants tuteurs, ou les souffrances de quelque jeune fille noble et pauvre, retrouvant enfin ses vrais parents ou un oncle bienfaisant, qui l'adopte au dernier chapitre" (660-61).

Chapter 7: Friendship Transformed

[1] *Le Charivari,* Oct. 12, 1845, p. 2. One critic maintained that running *Le Péché de M. Antoine* had spelled the death of *L'Epoque* which in fact collapsed soon thereafter (*La Mode* 984).

[2] See Josef Mayr's valuable assessment of critical opinion on George Sand.

[3] Sand insisted she saw no difference between the *roman de mœurs* and the *roman d'idées* (*Correspondance* 7: 56).

[4] I do not agree with Richard Grant's assessment that "*La Mare au diable* can hardly be considered a socialist protest novel because nowhere in the story is there any evidence of grinding poverty" (212). Poverty was not the only object of Sand's social protest; it is not the main focus here, but is present in the depiction of Marie's family.

[5] It seems to me that Grant does not appreciate to what extent family considerations actually dictate behavior in the kind of peasant patriarchal society presented here. He believes Germain's instant submission to Maurice's suggestion that he marry points to "some kind of psychological complex" (214) and speculates on the nature of Germain's relationship to his mother, who is not even mentioned in the novel (216).

[6] See Biermann 99. He points out that in Sand's novels of the 1840s there are no sharp distinctions among *prolétaire,* *paysan* and *artisan* (83); thus a peasant like Germain could represent the common people as well as a carpenter like Jean Jappeloup or Pierre Huguenin.

[7] This is, in fact, one of the principal aspects of Mayr's book.

[8] *Jeanne* was published in *Le Constitutionnel* (1844), *Le Meunier d'Angibault* in *La Réforme* (1845), *Le Péché de M. Antoine* in *L'Epoque* (1845) and *La Mare au diable* in *Le Courrier français* (1846)

[9] Mireille Bossis discusses the similarities between *Consuelo* and popular fiction, in particular *Les Mystères de Paris.*

[10] This is the view of Reinhold Grimm (237). Grimm argues that class distinctions play an insignificant role in the rustic novels, but he bases this in part on a factual error, claiming that it is Catherine's father who tries to seduce Marie (231).

[11] Pierre Salomon points to the fact that fights in George Sand's novels are a concession to popular taste (84).

[12] Crecelius offers an interesting Freudian view of Sand's father figures that fits perfectly the situation in *La Mare au diable,* namely that the oppressive father figure serves a double purpose: "On one level, he incorporates the male society from which George Sand wanted to escape. On a deeper psychological level, though, he symbolizes her denial and fear of the very same incestuous union she sets up later in the novel. By heaping opprobrium on this paternal

character and showing him to be the representative of all she disdains, Sand temporarily distances herself from forbidden desires and is then free to satisfy them with a character who is the antithesis of the scorned male. A denial in Freudian terms is an affirmation, however, so that Sand's novels in fact twice postulate a desired union with the father, first as anxious denial and then as positive fulfillment" (18). The oppressive figure is the Ormeaux farmer, while Germain plays the role of the rescuer.

[13] There were still enough dialect terms left to cause Turgenev to object strongly, according to W. Karénine (670).

[14] See Frappier-Mazur's discussion, 53ff.

Chapter 8: Other Winds Blowing

[1] This emerges clearly from a letter to Mazzini: "Ce public froid et lâche qui a laissé égorger la liberté et souiller la ville éternelle redevenue sainte, ce public égoïste, aveugle, ingrat, qui ne s'émeut pas aux exploits de la Hongrie et qui ne s'alarme pas même des efforts de la Russie et de l'Autriche, se réveillerait-il devant un livre, un journal, un écrit quelconque? Ce serait un devoir pourtant de poursuivre l'œuvre par tous les moyens. Il y en a d'autres peut-être que celui-là, et je ne les néglige pas, je vous les dirai plus tard. Quant à écrire, discuter, prêcher, je crois que la mission des gens de lettre de ce temps-ci est finie ou ajournée en France, et que les plus sincères sont les plus taciturnes" (*Correspondance* 9: 243).

[2] I disagree with Gretchen van Slyke's analysis of *La petite Fadette* as preaching patriarchal values; this is the starting point in the novel, but the whole narrative strategy is built around showing the reader the limitations of that world view.

[3] Mireille Bossis has pointed out how women in Sand's fiction have a privileged kind of communion with nature (*La Femme* 263).

[4] Here again I take exception to Gretchen van Slyke's view that the novel shows Fadette undergoing significant changes; it is Landry who really is transformed.

[5] The original title of the novel was "La mère et l'enfant" (Dauphiné 185).

Chapter 9: Helping Sweet Providence

[1] Langlade 48; his book is the only extensive study on Sand's late novels but his attention centers mostly on the novels dealing with Auvergne.

[2] According to Langlade becoming a grandmother liberated Sand's "âme bourgeoise" (15) which had always been lurking in the background and evinced by her attachment to home and the importance of family.

[3] See Jean Courrier's introduction to his edition of *La ville noire* in which he gives an account of the condition of factory workers in Thiers at the time (x-xvi).

[4] Biermann 200; Biermann points out that *La ville noire* was not well received. The middle class reader assumed the problem was being solved by the government, thus it was not seen as a major issue.

[5] Cited in Biermann 199.

[6] Langlade has an informative discussion of Sand's realism (33-41). He sees the (limited) realist tendencies in her later fiction as a reflection of her life in the country and her travels (60-63).

[7] Courrier sees the novel as one of the earliest documents on industrial workers in France (xxx).

[8] As Courrier points out there is a similarity between Sept-Epées and Pierre Leroux, who was also an inventor.

[9] Courrier points out the extent to which Sept-Epées's dilemma represents the stage that industrial development in France had reached in 1860 (xviii).

[10] The name Creux-Perdu was one Sand encountered on her trip to Thiers (Courrier viii).

[11] I thus disagree with Stefan Max's statement that in the novel Sand sees money "comme une malédiction" (85). Her attitude is not that simplistic.

[12] This has been seen as evidence of Lamennais's influence (Courrier xvii, Max 88).

[13] This is the view of Wolfenzettel (62).

[14] On Saint-Simonian influence, see Courrier xix and Max 88. It seems to me, however, that there may well be a some satire in the final vision, particularly through Audebert's long poem. There is certainly a strong sense in which he incorporates the Saint-Simonian vision of the poet in society (see Courrier xx).

[15] Langlade's general characterization of Sand's late novels fits the *Le Marquis de Villemer* better than it does *La ville noire*: "Une intrigue romanesque, des sentiments nobles, une nature poétique unies à un réalisme discret mais sûr dans la peinture des lieux, des milieux et des comparses" (5). His definition is based above all on the Auvergne novels.

[16] Even the Marquis defends the Duke: "Un homme de qualité qui n'a jamais forfait à l'honneur a le droit de se ruiner, qu'une vie de plaisir a toujours été bien portée dans le grand monde lorsqu'on sait s'arrêter à temps, accepter noblement l'indigence et se montrer tout à coup supérieur à soi-même" (240).

[17] Langlade sees Sand striving in her late novels to offer a little of everything and not too much of any one thing: "Elle tâchera d'instruire, mais aussi elle aimera les belles aventures et les sentiments tendres. Elle fuira la réalité vulgaire mais ne se perdra pas dans les nuages. Elle sera poète, elle chantera la

nature, mais elle sera peintre ausi, et conteur, et psychologue. Elle n'écrira ni des romans à thèse, ni des féeries, ni des romans lyriques, mais ce que, faute d'un autre terme, on appelle des romans romanesques" (41).

[18] Langlade qualifies such remarks as "bavardage de l'auteur" and finds them insufferable (100). The variety of subjects on which the narrator comments, sometimes in the form of travel descriptions, he sees as evidence of the lack of unity in the novel (97).

Chapter 10: The Freedom to Love

[1] According to Jacques Langlade the fight against the danger represented by the Catholic Church was the one principal idea Sand championed in her late novels (231).

[2] Suleiman describes this type of *roman à thèse* as having a confrontational structure: "The rhetorical strategy consists not in leading the reader gradually toward a predetermined truth, but in treating him from the start as a possessor of that truth, or at last as someone whose sympathies are on the side of those who possess the truth and are fighting in its name. One might call this strategy persuasion by cooptation: the reader, coopted from the start into the ranks of the hero, finds himself structurally—that is, necessarily—on the "right" side. He *must* desire the triumph of the hero, and hence of the latter's values" (143). This is precisely what happens in *Mademoiselle La Quintinie*.

[3] Suleiman points to this as typical of the rhetoric of the *roman à thèse*, multiplying redundancies in order to reduce the "openings" available to the reader that might make a plural reading possible (55).

[4] Suleiman comments: "Paradox of this genre: the more closely a work conforms to it, and to it alone, the more the work is destined to disappear. The *romans à thèse* that survive their own period do so *despite* their belonging to the genre, not because of it" (148).

[5] Sand felt strongly on this issue partially since schools did not offer the kind of social education she saw as necessary along with traditional education. She also demonstrated in her own travels how much could be learned if one had the will; see Langlade 72-78.

[6] Langlade sees as representative qualities of Sand's heroines in her late novels their knowledge and intelligence (43). While this is important in the superiority of Caroline in *Le Marquis de Villemer* over other women, qualities that she had and shares with more female protagonists of these novels seem to be resourcefulness and dedication.

[7] Sand had a profound dislike of violence in any form and was very distressed by the violent events in the 1848 revolution and in the Commune; see Mallet 27.

[8] Mallet rightly points out that this was not a position Sand took up suddenly in response to the Commune. She was in 1848 as well opposed to extreme positions, such as those represented by Blanqui (32).

[9] Once again Mallet has noted that this does not represent a change in position (19).

[10] Sand, despite her socialist beliefs, was never in favor of the total abolition of private property; see Mallet 25.

[11] Langlade sees this as the one constant in Sand's fiction (27-29).

Conclusion

[1] There is unfortunately no effective way to ascertain who Sand's real readers were and precisely what strata of the population actually read her novels. It may be possible to make conjectures based on comments in reviews and letters and on the readership of French journals in which the novels first appeared. Such a study would be helpful in evaluating the evolution of Sand's approach to fiction.

[2] Susan Suleiman points this out in reference to this type of *roman à thèse*: "The actanial role assigned to the reader of a confrontation story is that of a pseudo-helper: he does not participate as an actor in the story (to be extradiegetic is the sad lot of any reader), but as a witness to the struggle being waged by the hero, he is not indifferent" (144).

[3] Sand points this out herself in a letter of August 28, 1842: "Que la femme, pour échapper à la souffrance et à l'humiliation, se préserve de l'amour et de la maternité, c'est une conclusion romanesque que j'ai essayée dans le roman de *Lélia*, non pas comme un exemple à suivre, mais comme la peinture d'un martyre qui peut donner à penser aux juges et aux bourreaux, aux hommes qui font la loi et à ceux qui l'appliquent" (*Correspondance* 5: 757-58).

[4] This is also evoked in Sand's correspondance: "Il me vient souvent dans l'idée (et c'est une espèce de consolation que je me permets) que la cause pour laquelle les âmes passionnées subissent leur martyre en ce monde est une noble et sainte cause. Aimer, c'est de tout ce que nous connaissons, ce qu'il y a encore de plus large et [de] plus ennoblissant; c'est là qu'on trouve encore la volonté et le pouvoir de se sacrifier. Malheur à ceux qui repoussent le sacrifice et qui forcent une âme en feu, à se reprendre et à s'éteindre. Ceux-là, sont les bêtes féroces qui déchirent le patient, mais le Dieu pour qui le martyre s'accomplit n'en est pas moins digne de bénédictions et ceux qui le blasphèment en mourant sont des lâches" (*Correspondance* 2: 825).

[5] Once again this is echoed in Sand's correspondance: "Je trouve la société livrée au plus affreux désordre, et, entre toutes les iniquités que je lui vois consacrer, je regarde, en première ligne, les rapports de l'homme avec la femme

établis d'une manière injuste et absurde. Je ne puis donc conseiller à personne un mariage sanctionné par une loi civile qui consacre la dépendance, l'infériorité et la nullité sociale de la femme. J'ai passé dix ans à réfléchir là-dessus, et, après m'être demandé pourquoi tous les amours de ce monde, légitimés ou non légitimés pas la société, étaient tous plus ou moins malheureux, quelles que fussent les qualités et les vertus des âmes ainsi associées, je me suis convaincue de l'impossibilité radicale de ce parfait bonheur, idéal de l'amour, dans des conditions d'inégalité, d'infériorité et de dépendance d'un sexe vis-à-vis de l'autre. Que ce soit la loi, que ce soit la morale reconnue généralement, que ce soient l'opinion ou le préjugé, la femme, en se donnant à l'homme, est nécessairement ou enchaînée ou coupable" (*Correspondance* 5: 756).

[6] One reviewer in *Le Siècle* commented, for example, "Je vois dans une union de ce genre peu de garantie de solide félicité" (Kujaw 84).

[7] Arlette Michel sees this in terms of an apprenticeship the women must undergo (39).

[8] See Simone Vierne and Wolfenzettel. J.-P. Lacassagne argues similarly when he proposes the idea that the reader in Sand is frequently a "révélateur" who becomes initiated by the book and then in turn is supposed to initiate others (91).

Works Cited

Biermann, Karlheinrich. *Literarisch-politische Avantgarde in Frankreich. 1830-1870: Hugo, Sand, Baudelaire und andere.* Stuttgart: Kohlhammer, 1982.

Bossis, Mireille. "La Femme prêtresse dans les romans de George Sand." Ed. Janis Glasgow. *George Sand: Collected Essays.* Troy, NY: Whitston, 1985. 250-70.

———. "La Tentation du roman populaire chez Sand." Ed. R. Guise and H. -J. Neuschäfer. *Richesse du roman populaire.* Nancy: Centre de Recherches sur le Roman Populaire, 1986. 315-33.

Bourdet-Guillerault, Henri. *George Sand: Ce qu'elle croyait.* Marseille: Editions Rijois, 1979.

Bozon-Scalzitti, Yvette. "George Sand: Le bruit et la musique." *Orbis Litterarum* 41 (1986): 139-56.

Buis, Lucien. *Les Théories sociales de George Sand.* Paris: Pedone, 1910.

Cate, Curtis. *George Sand: A Biography.* New York: Avon, 1975.

Chastagnaret, Yves. "George Sand et la Revolution française." *Dix-huitième siècle* 20 (1988): 431-48.

Crecelius, Kathryn J. *Family Romances: George Sand's Early Novels.* Bloomington: Indiana UP, 1987.

Czyba, Lucette. "La femme et le prolétaire dans *Le Compagnon du tour de France.*" *George Sand. Colloque de Cérisy.* Paris: CDU/SEDES, 1983. 21-29.

Daly, Pierrette. "Consuelo et les contes de fée." Ed. Janis Glasgow. *George Sand: Collected Essays.* Troy, NY: Whitston, 1985. 20-28.

———. "The Problem of Language in George Sand's *Indiana.*" *West Virginia George Sand Conference Papers.* Morgantown: West Virginia UP, 1981. 22-27.

Dauphiné, James. "Ecriture et musique dans *Les Maîtres Sonneurs* de George Sand." *Nineteenth-Century French Studies* 9.3/4 (1981): 185-91.

Derré, Jean-René. *Lamennais, ses amis et le mouvement d'idées à l'époque romantique.* Paris: Klincksieck, 1962.

Dickenson, Donna. *George Sand: A Brave Man—The Most Womanly Woman.* Oxford: Berg, 1988.

Didier, Béatrice. "Rôles et figures du lecteur chez George Sand." *Etudes littéraires* 17.2 (1984): 239-59.

Dolléans, Edouard. *George Sand*. Paris: Editions Ouvrières, 1951.

Godwin-Jones, Robert. "The Representation of Economic Reality in George Sand's Rural Novels." *Studies in the Literary Imagination*, vol. 12, no. 2 (1979): (53-60).

Grant, Richard B. "George Sand's *La Mare Au Diable*: A Study in Male Passivity." *Nineteenth-Century French Studies* 13.4 (1985): 211-23.

Grimm, Reinhold R. "Les romans champêtres de George Sand: L'échec du renouvellement d'un genre littéraire." *Romantisme* 16 (1977): 64-70.

Hirsch, Michèle. "George Sand: Jeanne, esquisse d'une théorie de la magie." Ed. Margaret Jones-Davies. *La Magie et ses langages*. Lille: Presses Universitaires de Lille, 1980. 119-26.

Iknayan, Marguerite. *The Idea of the Novel in France: The Critical Reaction 1815-1848*. Geneva: Droz, 1961.

Iser, Wolfgang. *Prospecting: From Reader Response to Literary Anthropology*. Baltimore: Johns Hopkins UP, 1989.

Karénine, Wladimir. *George Sand: Sa vie et ses œuvres*. Paris: Plon, 1899-1912.

Knibiehler, Yvonne, and Catherine Fouquet. *L'histoire des mères du moyen âge à nos jours*. Paris: Editions Montalba, 1980.

Kujaw, Jörg. *George Sand im Urteil der Presse* (1831-1852). Bochum: N.p., 1970.

Lacassagne, Jean-Pierre. "George Sand et la 'vérité sociale' " *RHLF* July-Aug. 1976.

Langlade, Jacques. *La dernière manière de George Sand: Essai sur le déclin du romantisme*. Paris: E. Champion, 1925.

Larnac, Jean. *George Sand Révolutionnaire*. Paris: Editions Hier et Aujourd'hui, 1948.

Mayr, Josef. *Studien zur Rezeption des art social: Die Sozialromane George Sands in der zeitgenössischen Kritik*. Bern: Peter Lang, 1984.

Michel, Arlette. "Structures romanesques et problèmes du mariage d'*Indiana* à *La comtesse de Rudolstadt*." *Romantisme* 16 (1977): 34-45.

Modum, Egbuna. "Une initiation à caractère maçonnique: L'exemple de *Consuelo* et *La comtesse de Rudolstadt* de George Sand." *Nineteenth-Century Fiction* 11.3/4 (1983): 268-77.

Naginski, Isabelle Hoog. *George Sand: Writing for Her Life*. New Brunswick: Rutgers UP, 1991.

Neuschäfer, Hans-Jörg. *Populärromane im 19. Jahrhundert*. Munich: Wilhelm Fink Verlag, 1976.

Neuschäfer, Hans-Jörg, Dorothee Fritz-El Ahmad, and Klaus-Peter Walter. *Der französische Feuilletonroman*. Darmstadt: Wissenschaftliche Buchgesellschaft, 1986.

Pommier, Jean Joseph Marie. *George Sand et le rêve monastique: Spiridion*. Paris: Nizet, 1966.

Rea, Annabelle. "Toward a Definition of Women's Voice in Sand's Novels: The Siren and the Witch." Ed. Janis Glasgow. *George Sand: Collected Essays.* Troy, NY: Whitston, 1985. 227-38.

Riffaterre, Michael. *Fictional Truth.* Baltimore: The Johns Hopkins University Press, 1990.

Rogers, Nancy. *The Persuasive Style of the Young George Sand.* Diss. [Ann Arbor]: George Washington University, 1974.

Salomon, Pierre. *George Sand.* Paris: Hatier-Boivin, 1953.

Sand, George. *Le Compagnon du tour de France.* Paris: Editions d'aujourd'hui, 1976.

———. *Consuelo/La comtesse de Rudolstadt.* Paris: Garnier, 1959. 3 vols.

———. *Correspondance.* Ed. Georges Lubin. Paris: Garnier, 1964-90.

———. *François le Champi.* Paris: Garnier, 1962.

———. *Horace. Œuvres complètes.* Vol. 16. Geneva: Slatkine, 1980.

———. *Indiana.* Ed. Pierre Salomon. Paris: Garnier, 1962.

———. *Jacques. Œuvres complètes.* Vol. 18. Geneva: Slatkine, 1980.

———. *Jeanne. Œuvres complètes.* Vol. 29. Geneva: Slatkine 1980.

———. *Lélia.* Ed. Pierre Reboul. Edition revue et corrigée. Paris: Garnier, 1985.

———. *Mademoiselle la Quintinie. Œuvres complètes.* Vol. 22. Geneva: Slatkine, 1980.

———. *Les Maîtres Sonneurs.* Paris: Gallimard, 1979.

———. *La Mare au Diable.* Paris: Garnier, 1962.

———. *Le Marquis de Villemer. Œuvres complètes.* Geneva: Slatkine, 1980,

———. *Mauprat.* Paris: Garnier-Flammarion, 1969.

———. *Le Meunier d'Angibault.* Paris: Livre de Poche, 1985.

———. *Nanon. Œuvres complètes.* Vol. 26. Geneva: Slatkine, 1980.

———. *Le Péché de M. Antoine. Ouevres complètes.* Vol. 28. Geneva: Slatkine, 1980. 2 vols.

———. *La petite Fadette.* Paris: Garnier, 1958.

———. *Spiridion. Œuvres complètes.* Vol. 16. Geneva: Slatkine, 1980.

———. *Valentine. Œuvres complètes.* Vol. 35. Geneva: Slatkine, 1980.

———. *La Ville noire. Œuvres complètes.* Vol. 35. Geneva: Slatkine, 1980.

Schenda, Rudolf. "Populäre Lesestoffe im 19. Jahrhundert." *Französiche Literatur in Einzeldarstellungen.* Vol. 2. Stuttgart: Metzler, 1982.

Schor, Naomi. "Idealism in the Novel: Recanonizing Sand." *Yale French Studies* 75 (1988): 56-73.

Schwartz, Lucy. "Sensibilité et sensualité: Rapports sexuels dans les premiers romans de George Sand (1831-43)." Ed. Simone Vierne. *George Sand.* Colloque de Cérisy. Paris: CDU/SEDES, 1983. 171-77.

Sourian, Eve. "Les opinions religieuses de George Sand: Pourquoi Consuelo a-t-elle perdu sa voix?" Ed. Janis Glasgow. *George Sand: Collected Essays.* Troy, NY: Whitston, 1985. 127-38.

Stefan, Max. "Quelques notes sur *La ville noire* de George Sand." Ed. Janis Glasgow. *George Sand: Collected Essays*. Troy, NY: Whitston, 1985. 84-91.

Suleiman, Susan. *Authoritarian Fictions. The Ideolgical Novel as a Literary Genre*. New York: Columbia University Press, 1983.

Van Rossum-Guyon, Françoise. "A propos d'*Indiana*: la préface de 1832. Problèmes du metadiscours." *George Sand*. Colloque de Cérisy. Paris: CDU/SEDES, 1983. 71-83.

Vermeylen, Pierre. *Les idées politiques et sociales de George Sand*. Brussels: Editions de L'Université de Bruxelles, 1985.

Vest, James M. "Dreams and Romance Tradition in George Sand's *Indiana*." *French Forum* 3 (1978): 35-47.

Vierne, Simone. "George Sand et le mythe initiatique." Ed. Janis Glasgow. *George Sand: Collected Essays*. Troy, NY: Whitston, 1985. 288-305.

Wingard Vareille, Kristina. *Socialité, sexualité et les impasses de l'histoire: l'évolution de la thématique sandienne d'Indiana (1832) à Mauprat (1837)*. Uppsala: Almqvist and Wiksell International, 1987.

———. "Thèmes et techniques narratives chez George Sand d'*Indiana* (1832) aux *Maîtres Sonneurs* (1853)." *Actes du 8ᵉ congrès des romanistes scandinaves*. Ed. Palle Spore. Etudes romanes de l'Université d'Odense. Odense, Denmark: Odense UP, 1983.

Wolfzettel, Friedrich, ed. *Der französische Sozialroman des 19. Jahrhunderts*. Wege der Forschung (vol. 364). Darmstadt: Wissenschaftliche Buchgesellschaft, 1981.

———. "George Sand: Liebesroman—Sozialroman. Zum Problem der Romantypologie." *Romanistische Zeitschrift für Literaturgeschichte* 1.4 (1980): 36-64.

843
S 2133
G